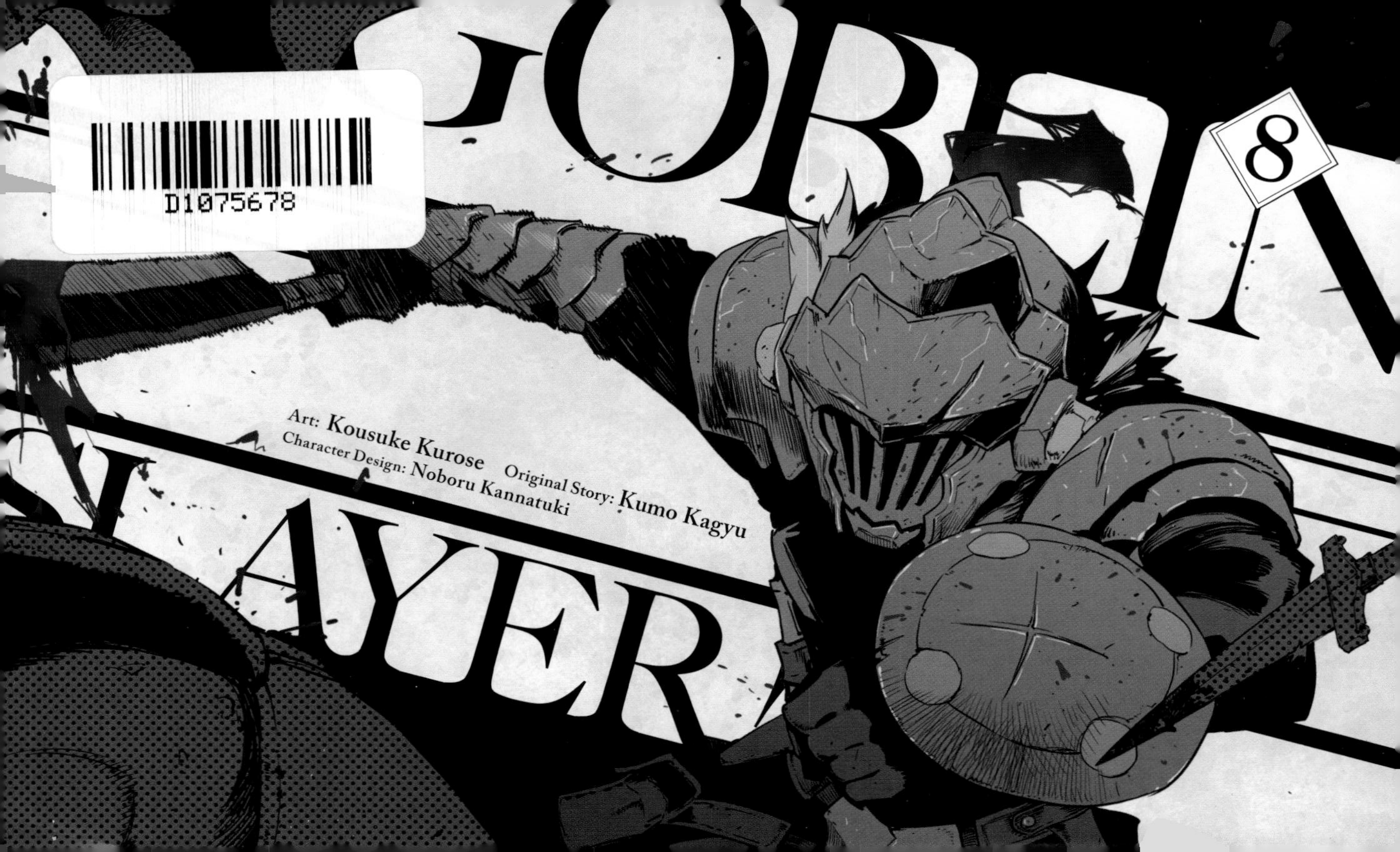
8
Art: Kousuke Kurose
Original Story: Kumo Kagyu
Character Design: Noboru Kannatuki
D1075678

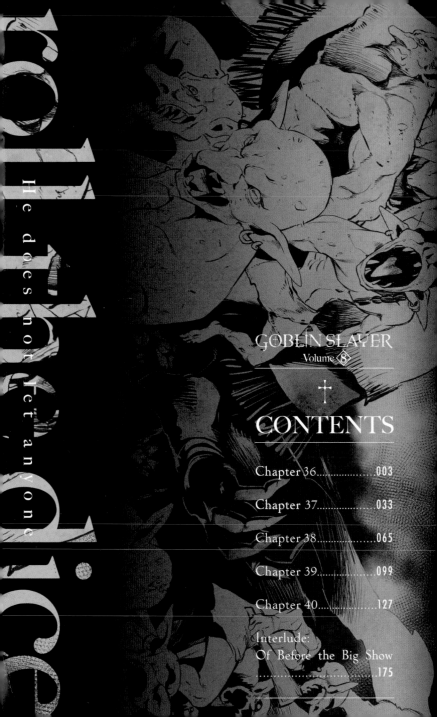

roll the dice

He does not let anyone

GOBLIN SLAYER
Volume 8

†

CONTENTS

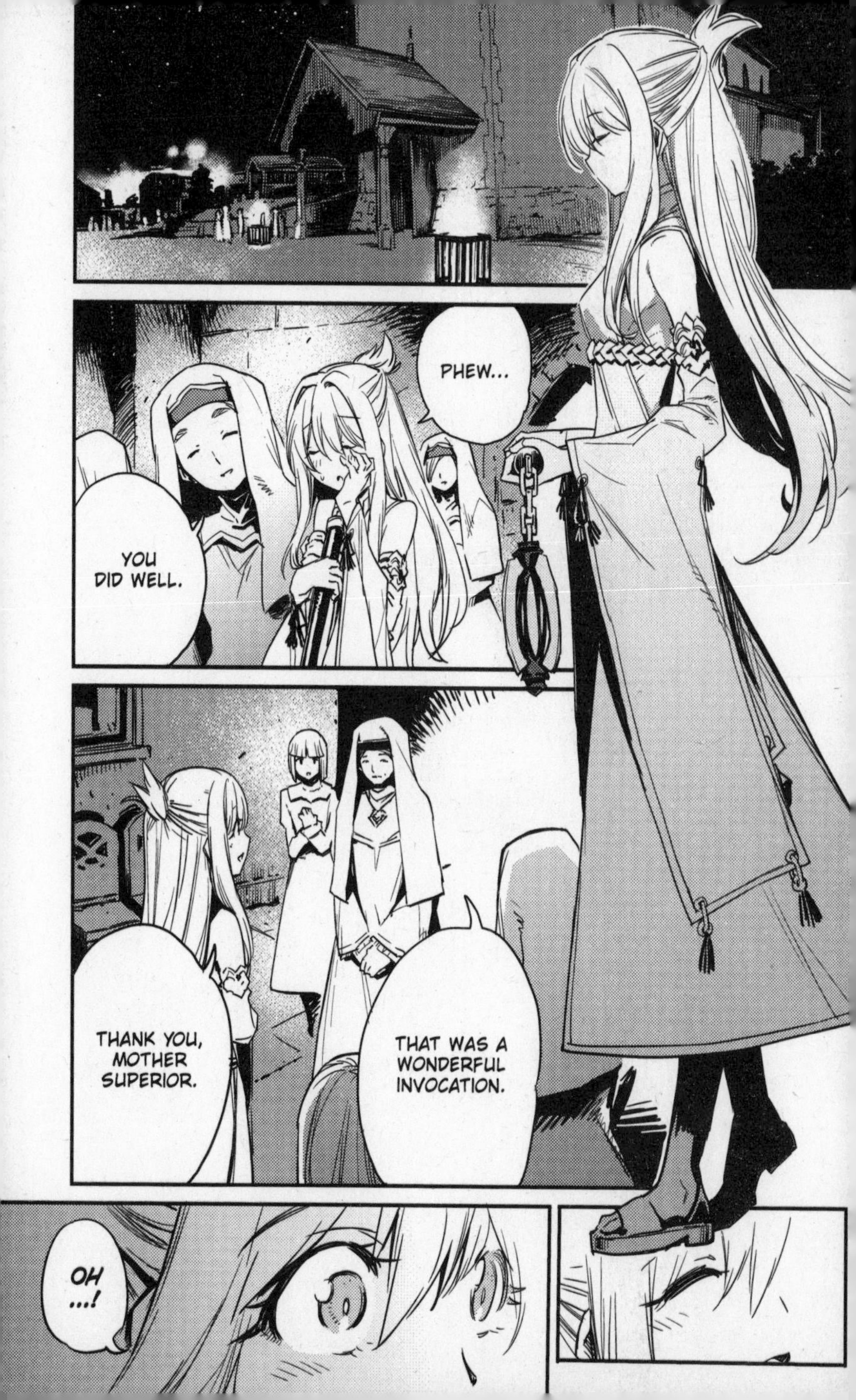
PHEW...
YOU DID WELL.
THAT WAS A WONDERFUL INVOCATION.
THANK YOU, MOTHER SUPERIOR.
OH ...!

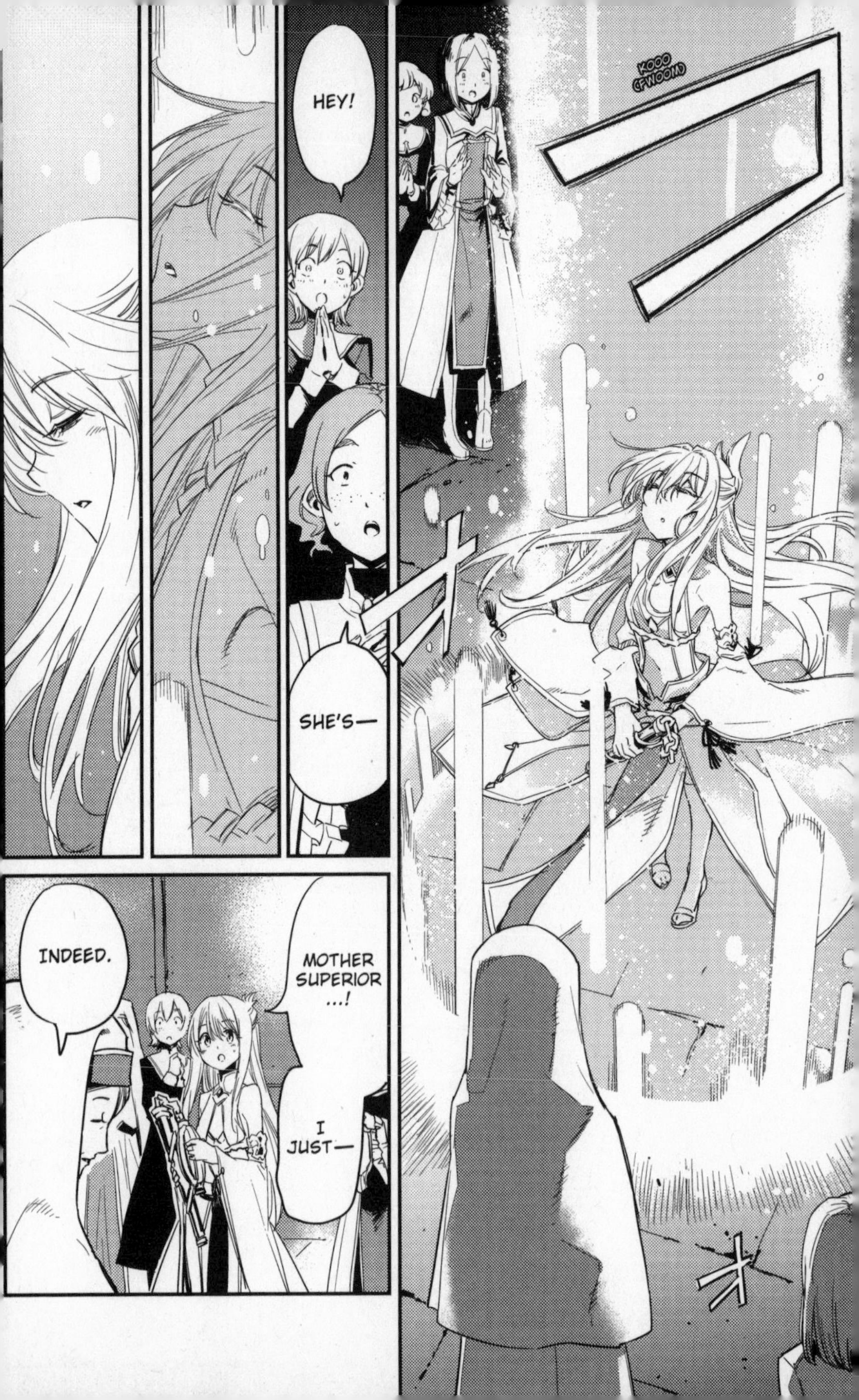
KOOO (FWOOM)
HEY!
SHE'S—
MOTHER SUPERIOR ...!
I JUST—
INDEED.

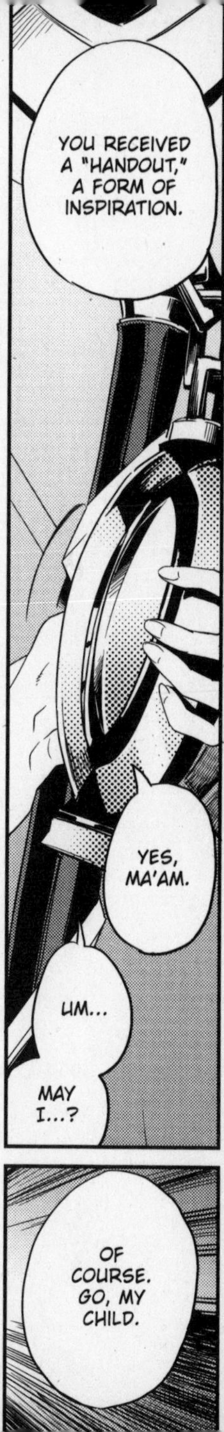
YOU RECEIVED A "HANDOUT," A FORM OF INSPIRATION.
YES, MA'AM.
UM...
MAY I...?
OF COURSE. GO, MY CHILD.

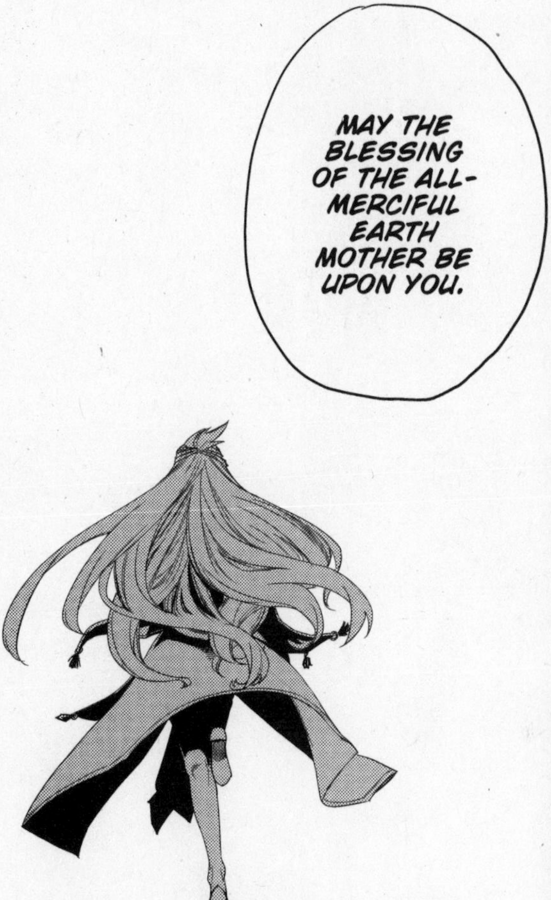
MAY THE BLESSING OF THE ALL-MERCIFUL EARTH MOTHER BE UPON YOU.

CHAPTER 36

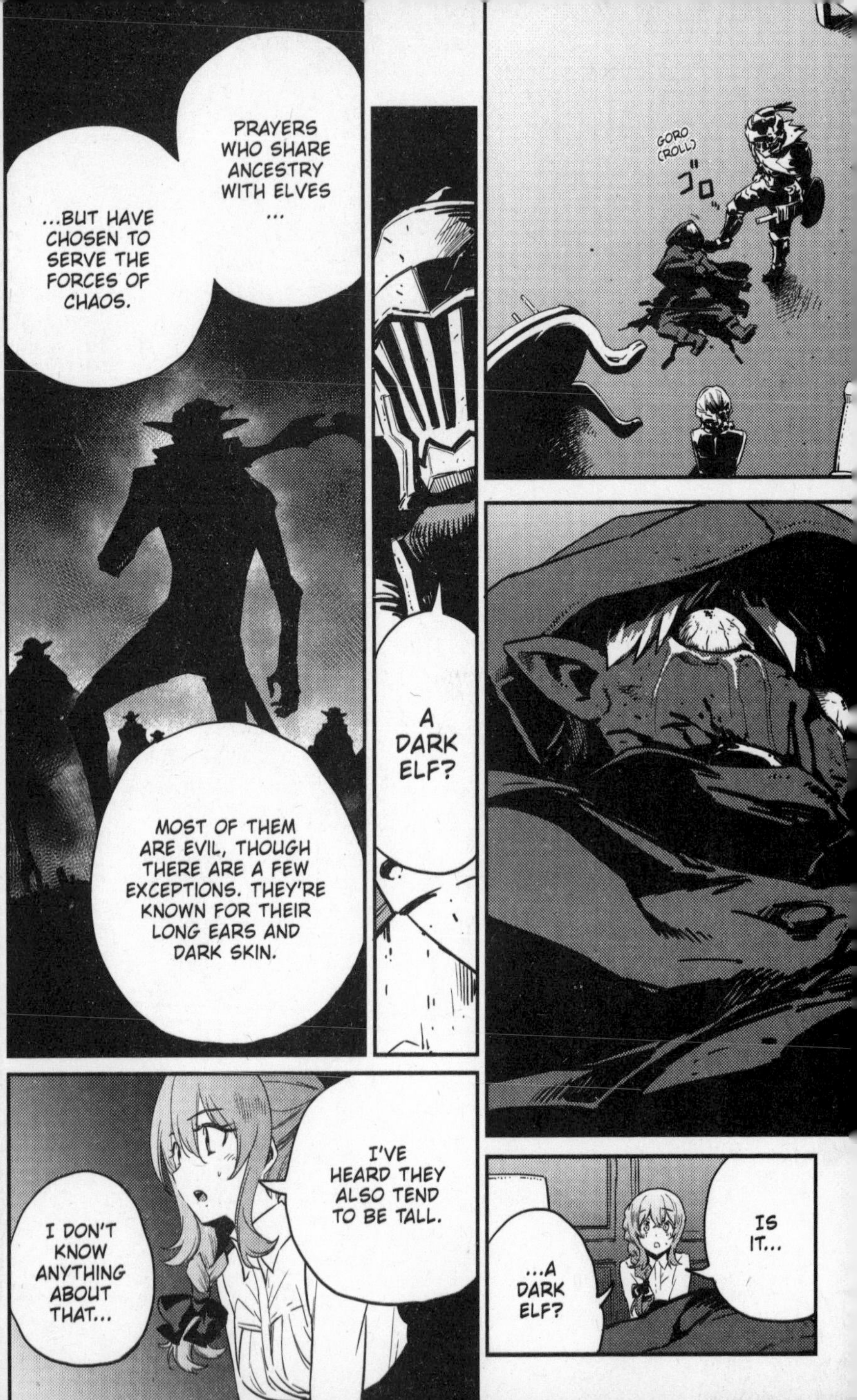
ゴロ
GORO (ROLL)
A DARK ELF?
PRAYERS WHO SHARE ANCESTRY WITH ELVES ...
...BUT HAVE CHOSEN TO SERVE THE FORCES OF CHAOS.
MOST OF THEM ARE EVIL, THOUGH THERE ARE A FEW EXCEPTIONS. THEY'RE KNOWN FOR THEIR LONG EARS AND DARK SKIN.
IS IT...
...A DARK ELF?
I'VE HEARD THEY ALSO TEND TO BE TALL.
I DON'T KNOW ANYTHING ABOUT THAT...

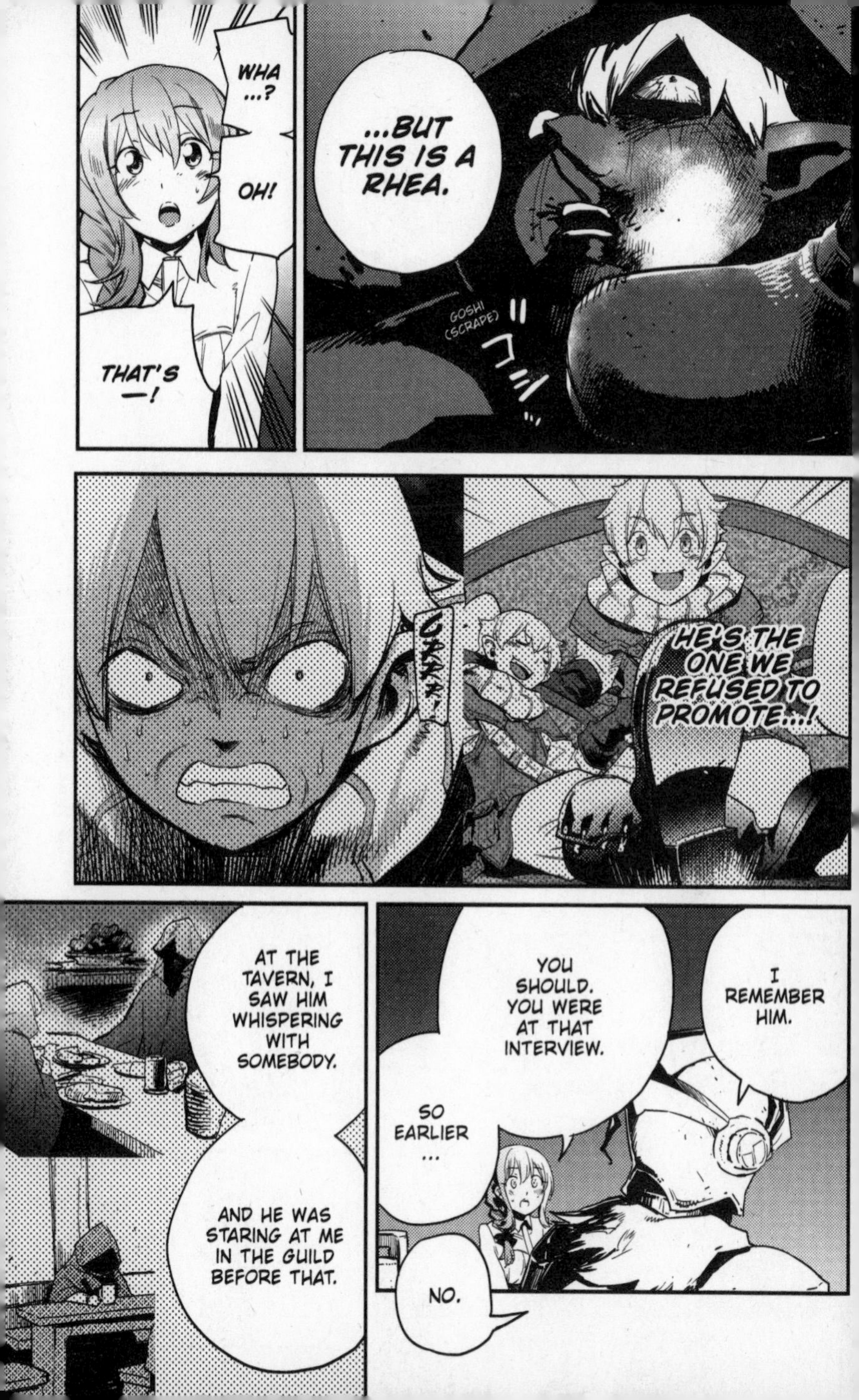
...BUT THIS IS A RHEA.
GOSHI (SCRAPE)
WHA ...?
OH!
THAT'S —!
HE'S THE ONE WE REFUSED TO PROMOTE...!
I REMEMBER HIM.
YOU SHOULD. YOU WERE AT THAT INTERVIEW.
SO EARLIER ...
NO.
AT THE TAVERN, I SAW HIM WHISPERING WITH SOMEBODY.
AND HE WAS STARING AT ME IN THE GUILD BEFORE THAT.

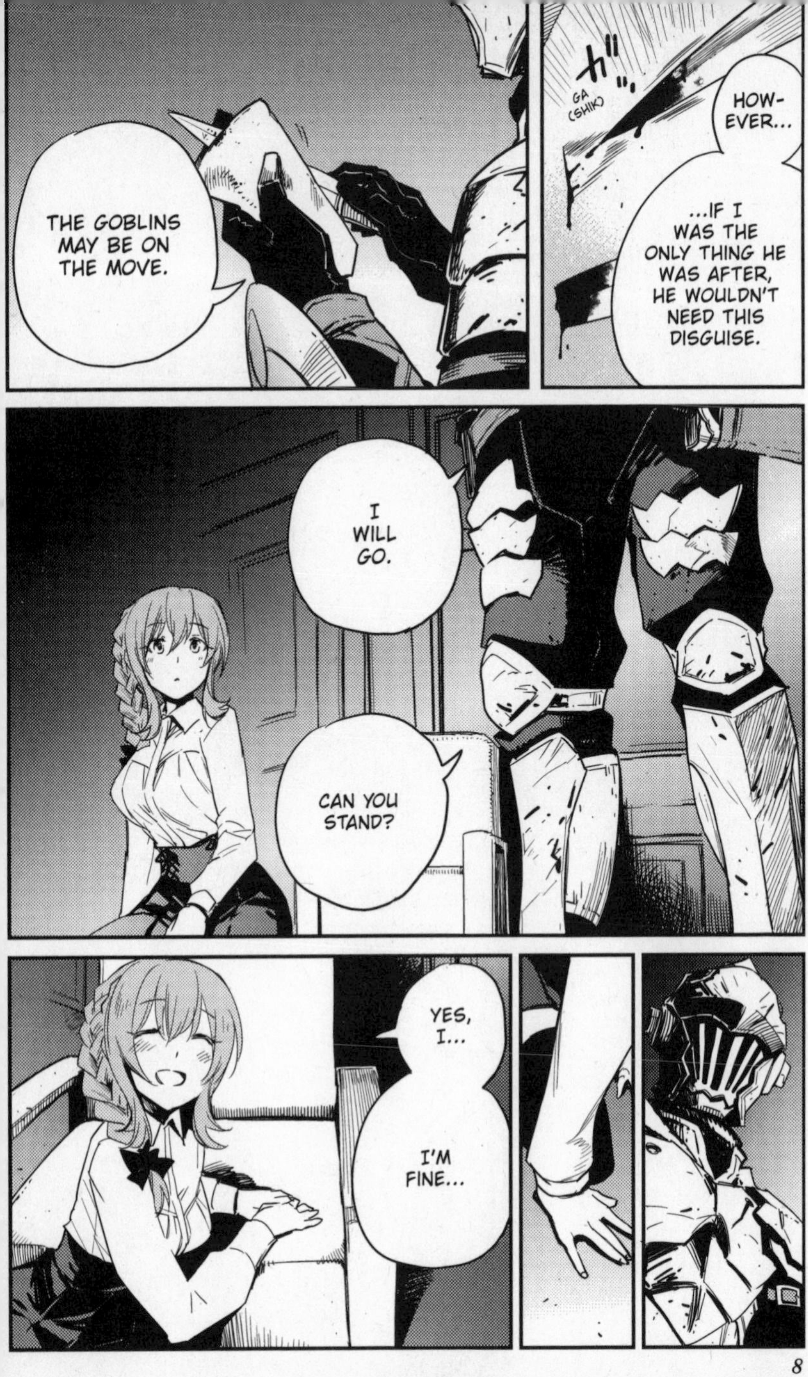
ガッ
GA (SHIK)
HOW-EVER...
...IF I WAS THE ONLY THING HE WAS AFTER, HE WOULDN'T NEED THIS DISGUISE.
THE GOBLINS MAY BE ON THE MOVE.
I WILL GO.
CAN YOU STAND?
YES, I...
I'M FINE...

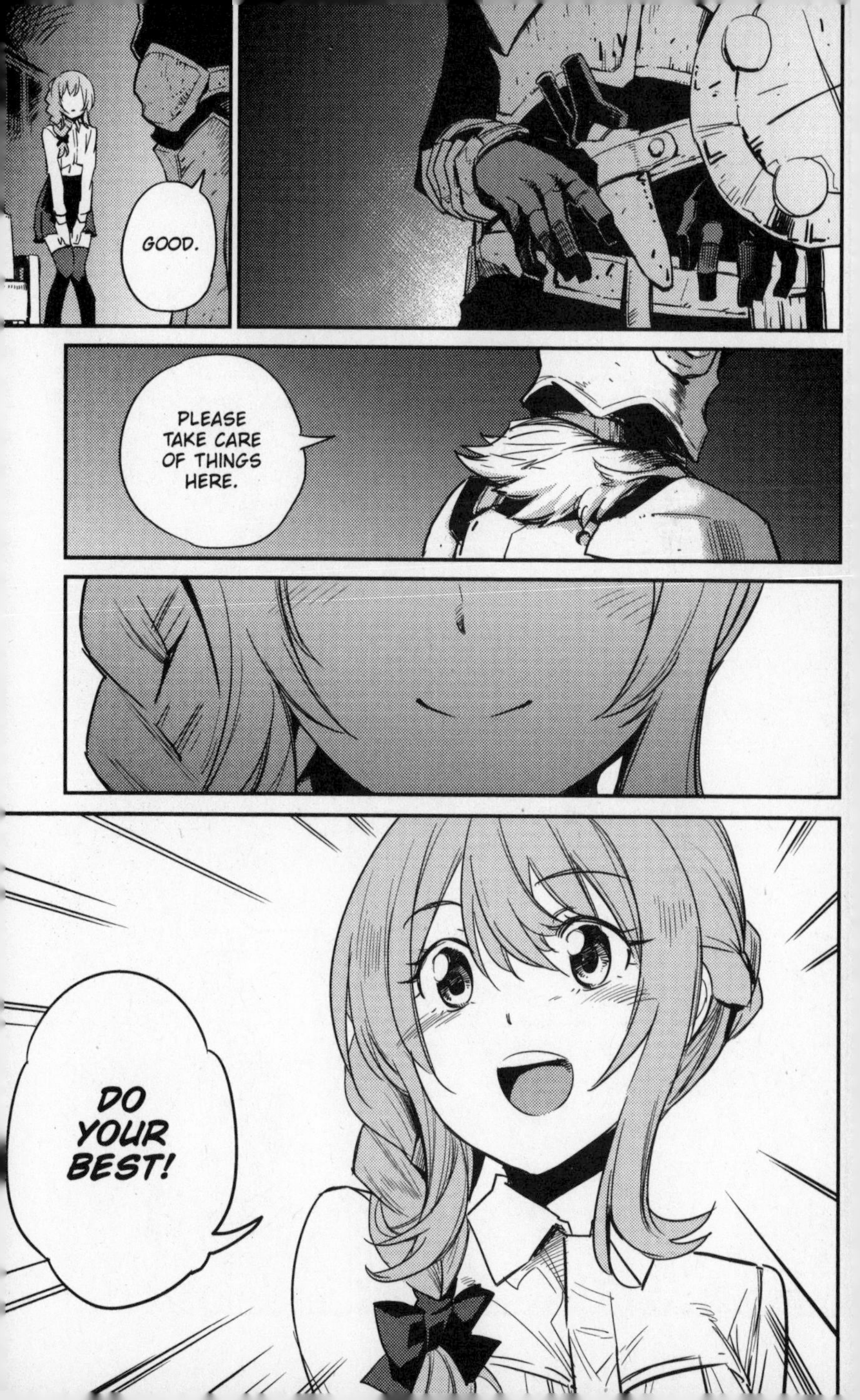
GOOD.
PLEASE TAKE CARE OF THINGS HERE.
DO YOUR BEST!

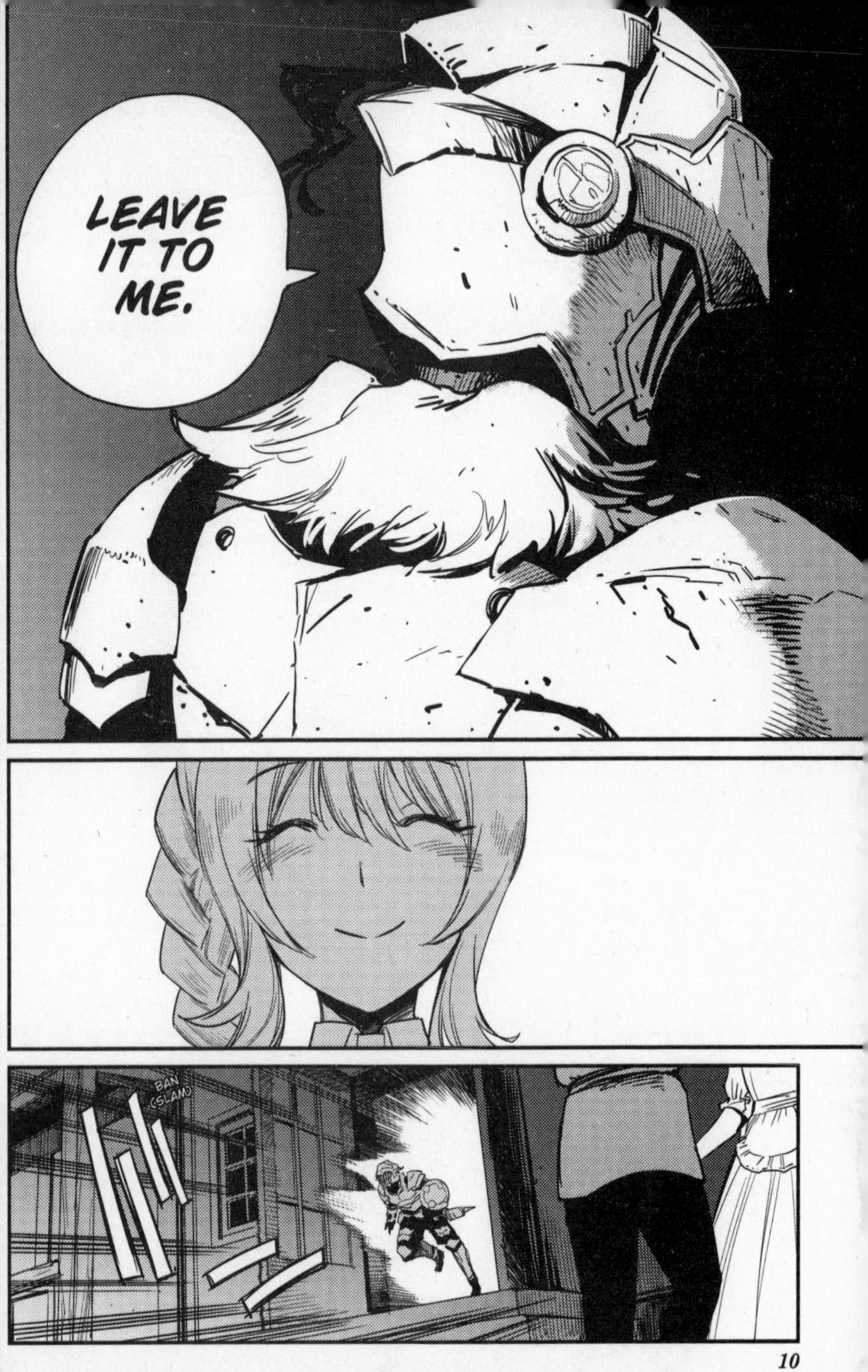
LEAVE IT TO ME.
BAN (SLAM)

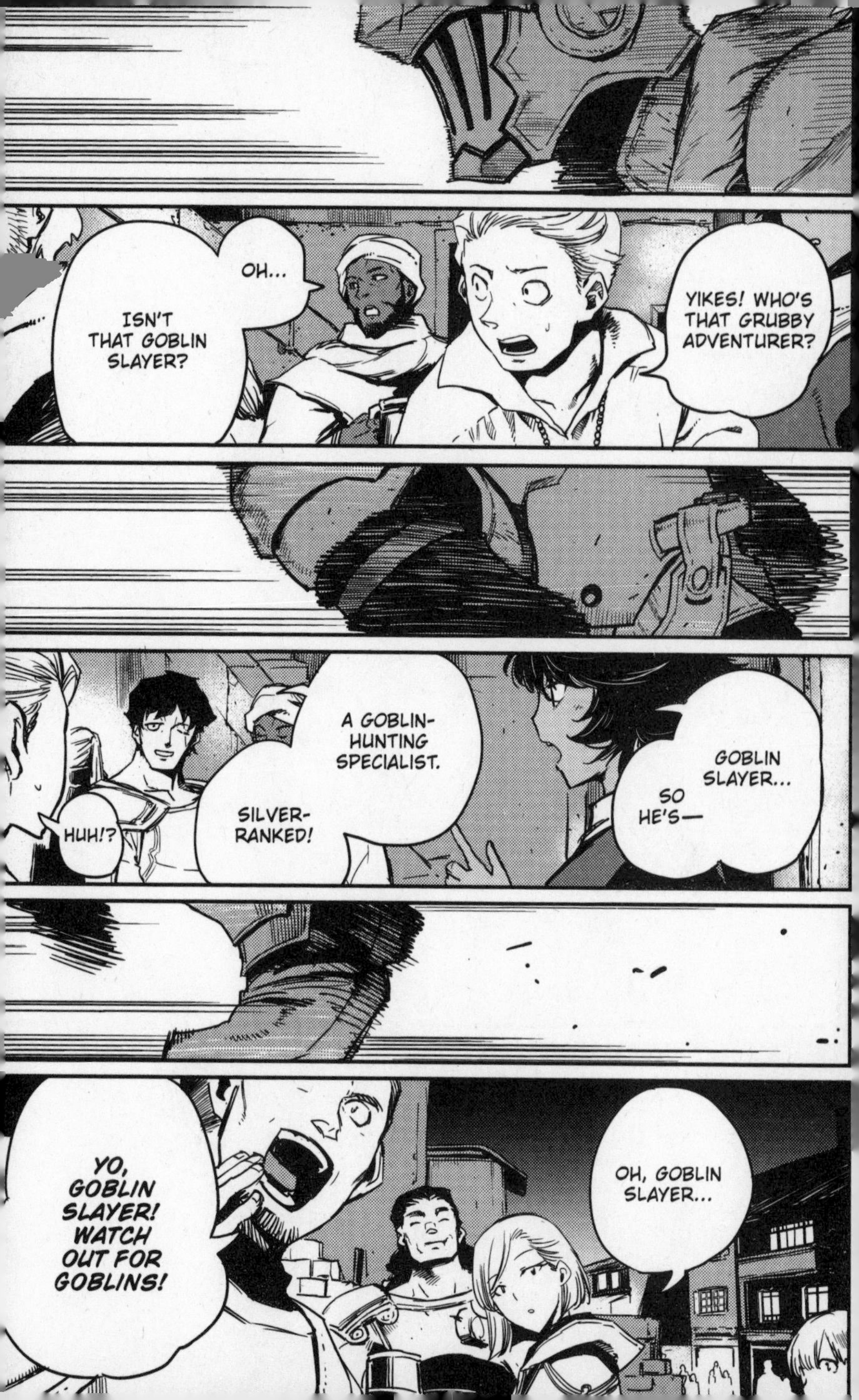
YIKES! WHO'S THAT GRUBBY ADVENTURER?
OH...
ISN'T THAT GOBLIN SLAYER?
GOBLIN SLAYER...
SO HE'S—
A GOBLIN-HUNTING SPECIALIST.
SILVER-RANKED!
HUH!?
OH, GOBLIN SLAYER...
YO, GOBLIN SLAYER! WATCH OUT FOR GOBLINS!

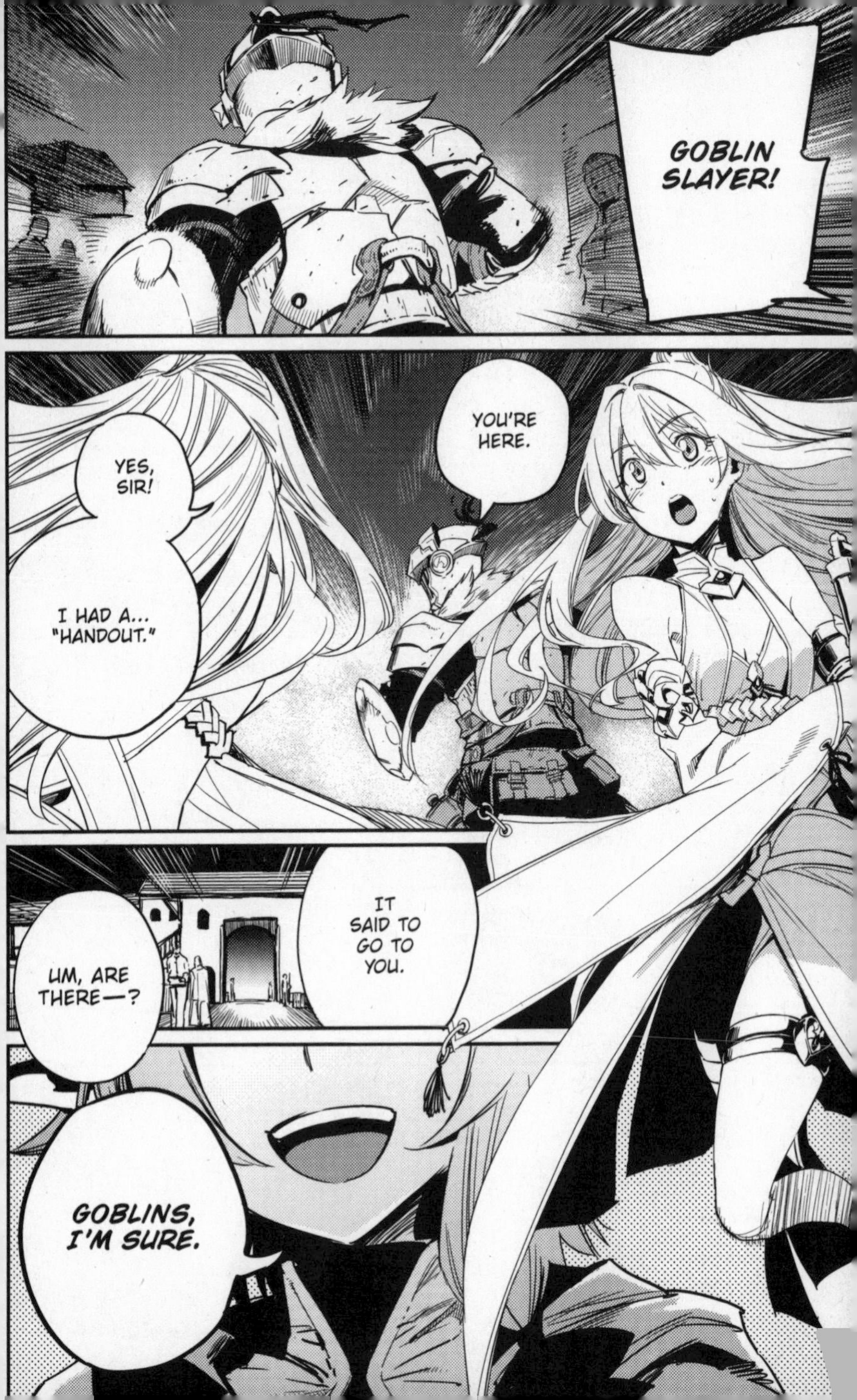
GOBLIN SLAYER!
YOU'RE HERE.
YES, SIR!
I HAD A... "HANDOUT."
IT SAID TO GO TO YOU.
UM, ARE THERE—?
GOBLINS, I'M SURE.

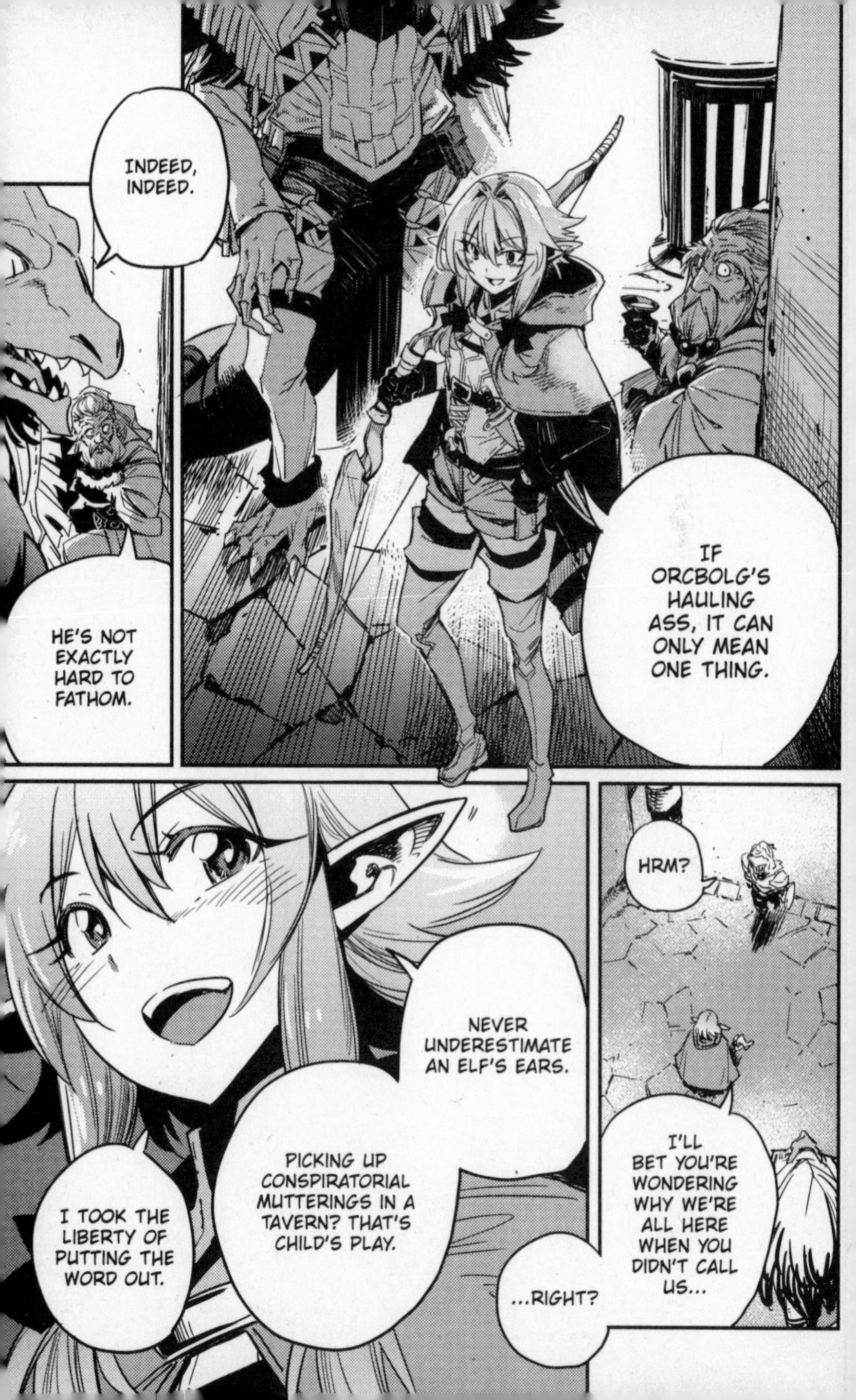
IF ORCBOLG'S HAULING ASS, IT CAN ONLY MEAN ONE THING.
INDEED, INDEED.
HE'S NOT EXACTLY HARD TO FATHOM.
HRM?
I'LL BET YOU'RE WONDERING WHY WE'RE ALL HERE WHEN YOU DIDN'T CALL US...
...RIGHT?
NEVER UNDERESTIMATE AN ELF'S EARS.
PICKING UP CONSPIRATORIAL MUTTERINGS IN A TAVERN? THAT'S CHILD'S PLAY.
I TOOK THE LIBERTY OF PUTTING THE WORD OUT.

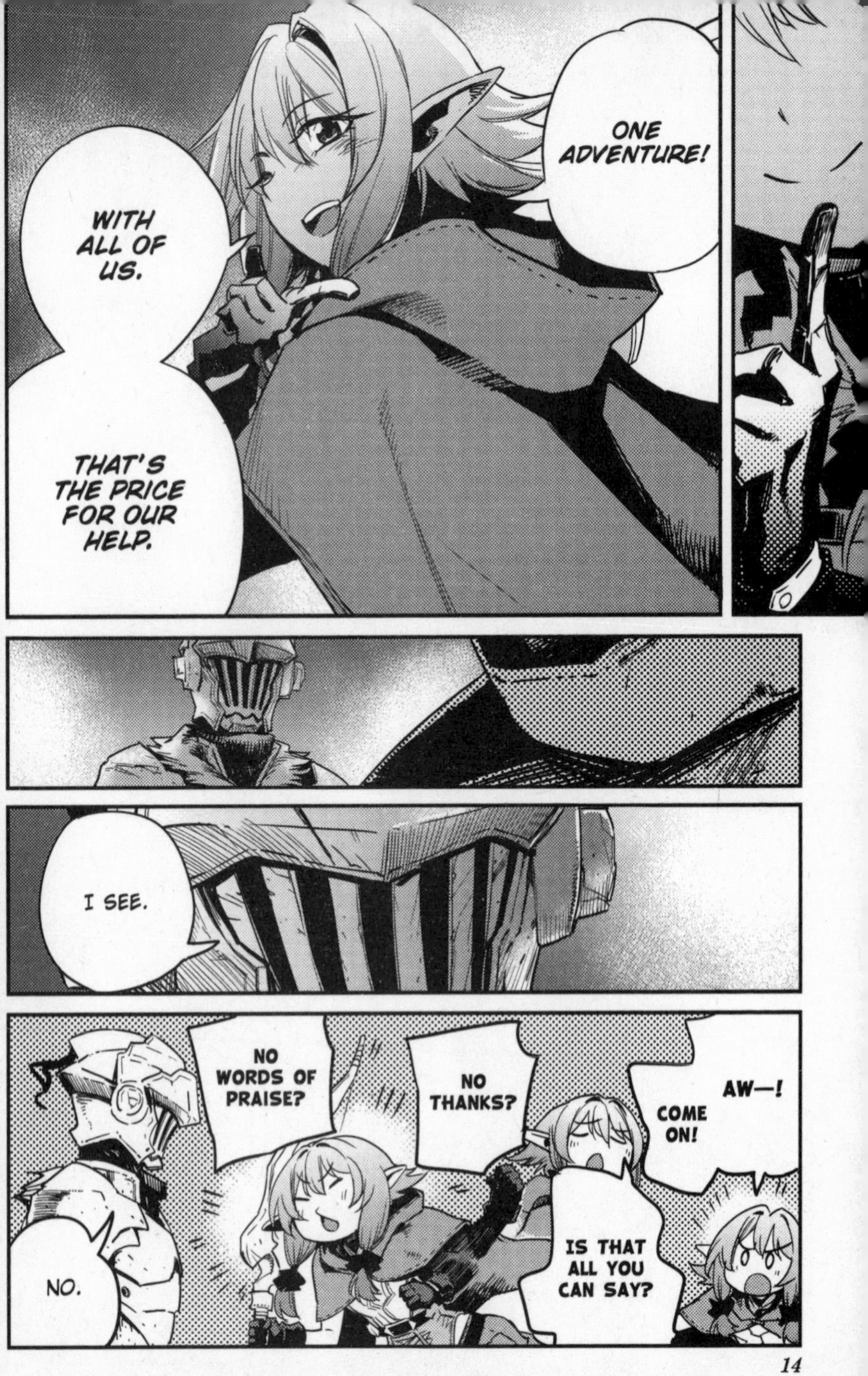
ONE ADVENTURE!
WITH ALL OF US.
THAT'S THE PRICE FOR OUR HELP.
I SEE.
AW—!
COME ON!
NO THANKS?
NO WORDS OF PRAISE?
IS THAT ALL YOU CAN SAY?
NO.

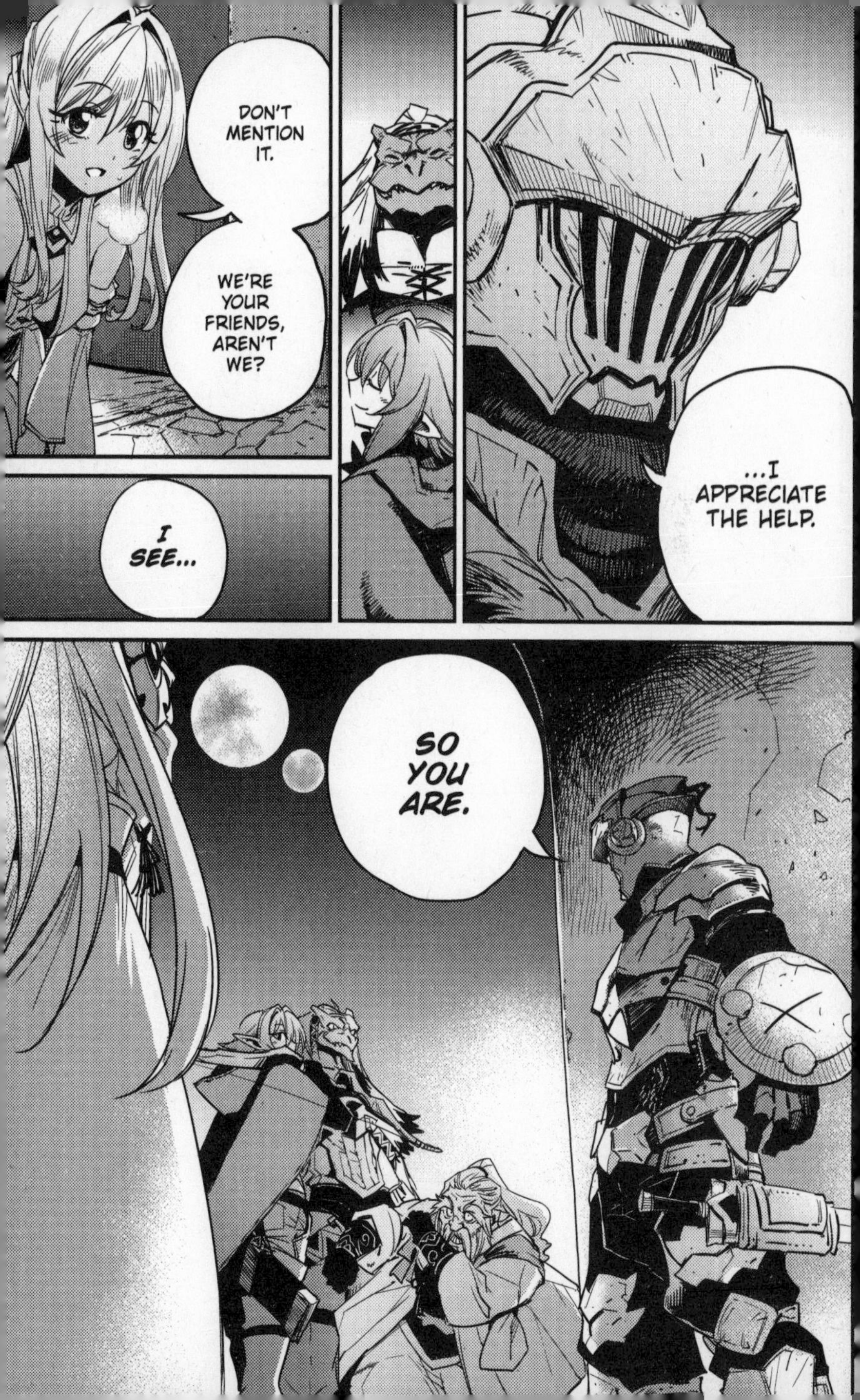
...I APPRECIATE THE HELP.
DON'T MENTION IT.
WE'RE YOUR FRIENDS, AREN'T WE?
I SEE...
SO YOU ARE.

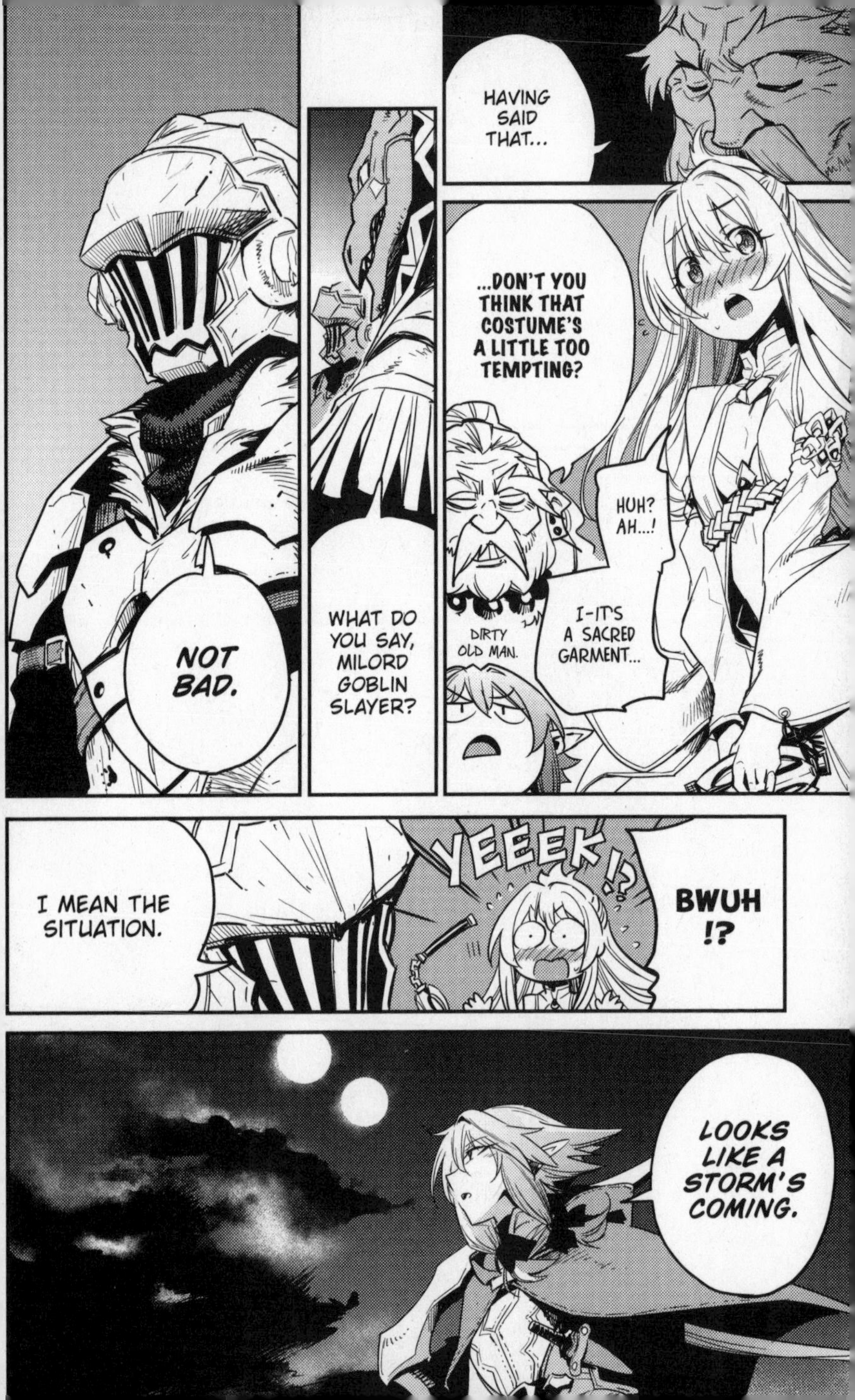
HAVING SAID THAT...
...DON'T YOU THINK THAT COSTUME'S A LITTLE TOO TEMPTING?
HUH? AH...!
I-IT'S A SACRED GARMENT...
DIRTY OLD MAN.
WHAT DO YOU SAY, MILORD GOBLIN SLAYER?
NOT BAD.
BWUH !?
YEEEK!?
I MEAN THE SITUATION.
LOOKS LIKE A STORM'S COMING.

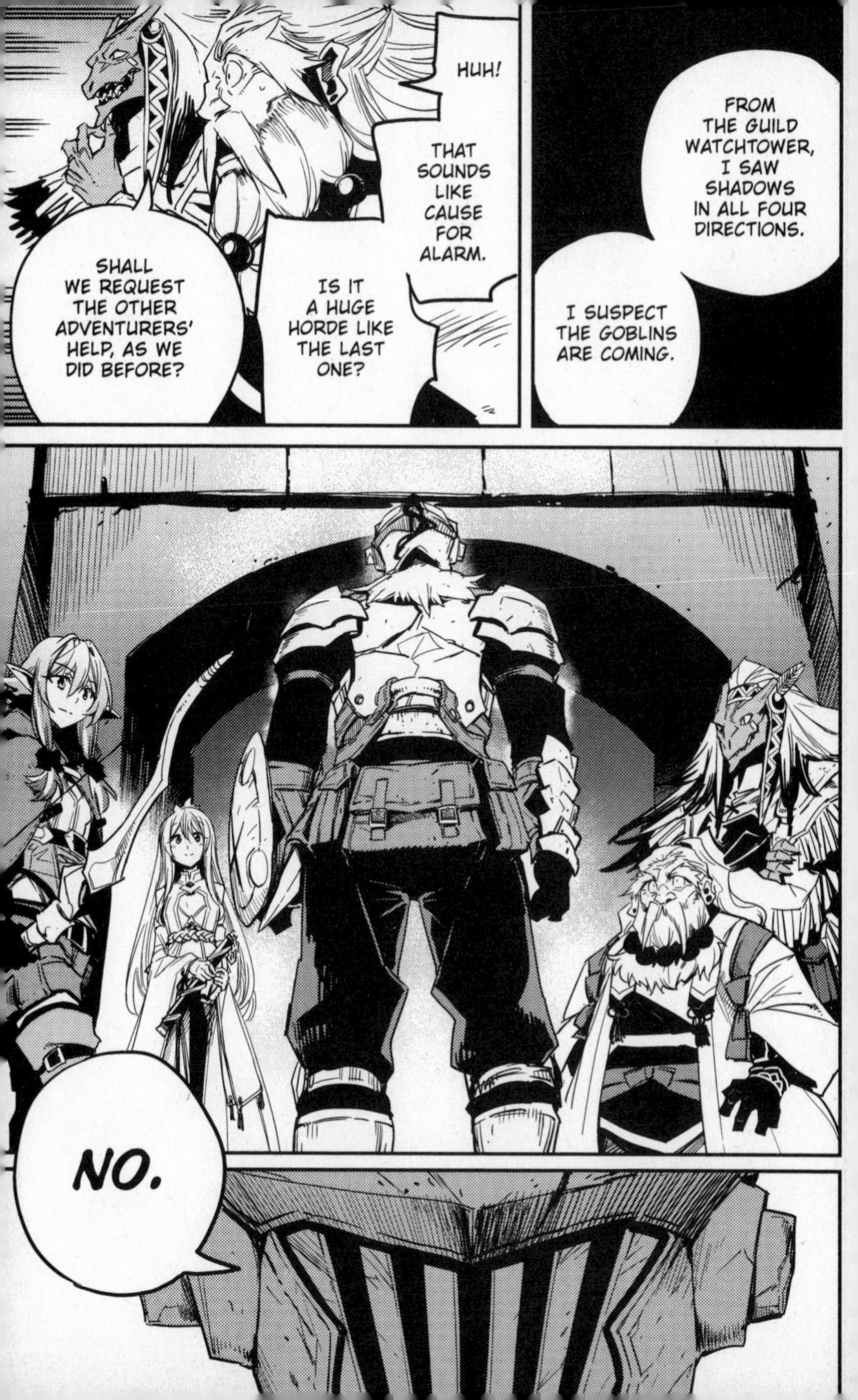
FROM THE GUILD WATCHTOWER, I SAW SHADOWS IN ALL FOUR DIRECTIONS.
I SUSPECT THE GOBLINS ARE COMING.
HUH!
THAT SOUNDS LIKE CAUSE FOR ALARM.
IS IT A HUGE HORDE LIKE THE LAST ONE?
SHALL WE REQUEST THE OTHER ADVENTURERS' HELP, AS WE DID BEFORE?
NO.

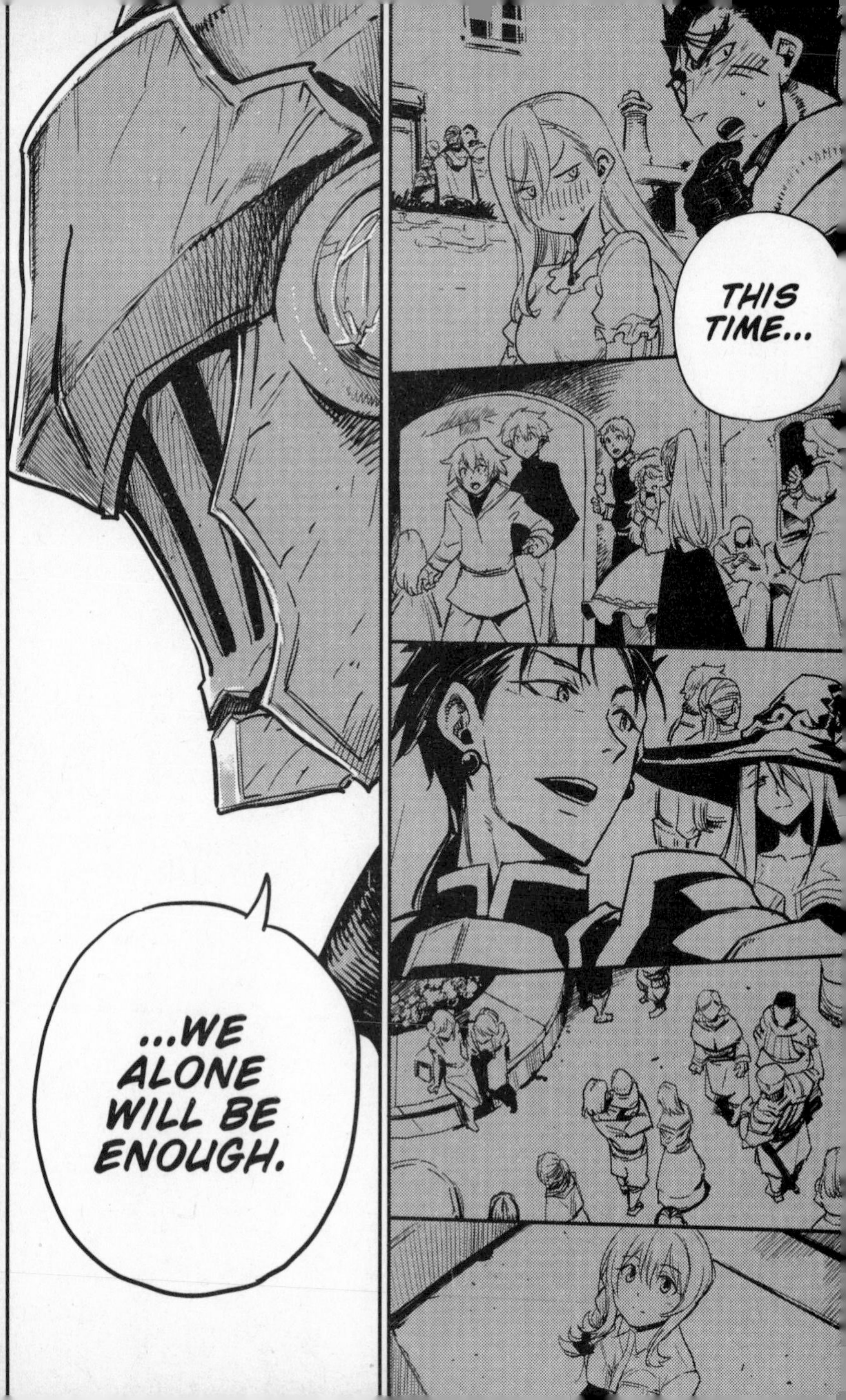
THIS TIME...
...WE ALONE WILL BE ENOUGH.

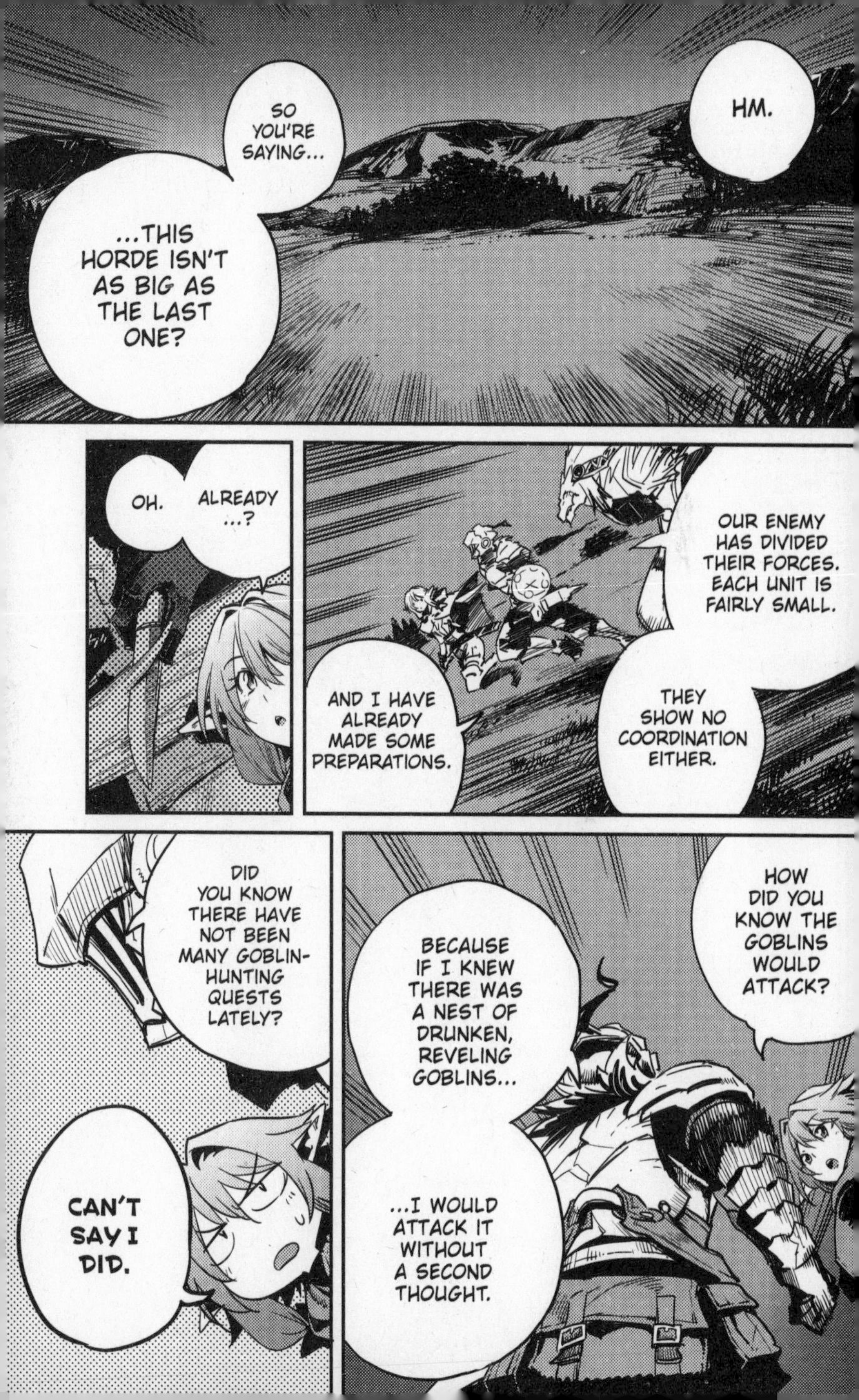
HM.
SO YOU'RE SAYING...
...THIS HORDE ISN'T AS BIG AS THE LAST ONE?
OUR ENEMY HAS DIVIDED THEIR FORCES. EACH UNIT IS FAIRLY SMALL.
THEY SHOW NO COORDINATION EITHER.
AND I HAVE ALREADY MADE SOME PREPARATIONS.
ALREADY ...?
OH.
HOW DID YOU KNOW THE GOBLINS WOULD ATTACK?
BECAUSE IF I KNEW THERE WAS A NEST OF DRUNKEN, REVELING GOBLINS...
...I WOULD ATTACK IT WITHOUT A SECOND THOUGHT.
DID YOU KNOW THERE HAVE NOT BEEN MANY GOBLIN-HUNTING QUESTS LATELY?
CAN'T SAY I DID.

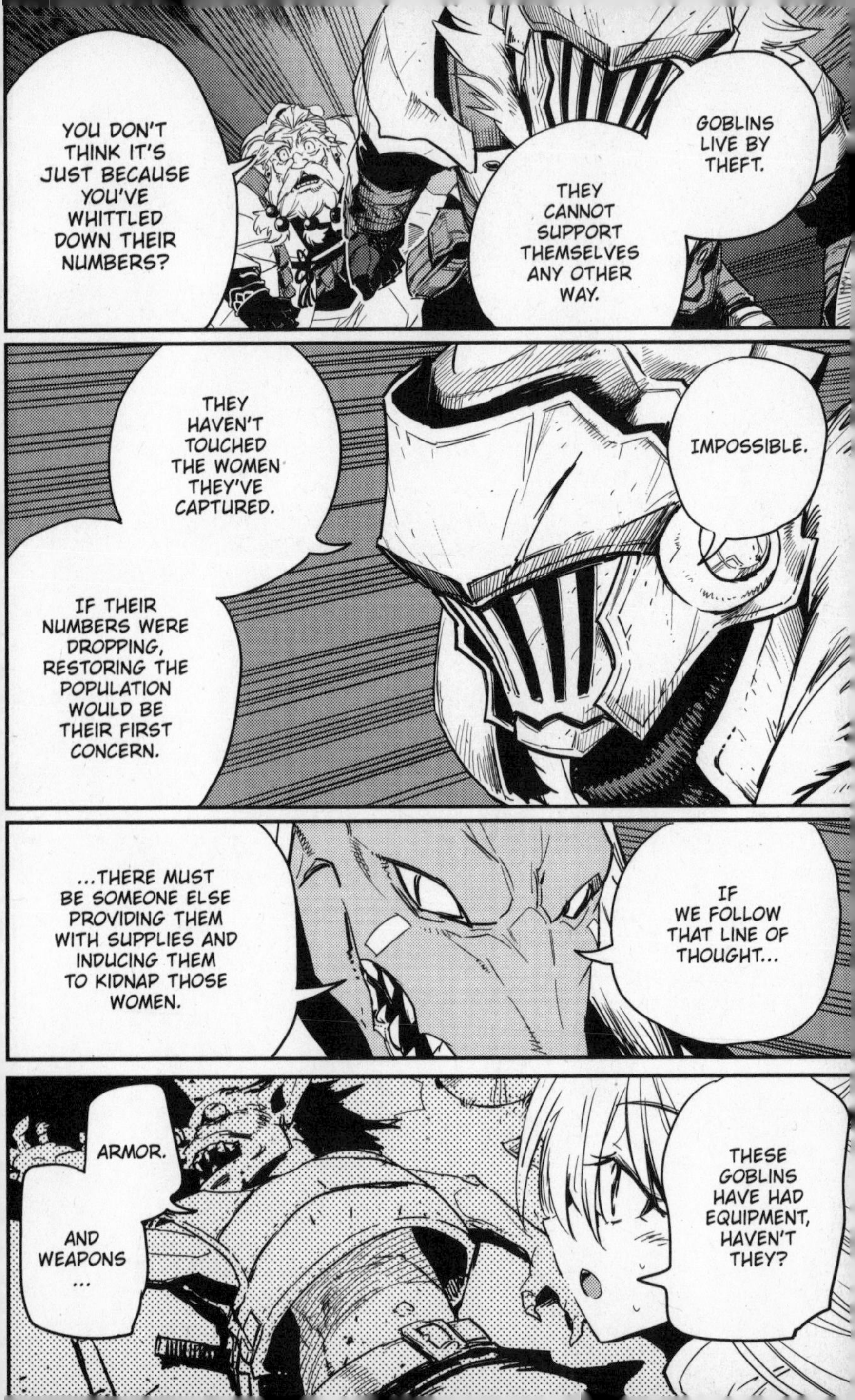
GOBLINS LIVE BY THEFT.
THEY CANNOT SUPPORT THEMSELVES ANY OTHER WAY.
YOU DON'T THINK IT'S JUST BECAUSE YOU'VE WHITTLED DOWN THEIR NUMBERS?
IMPOSSIBLE.
THEY HAVEN'T TOUCHED THE WOMEN THEY'VE CAPTURED.
IF THEIR NUMBERS WERE DROPPING, RESTORING THE POPULATION WOULD BE THEIR FIRST CONCERN.
IF WE FOLLOW THAT LINE OF THOUGHT...
...THERE MUST BE SOMEONE ELSE PROVIDING THEM WITH SUPPLIES AND INDUCING THEM TO KIDNAP THOSE WOMEN.
THESE GOBLINS HAVE HAD EQUIPMENT, HAVEN'T THEY?
ARMOR.
AND WEAPONS ...

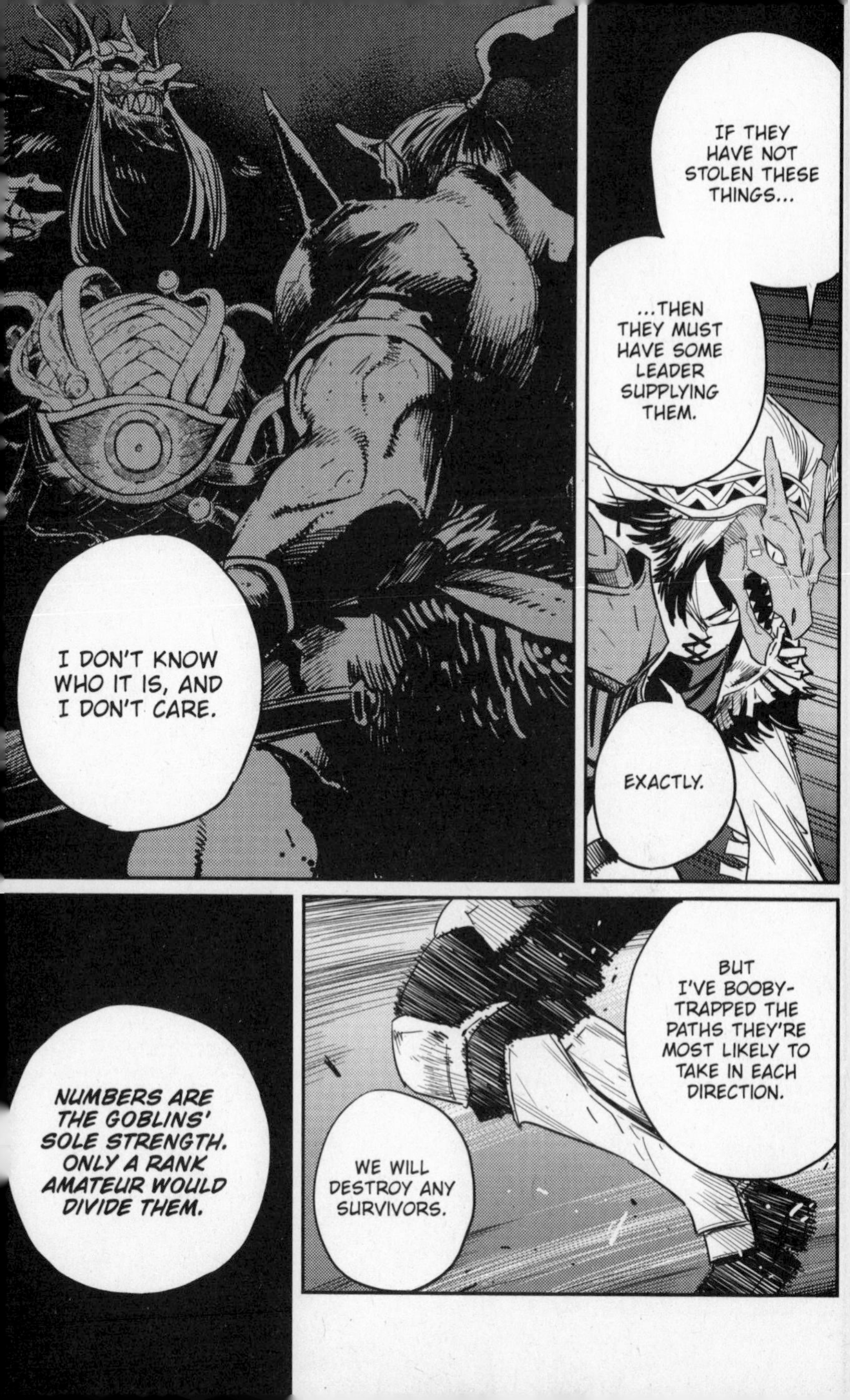
IF THEY HAVE NOT STOLEN THESE THINGS...
...THEN THEY MUST HAVE SOME LEADER SUPPLYING THEM.
EXACTLY.
I DON'T KNOW WHO IT IS, AND I DON'T CARE.
BUT I'VE BOOBY-TRAPPED THE PATHS THEY'RE MOST LIKELY TO TAKE IN EACH DIRECTION.
WE WILL DESTROY ANY SURVIVORS.
NUMBERS ARE THE GOBLINS' SOLE STRENGTH. ONLY A RANK AMATEUR WOULD DIVIDE THEM.

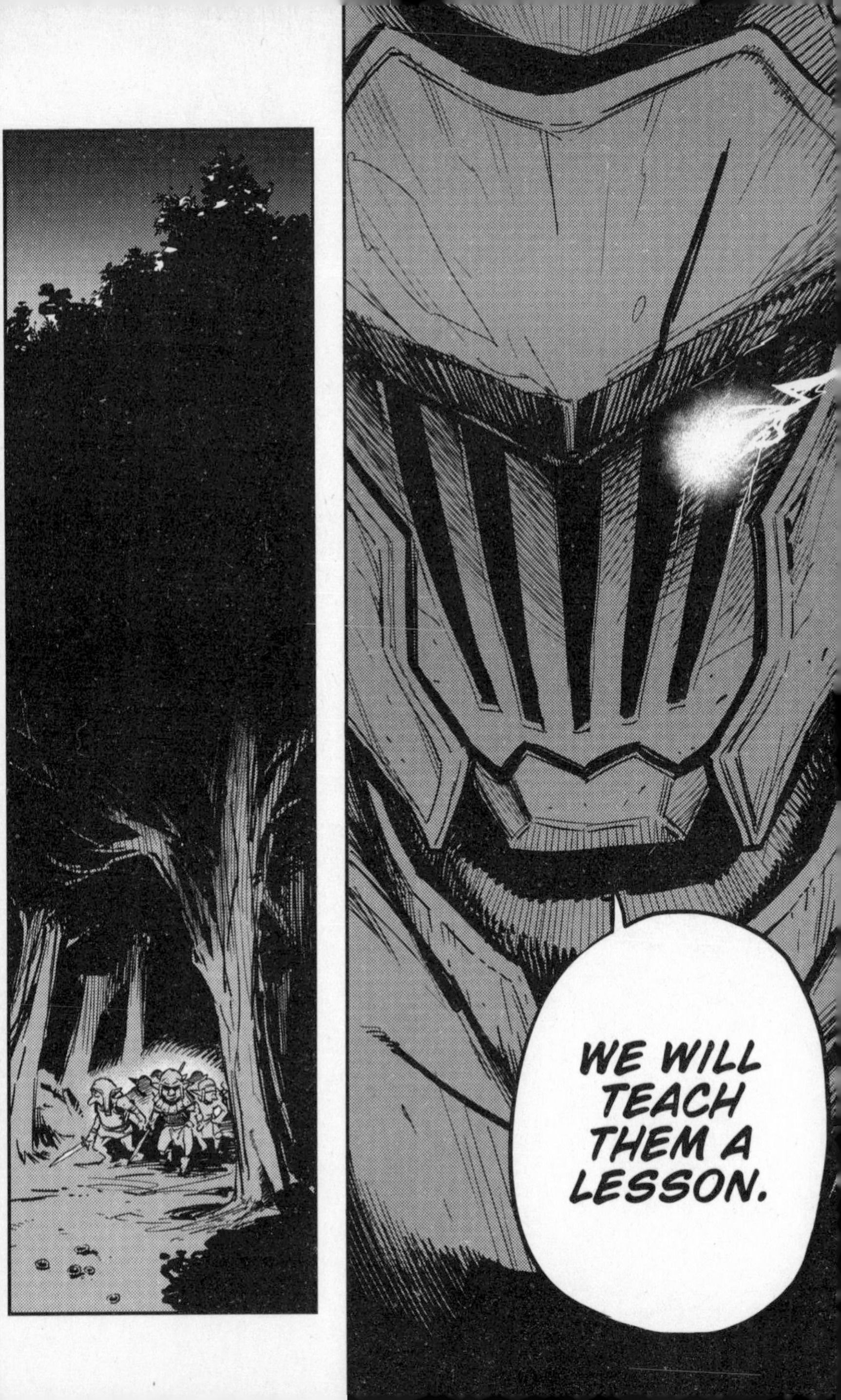
WE WILL TEACH THEM A LESSON.

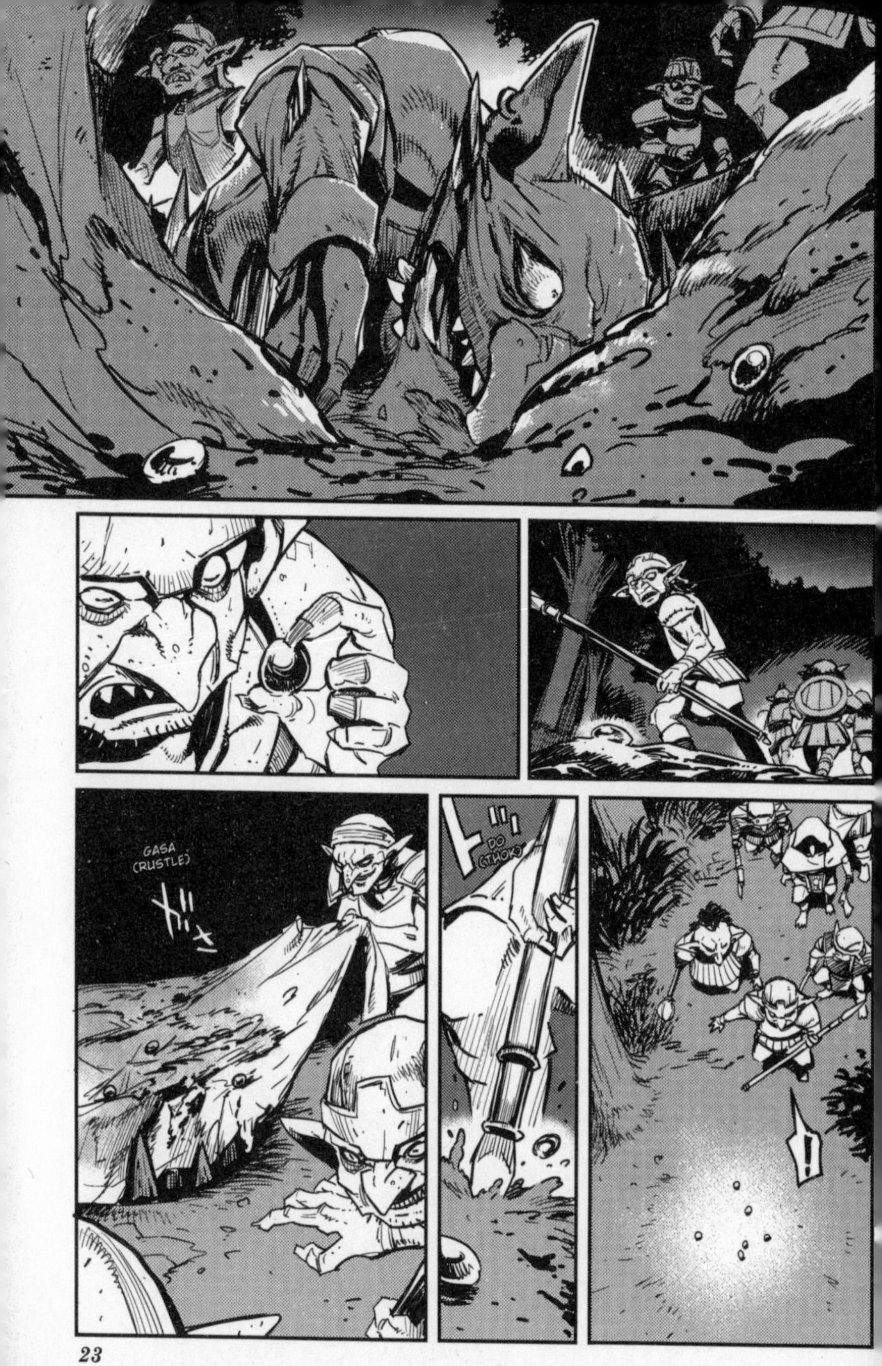
DO (THOK)
GASA (RUSTLE)
!

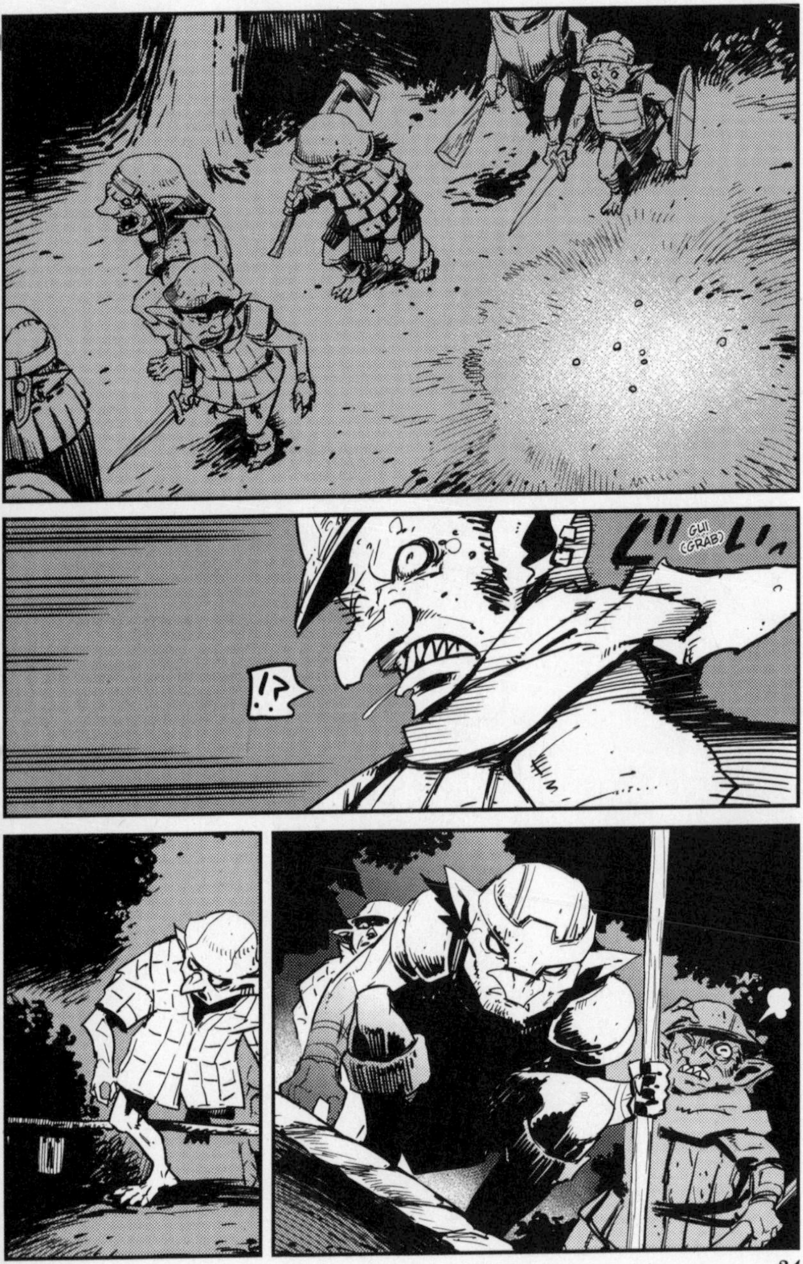
GUI
(GRAB)
!?

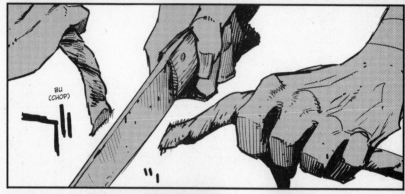

BU
(CHOP)

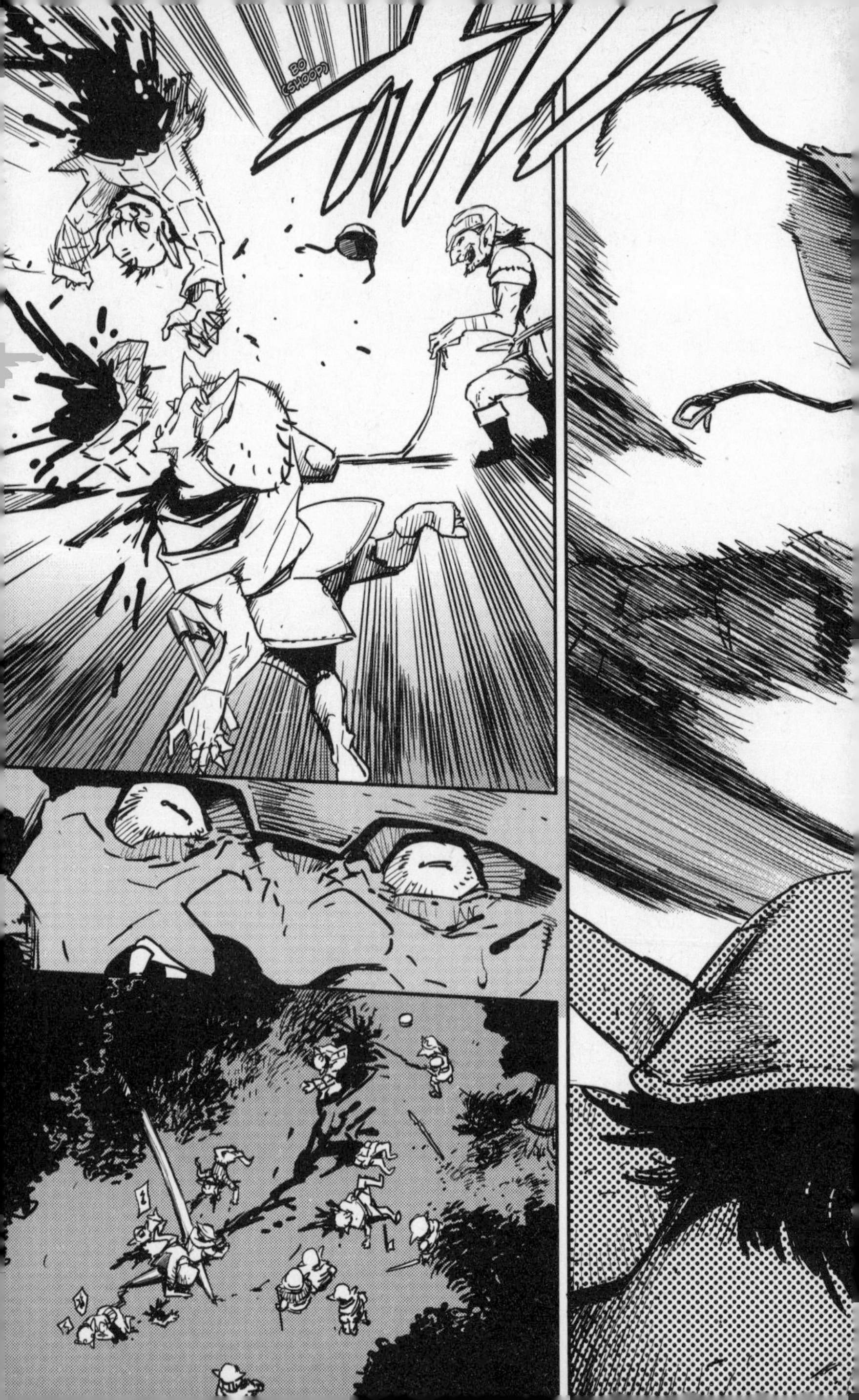
BO (SHOOP)

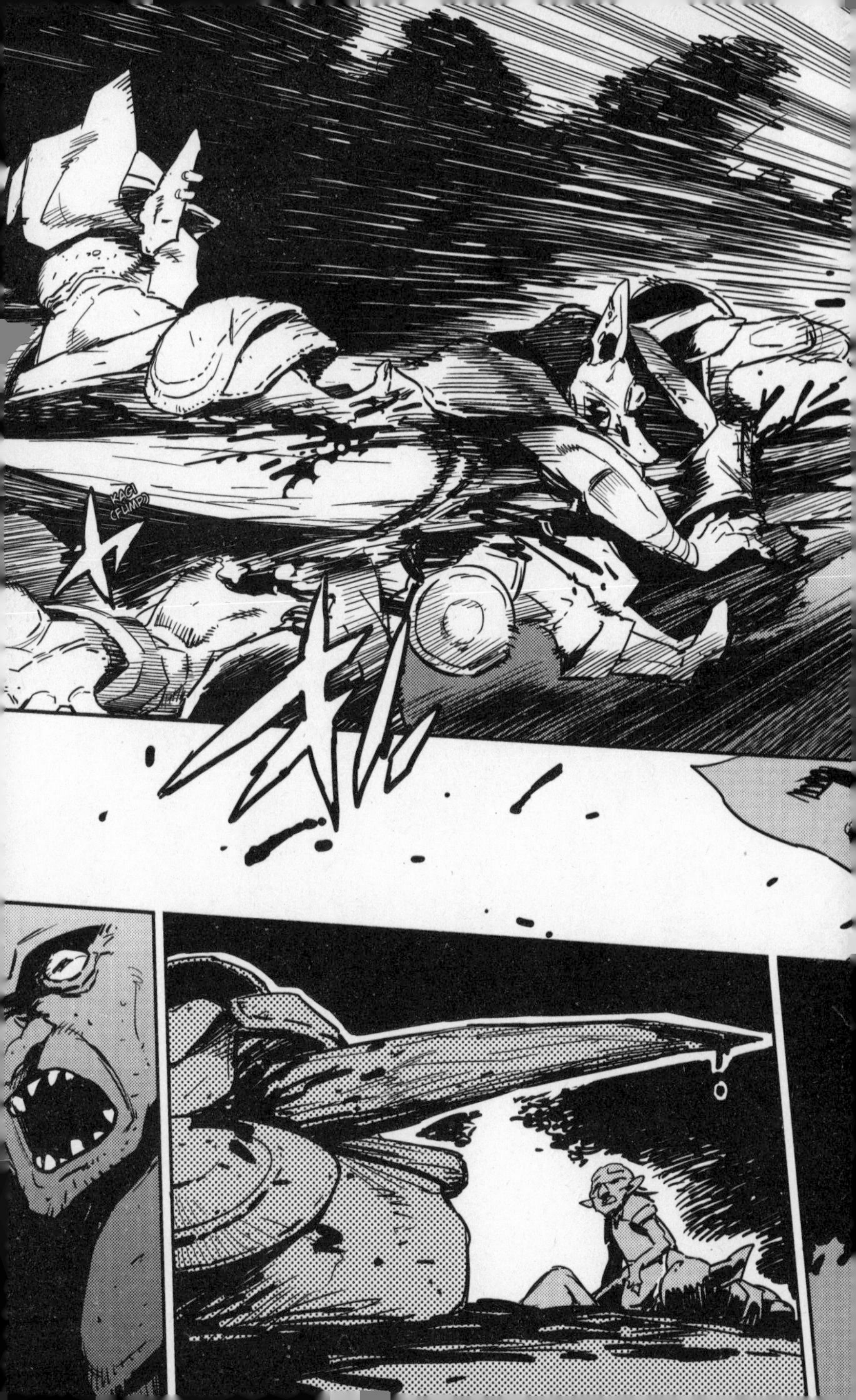
KAGI
(FUMP)

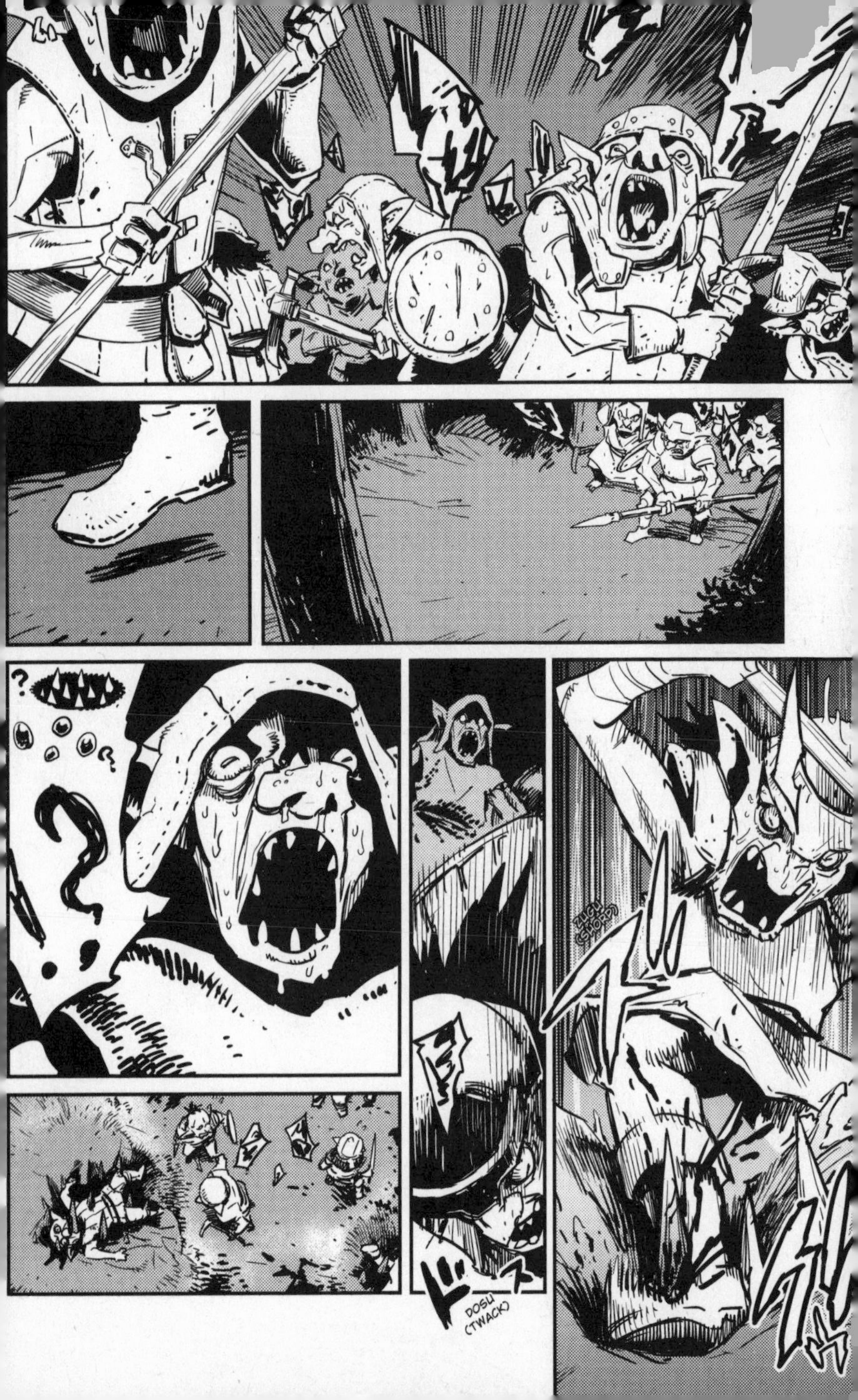
ZUGU (SHORP)
DOSU (TWACK)

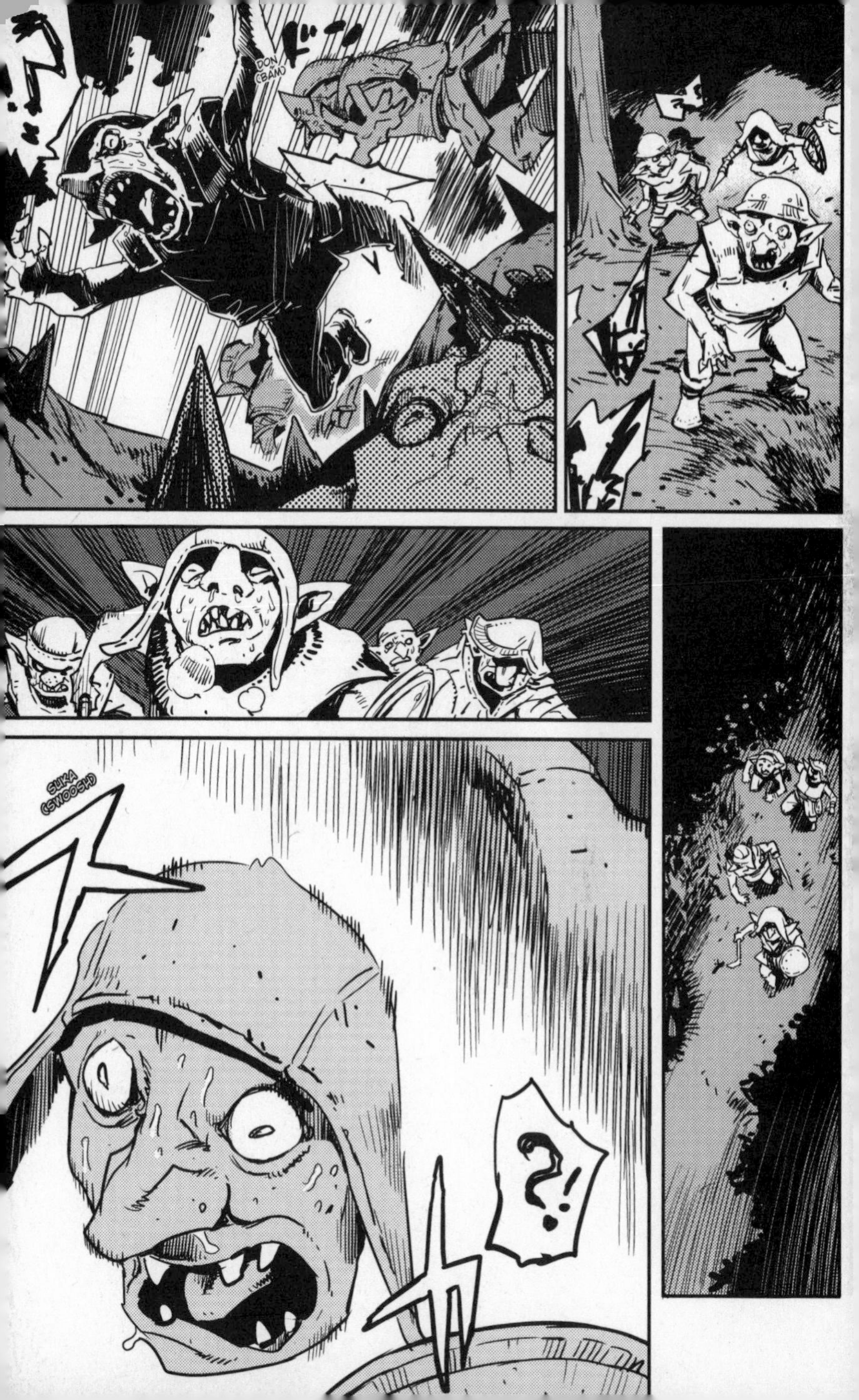
?
DON (BAM)
SUKA (SWOOSH)
?!

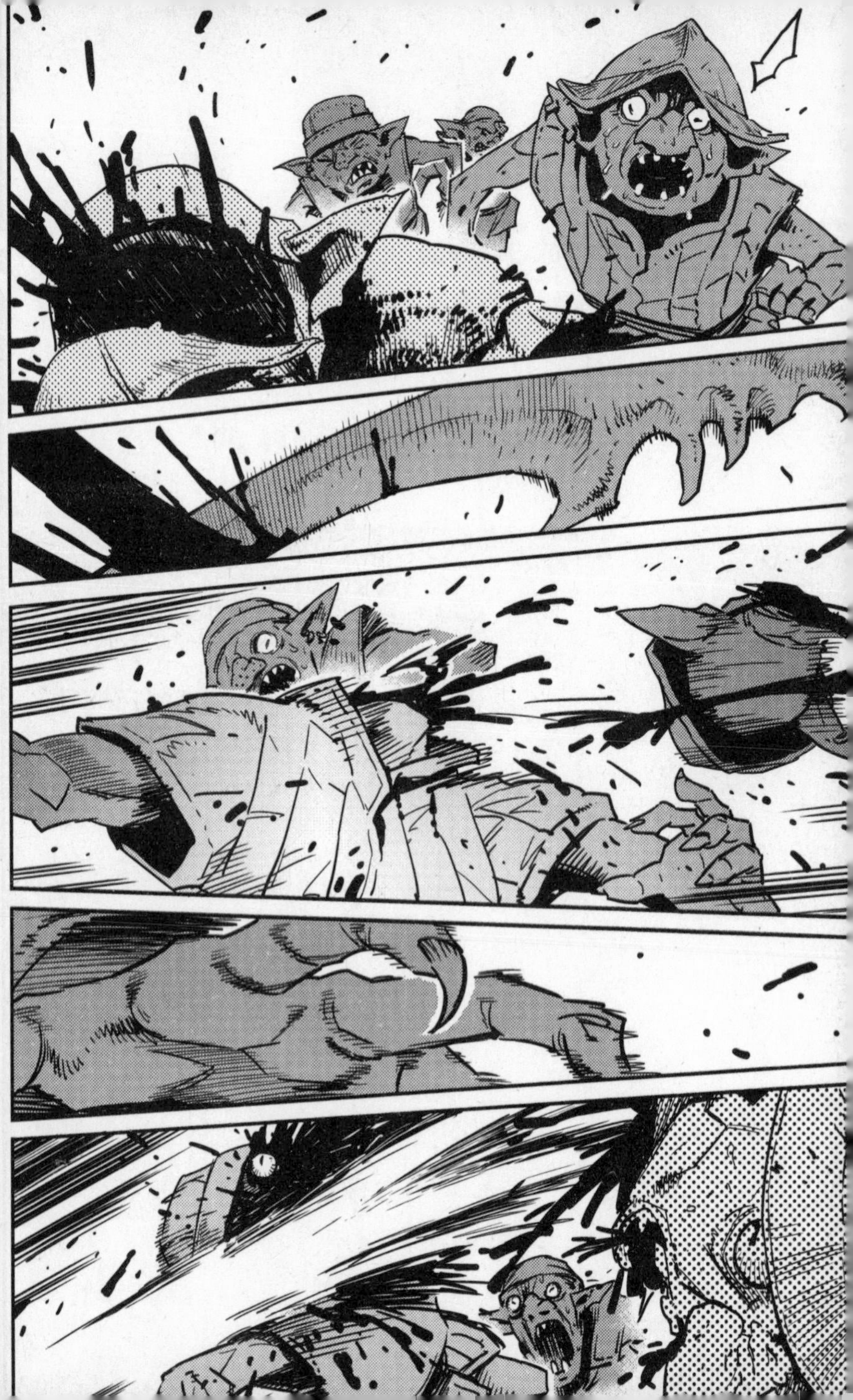

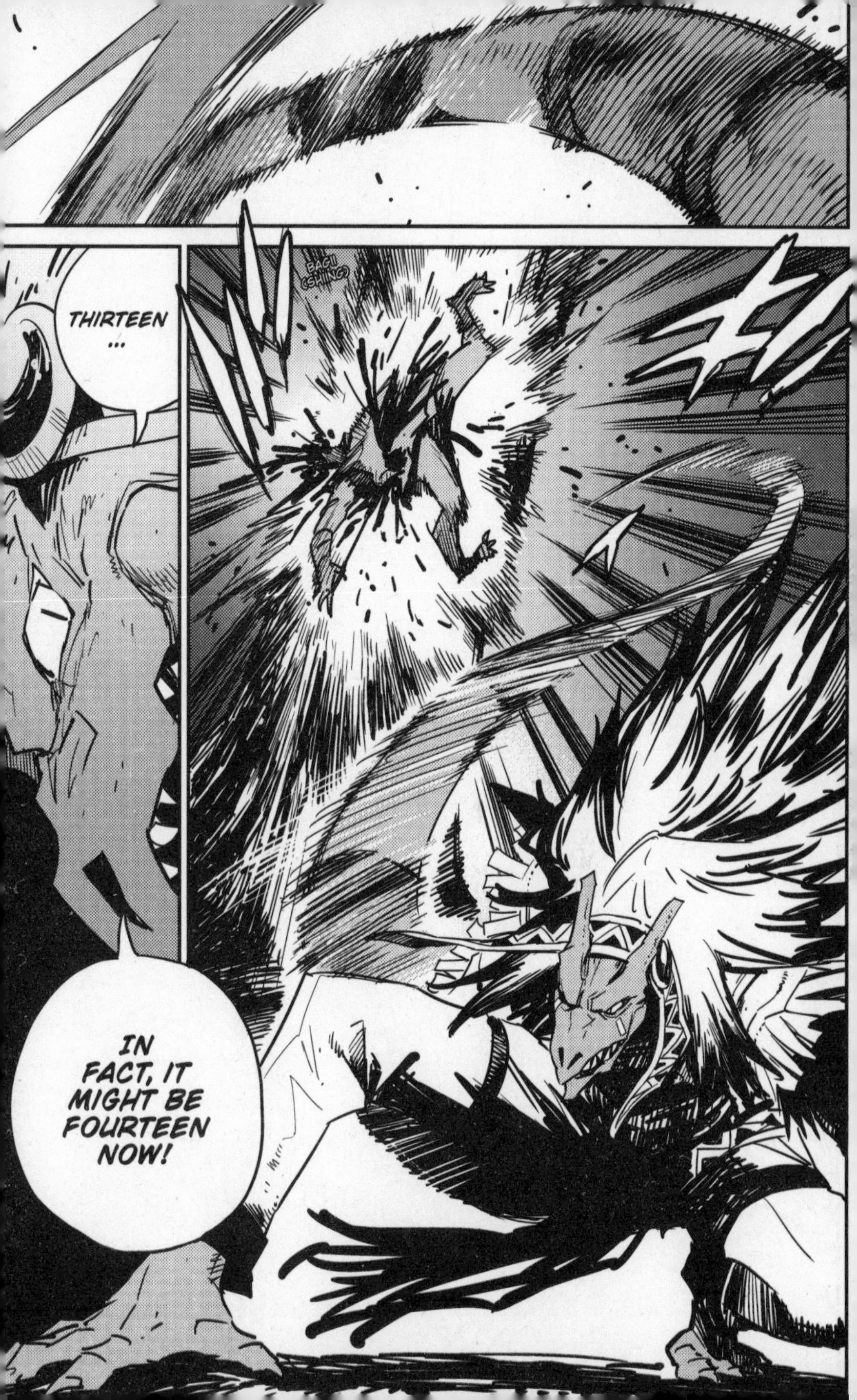
BAGI! (SHIING)
THIRTEEN ...
IN FACT, IT MIGHT BE FOURTEEN NOW!

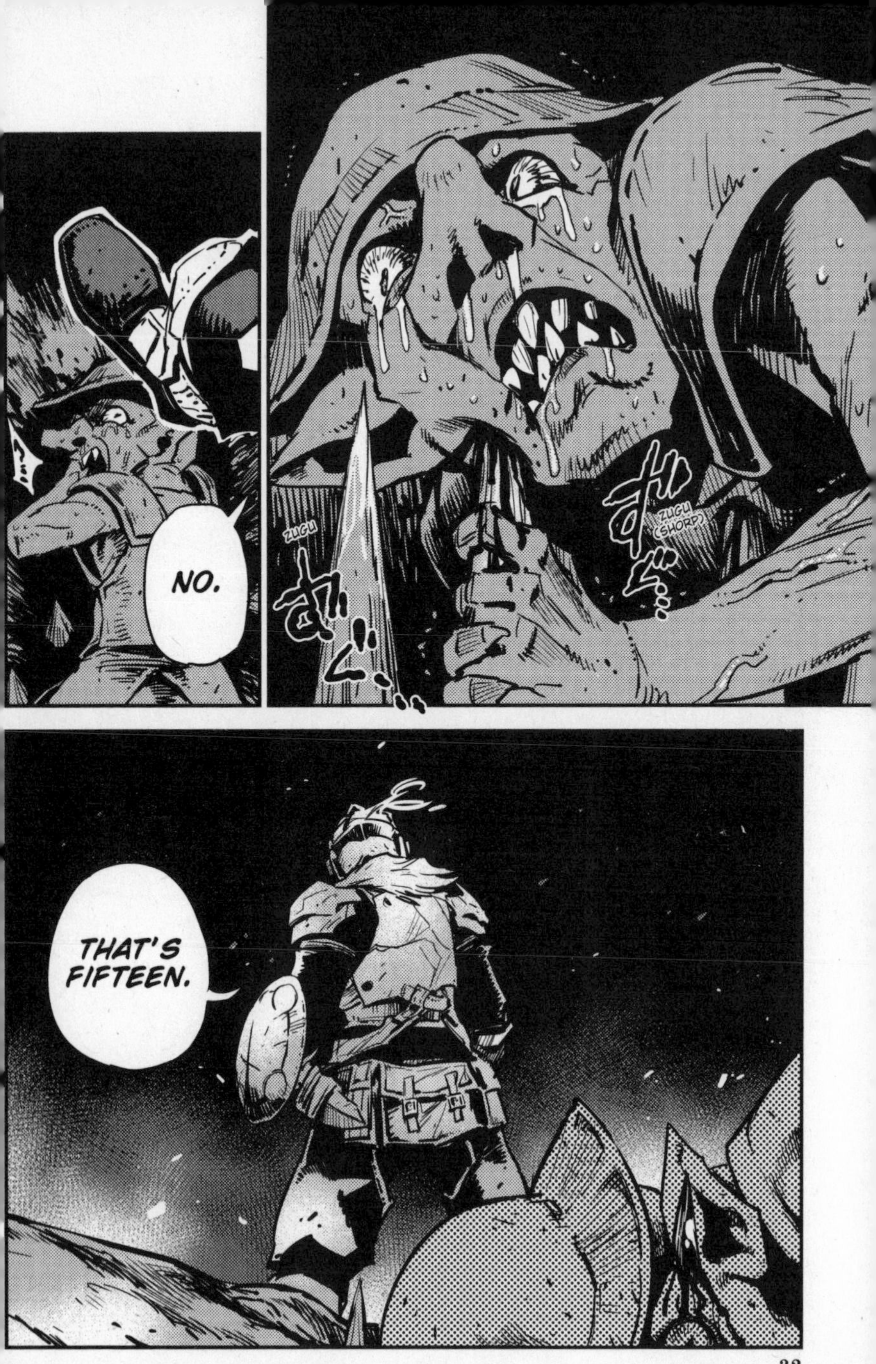
ZUGU (SHORP)
ZUGU
?!
NO.
THAT'S FIFTEEN.

CHAPTER 37

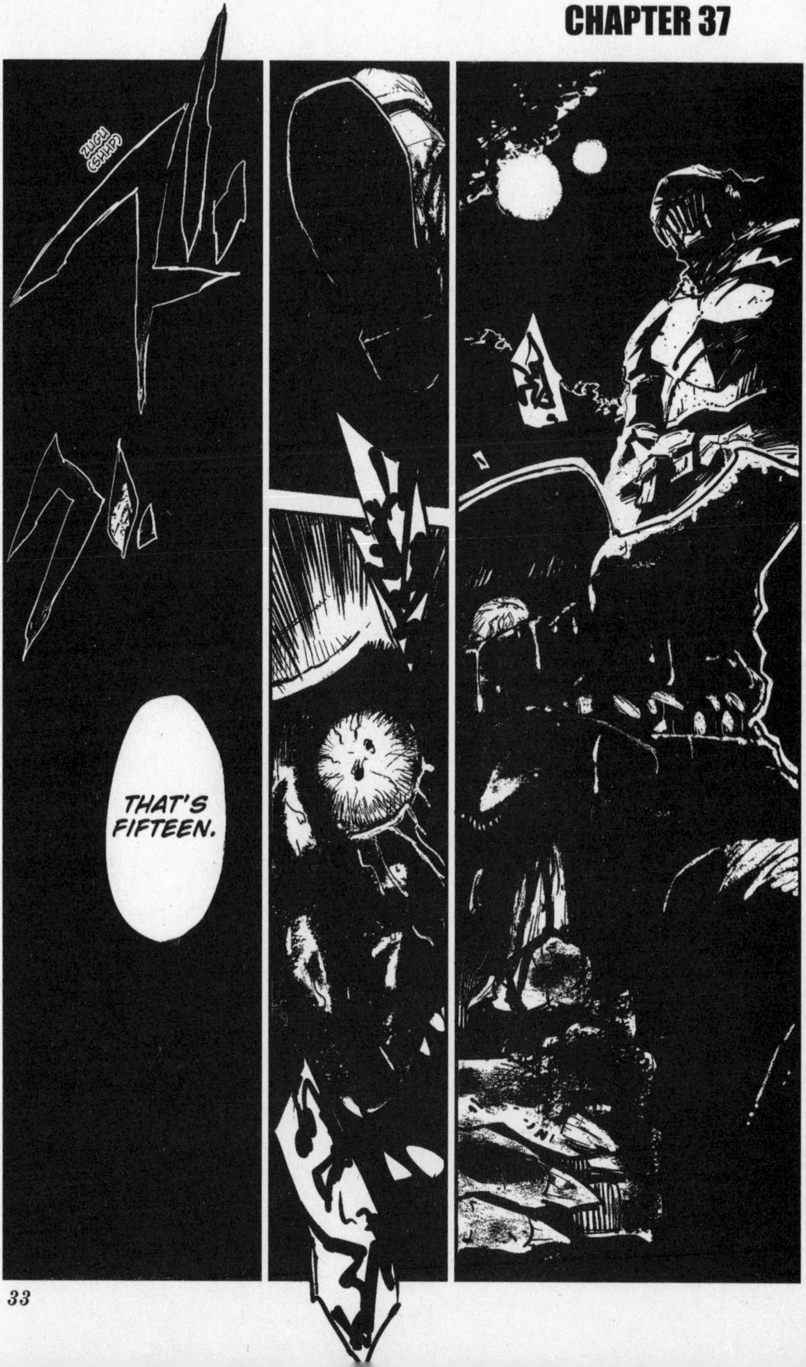
ZUGU
(SHP)
THAT'S FIFTEEN.

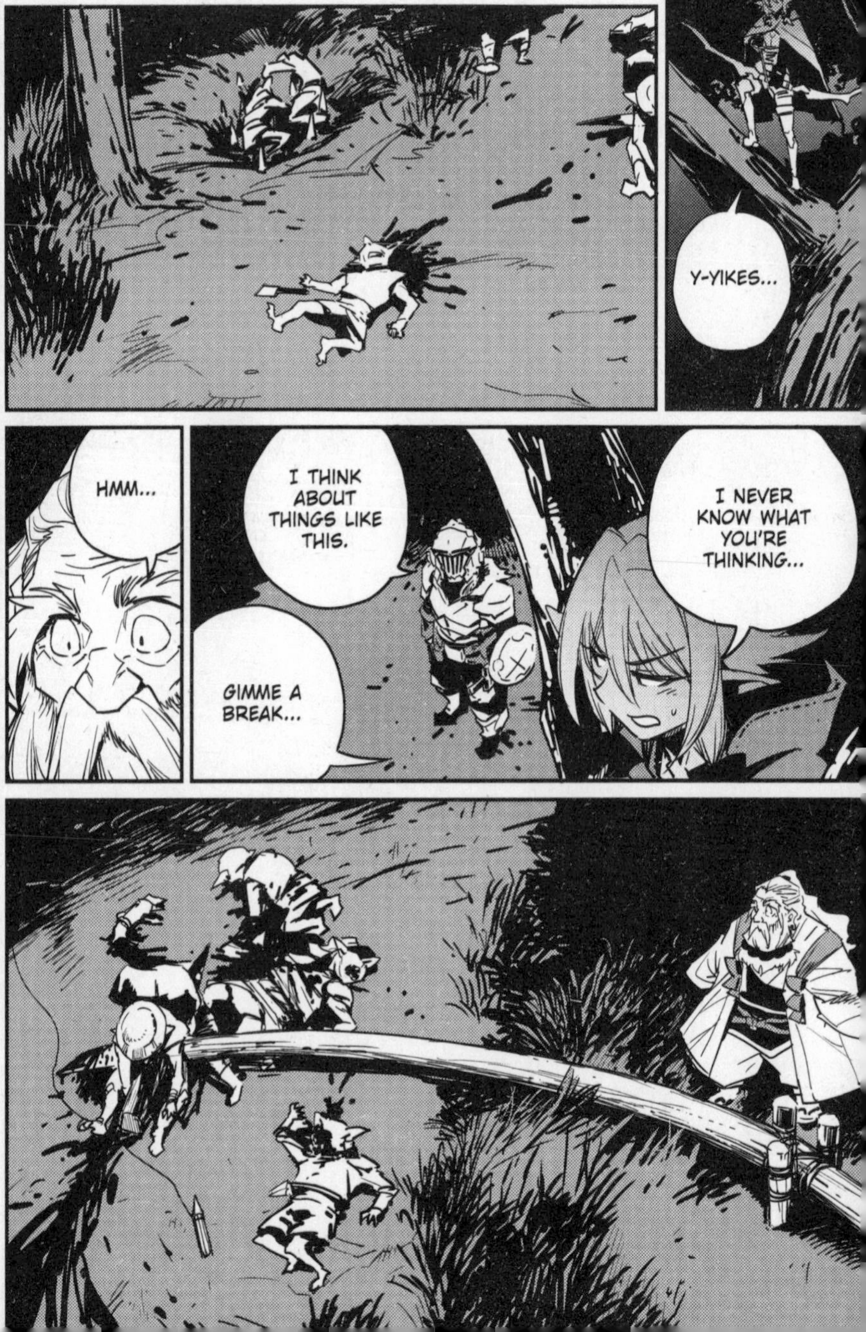
Y-YIKES...
I NEVER KNOW WHAT YOU'RE THINKING...
I THINK ABOUT THINGS LIKE THIS.
GIMME A BREAK...
HMM...

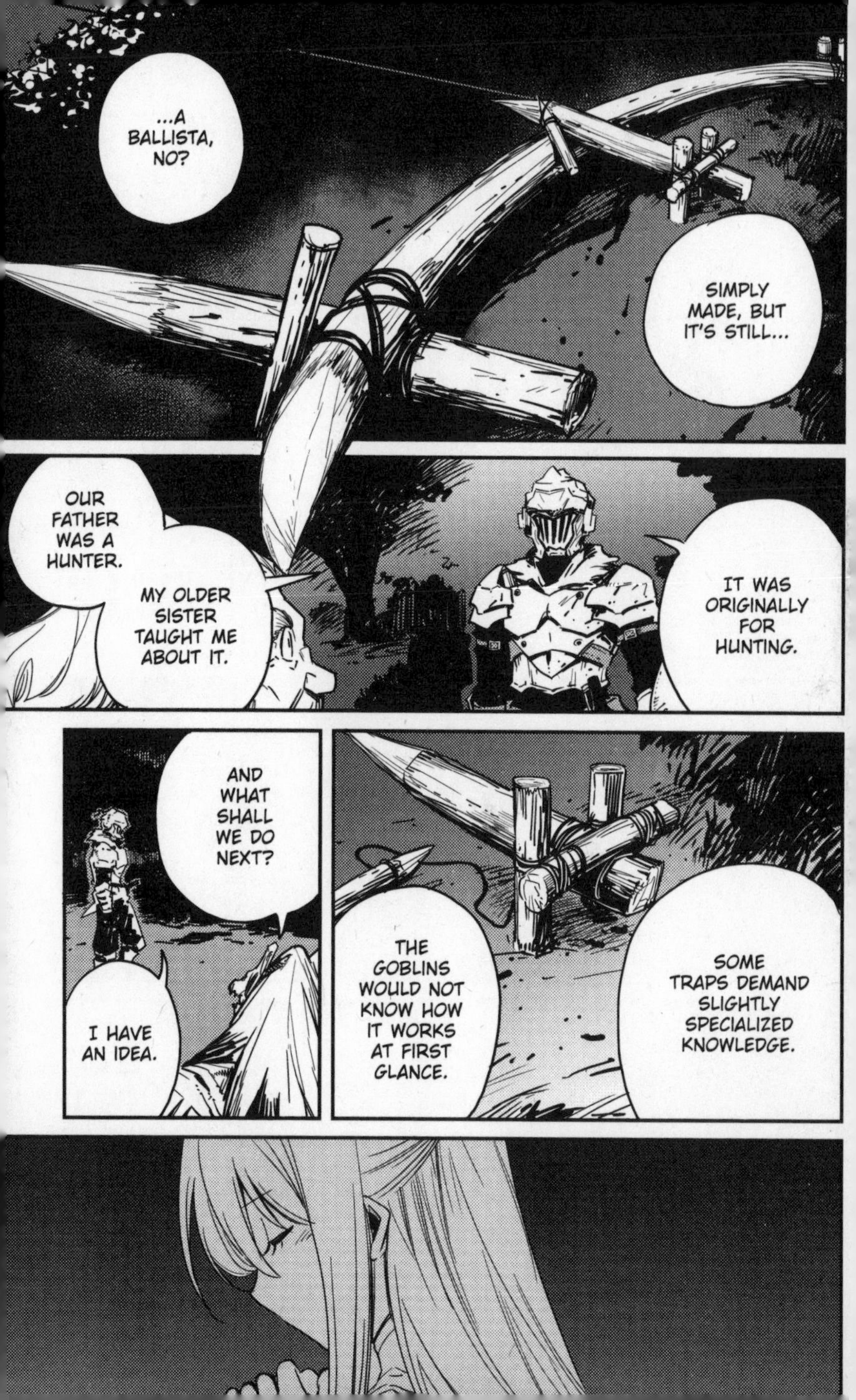
...A BALLISTA, NO?
SIMPLY MADE, BUT IT'S STILL...
IT WAS ORIGINALLY FOR HUNTING.
OUR FATHER WAS A HUNTER.
MY OLDER SISTER TAUGHT ME ABOUT IT.
SOME TRAPS DEMAND SLIGHTLY SPECIALIZED KNOWLEDGE.
THE GOBLINS WOULD NOT KNOW HOW IT WORKS AT FIRST GLANCE.
AND WHAT SHALL WE DO NEXT?
I HAVE AN IDEA.

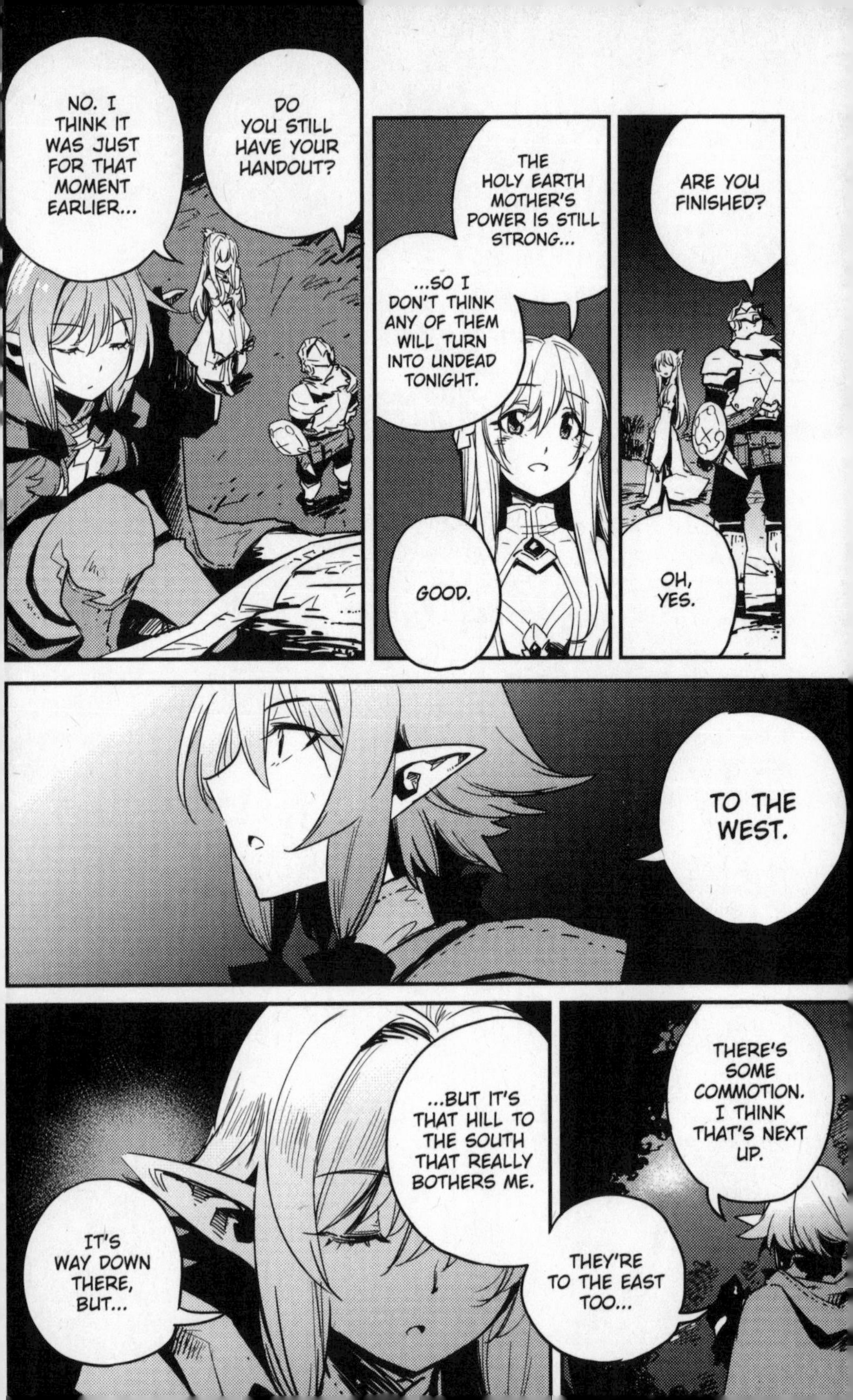
ARE YOU FINISHED?
OH, YES.
THE HOLY EARTH MOTHER'S POWER IS STILL STRONG...
...SO I DON'T THINK ANY OF THEM WILL TURN INTO UNDEAD TONIGHT.
GOOD.
DO YOU STILL HAVE YOUR HANDOUT?
NO. I THINK IT WAS JUST FOR THAT MOMENT EARLIER...
TO THE WEST.
THERE'S SOME COMMOTION. I THINK THAT'S NEXT UP.
THEY'RE TO THE EAST TOO...
IT'S WAY DOWN THERE, BUT...
...BUT IT'S THAT HILL TO THE SOUTH THAT REALLY BOTHERS ME.

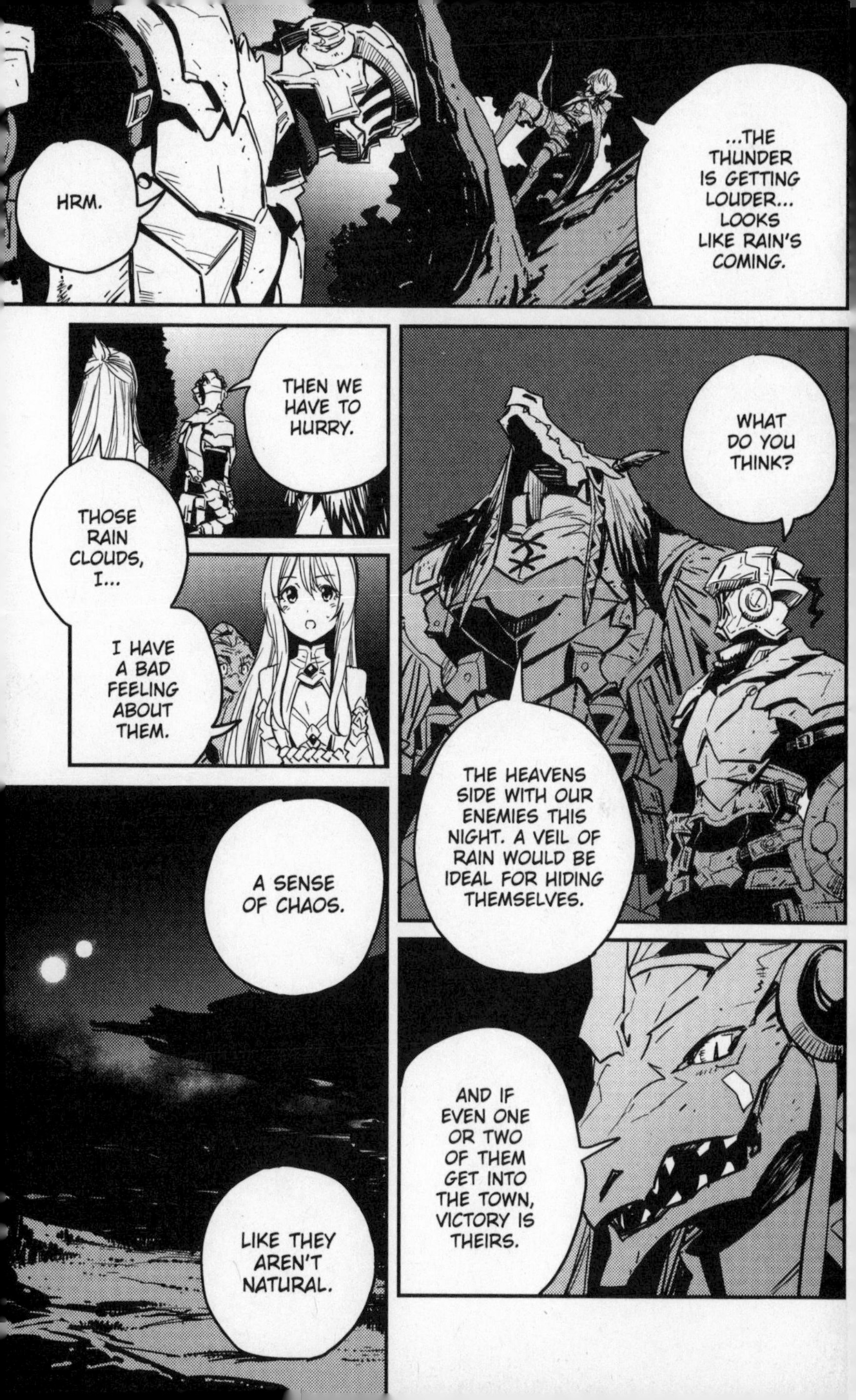
...THE THUNDER IS GETTING LOUDER... LOOKS LIKE RAIN'S COMING.
HRM.
WHAT DO YOU THINK?
THE HEAVENS SIDE WITH OUR ENEMIES THIS NIGHT. A VEIL OF RAIN WOULD BE IDEAL FOR HIDING THEMSELVES.
THEN WE HAVE TO HURRY.
THOSE RAIN CLOUDS, I...
I HAVE A BAD FEELING ABOUT THEM.
AND IF EVEN ONE OR TWO OF THEM GET INTO THE TOWN, VICTORY IS THEIRS.
A SENSE OF CHAOS.
LIKE THEY AREN'T NATURAL.

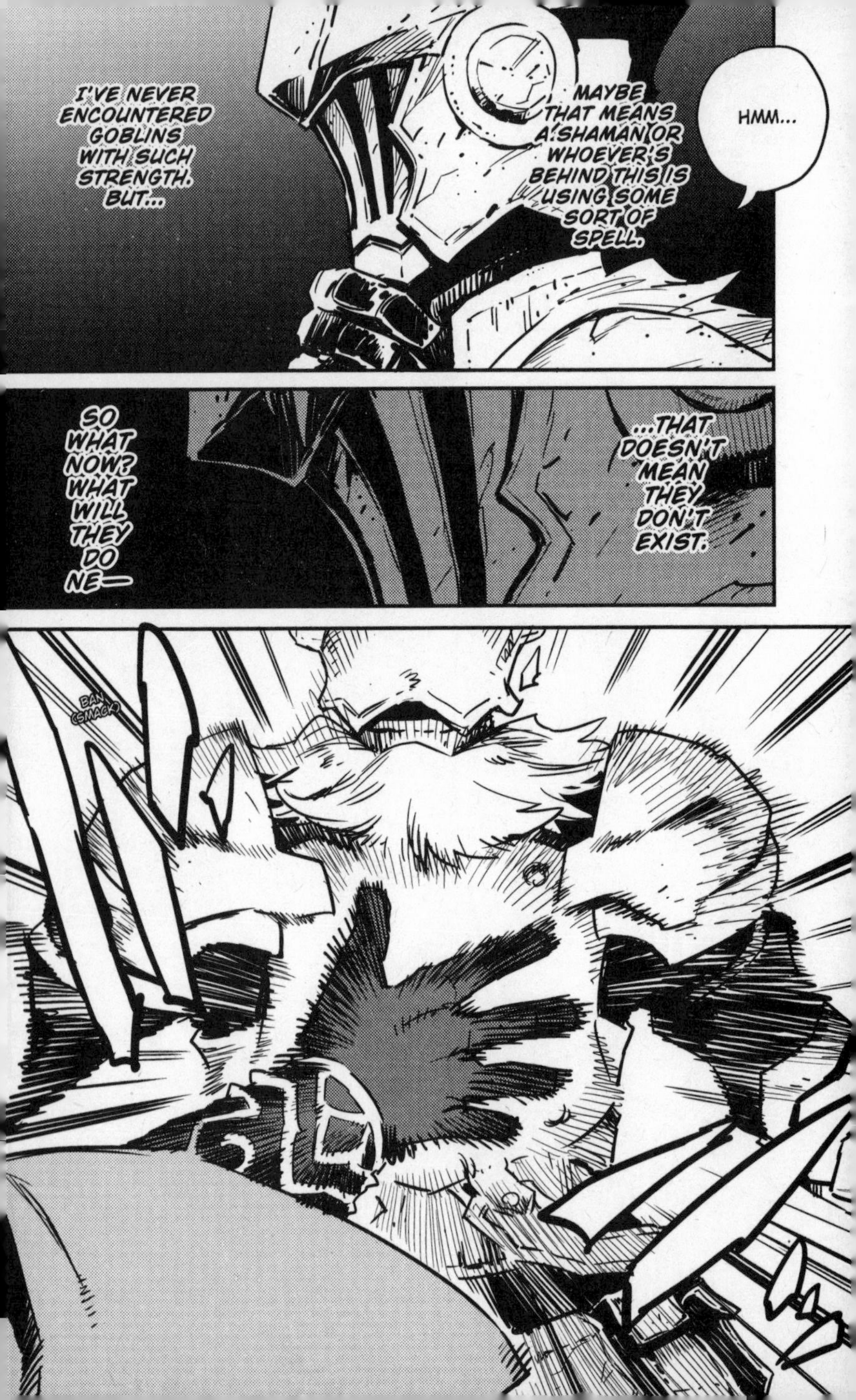
HMM...
MAYBE THAT MEANS A SHAMAN OR WHOEVER'S BEHIND THIS IS USING SOME SORT OF SPELL.
I'VE NEVER ENCOUNTERED GOBLINS WITH SUCH STRENGTH. BUT...
...THAT DOESN'T MEAN THEY DON'T EXIST.
SO WHAT NOW? WHAT WILL THEY DO NE—
BAN (SMACK)

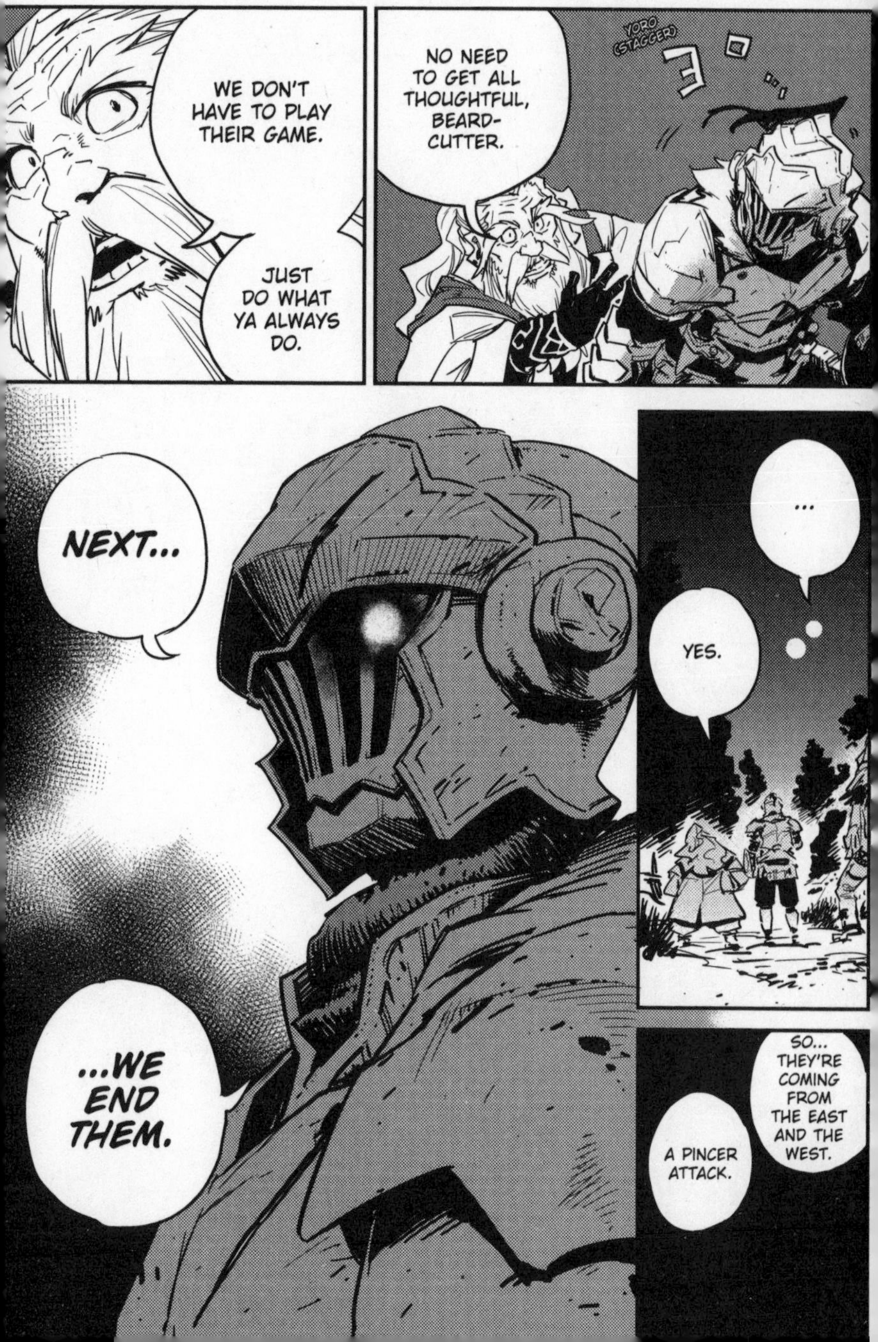
YORO (STAGGER)
NO NEED TO GET ALL THOUGHTFUL, BEARD-CUTTER.
WE DON'T HAVE TO PLAY THEIR GAME.
JUST DO WHAT YA ALWAYS DO.
...
YES.
SO... THEY'RE COMING FROM THE EAST AND THE WEST.
A PINCER ATTACK.
NEXT...
...WE END THEM.

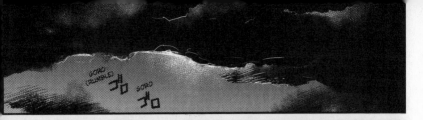

GORO
(RUMBLE)
ゴロ
ゴロ
GORO

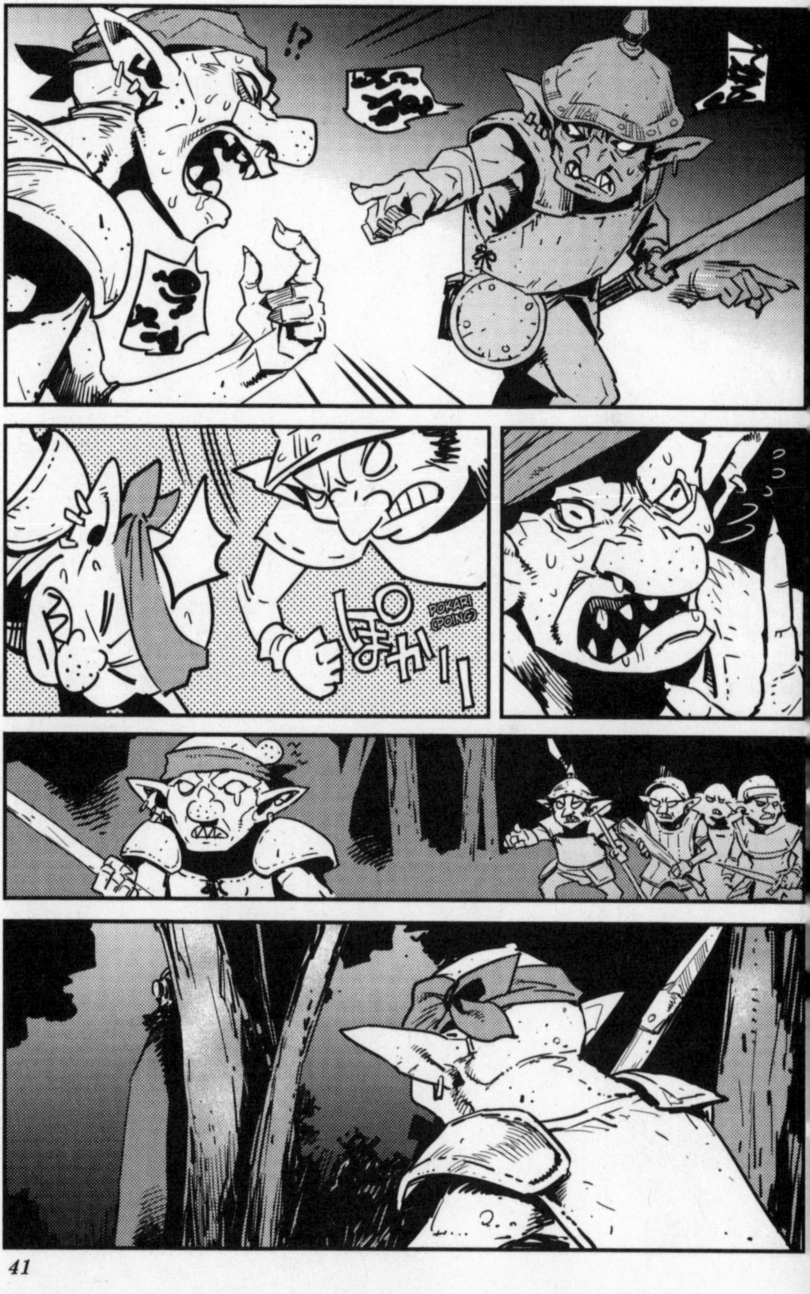
!?
POKARI
(POING)

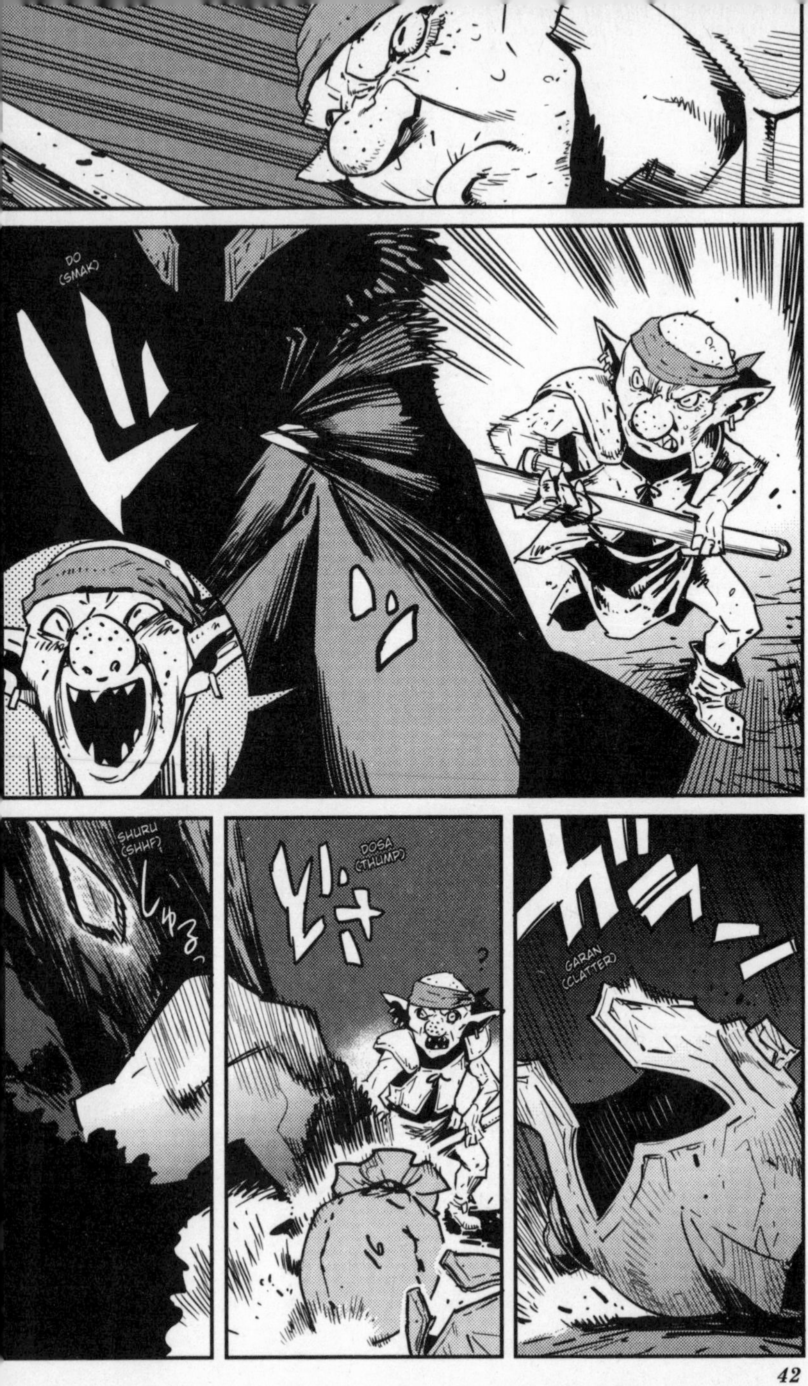
DO
(SMAK)
GARAN
(CLATTER)
DOSA
(THUMP)
SHURU
(SHHF)

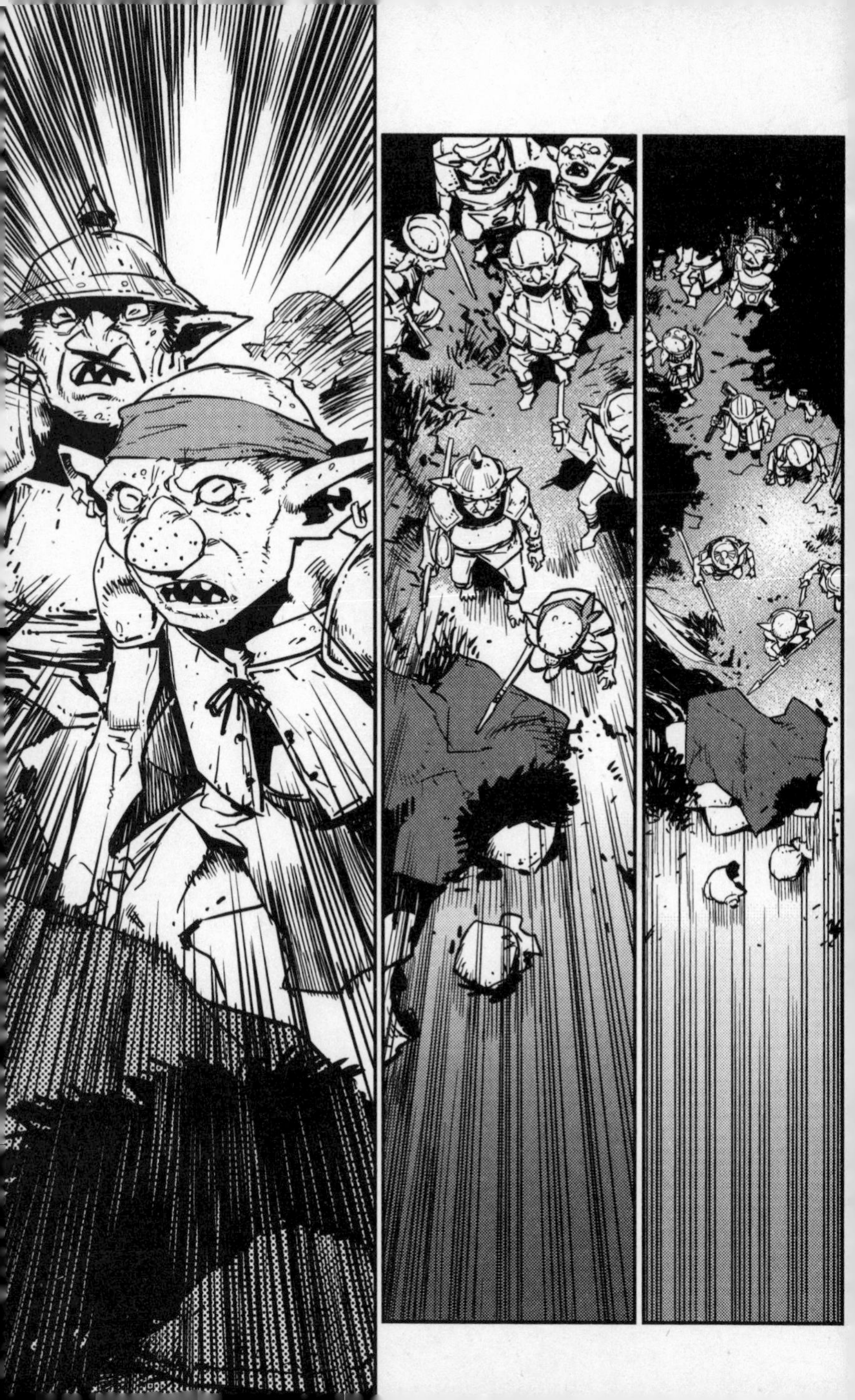

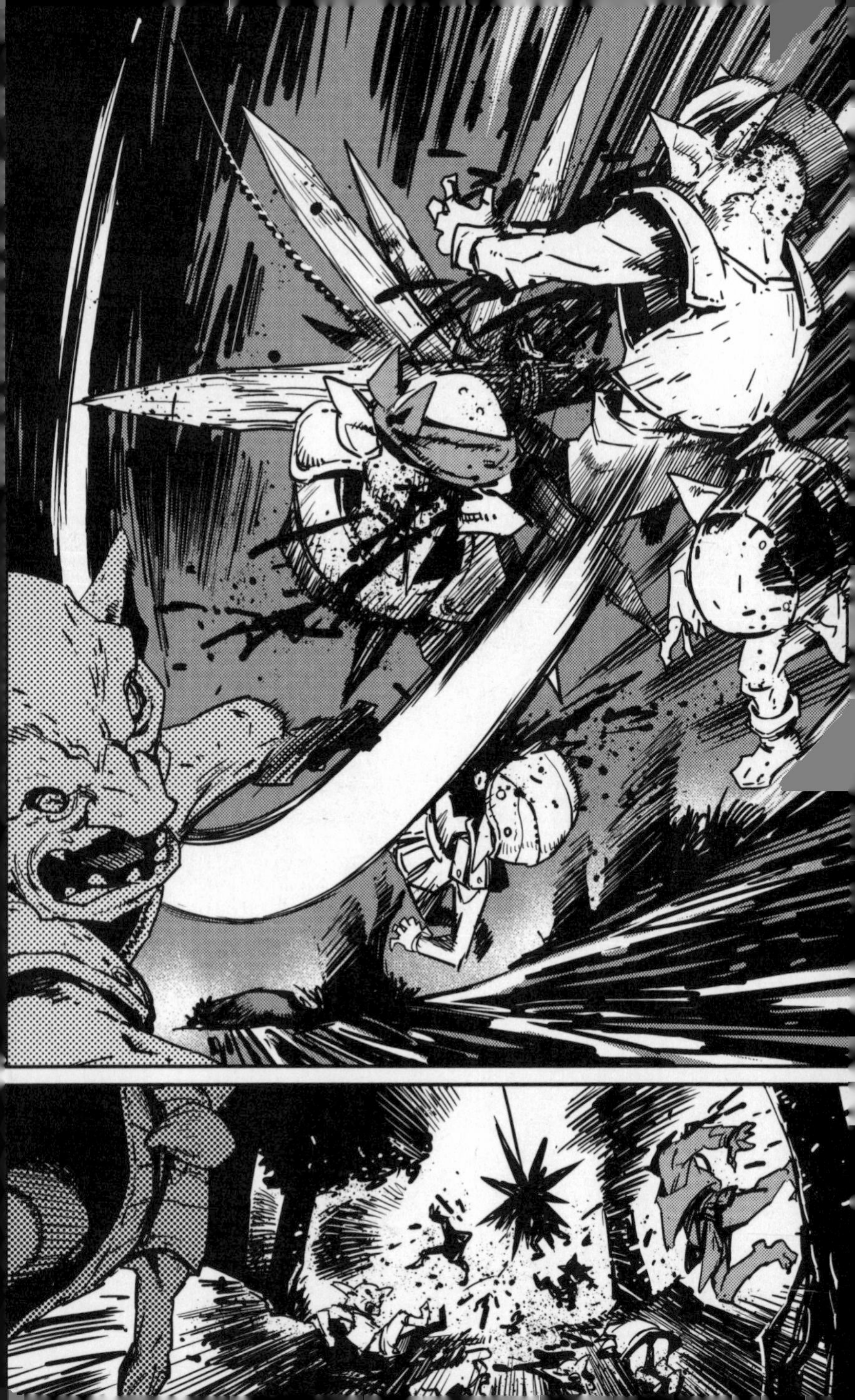

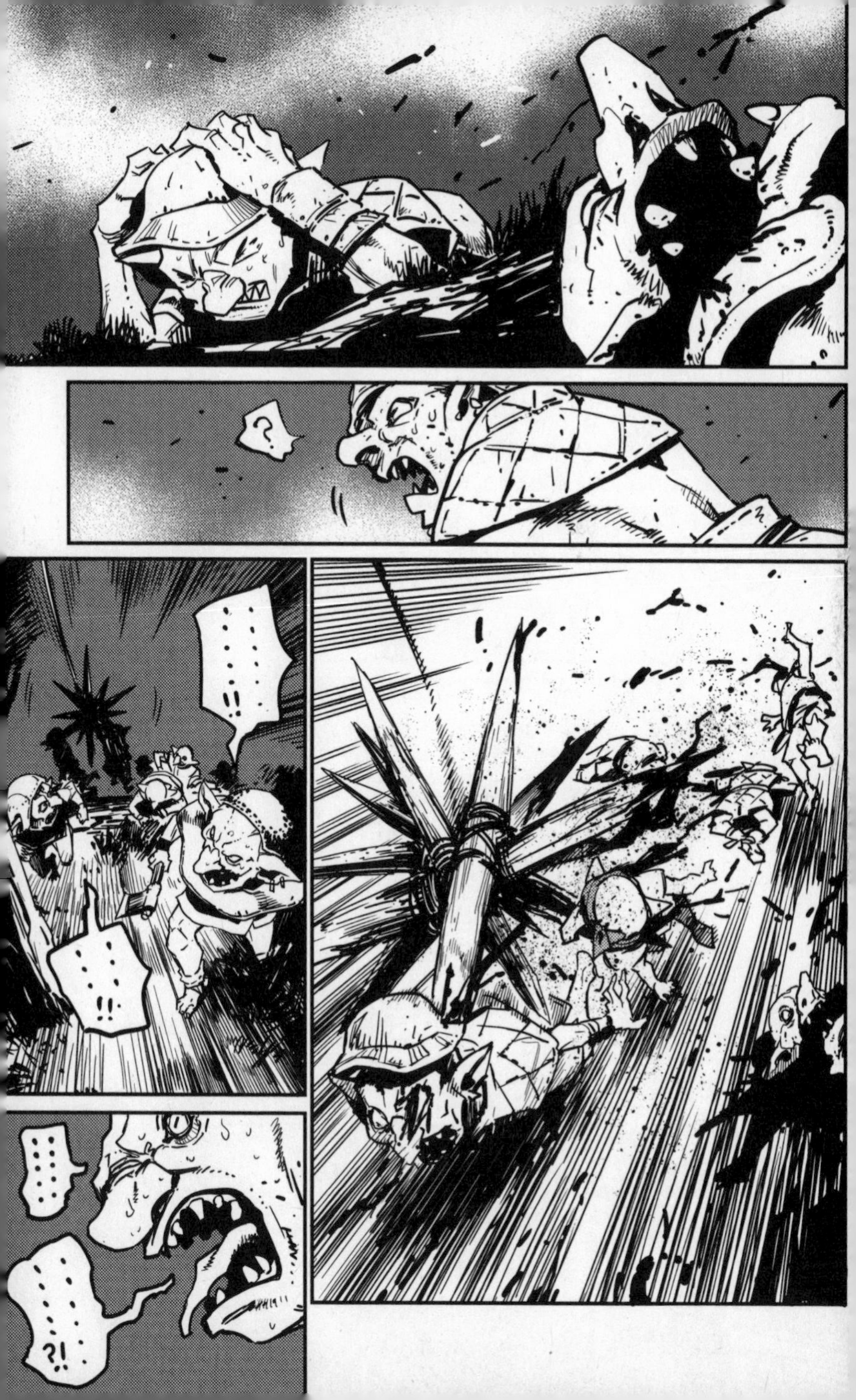
?
......!!
......!!
......
......?!

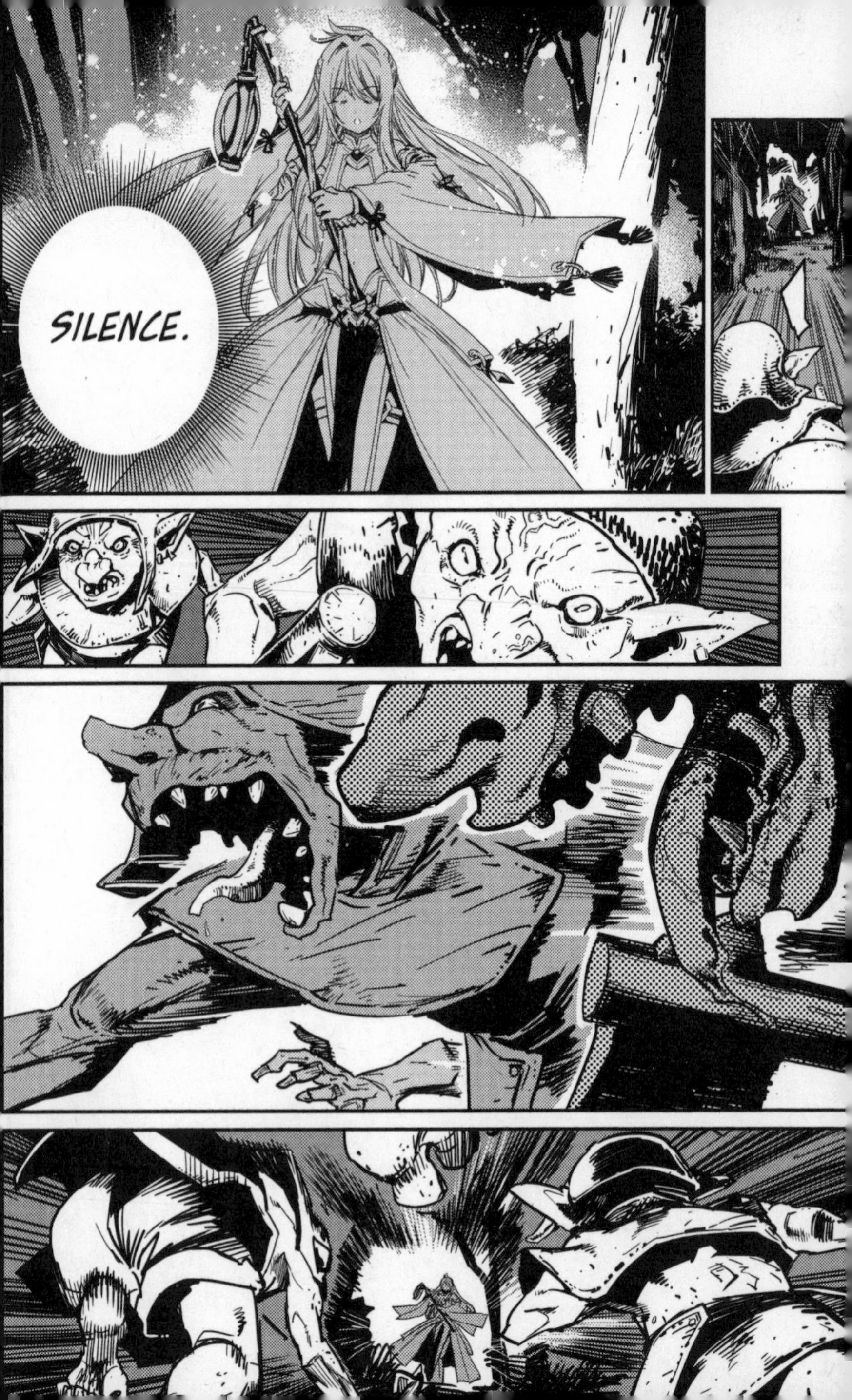
SILENCE.

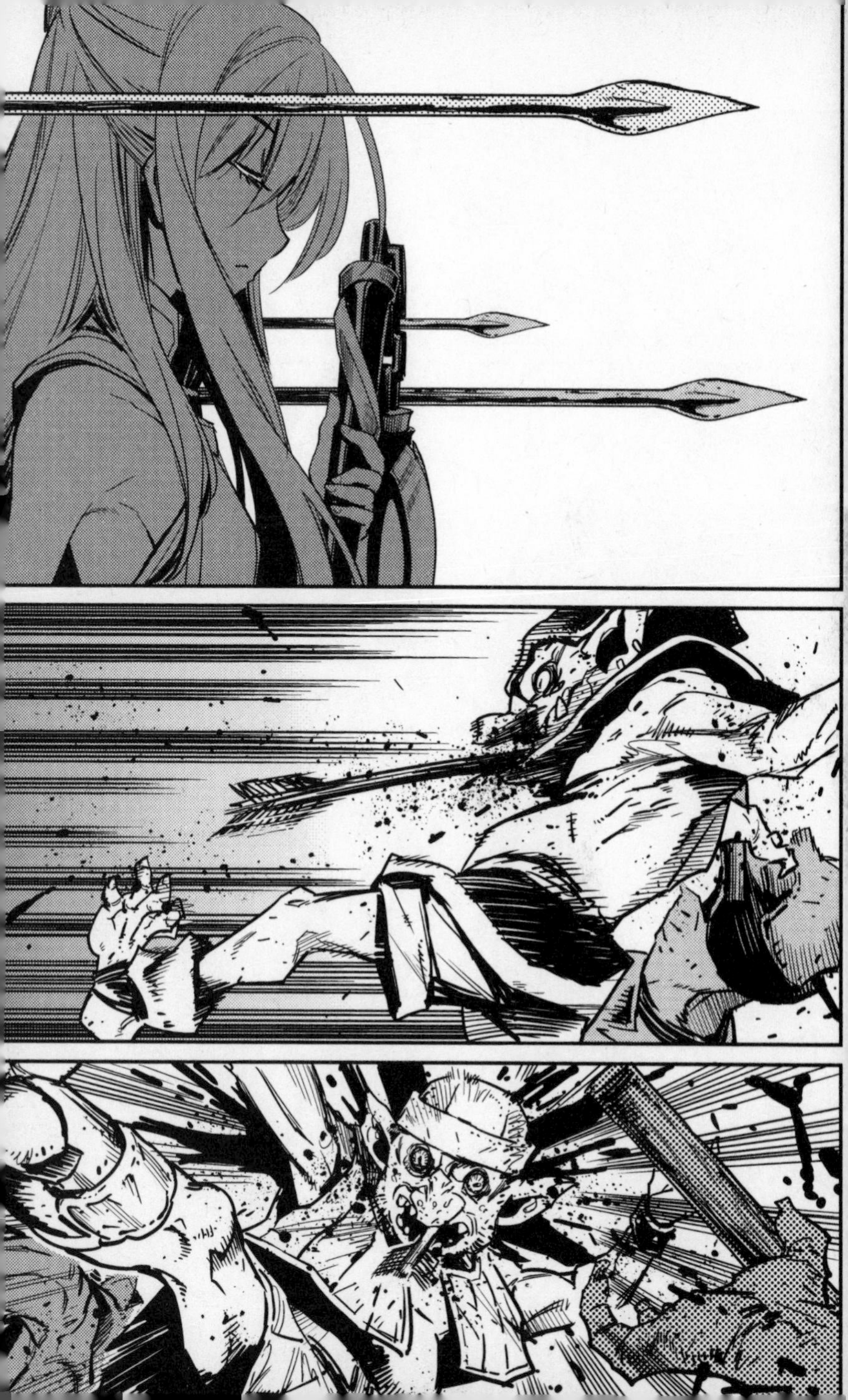

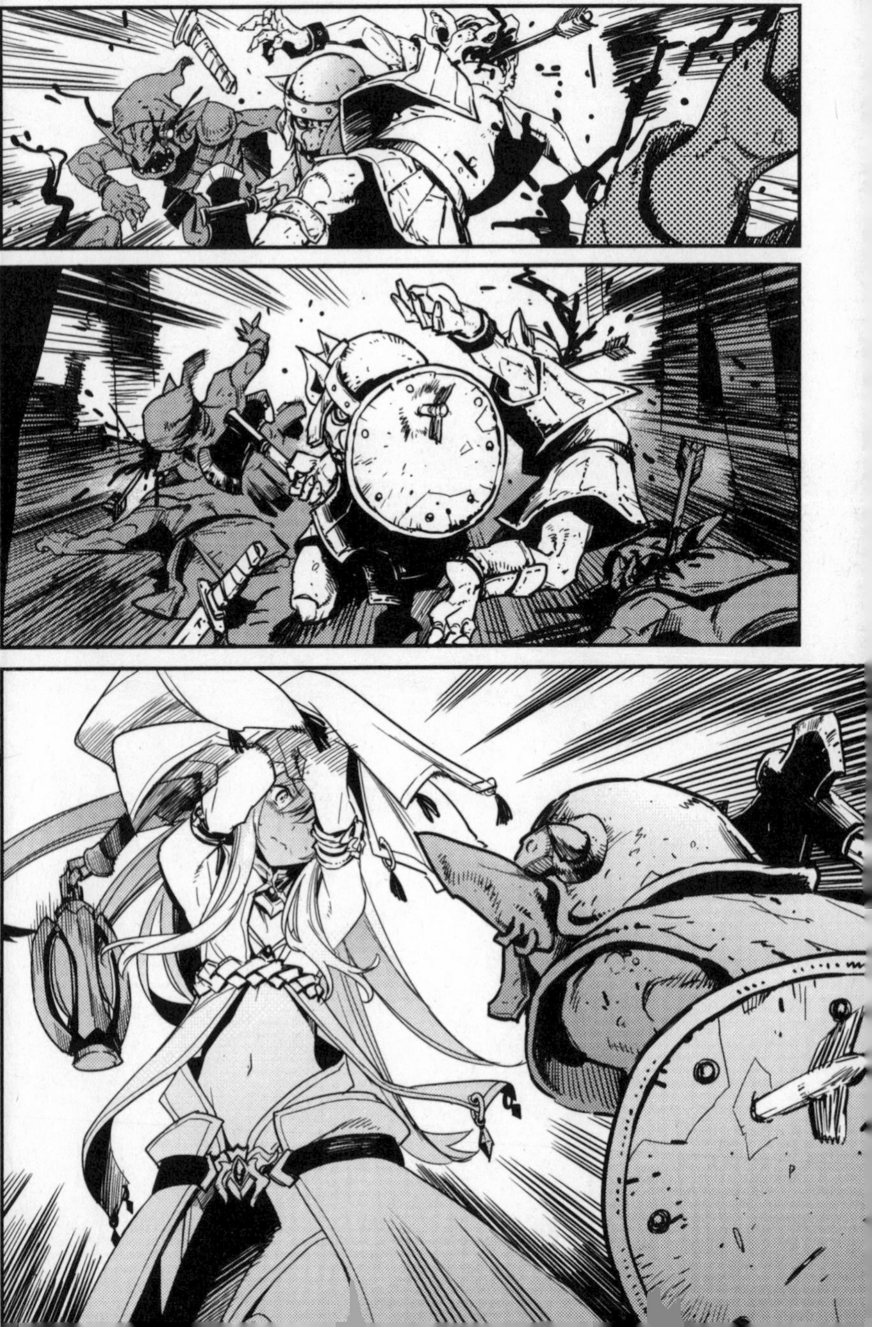

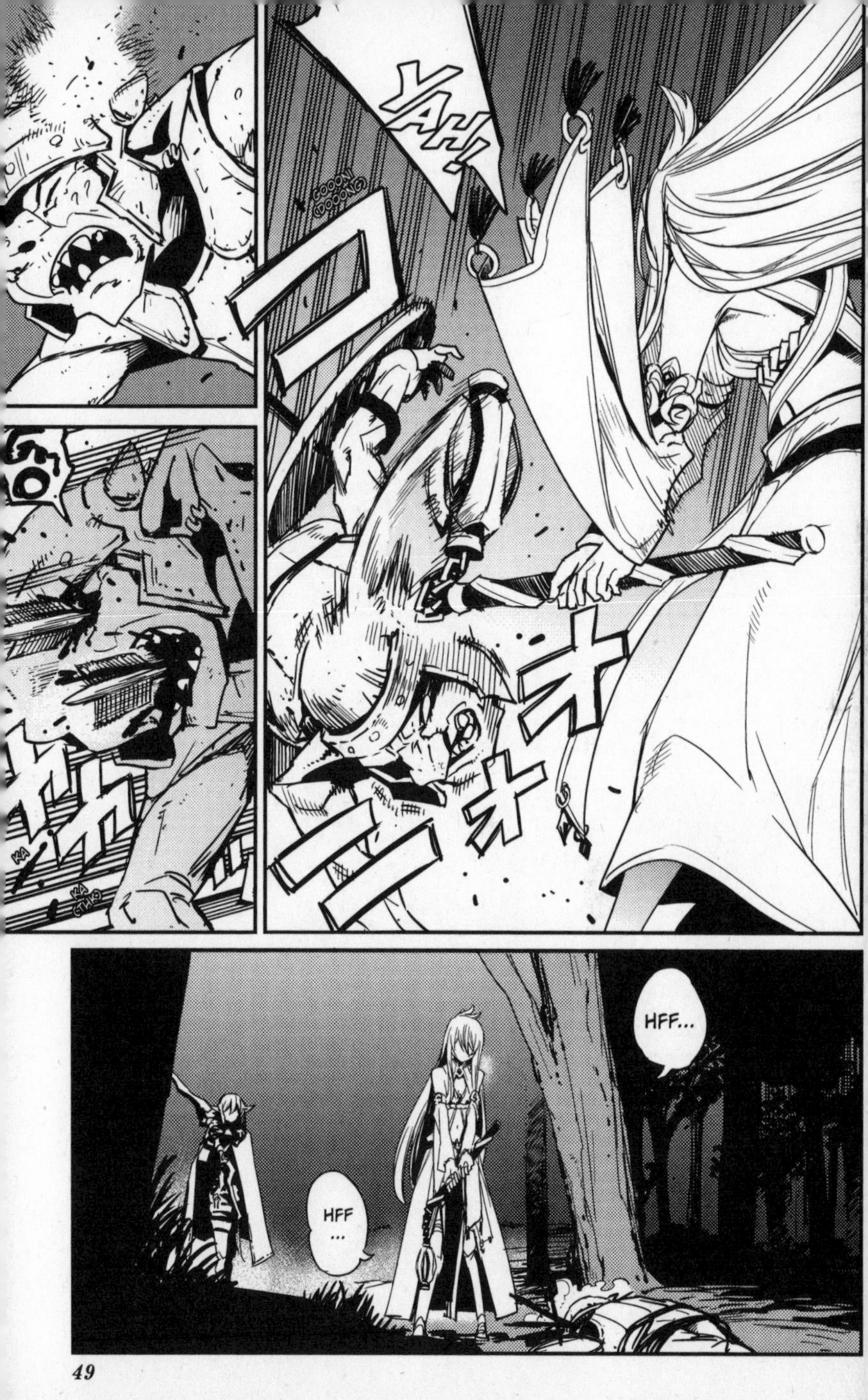
YAH!
GOOON (DOOONG)
KA
KA (THK)
HFF...
HFF ...

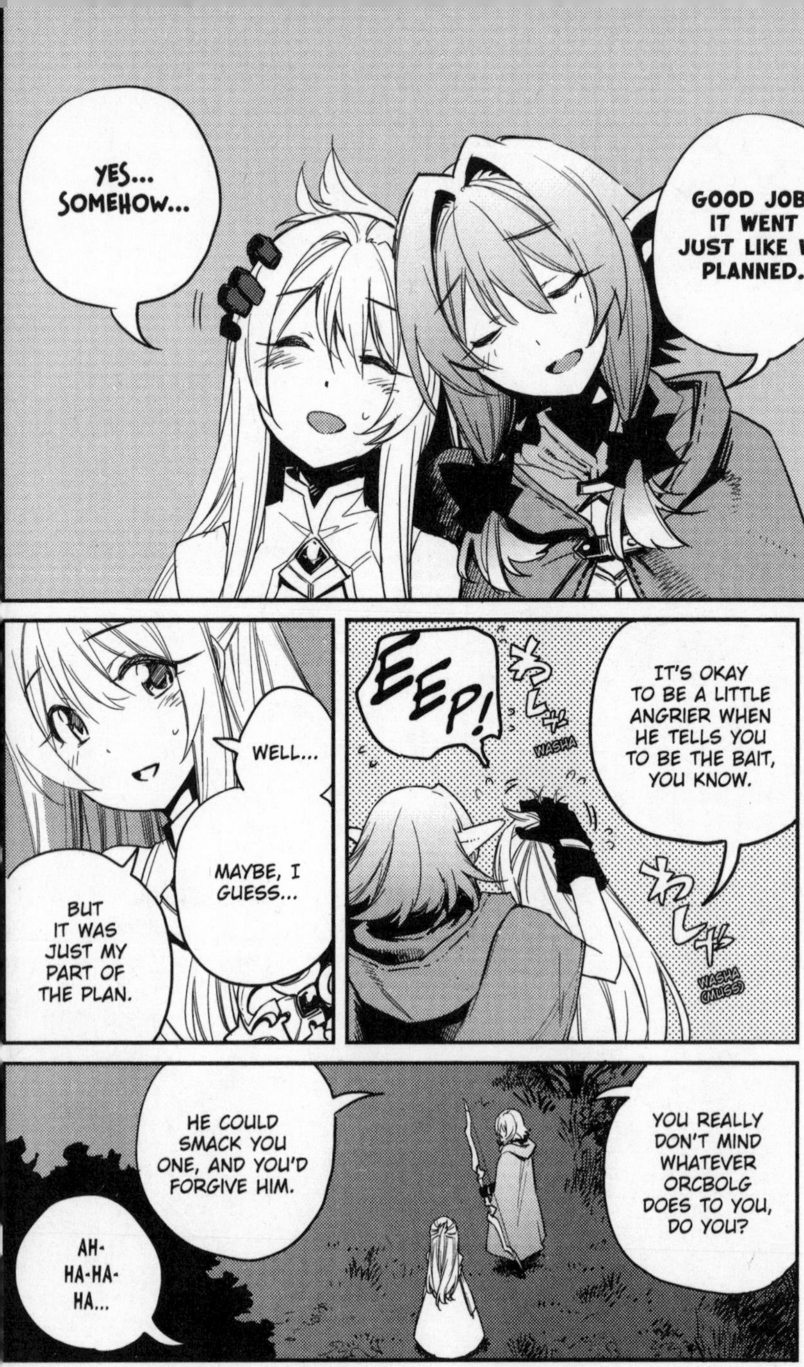
GOOD JOB. IT WENT JUST LIKE WE PLANNED.
YES... SOMEHOW...
IT'S OKAY TO BE A LITTLE ANGRIER WHEN HE TELLS YOU TO BE THE BAIT, YOU KNOW.
EEP!
WASHA
WASHA (MUSS)
WELL...
MAYBE, I GUESS...
BUT IT WAS JUST MY PART OF THE PLAN.
YOU REALLY DON'T MIND WHATEVER ORCBOLG DOES TO YOU, DO YOU?
HE COULD SMACK YOU ONE, AND YOU'D FORGIVE HIM.
AH-HA-HA-HA...

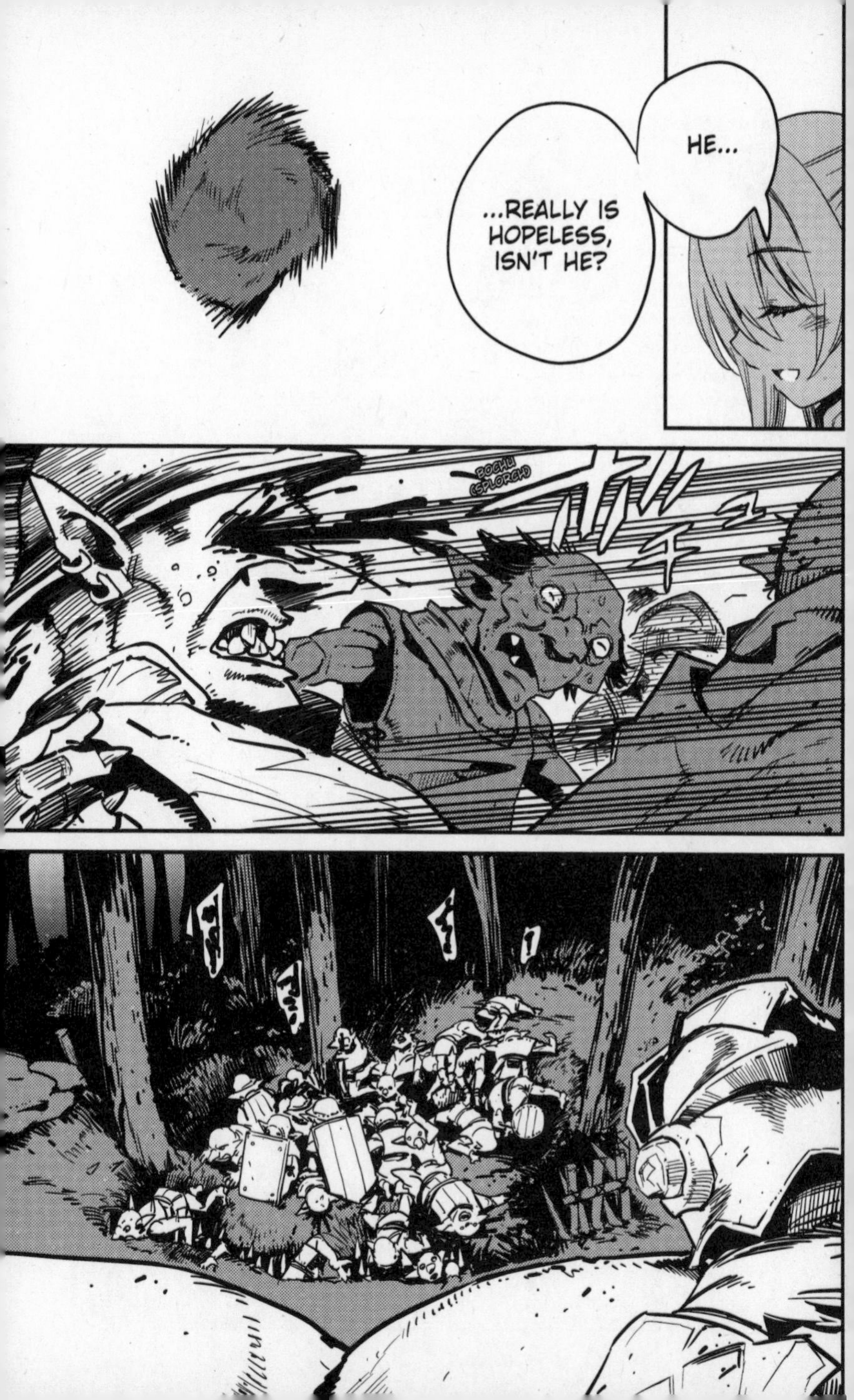
HE...
...REALLY IS HOPELESS, ISN'T HE?
BOCHU (SPLORCH)

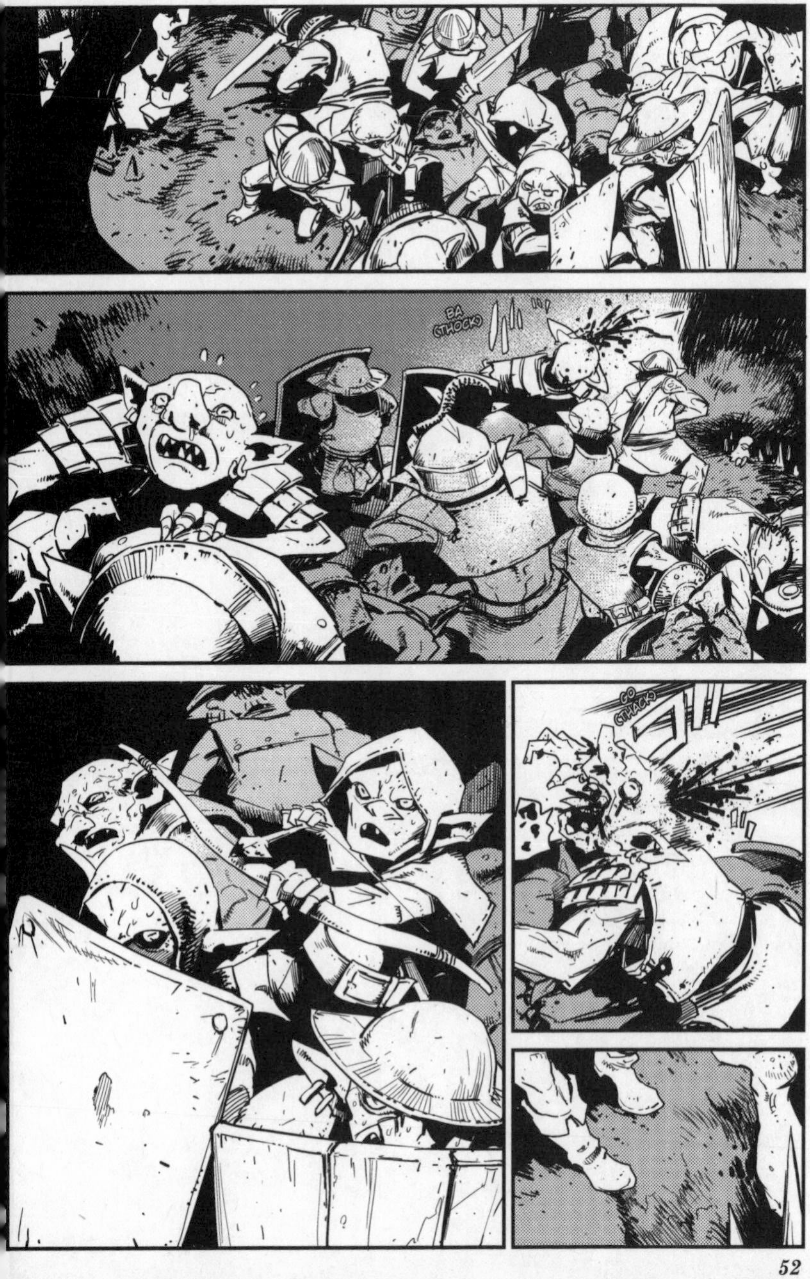
BA (THOCK)
GO (THACK)

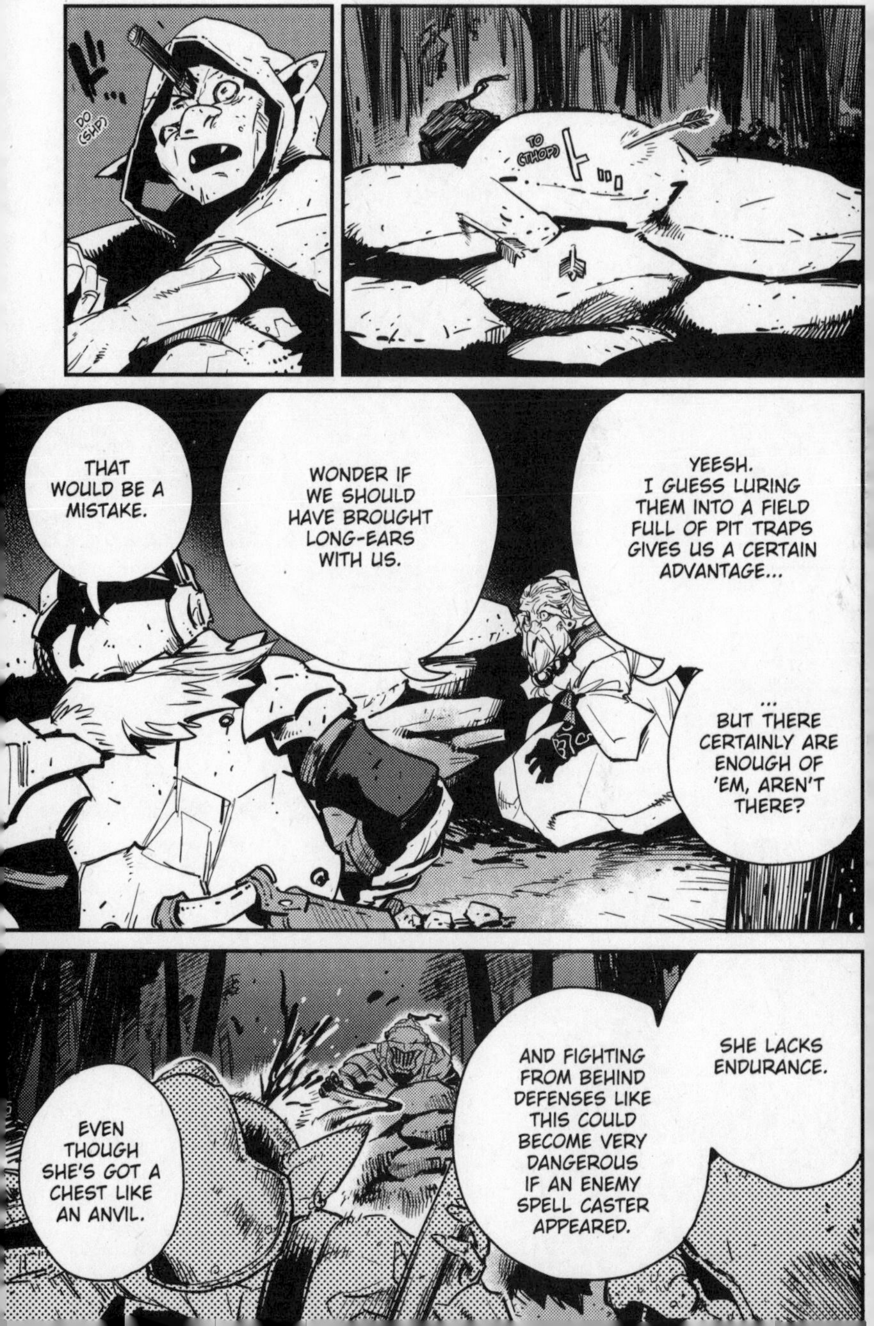
TO (THOP)
DO (SHP)
YEESH. I GUESS LURING THEM INTO A FIELD FULL OF PIT TRAPS GIVES US A CERTAIN ADVANTAGE...
... BUT THERE CERTAINLY ARE ENOUGH OF 'EM, AREN'T THERE?
WONDER IF WE SHOULD HAVE BROUGHT LONG-EARS WITH US.
THAT WOULD BE A MISTAKE.
SHE LACKS ENDURANCE.
AND FIGHTING FROM BEHIND DEFENSES LIKE THIS COULD BECOME VERY DANGEROUS IF AN ENEMY SPELL CASTER APPEARED.
EVEN THOUGH SHE'S GOT A CHEST LIKE AN ANVIL.

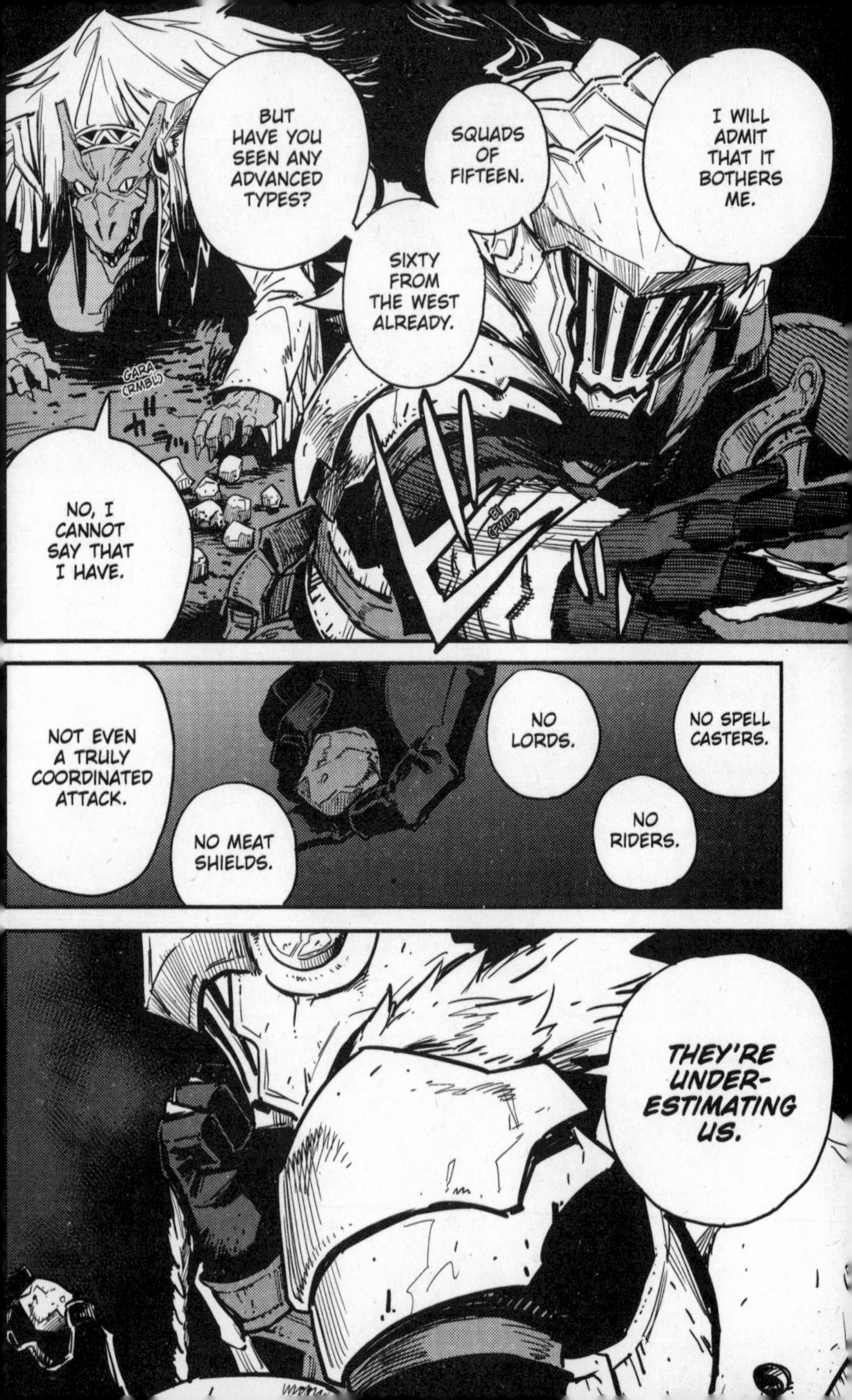
I WILL ADMIT THAT IT BOTHERS ME.
SQUADS OF FIFTEEN.
SIXTY FROM THE WEST ALREADY.
BUT HAVE YOU SEEN ANY ADVANCED TYPES?
BI (FWIP)
GARA (RMBL)
NO, I CANNOT SAY THAT I HAVE.
NO SPELL CASTERS.
NO LORDS.
NO RIDERS.
NO MEAT SHIELDS.
NOT EVEN A TRULY COORDINATED ATTACK.
THEY'RE UNDER-ESTIMATING US.

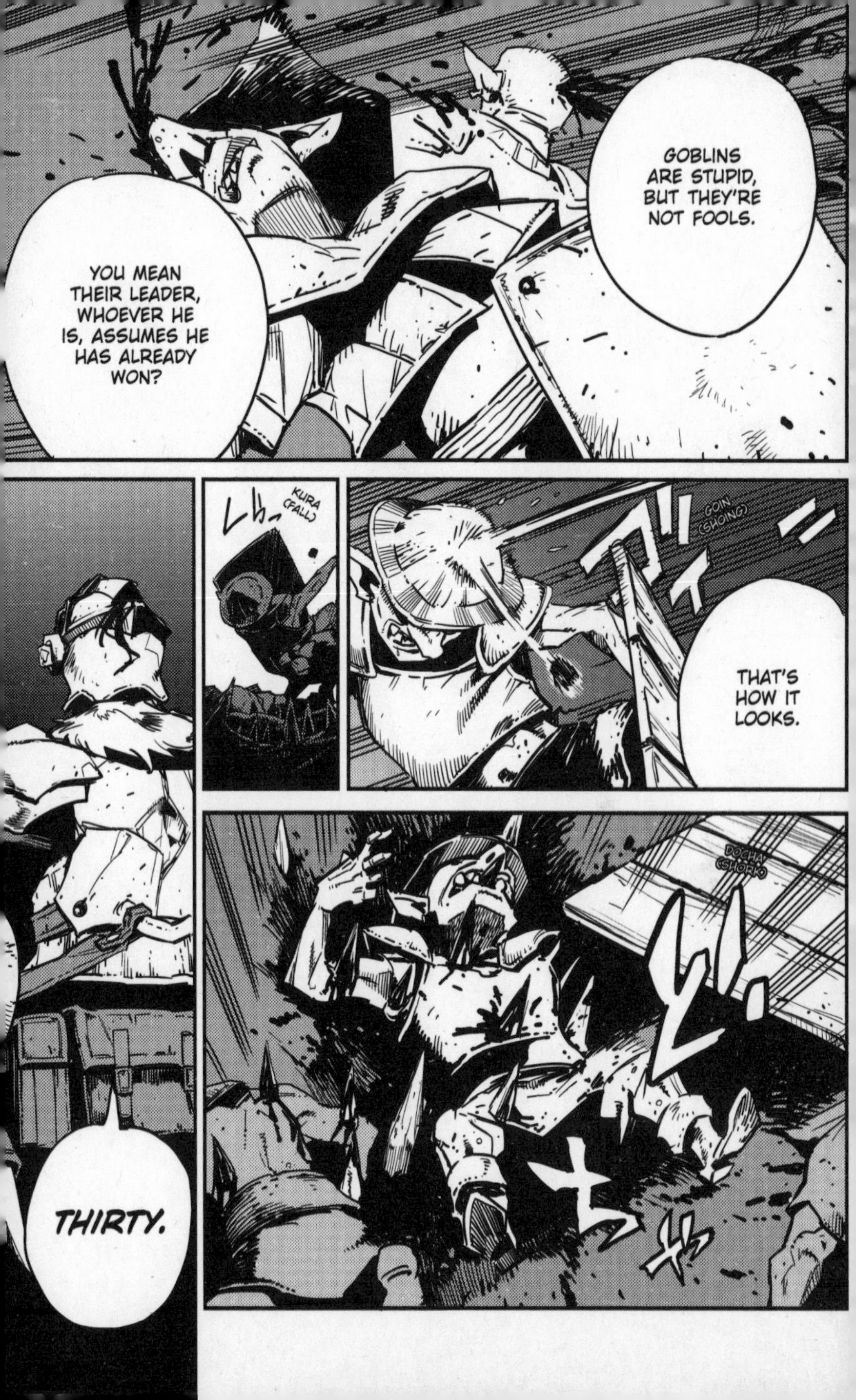
GOBLINS ARE STUPID, BUT THEY'RE NOT FOOLS.
YOU MEAN THEIR LEADER, WHOEVER HE IS, ASSUMES HE HAS ALREADY WON?
GOIN (SHOING)
THAT'S HOW IT LOOKS.
KURA (FALL)
DOCHA (SHORK)
THIRTY.

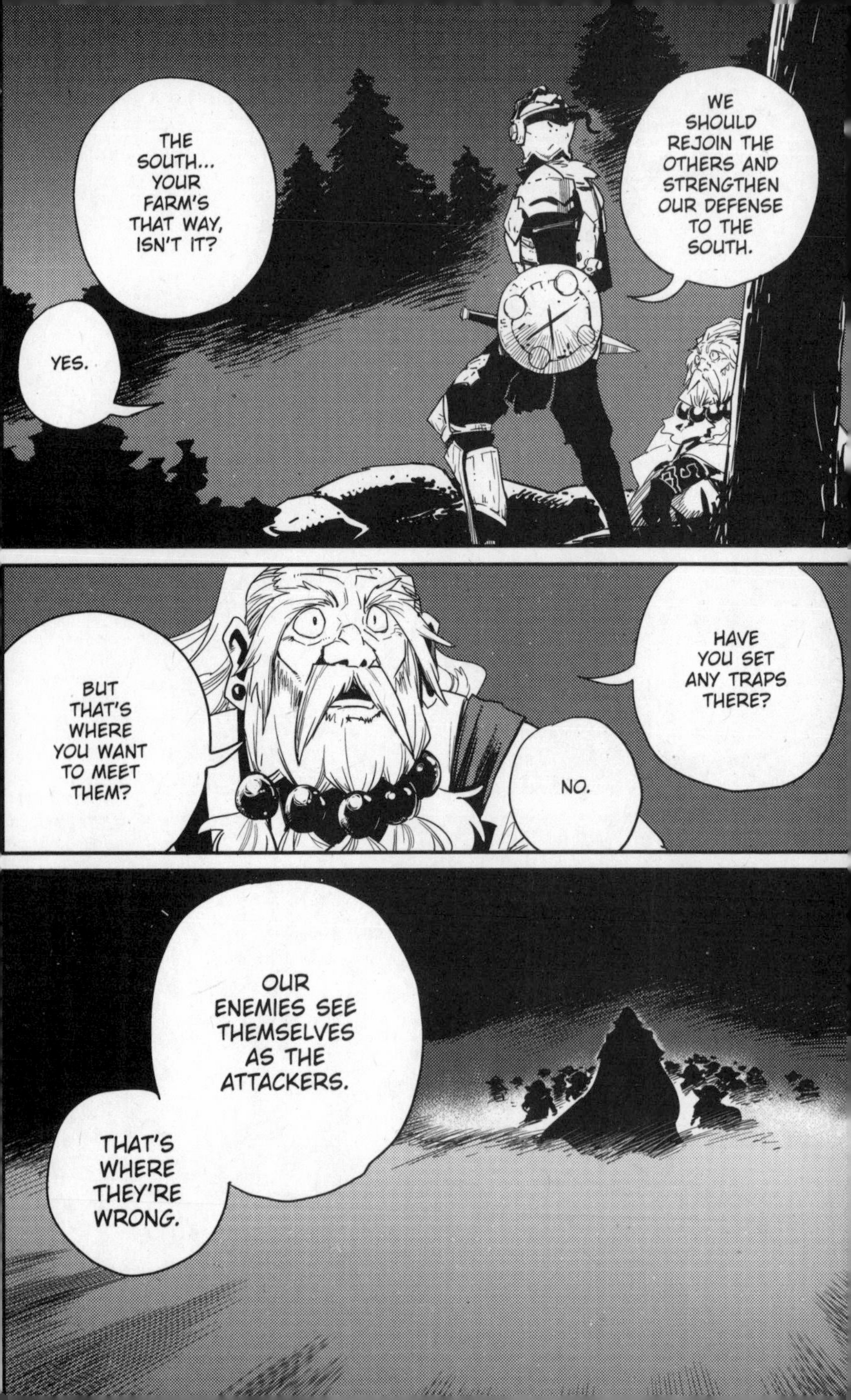
WE SHOULD REJOIN THE OTHERS AND STRENGTHEN OUR DEFENSE TO THE SOUTH.
THE SOUTH... YOUR FARM'S THAT WAY, ISN'T IT?
YES.
HAVE YOU SET ANY TRAPS THERE?
NO.
BUT THAT'S WHERE YOU WANT TO MEET THEM?
OUR ENEMIES SEE THEMSELVES AS THE ATTACKERS.
THAT'S WHERE THEY'RE WRONG.

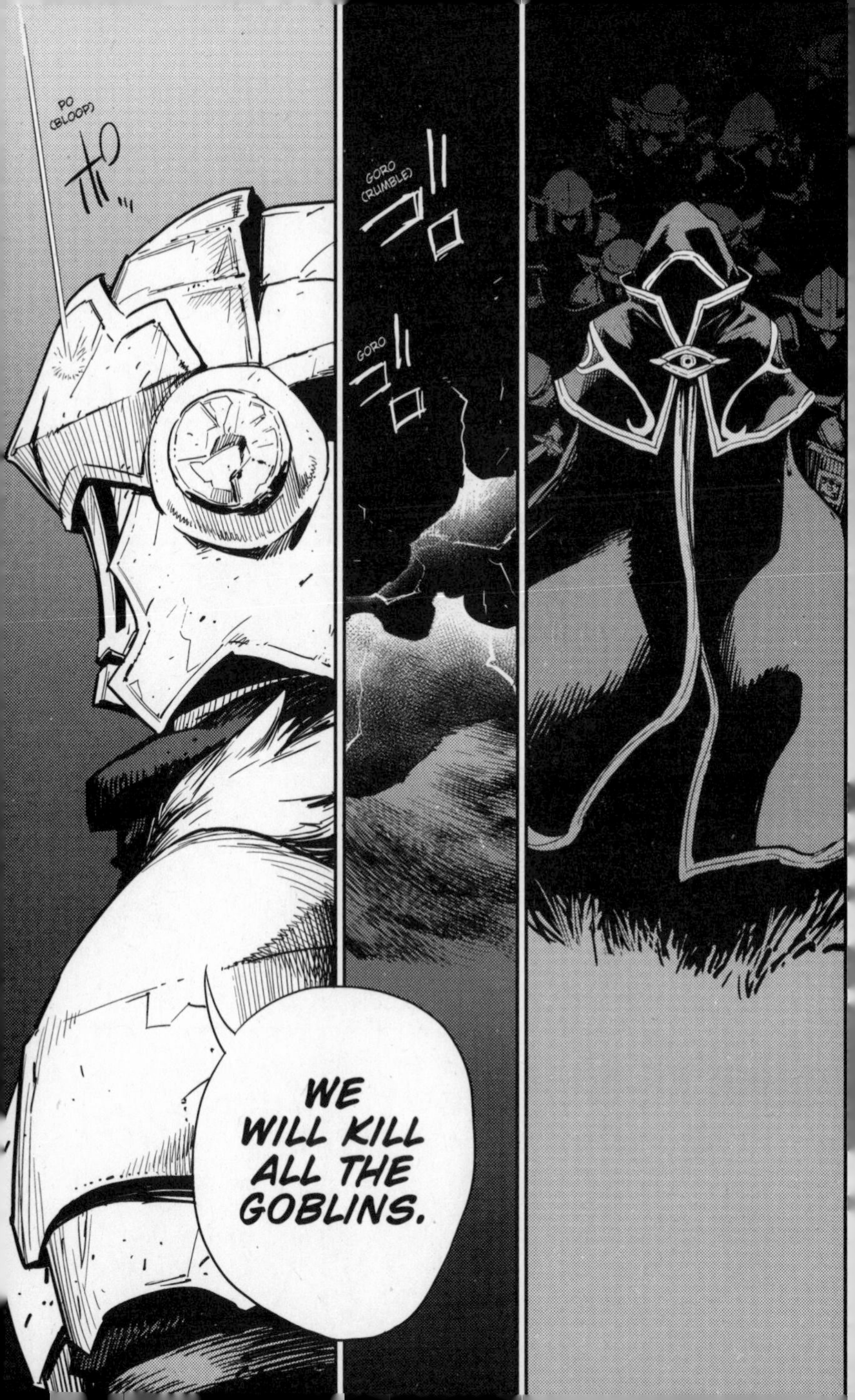
GORO (RUMBLE)
GORO
PO (BLOOP)
WE WILL KILL ALL THE GOBLINS.

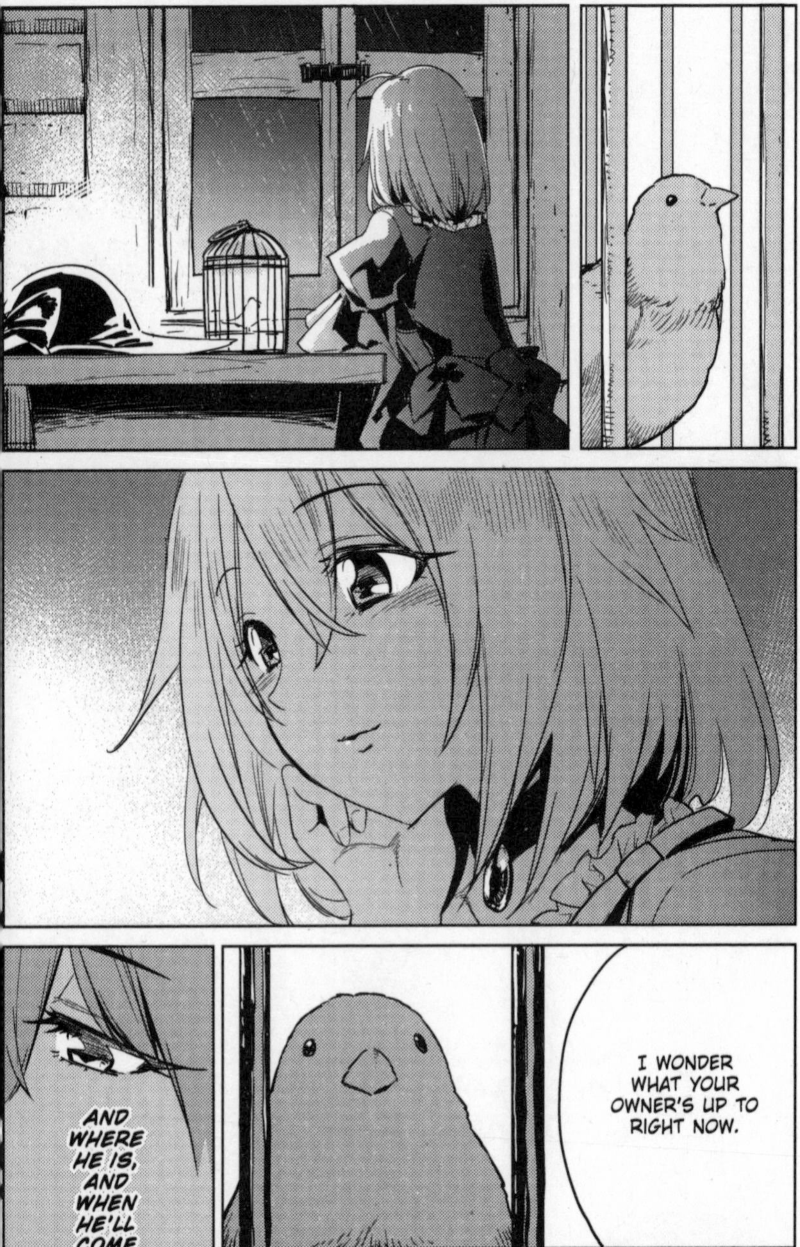
I WONDER WHAT YOUR OWNER'S UP TO RIGHT NOW.
AND WHERE HE IS, AND WHEN HE'LL COME HOME...

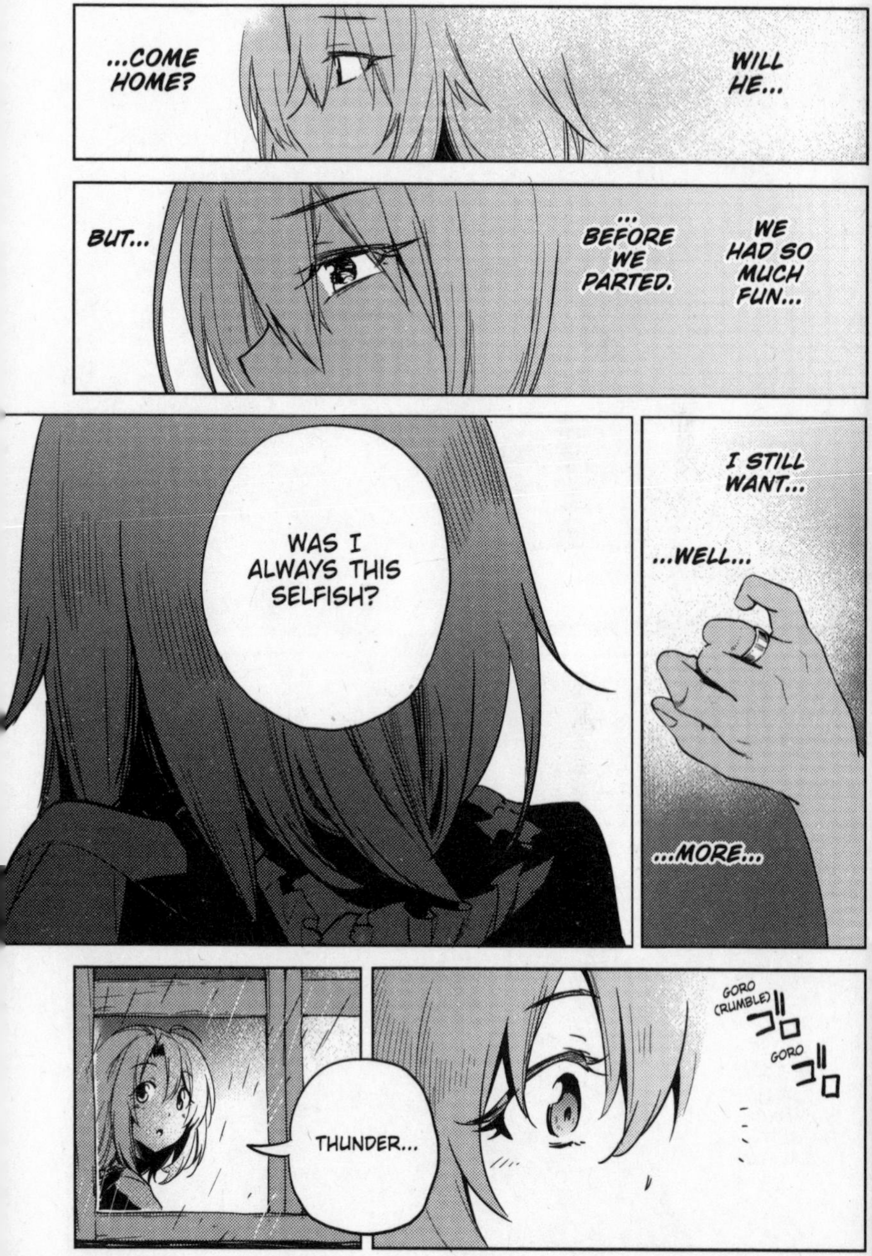
WILL HE...
...COME HOME?
WE HAD SO MUCH FUN...
...BEFORE WE PARTED.
BUT...
I STILL WANT...
...WELL...
...MORE...
WAS I ALWAYS THIS SELFISH?
GORO (RUMBLE) ゴロ
GORO ゴロ
THUNDER...

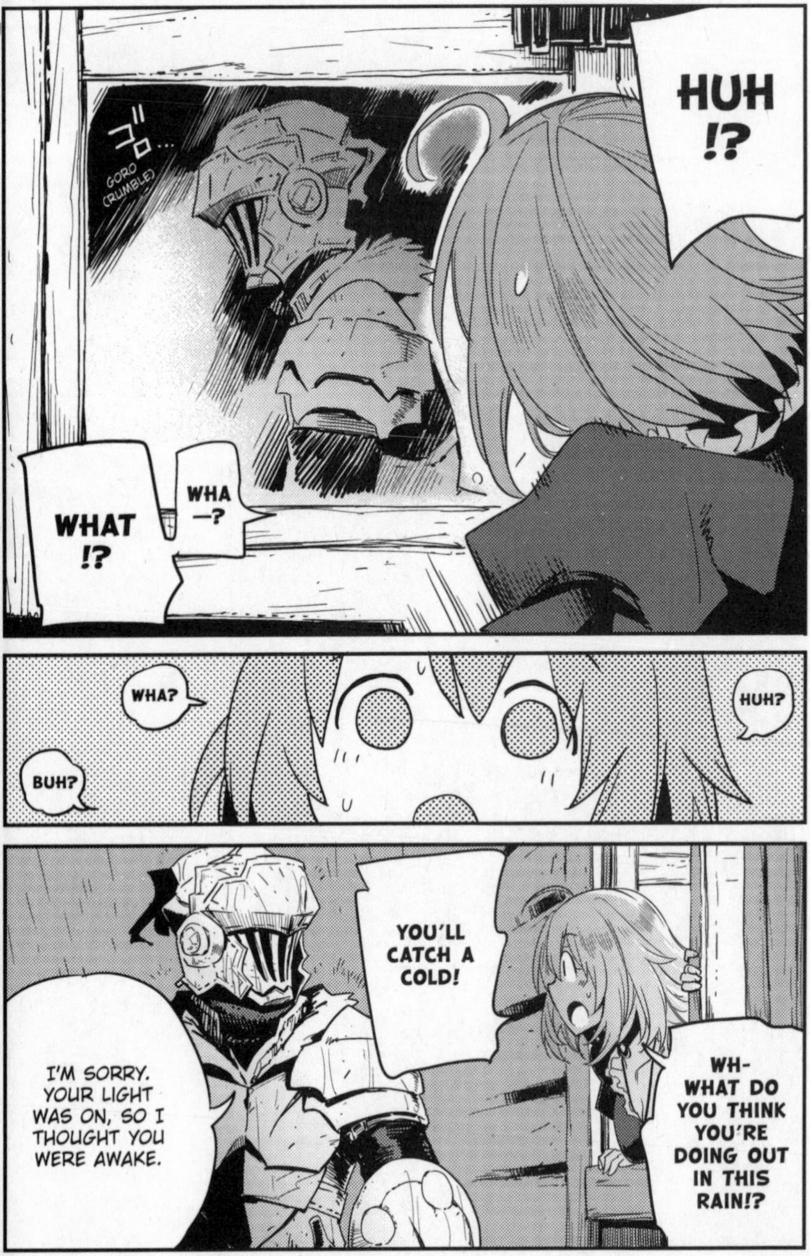
HUH!?
ゴロ…
GORO (RUMBLE)
WHA—?
WHAT!?
HUH?
WHA?
BUH?
WH-WHAT DO YOU THINK YOU'RE DOING OUT IN THIS RAIN!?
YOU'LL CATCH A COLD!
I'M SORRY. YOUR LIGHT WAS ON, SO I THOUGHT YOU WERE AWAKE.

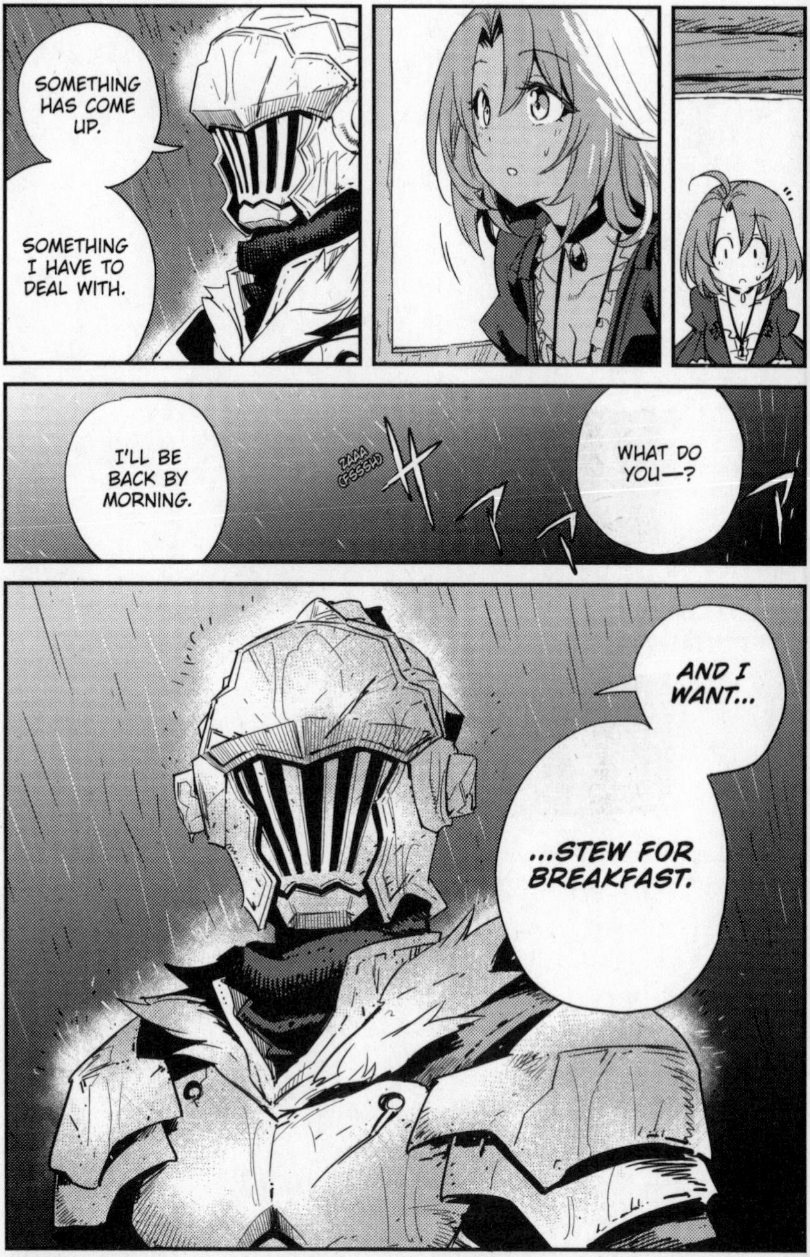
SOMETHING HAS COME UP.
SOMETHING I HAVE TO DEAL WITH.
WHAT DO YOU—?
ZAAA (FSSSH)
I'LL BE BACK BY MORNING.
AND I WANT...
...STEW FOR BREAKFAST.

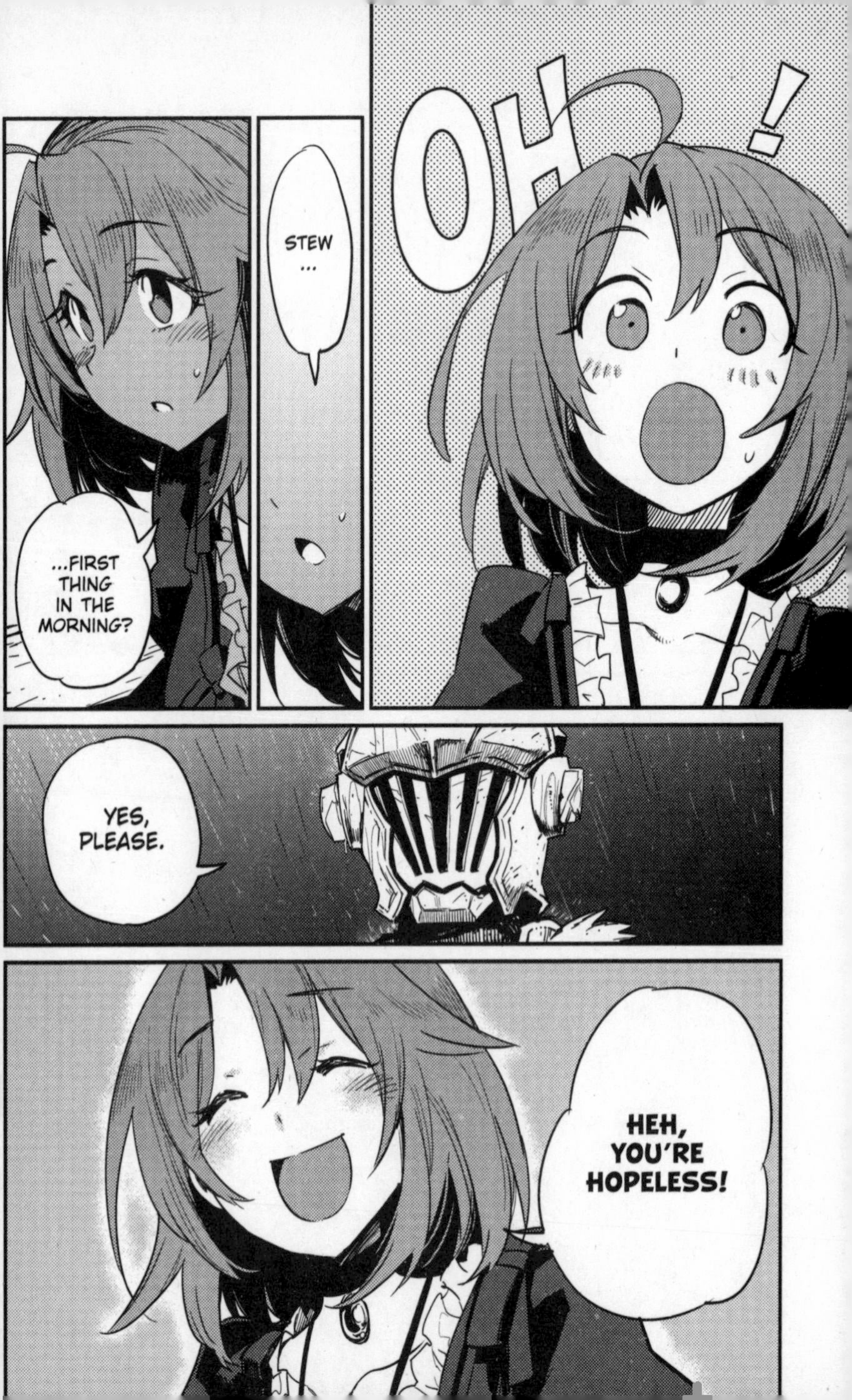
OH!
STEW ...
...FIRST THING IN THE MORNING?
YES, PLEASE.
HEH, YOU'RE HOPELESS!

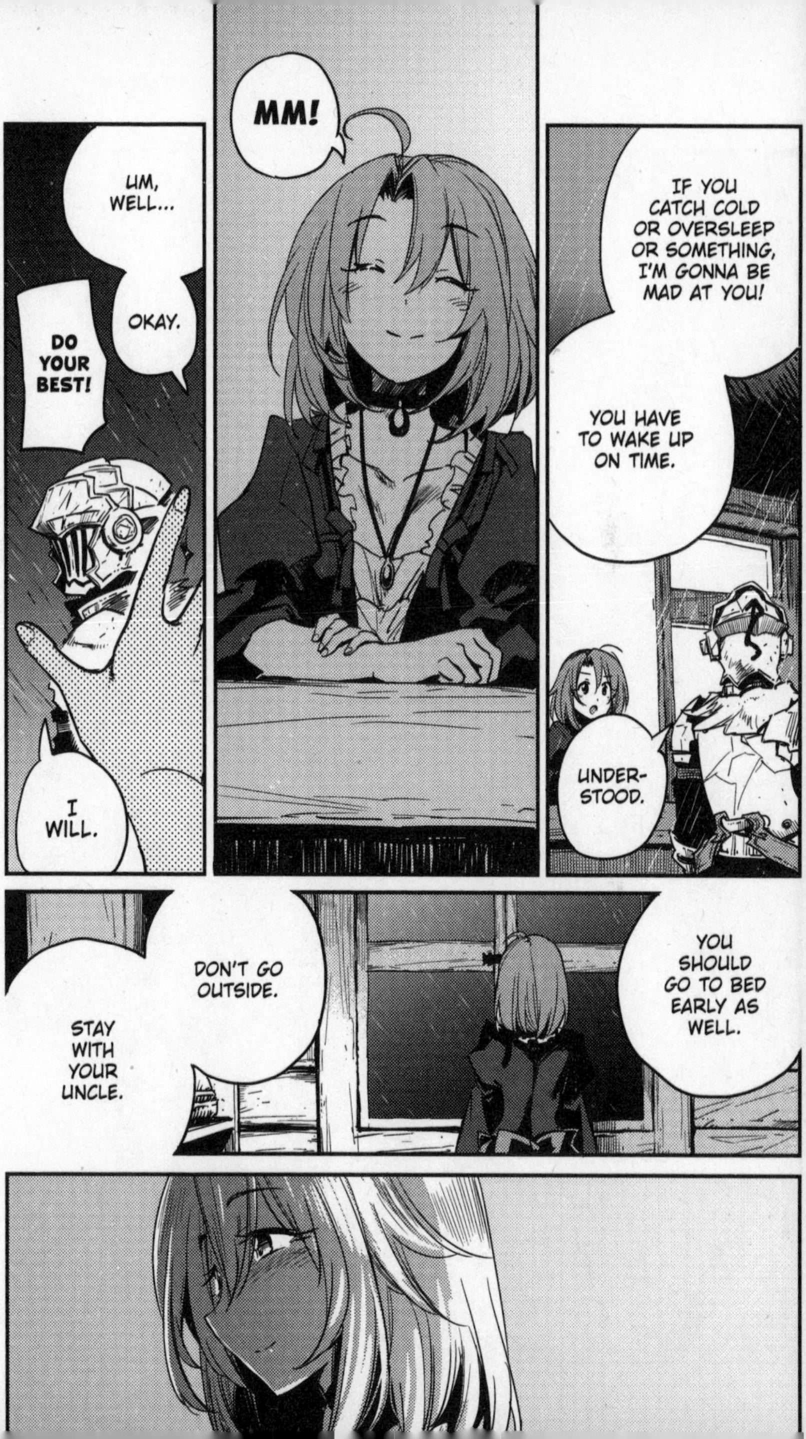
IF YOU CATCH COLD OR OVERSLEEP OR SOMETHING, I'M GONNA BE MAD AT YOU!
YOU HAVE TO WAKE UP ON TIME.
UNDER-STOOD.
MM!
UM, WELL...
OKAY.
DO YOUR BEST!
I WILL.
YOU SHOULD GO TO BED EARLY AS WELL.
DON'T GO OUTSIDE.
STAY WITH YOUR UNCLE.

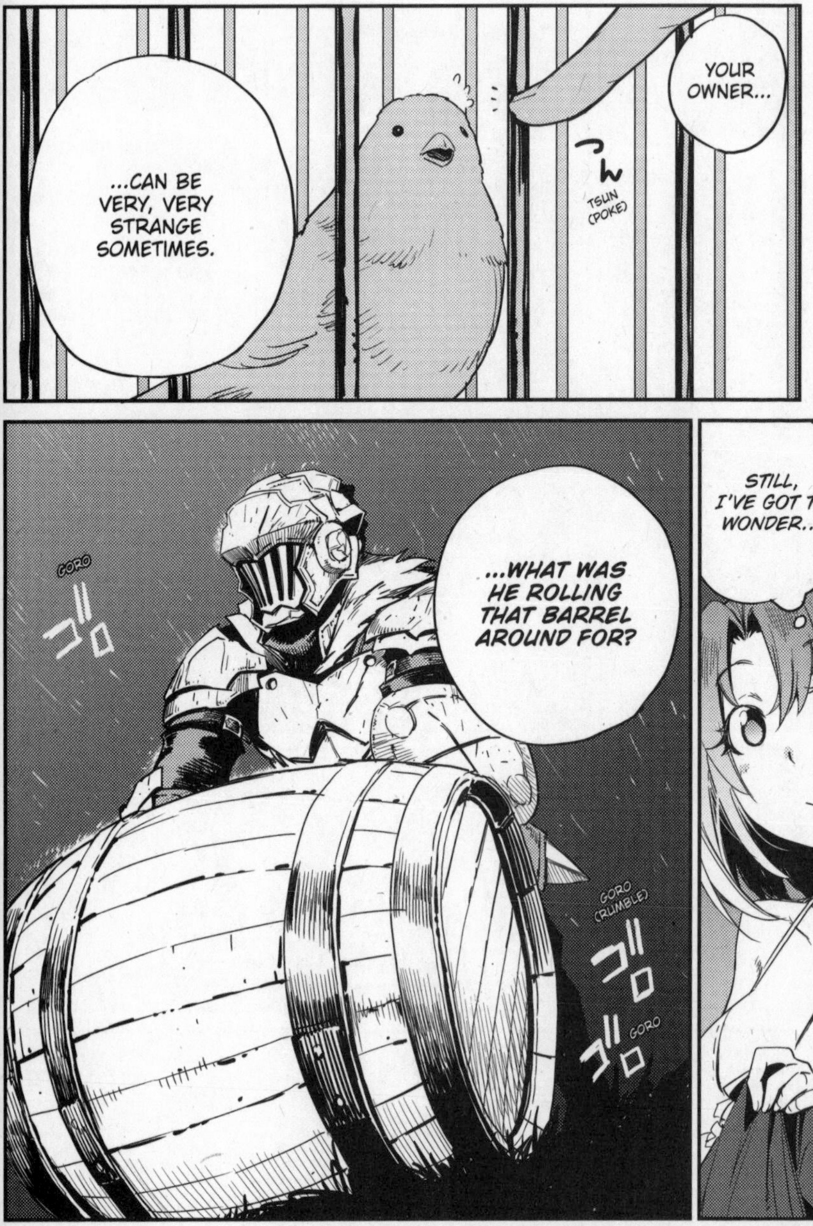
YOUR OWNER...
TSUN (POKE)
...CAN BE VERY, VERY STRANGE SOMETIMES.
STILL, I'VE GOT TO WONDER...
...WHAT WAS HE ROLLING THAT BARREL AROUND FOR?
GORO
GORO (RUMBLE)
GORO

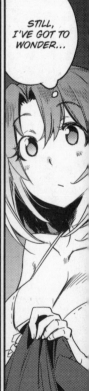

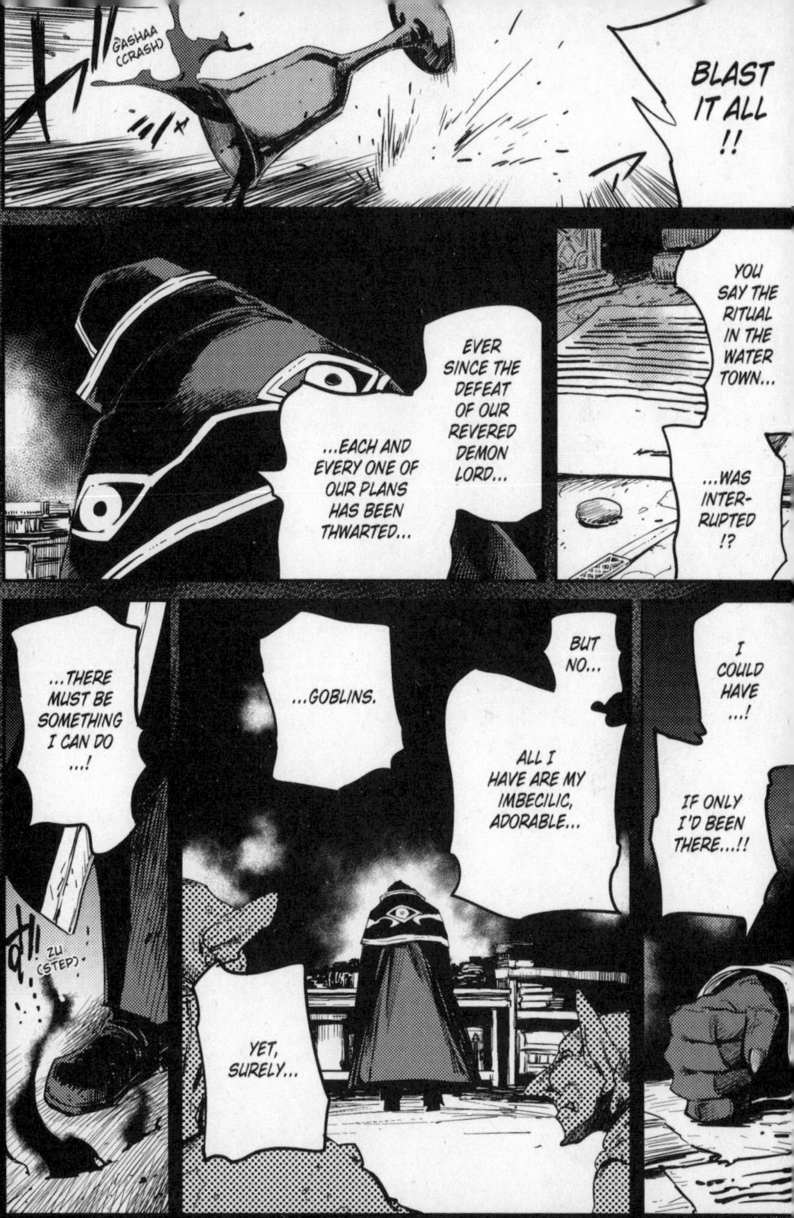
BLAST IT ALL!!
GASHAA (CRASH)
YOU SAY THE RITUAL IN THE WATER TOWN...
...WAS INTERRUPTED!?
EVER SINCE THE DEFEAT OF OUR REVERED DEMON LORD...
...EACH AND EVERY ONE OF OUR PLANS HAS BEEN THWARTED...
I COULD HAVE...!
IF ONLY I'D BEEN THERE...!!
BUT NO...
ALL I HAVE ARE MY IMBECILIC, ADORABLE...
...GOBLINS.
YET, SURELY...
...THERE MUST BE SOMETHING I CAN DO...!
ZU (STEP)

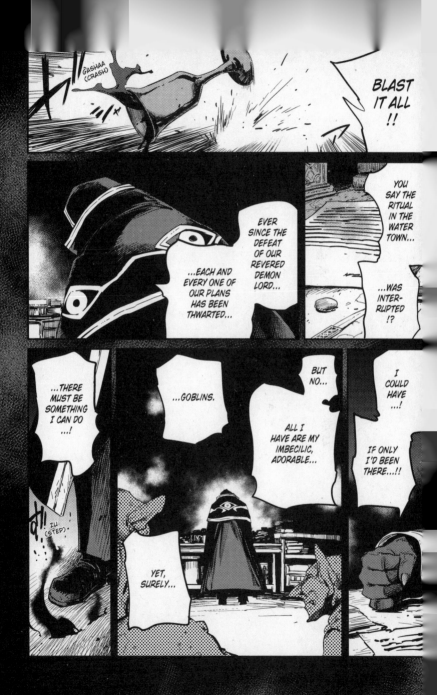

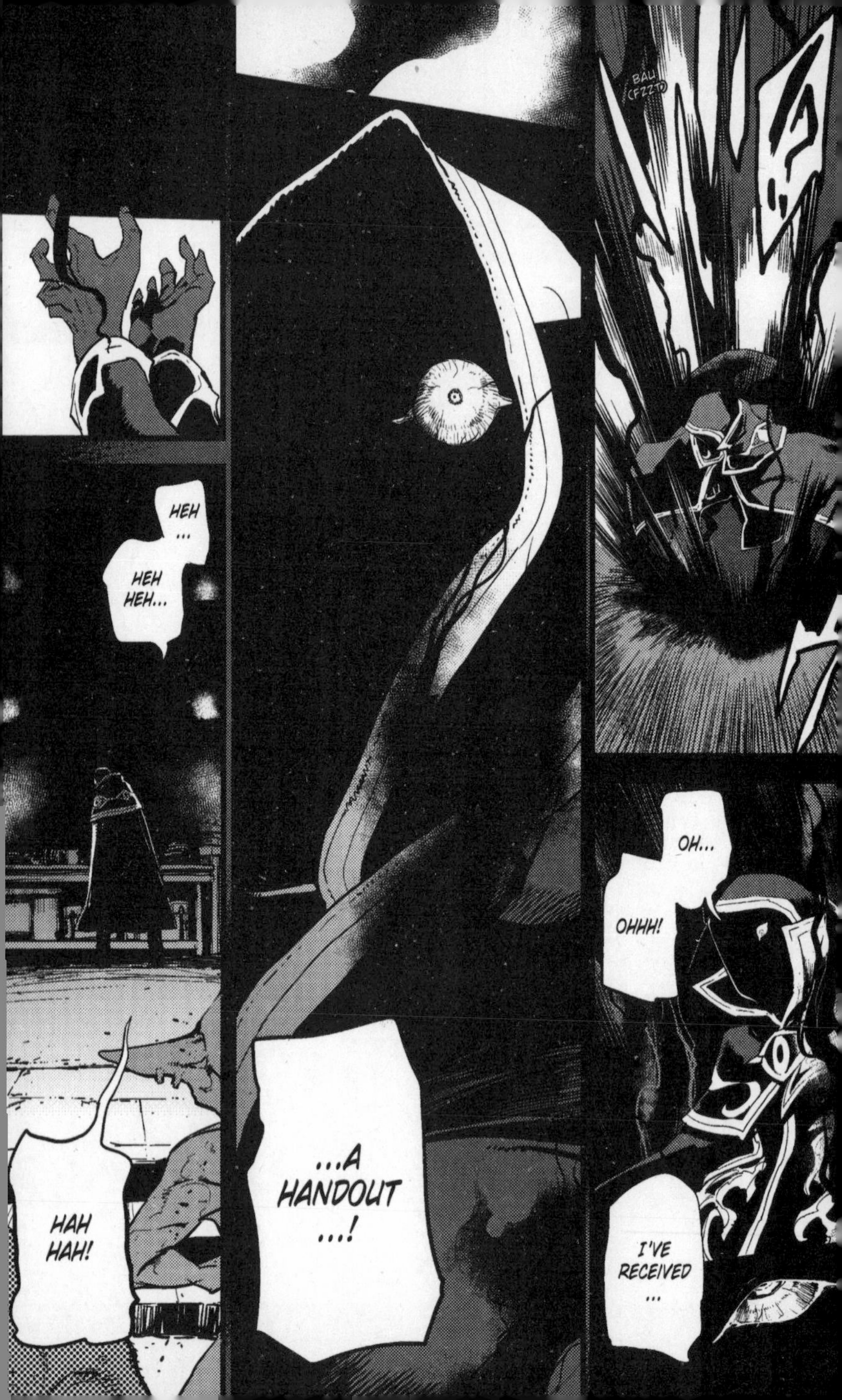
BAU (FZZT)
OH...
OHHH!
I'VE RECEIVED ...
...A HANDOUT ...!
HEH ... HEH HEH...
HAH HAH!

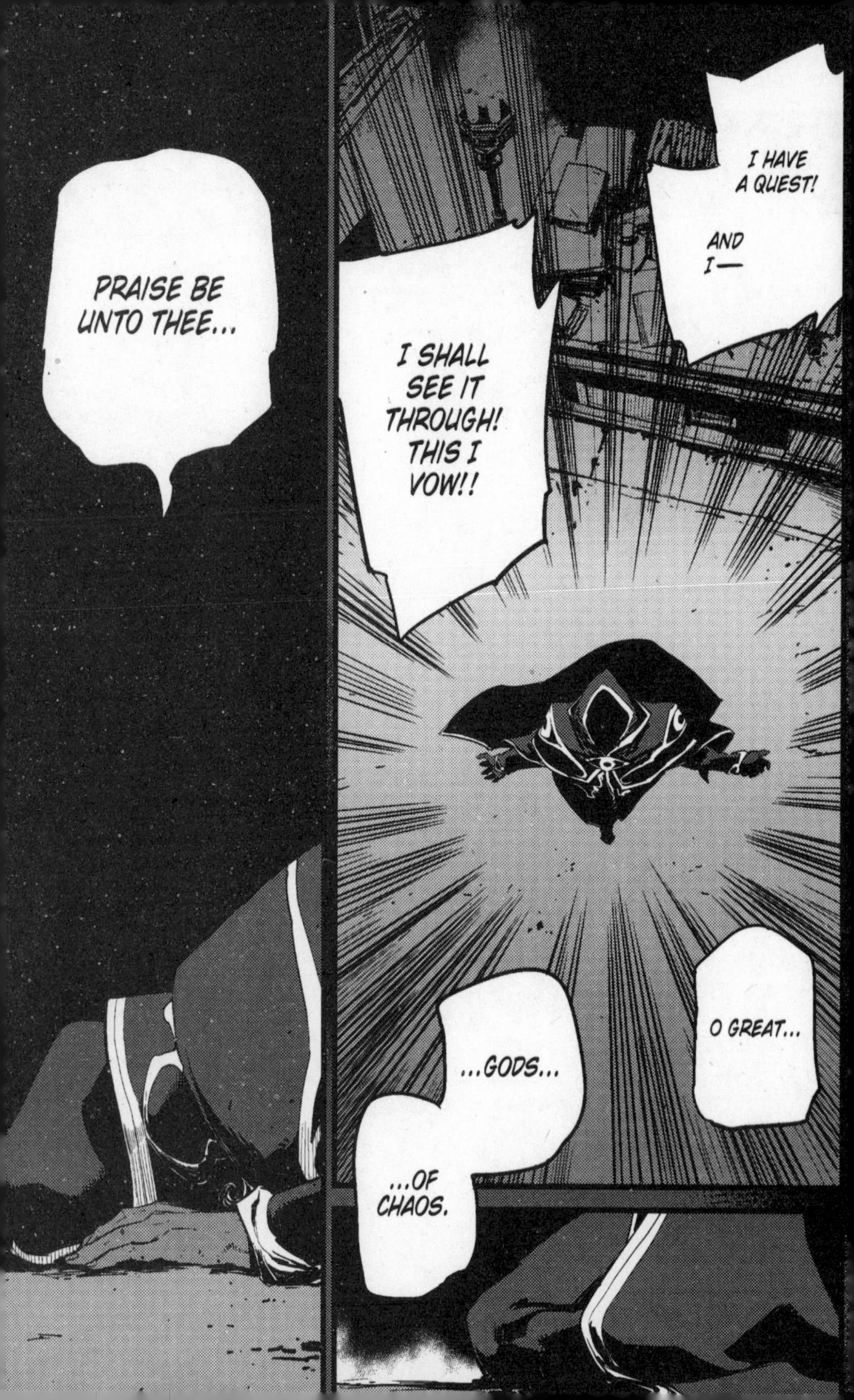
I HAVE A QUEST!
AND I—
I SHALL SEE IT THROUGH! THIS I VOW!!
O GREAT...
...GODS...
...OF CHAOS.
PRAISE BE UNTO THEE...

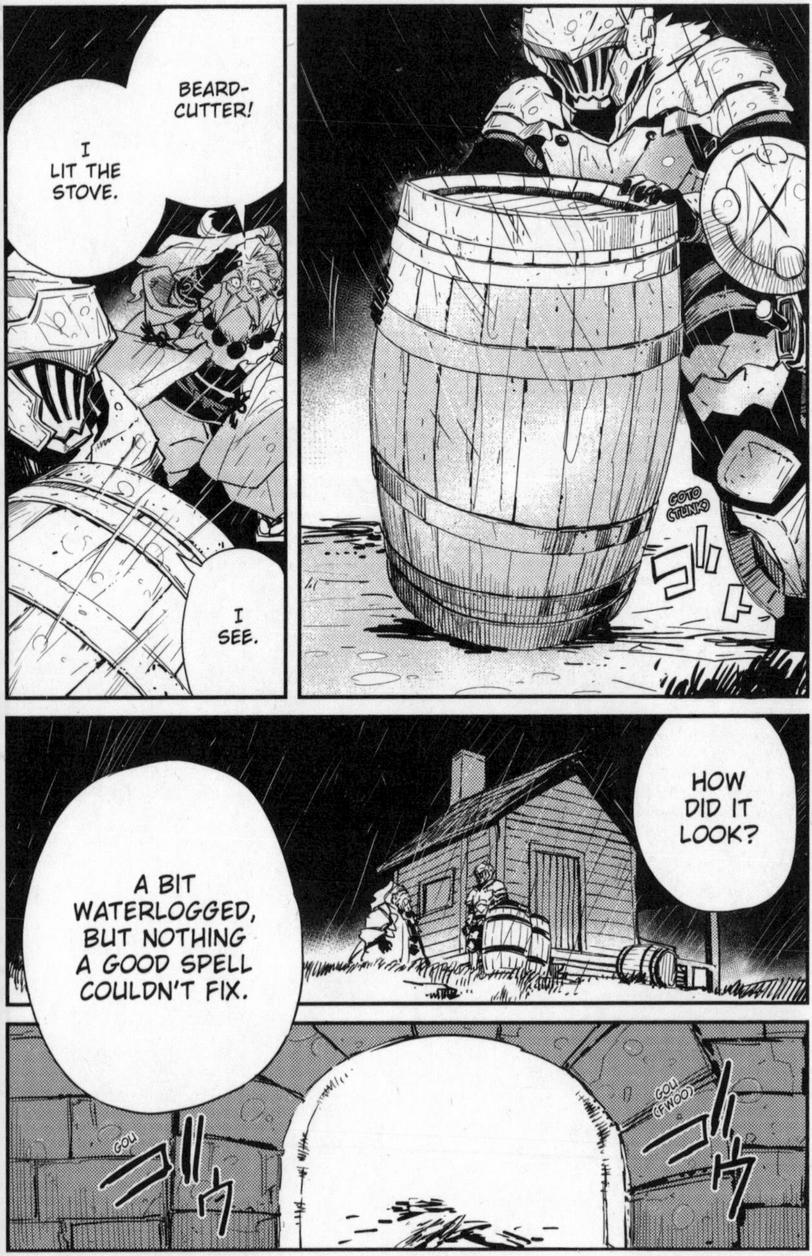
GOTO (TUNK)
BEARD-CUTTER!
I LIT THE STOVE.
I SEE.
HOW DID IT LOOK?
A BIT WATERLOGGED, BUT NOTHING A GOOD SPELL COULDN'T FIX.
GOU (FWOO)
GOU

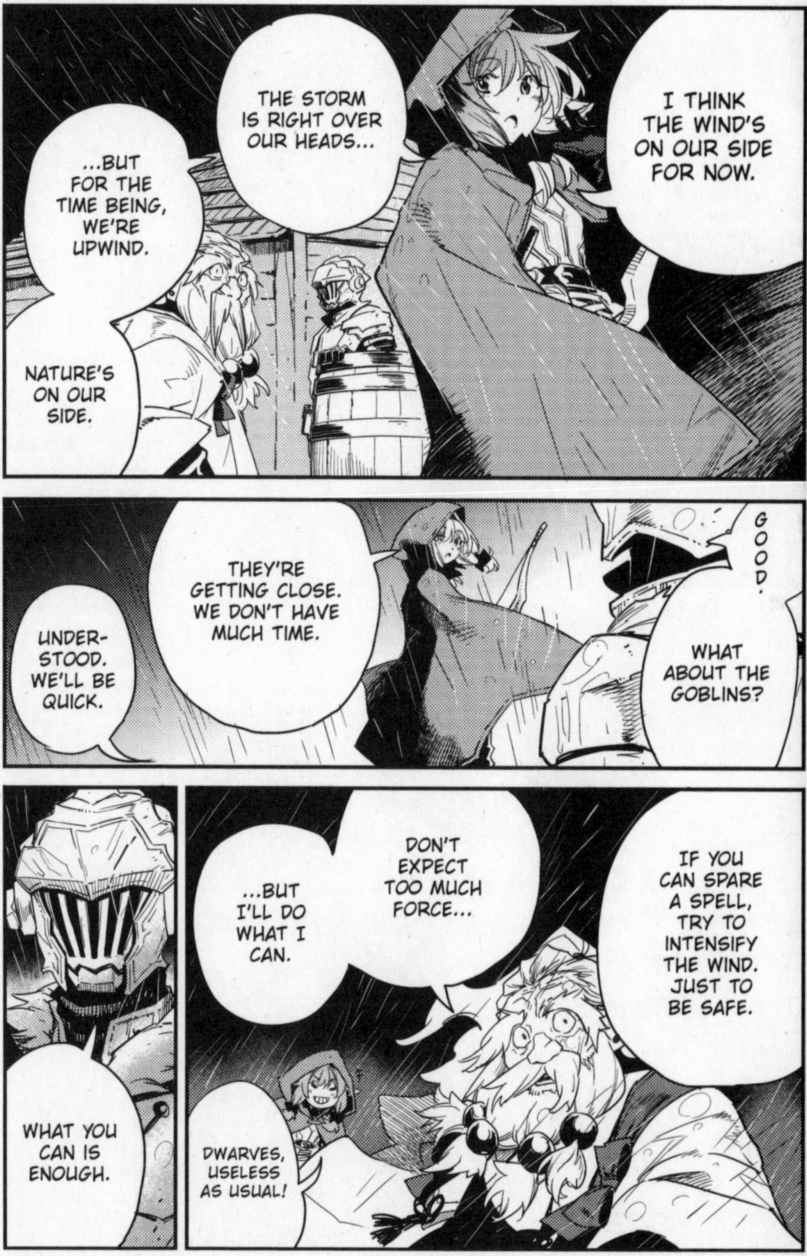
I THINK THE WIND'S ON OUR SIDE FOR NOW.
THE STORM IS RIGHT OVER OUR HEADS...
...BUT FOR THE TIME BEING, WE'RE UPWIND.
NATURE'S ON OUR SIDE.
GOOD.
WHAT ABOUT THE GOBLINS?
THEY'RE GETTING CLOSE. WE DON'T HAVE MUCH TIME.
UNDER-STOOD. WE'LL BE QUICK.
IF YOU CAN SPARE A SPELL, TRY TO INTENSIFY THE WIND. JUST TO BE SAFE.
DON'T EXPECT TOO MUCH FORCE...
...BUT I'LL DO WHAT I CAN.
DWARVES, USELESS AS USUAL!
WHAT YOU CAN IS ENOUGH.

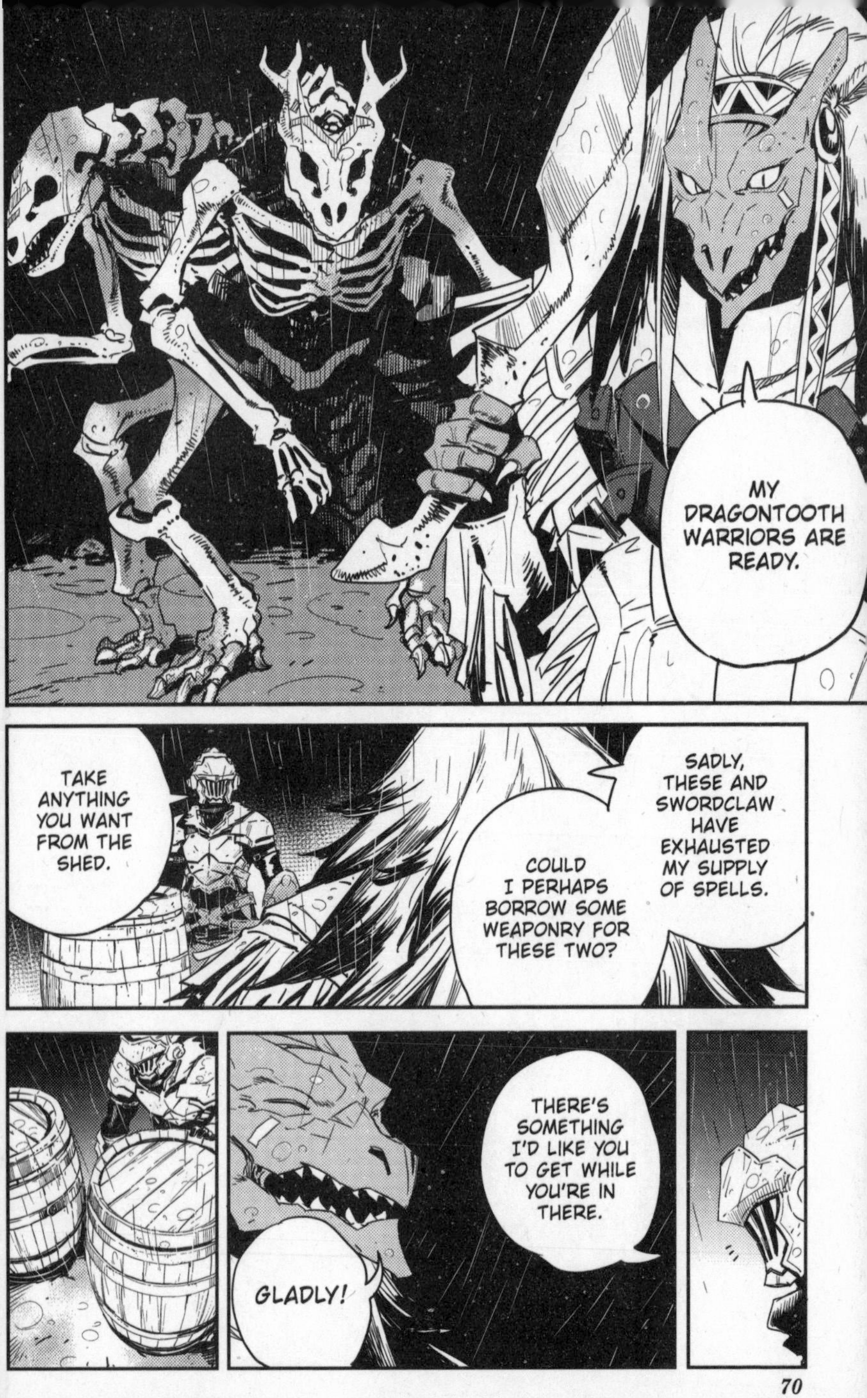
MY DRAGONTOOTH WARRIORS ARE READY.
SADLY, THESE AND SWORDCLAW HAVE EXHAUSTED MY SUPPLY OF SPELLS.
COULD I PERHAPS BORROW SOME WEAPONRY FOR THESE TWO?
TAKE ANYTHING YOU WANT FROM THE SHED.
THERE'S SOMETHING I'D LIKE YOU TO GET WHILE YOU'RE IN THERE.
GLADLY!

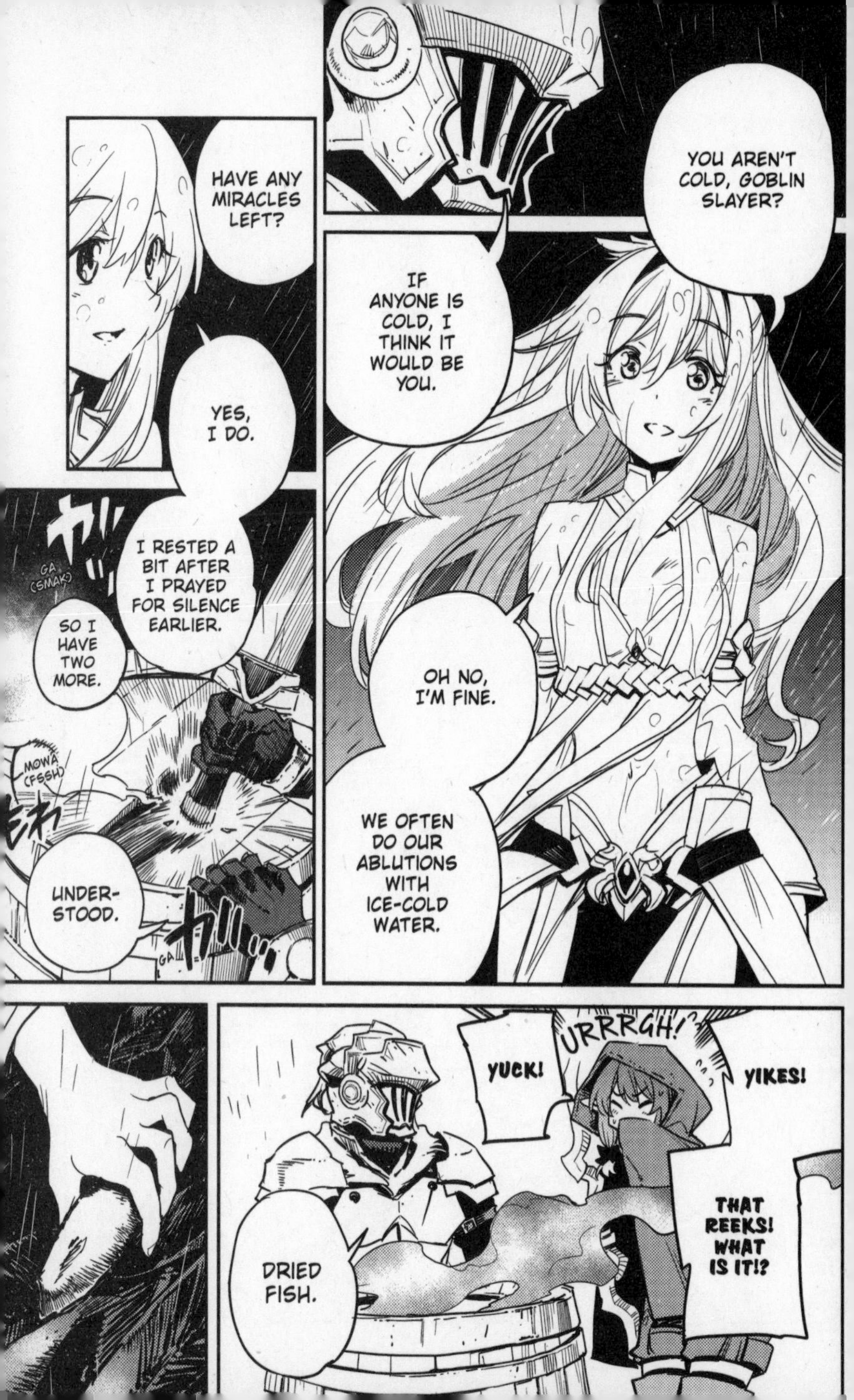

YOU AREN'T COLD, GOBLIN SLAYER?
IF ANYONE IS COLD, I THINK IT WOULD BE YOU.
OH NO, I'M FINE.
WE OFTEN DO OUR ABLUTIONS WITH ICE-COLD WATER.
HAVE ANY MIRACLES LEFT?
YES, I DO.
I RESTED A BIT AFTER I PRAYED FOR SILENCE EARLIER.
GA (SMAK)
SO I HAVE TWO MORE.
MOWA (FSSH)
UNDERSTOOD.
GA
URRRGH!
YIKES!
YUCK!
THAT REEKS! WHAT IS IT!?
DRIED FISH.

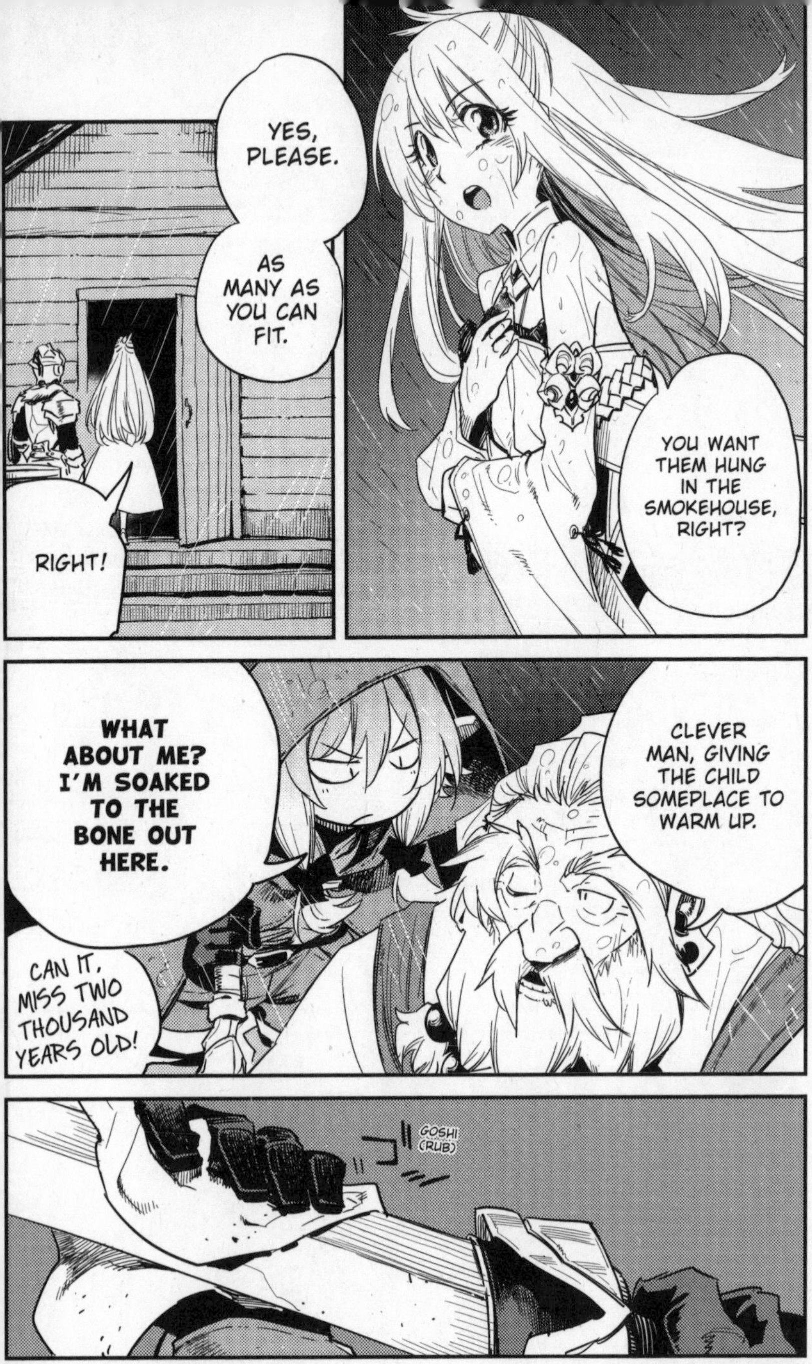
YOU WANT THEM HUNG IN THE SMOKEHOUSE, RIGHT?
YES, PLEASE.
AS MANY AS YOU CAN FIT.
RIGHT!
CLEVER MAN, GIVING THE CHILD SOMEPLACE TO WARM UP.
WHAT ABOUT ME? I'M SOAKED TO THE BONE OUT HERE.
CAN IT, MISS TWO THOUSAND YEARS OLD!
GOSHI (RUB)

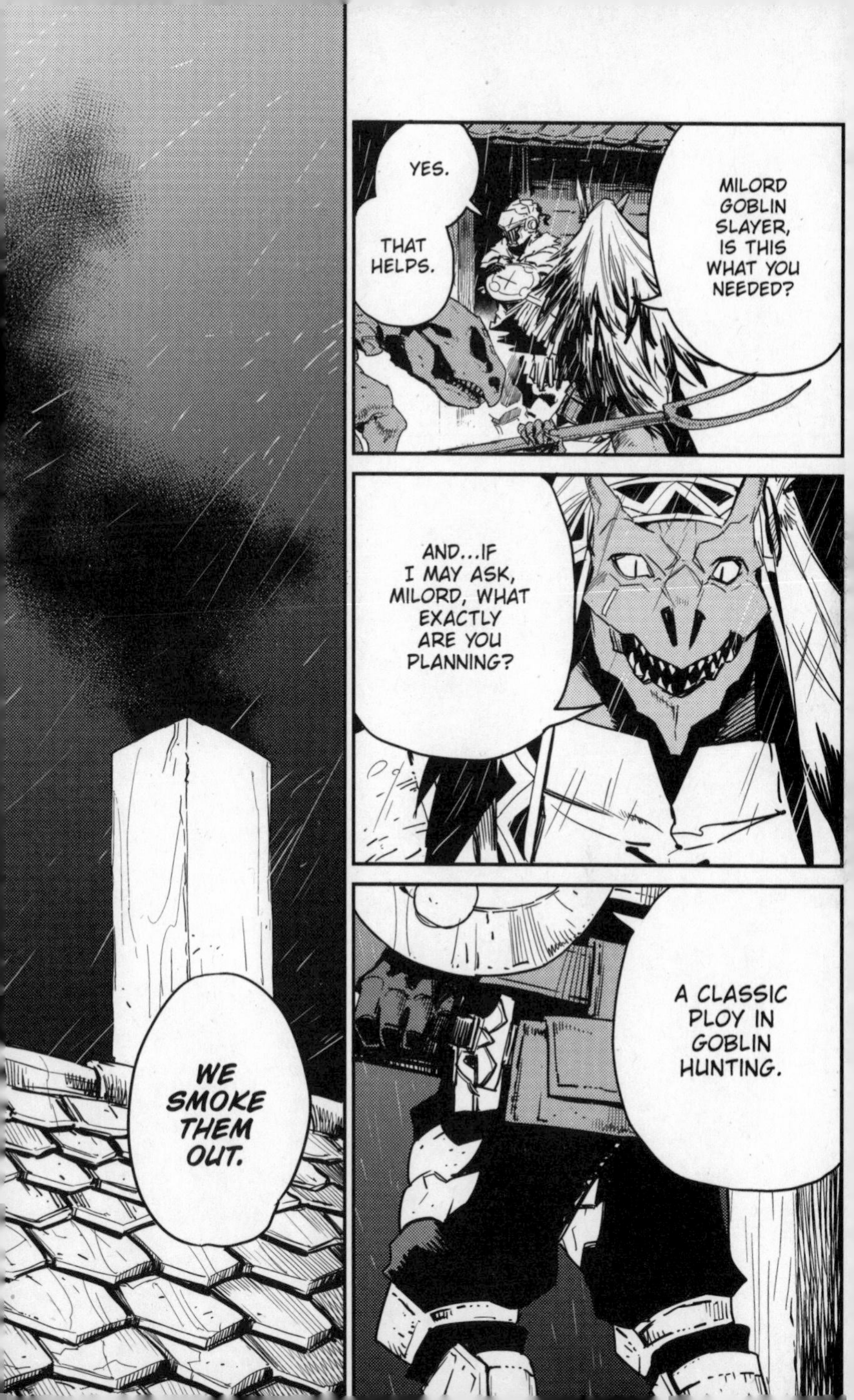
MILORD GOBLIN SLAYER, IS THIS WHAT YOU NEEDED?
YES.
THAT HELPS.
AND...IF I MAY ASK, MILORD, WHAT EXACTLY ARE YOU PLANNING?
A CLASSIC PLOY IN GOBLIN HUNTING.
WE SMOKE THEM OUT.

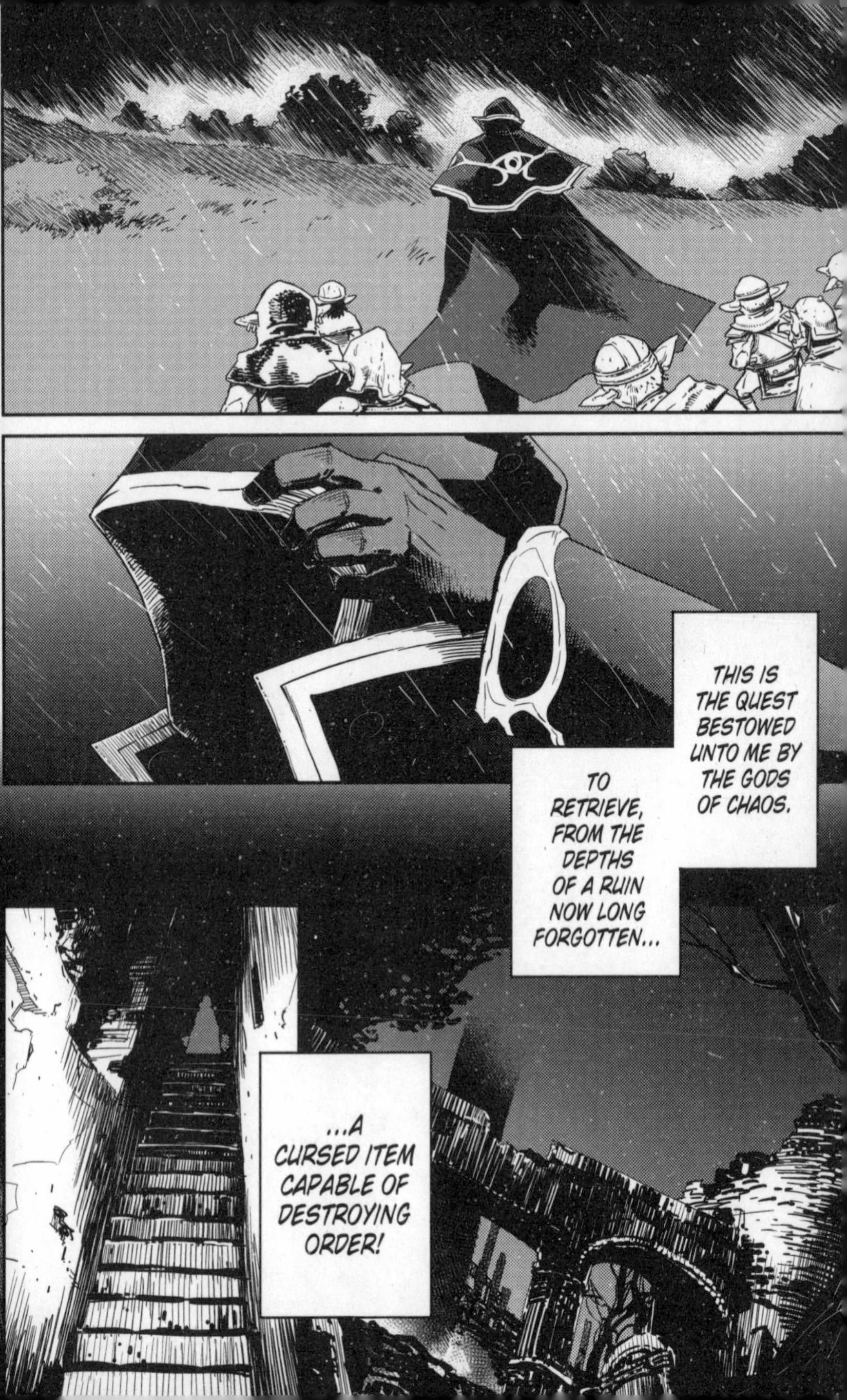
THIS IS THE QUEST BESTOWED UNTO ME BY THE GODS OF CHAOS.
TO RETRIEVE, FROM THE DEPTHS OF A RUIN NOW LONG FORGOTTEN...
...A CURSED ITEM CAPABLE OF DESTROYING ORDER!

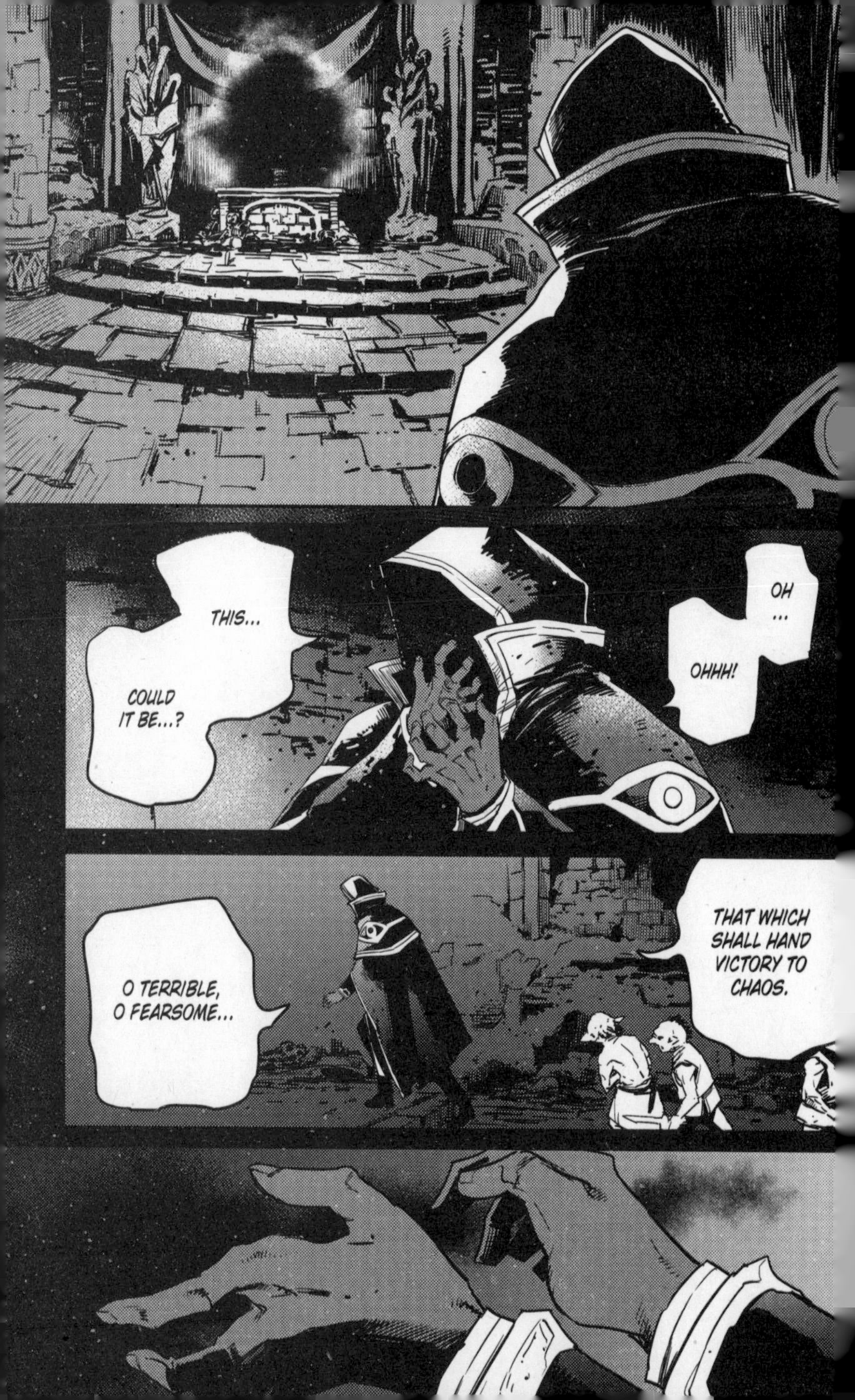
OH... OHHH!
THIS... COULD IT BE...?
THAT WHICH SHALL HAND VICTORY TO CHAOS.
O TERRIBLE, O FEARSOME...

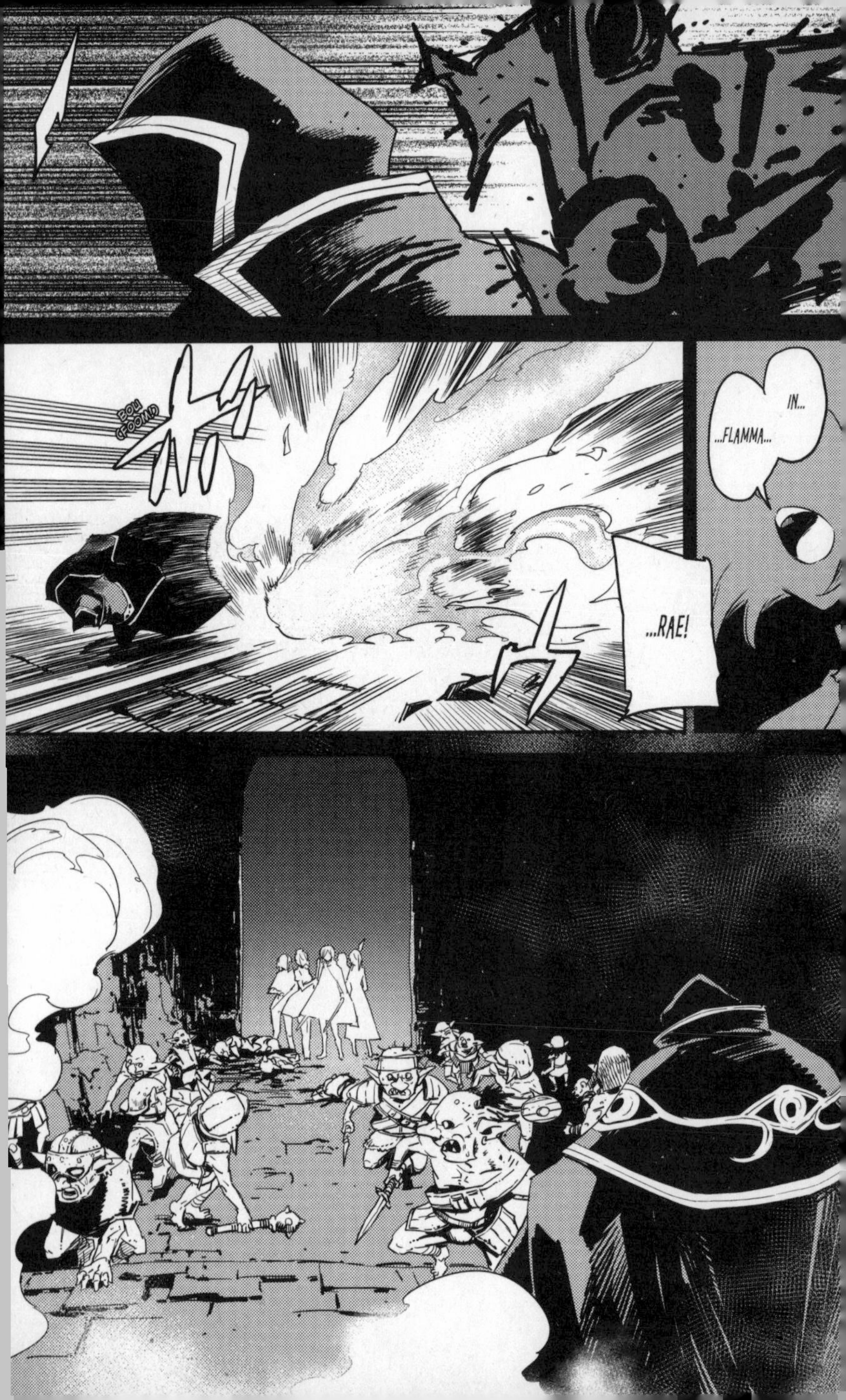
IN...
...FLAMMA...
...RAE!
BOU
(FOOM)

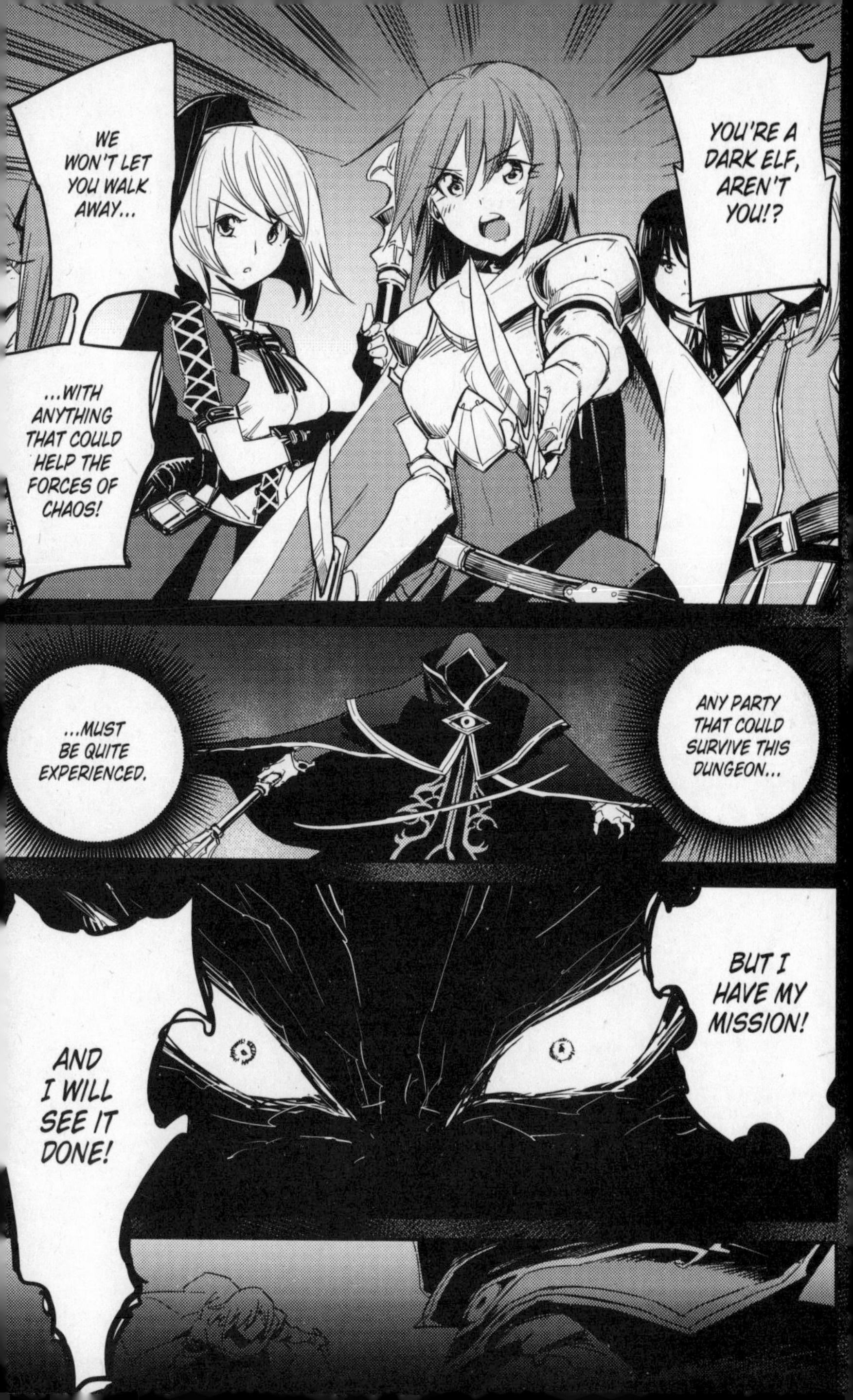
YOU'RE A DARK ELF, AREN'T YOU!?
WE WON'T LET YOU WALK AWAY...
...WITH ANYTHING THAT COULD HELP THE FORCES OF CHAOS!
ANY PARTY THAT COULD SURVIVE THIS DUNGEON...
...MUST BE QUITE EXPERIENCED.
BUT I HAVE MY MISSION!
AND I WILL SEE IT DONE!

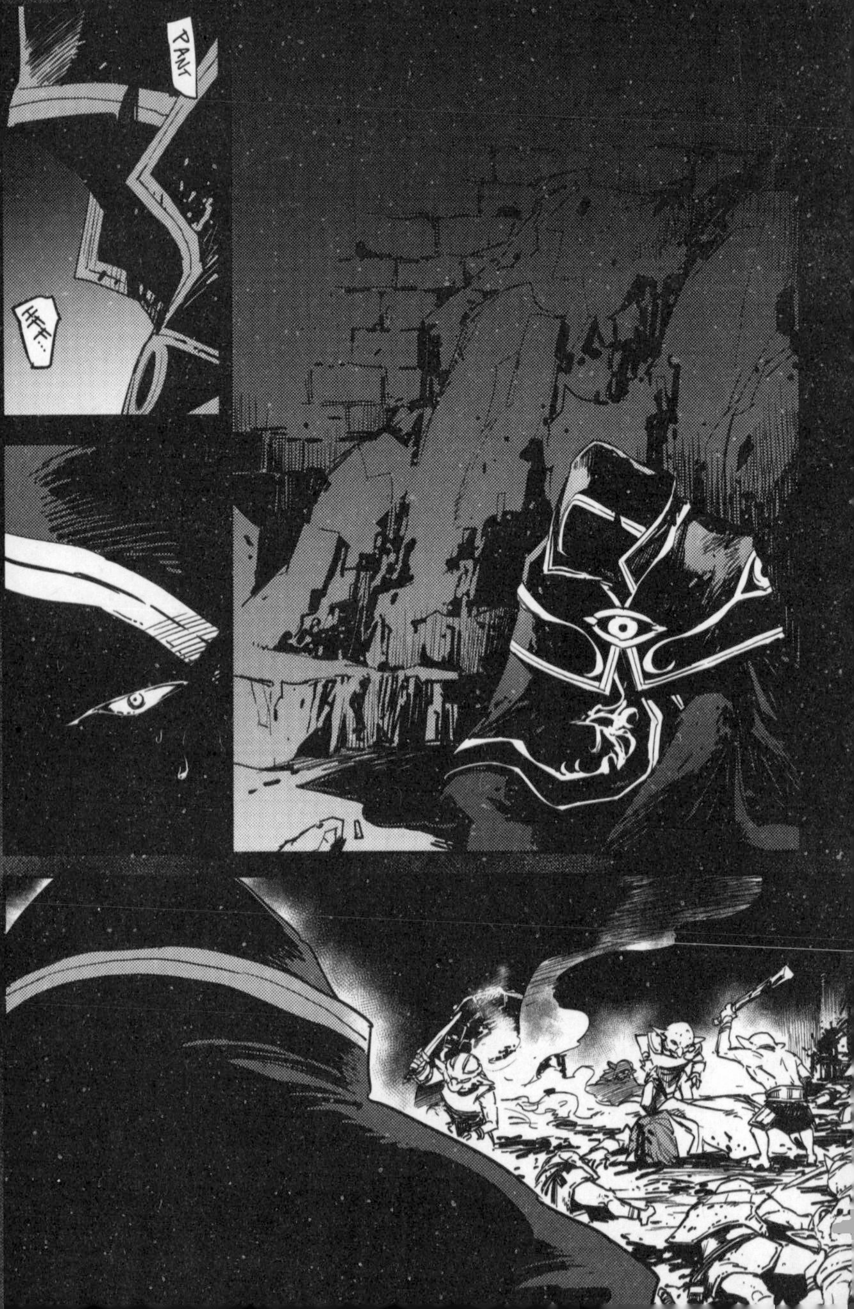
PANT
HFF...

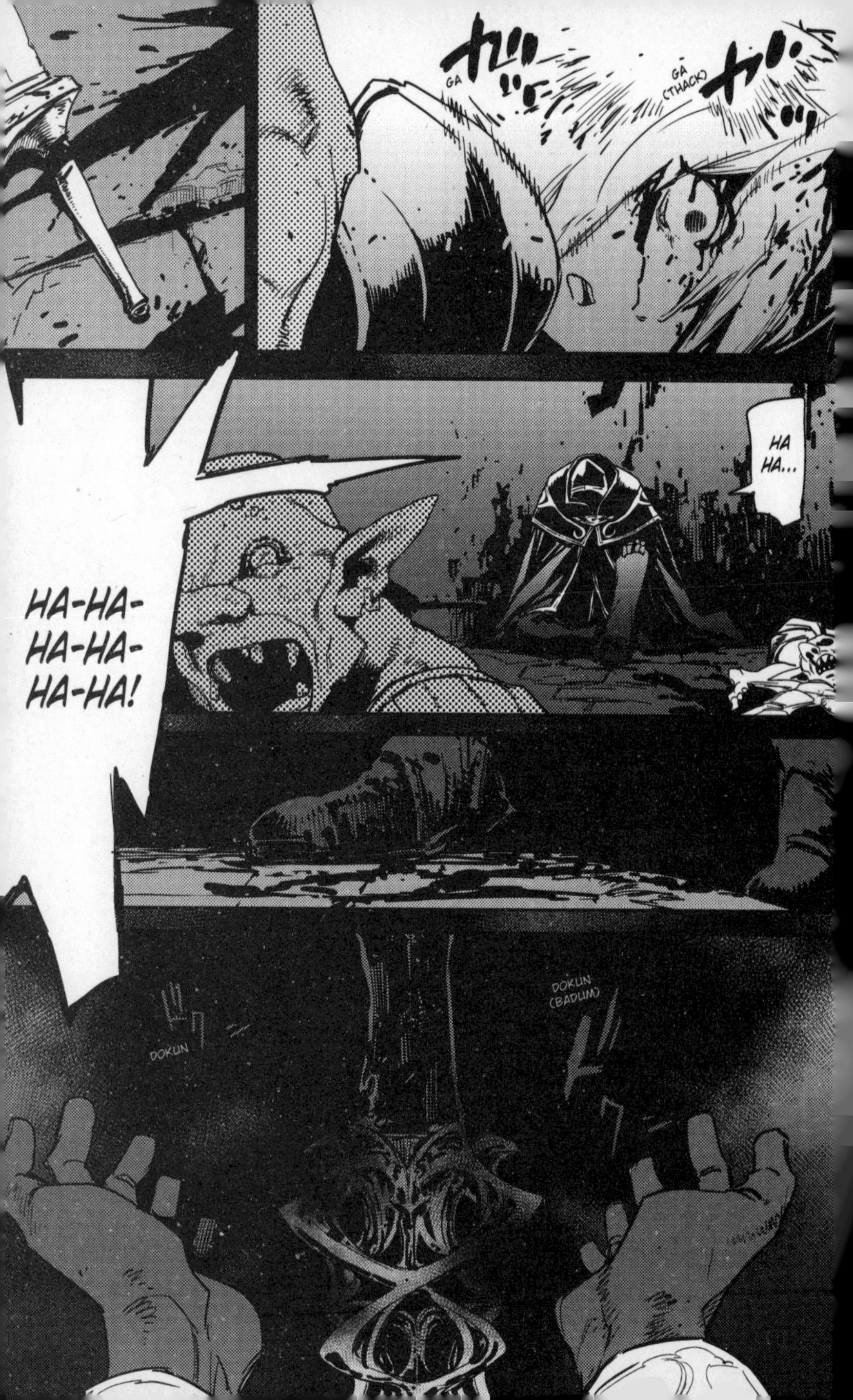
GA (THACK)
GA
HA HA...
HA-HA-HA-HA-HA-HA!
DOKUN (BADUM)
DOKUN

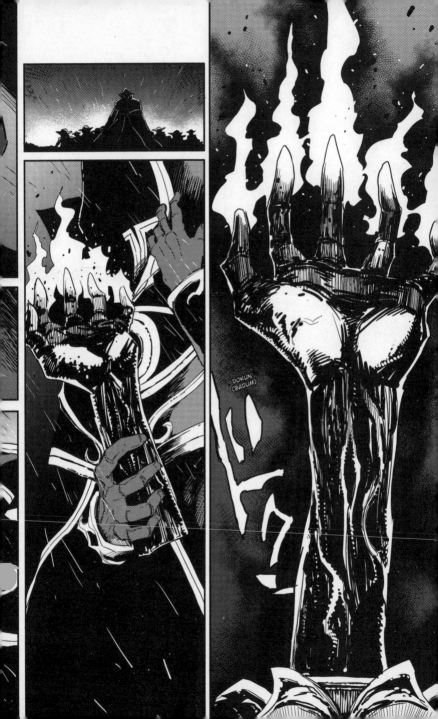

DOKUN
(BADUM)

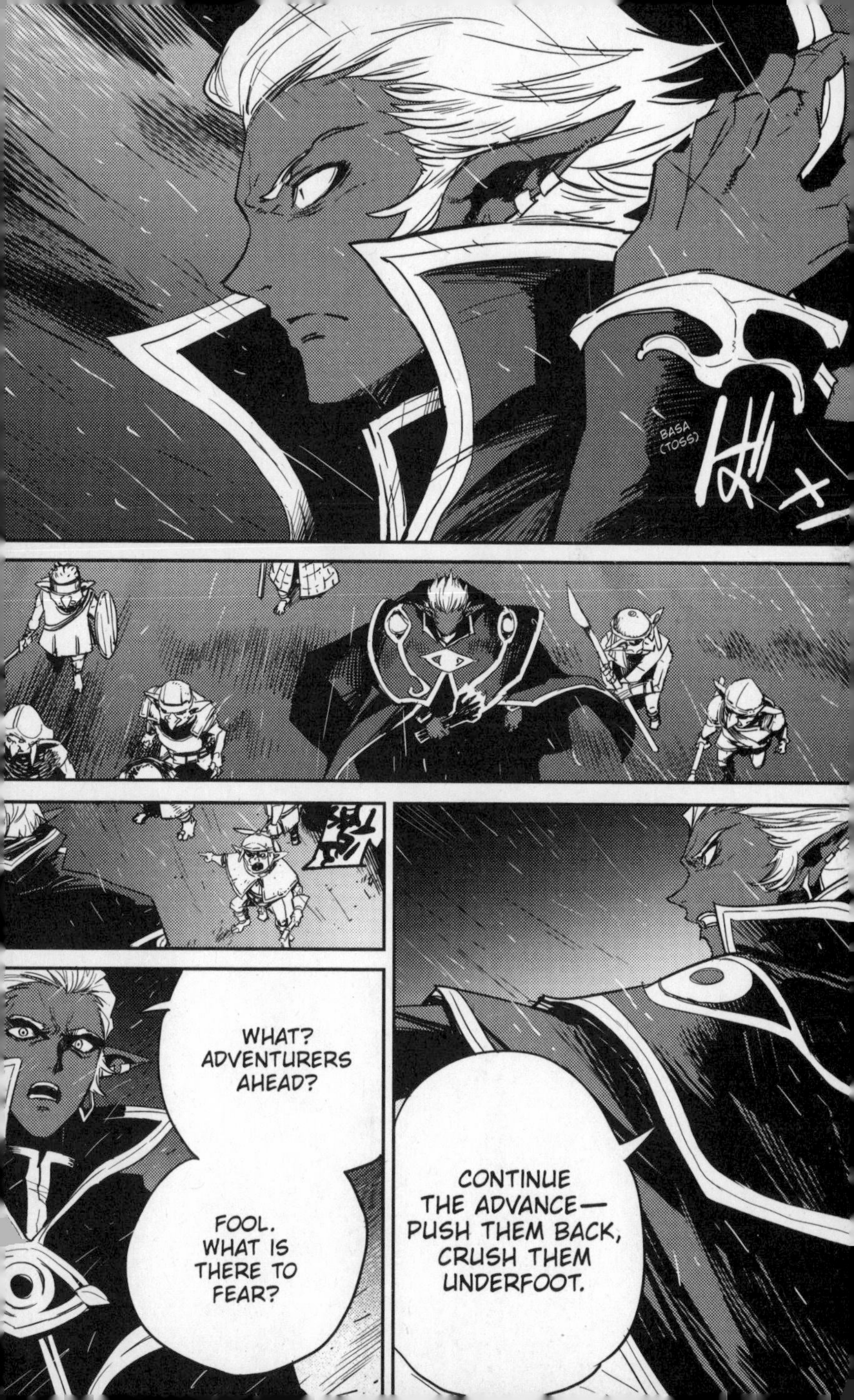
BASA (TOSS)
CONTINUE THE ADVANCE—PUSH THEM BACK, CRUSH THEM UNDERFOOT.
WHAT? ADVENTURERS AHEAD?
FOOL. WHAT IS THERE TO FEAR?

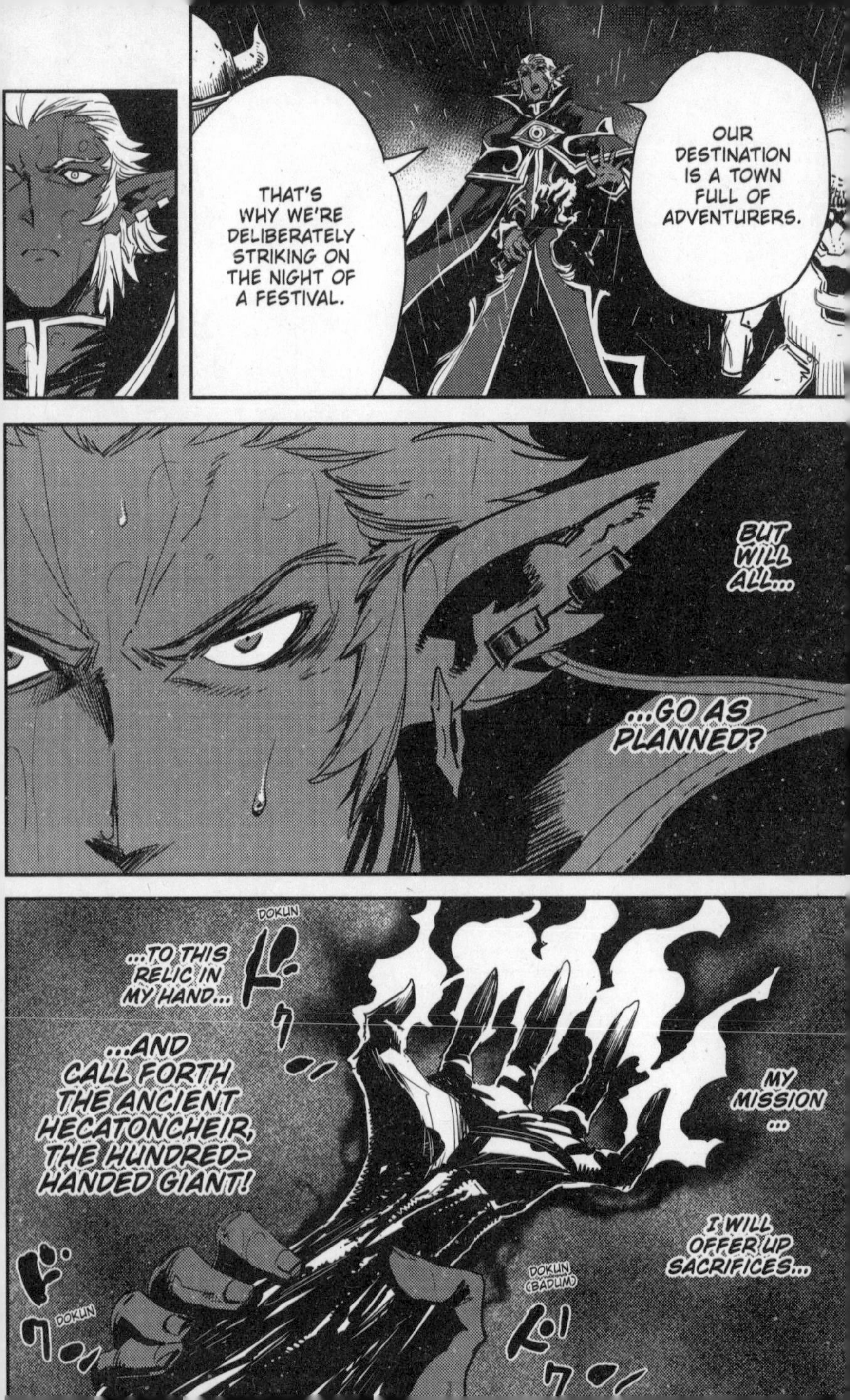
OUR DESTINATION IS A TOWN FULL OF ADVENTURERS.
THAT'S WHY WE'RE DELIBERATELY STRIKING ON THE NIGHT OF A FESTIVAL.
BUT WILL ALL...
...GO AS PLANNED?
MY MISSION...
I WILL OFFER UP SACRIFICES...
DOKUN (BADUM)
...TO THIS RELIC IN MY HAND...
DOKUN
...AND CALL FORTH THE ANCIENT HECATONCHEIR, THE HUNDRED-HANDED GIANT!
DOKUN

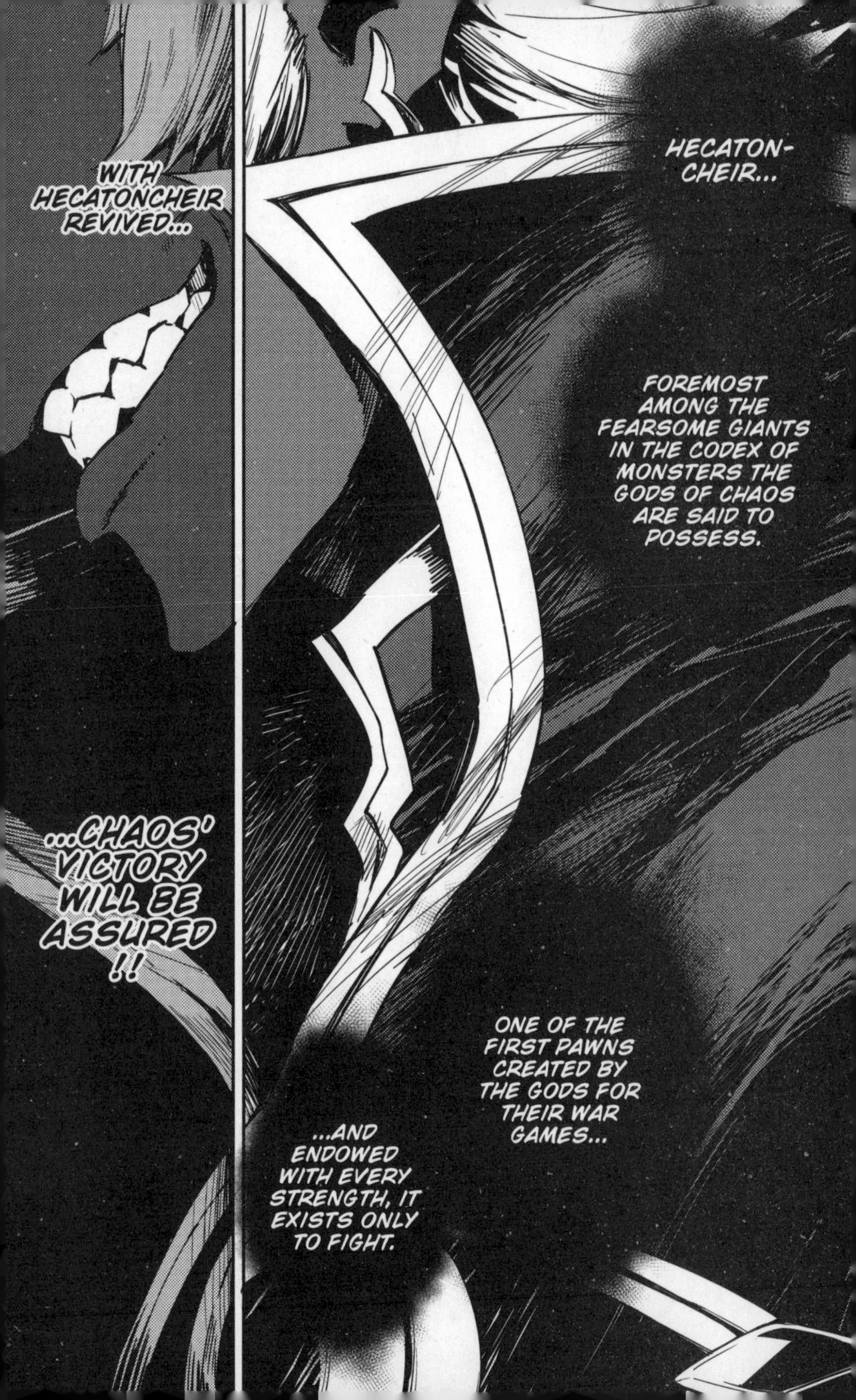
HECATON-CHEIR...
FOREMOST AMONG THE FEARSOME GIANTS IN THE CODEX OF MONSTERS THE GODS OF CHAOS ARE SAID TO POSSESS.
ONE OF THE FIRST PAWNS CREATED BY THE GODS FOR THEIR WAR GAMES...
...AND ENDOWED WITH EVERY STRENGTH, IT EXISTS ONLY TO FIGHT.
WITH HECATONCHEIR REVIVED...
...CHAOS' VICTORY WILL BE ASSURED!!

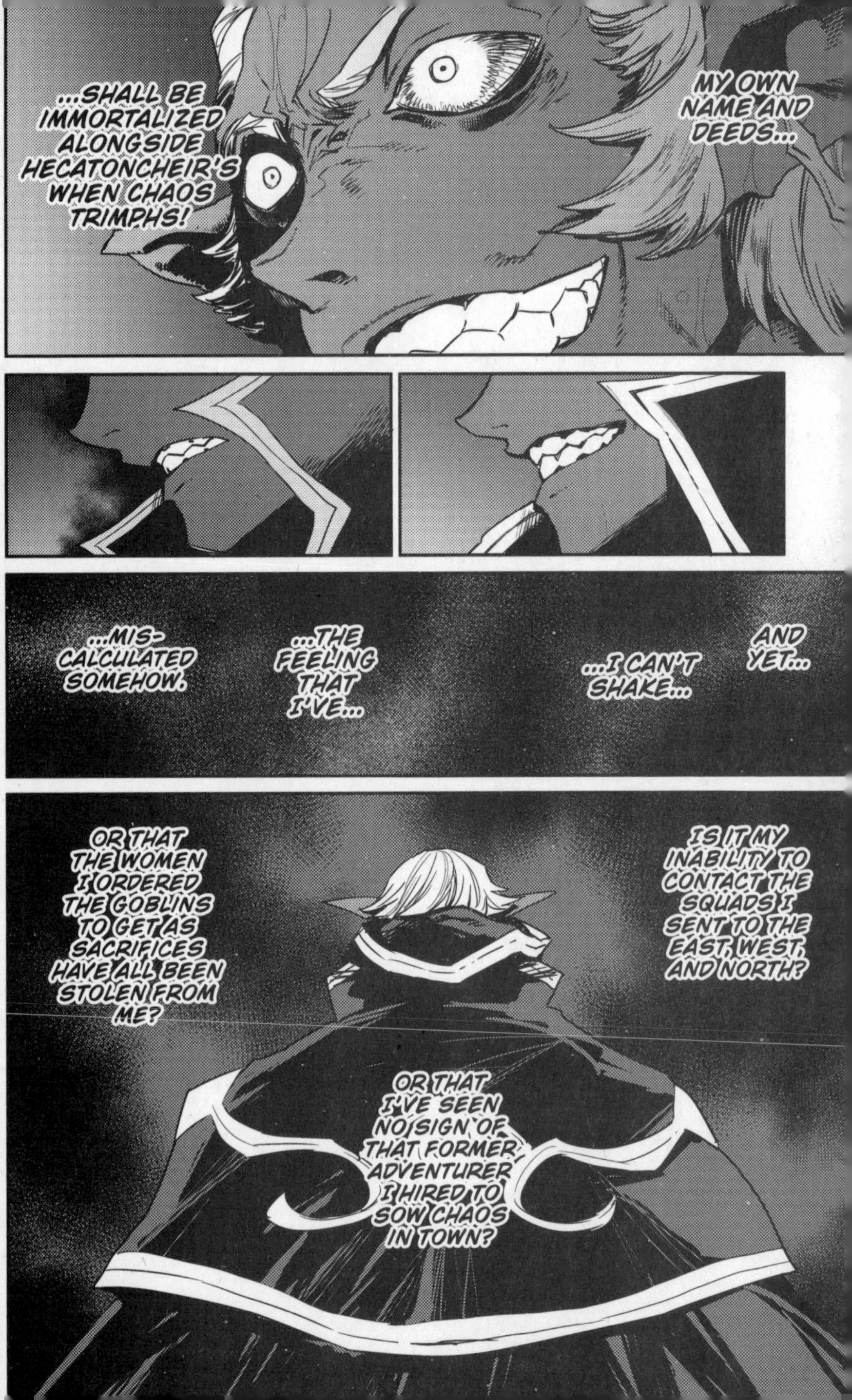
MY OWN NAME AND DEEDS...
...SHALL BE IMMORTALIZED ALONGSIDE HECATONCHEIR'S WHEN CHAOS TRIMPHS!
AND YET...
...I CAN'T SHAKE...
...THE FEELING THAT I'VE...
...MIS-CALCULATED SOMEHOW.
IS IT MY INABILITY TO CONTACT THE SQUADS I SENT TO THE EAST, WEST, AND NORTH?
OR THAT THE WOMEN I ORDERED THE GOBLINS TO GET AS SACRIFICES HAVE ALL BEEN STOLEN FROM ME?
OR THAT I'VE SEEN NO SIGN OF THAT FORMER ADVENTURER I HIRED TO SOW CHAOS IN TOWN?

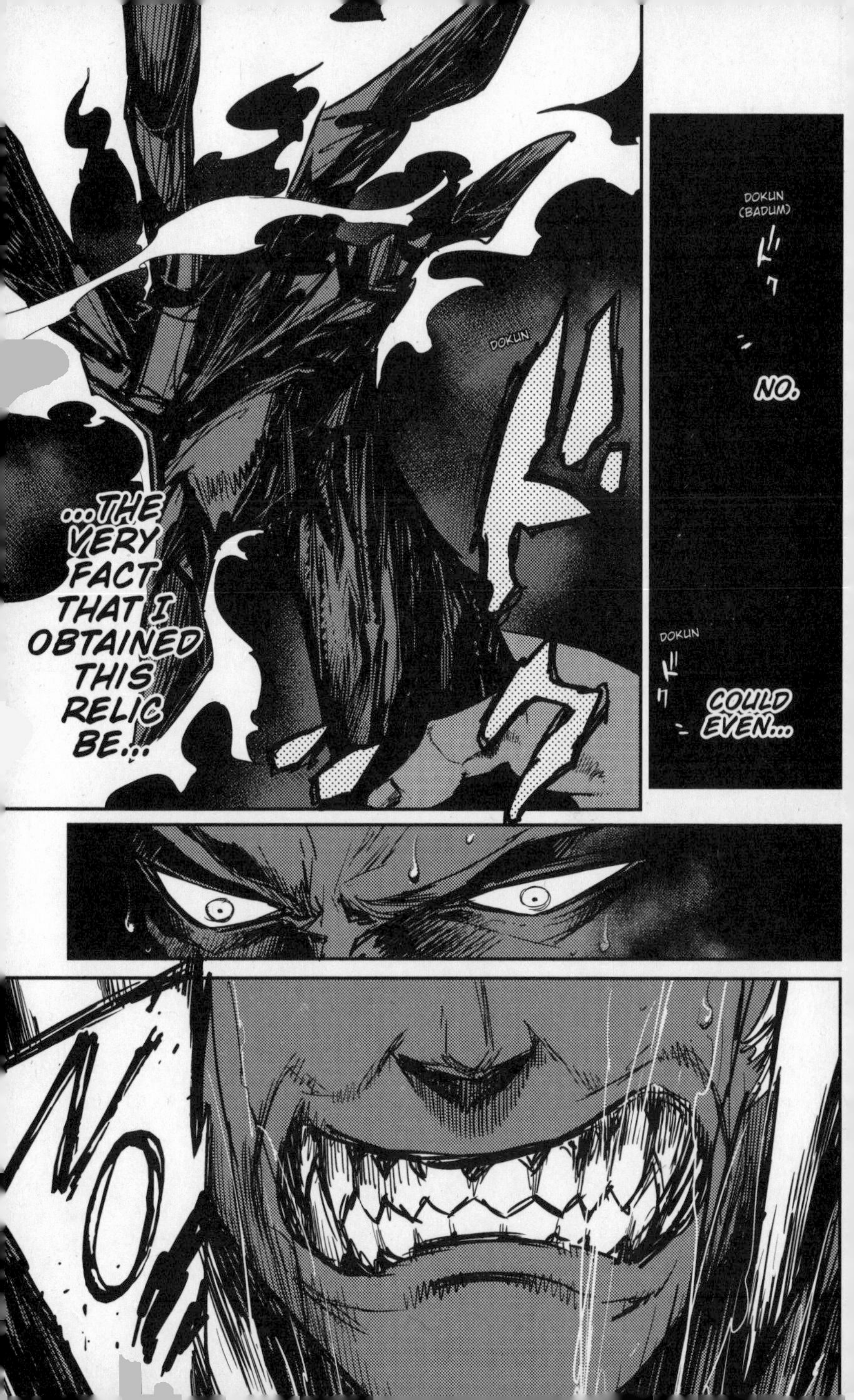
DOKUN (BADUM)
ドク
NO.
DOKUN
ドク
COULD EVEN...
DOKUN
...THE VERY FACT THAT I OBTAINED THIS RELIC BE...
NO

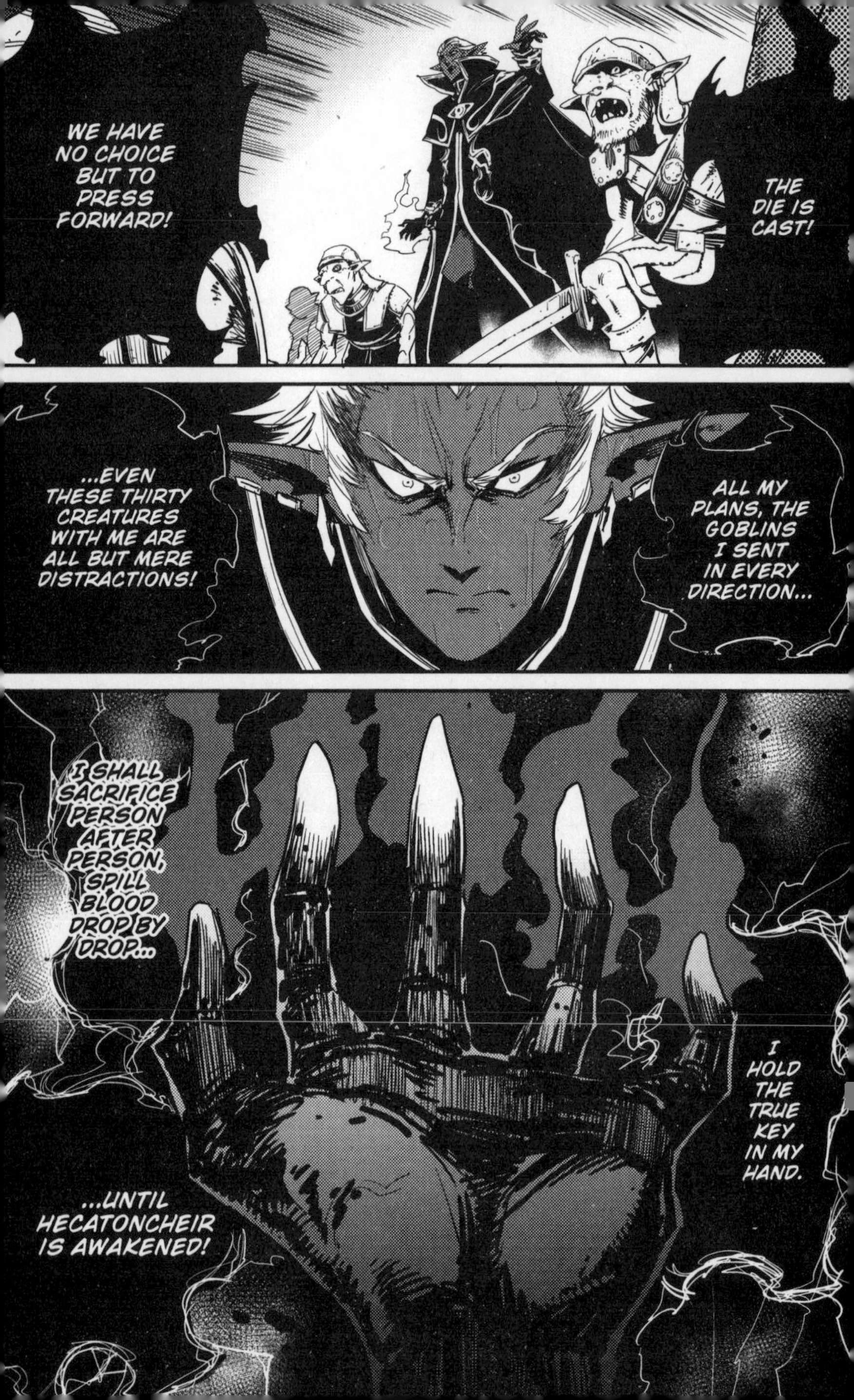
THE DIE IS CAST!
WE HAVE NO CHOICE BUT TO PRESS FORWARD!
ALL MY PLANS, THE GOBLINS I SENT IN EVERY DIRECTION...
...EVEN THESE THIRTY CREATURES WITH ME ARE ALL BUT MERE DISTRACTIONS!
I HOLD THE TRUE KEY IN MY HAND.
I SHALL SACRIFICE PERSON AFTER PERSON, SPILL BLOOD DROP BY DROP...
...UNTIL HECATONCHEIR IS AWAKENED!

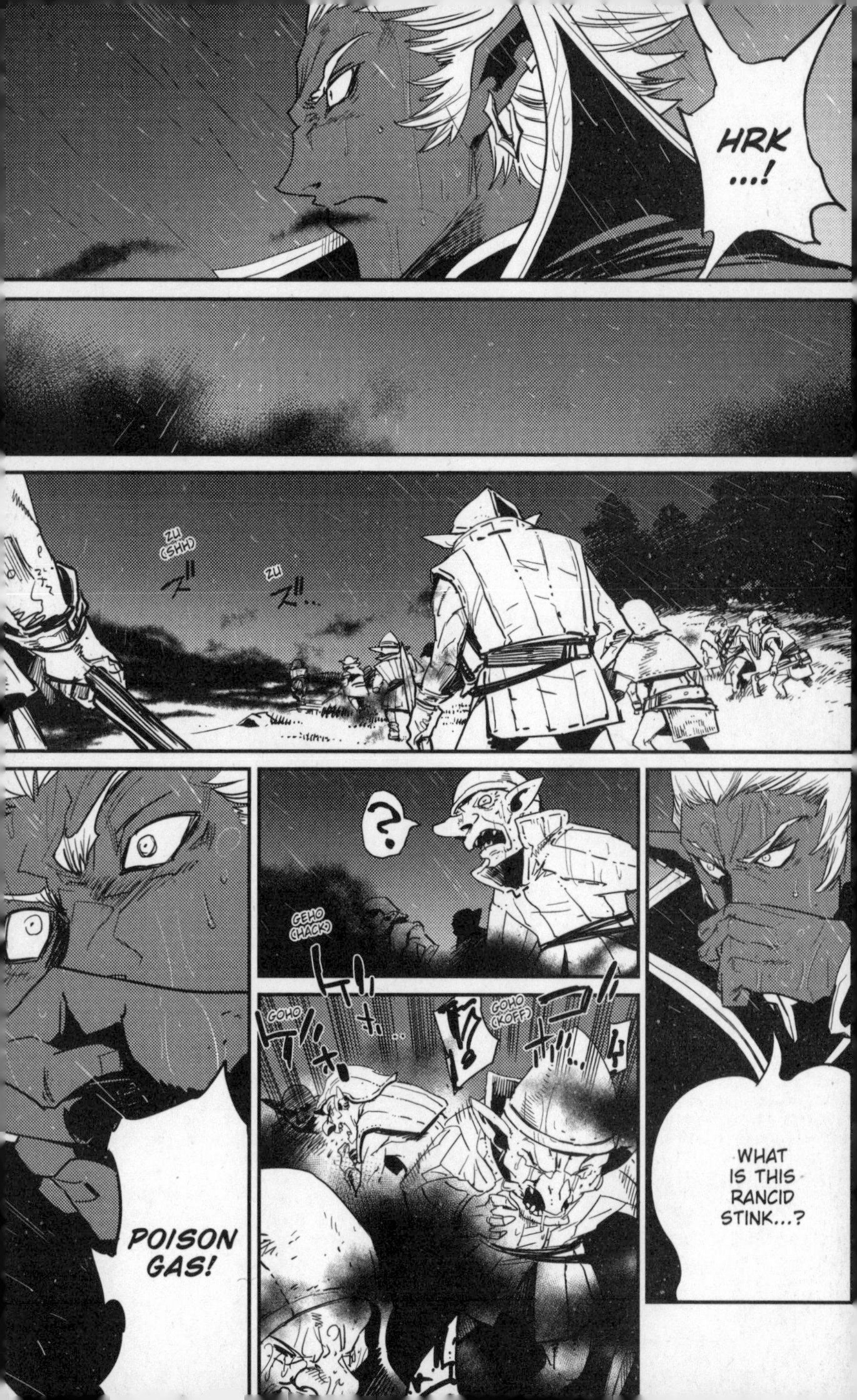

HRK...!
ZU (SHH)
ZU
WHAT IS THIS RANCID STINK...?
?
GEHO (HACK)
GOHO (KOFF)
GOHO
POISON GAS!

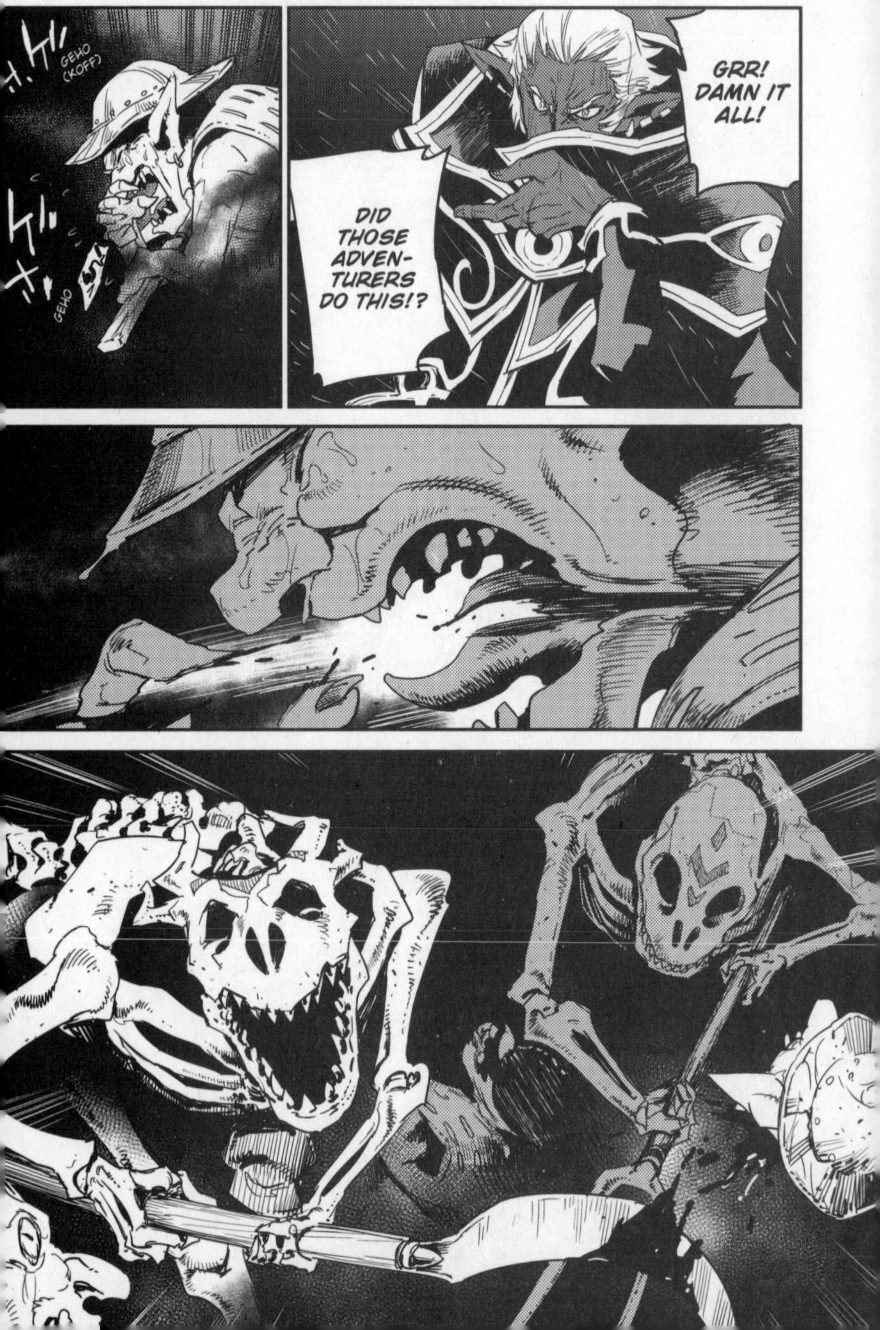
GRR! DAMN IT ALL!
DID THOSE ADVENTURERS DO THIS!?
GEHO (KOFF)
GEHO

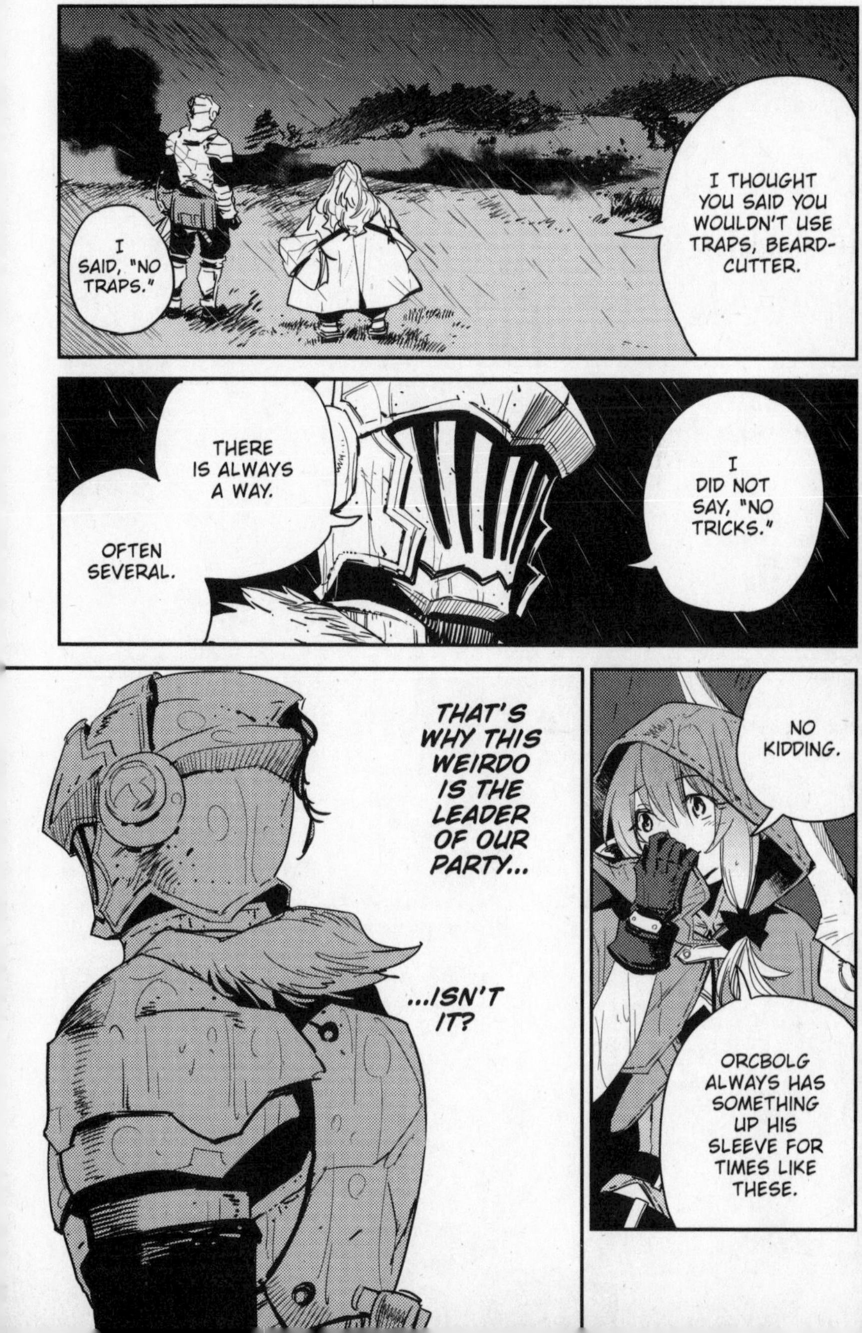
I THOUGHT YOU SAID YOU WOULDN'T USE TRAPS, BEARD-CUTTER.
I SAID, "NO TRAPS."
I DID NOT SAY, "NO TRICKS."
THERE IS ALWAYS A WAY.
OFTEN SEVERAL.
NO KIDDING.
ORCBOLG ALWAYS HAS SOMETHING UP HIS SLEEVE FOR TIMES LIKE THESE.
THAT'S WHY THIS WEIRDO IS THE LEADER OF OUR PARTY...
...ISN'T IT?

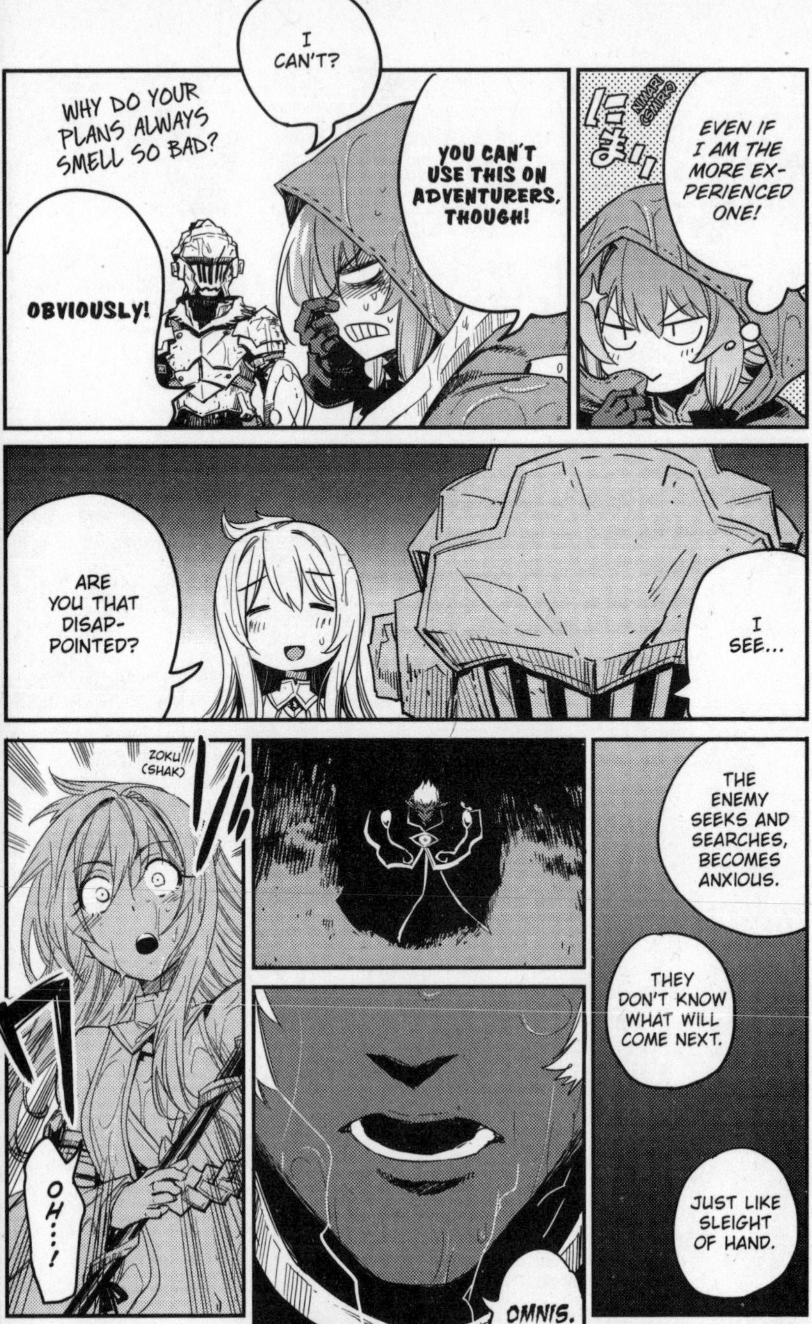

NIMARI (SMIRK)
EVEN IF I AM THE MORE EX-PERIENCED ONE!
YOU CAN'T USE THIS ON ADVENTURERS, THOUGH!
I CAN'T?
WHY DO YOUR PLANS ALWAYS SMELL SO BAD?
OBVIOUSLY!
I SEE...
ARE YOU THAT DISAP-POINTED?
THE ENEMY SEEKS AND SEARCHES, BECOMES ANXIOUS.
THEY DON'T KNOW WHAT WILL COME NEXT.
JUST LIKE SLEIGHT OF HAND.
OMNIS.
ZOKU (SHAK)
OH...!

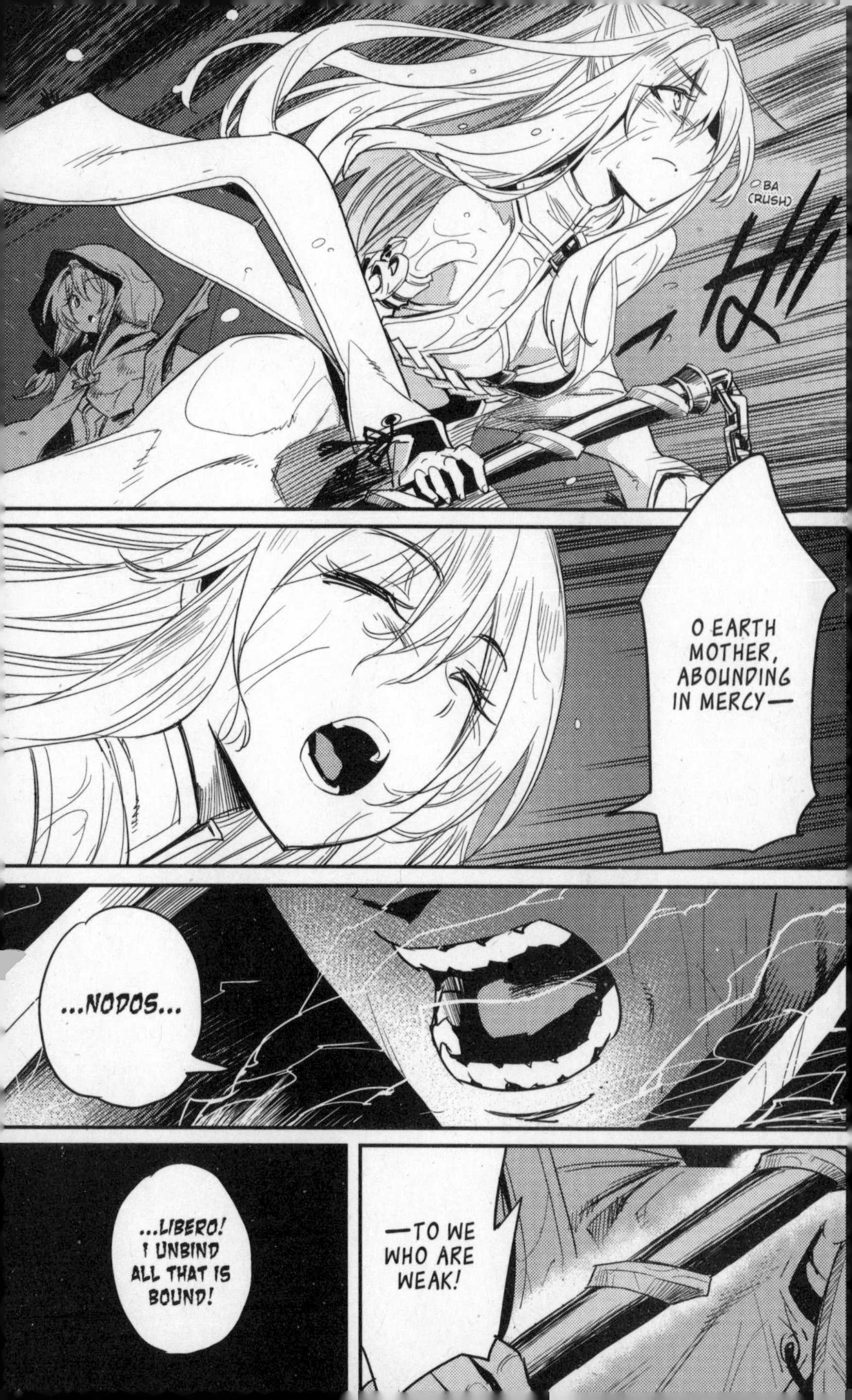
BA (RUSH)
O EARTH MOTHER, ABOUNDING IN MERCY—
...NODOS...
—TO WE WHO ARE WEAK!
...LIBERO! I UNBIND ALL THAT IS BOUND!

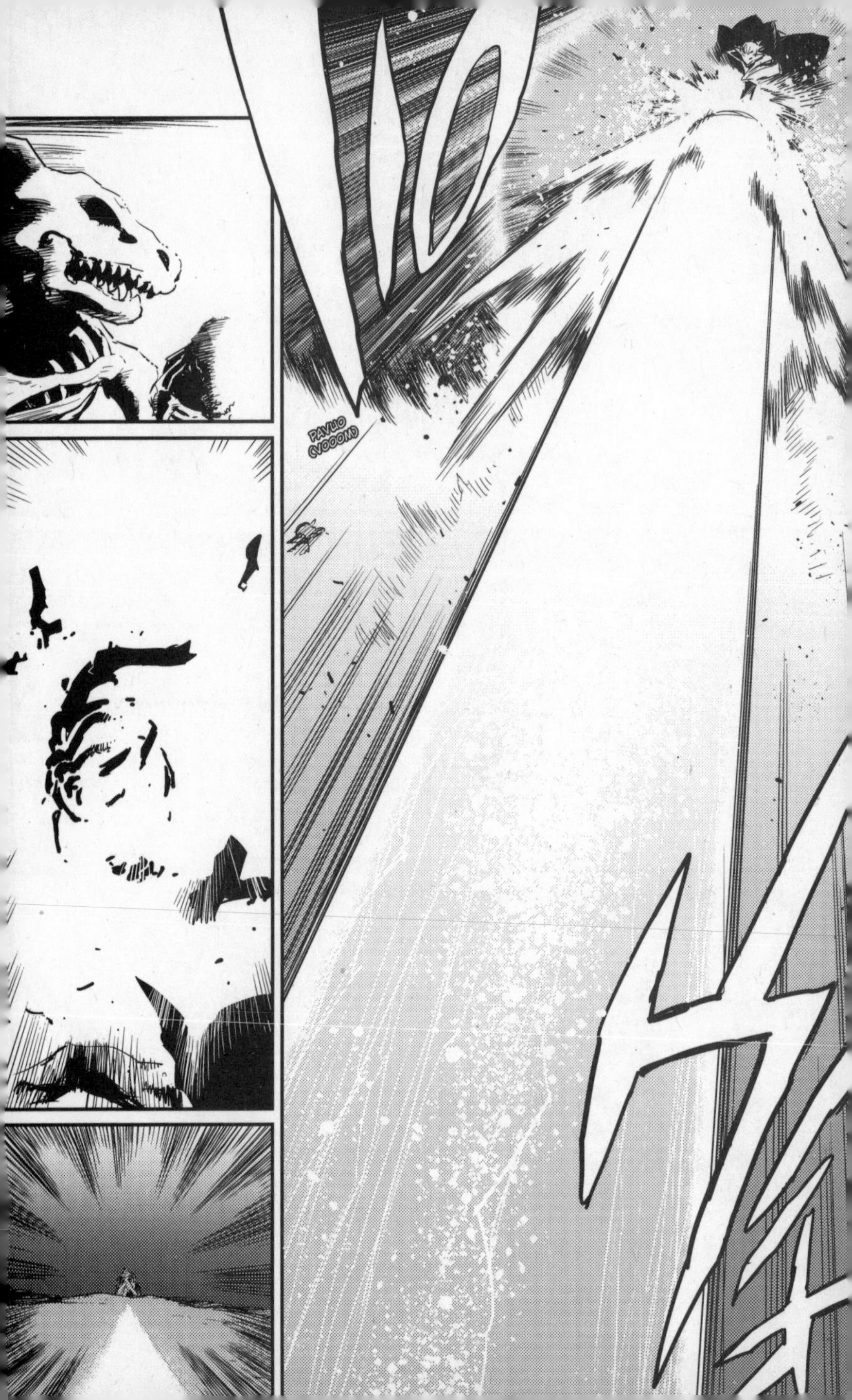
PAVUO
(VOOOM)

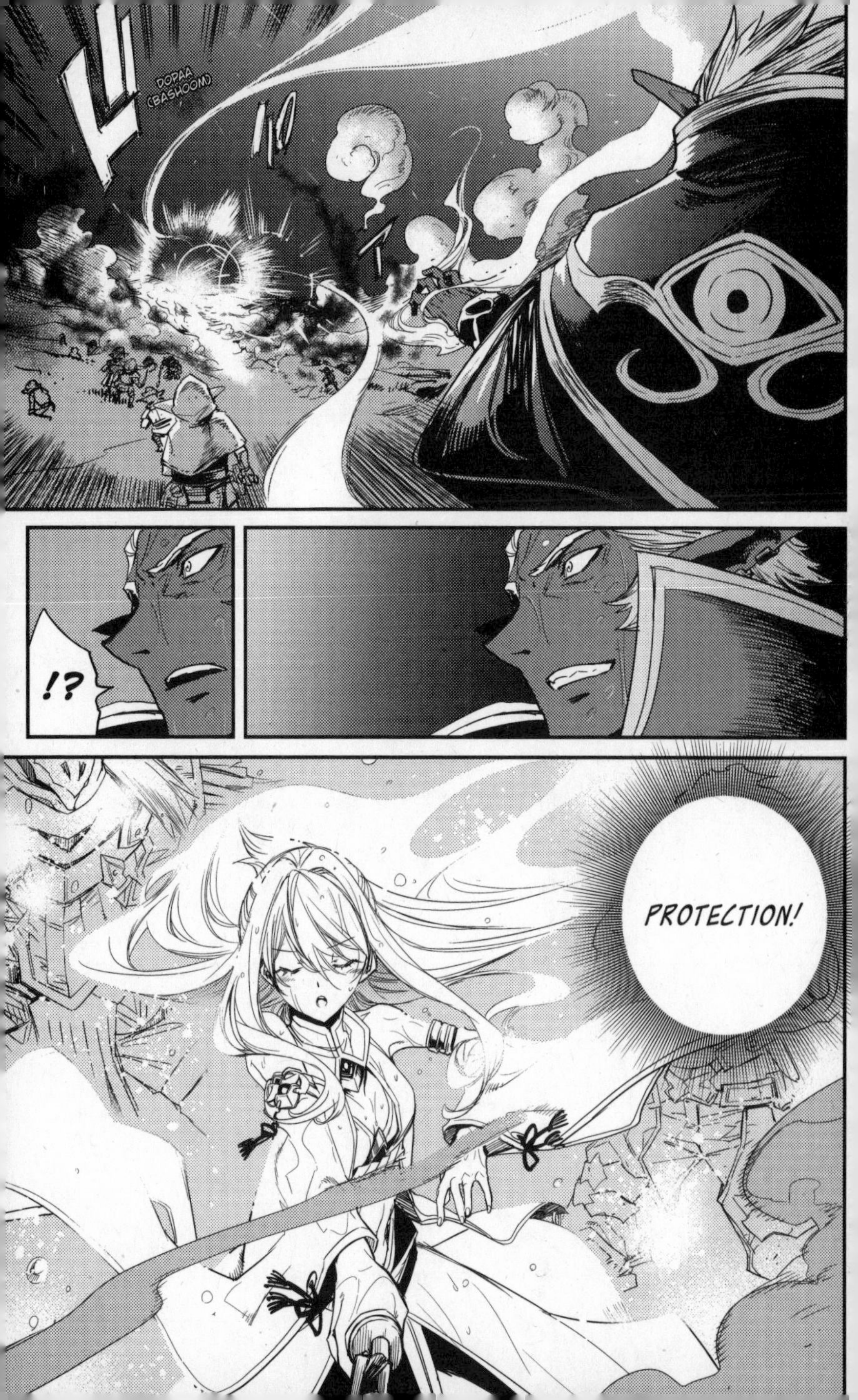
DOPAA (BASHOOM)
!?
PROTECTION!

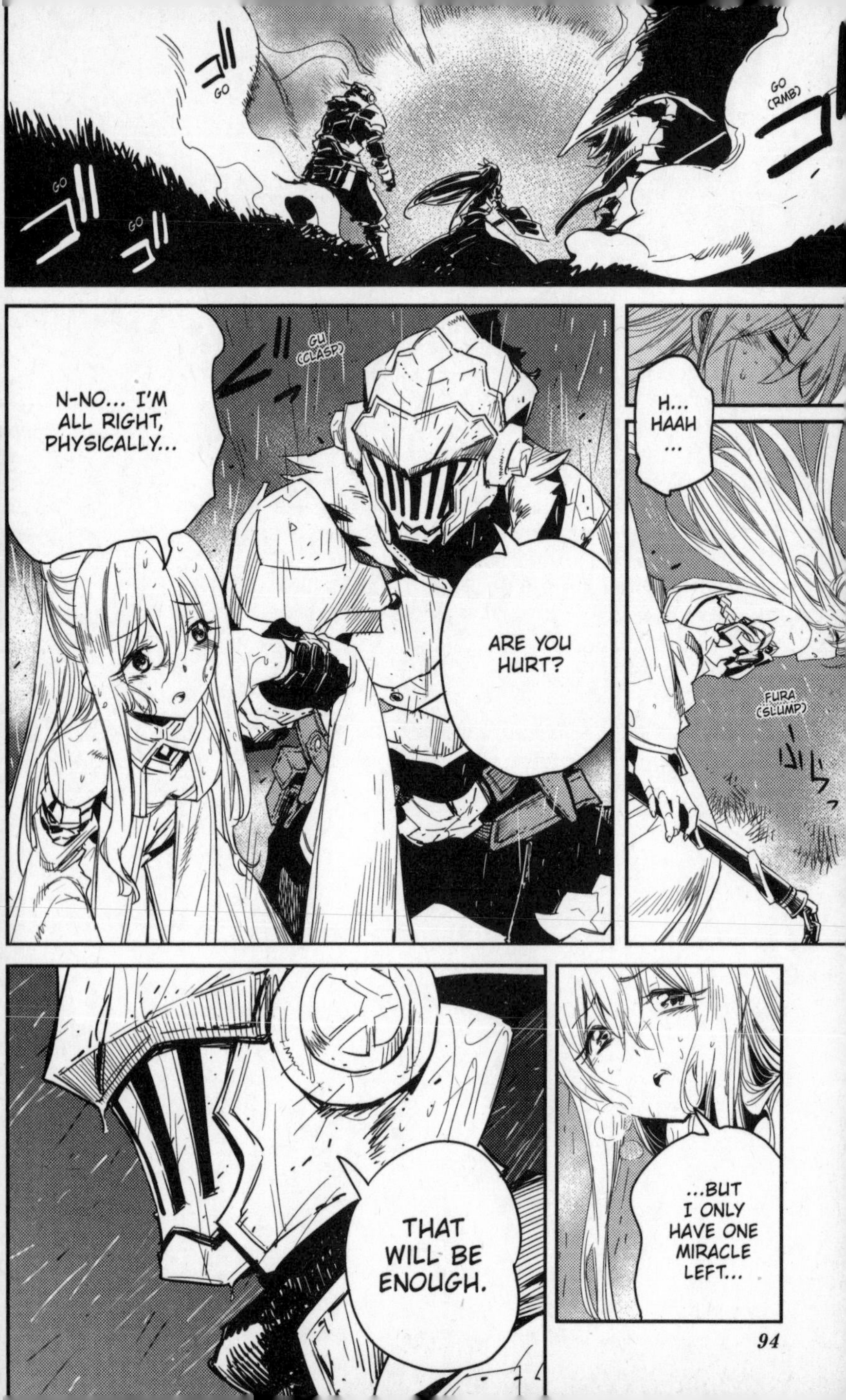
GO (RMB)
GO
GO
GO
H... HAAH ...
FURA (SLUMP)
GU (CLASP)
ARE YOU HURT?
N-NO... I'M ALL RIGHT, PHYSICALLY...
...BUT I ONLY HAVE ONE MIRACLE LEFT...
THAT WILL BE ENOUGH.

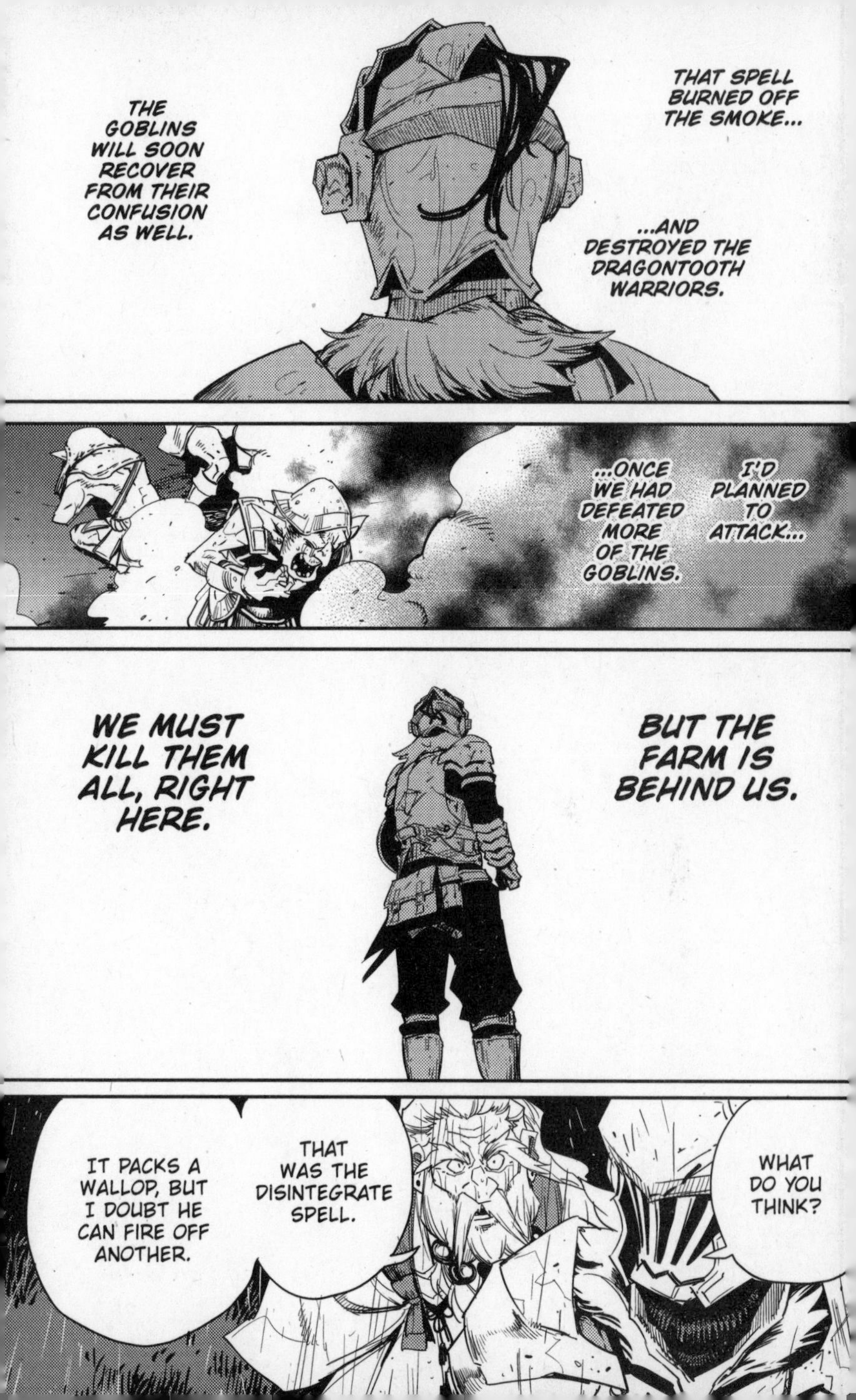
THAT SPELL BURNED OFF THE SMOKE...
...AND DESTROYED THE DRAGONTOOTH WARRIORS.
THE GOBLINS WILL SOON RECOVER FROM THEIR CONFUSION AS WELL.
I'D PLANNED TO ATTACK...
...ONCE WE HAD DEFEATED MORE OF THE GOBLINS.
BUT THE FARM IS BEHIND US.
WE MUST KILL THEM ALL, RIGHT HERE.
WHAT DO YOU THINK?
THAT WAS THE DISINTEGRATE SPELL.
IT PACKS A WALLOP, BUT I DOUBT HE CAN FIRE OFF ANOTHER.

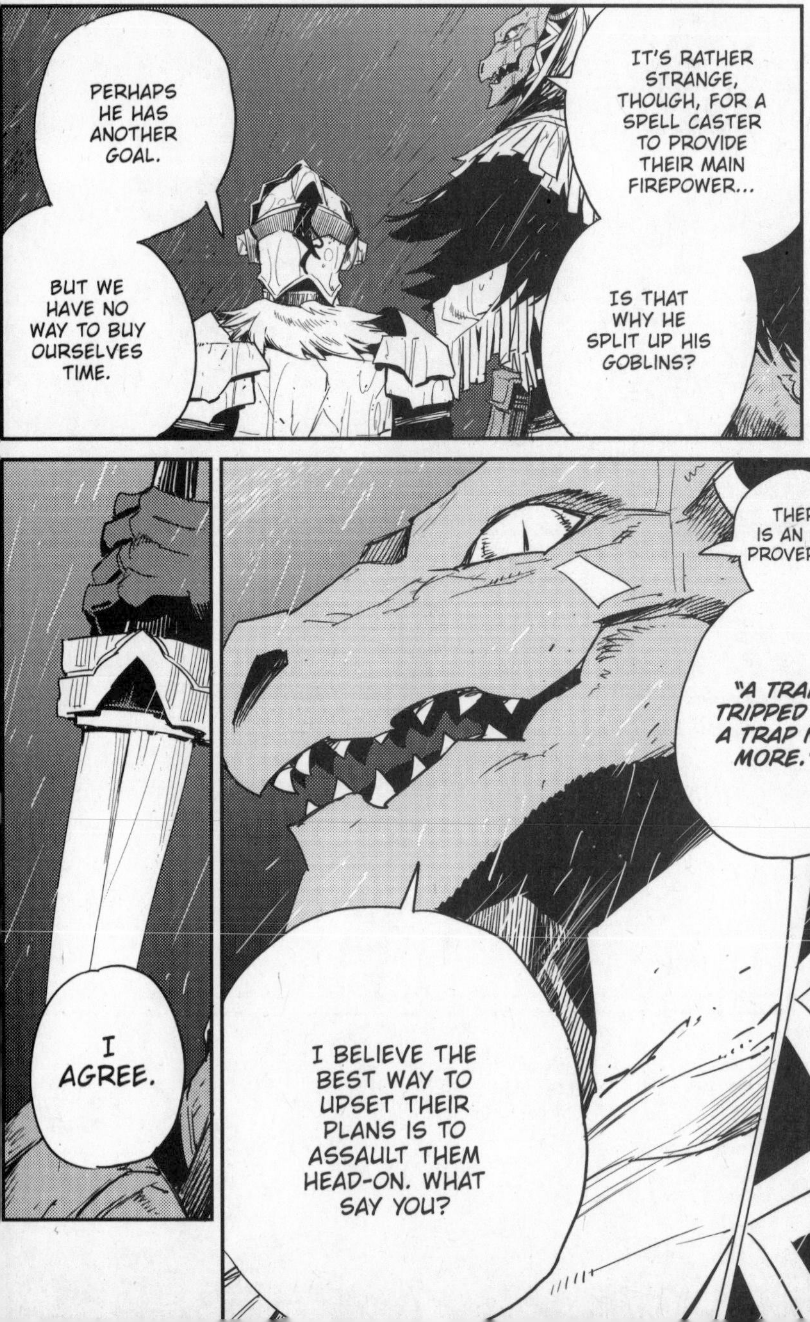
IT'S RATHER STRANGE, THOUGH, FOR A SPELL CASTER TO PROVIDE THEIR MAIN FIREPOWER...
IS THAT WHY HE SPLIT UP HIS GOBLINS?
PERHAPS HE HAS ANOTHER GOAL.
BUT WE HAVE NO WAY TO BUY OURSELVES TIME.
THERE IS AN OLD PROVERB—
"A TRAP TRIPPED IS A TRAP NO MORE."
I BELIEVE THE BEST WAY TO UPSET THEIR PLANS IS TO ASSAULT THEM HEAD-ON. WHAT SAY YOU?
I AGREE.

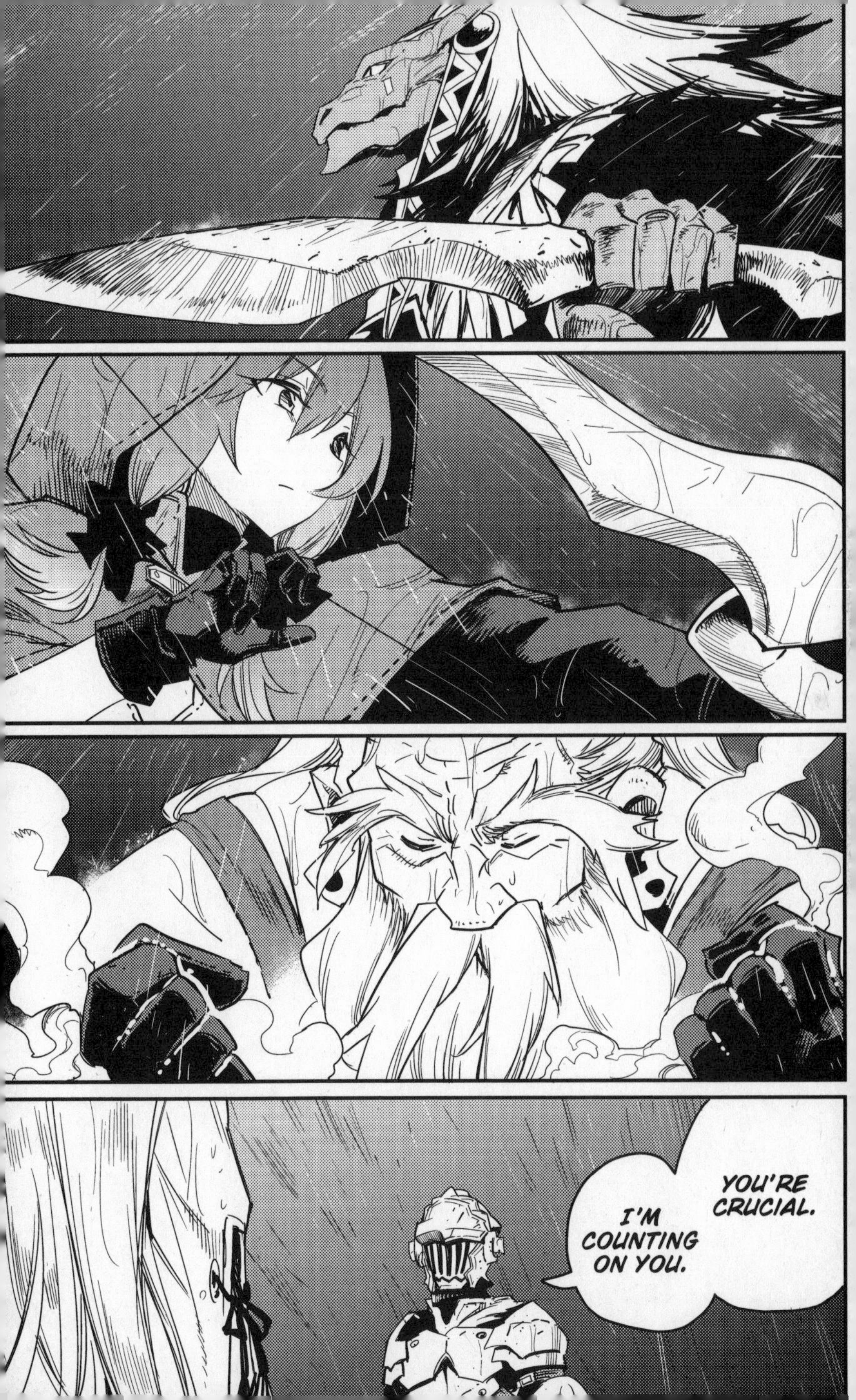
YOU'RE CRUCIAL.
I'M COUNTING ON YOU.

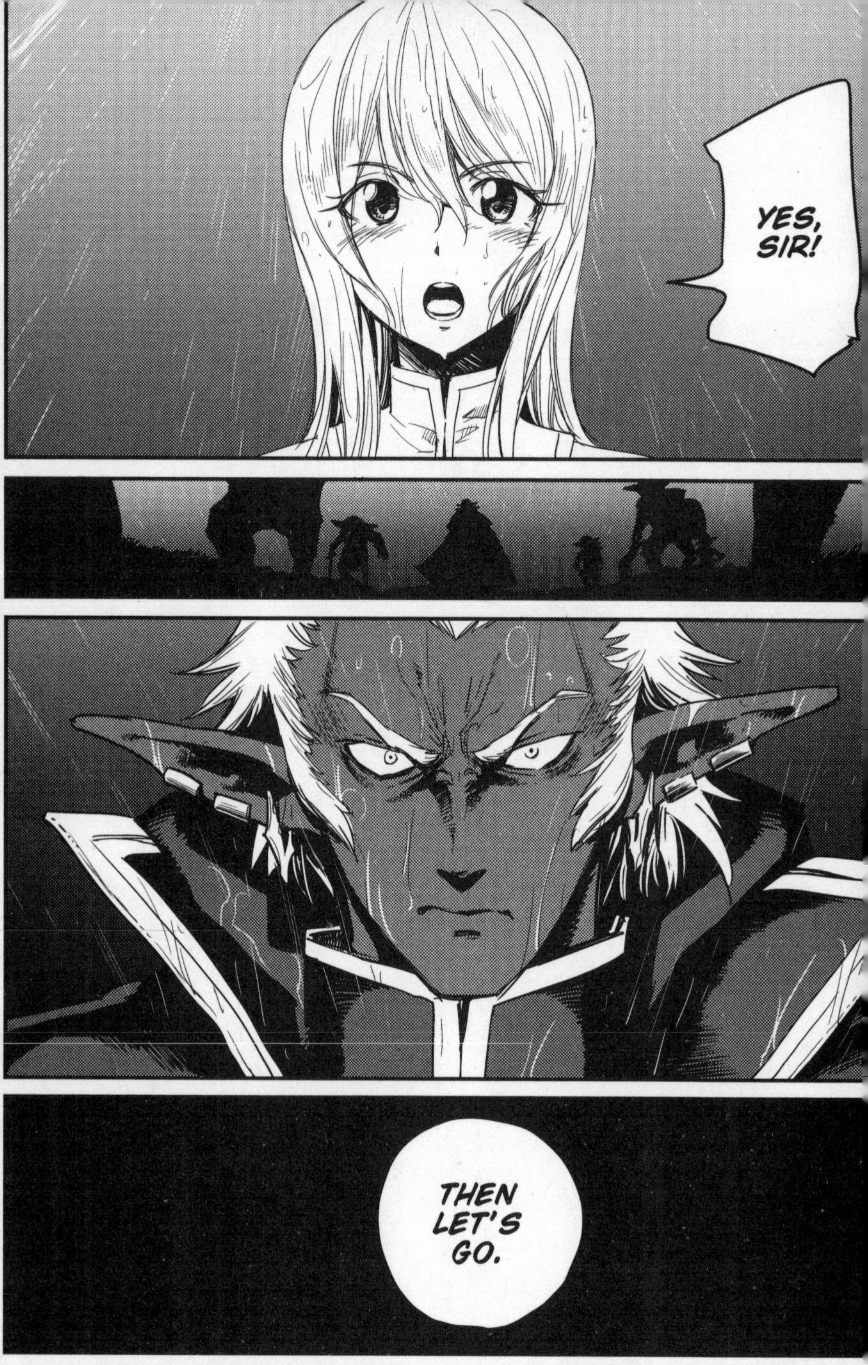
YES, SIR!
THEN LET'S GO.

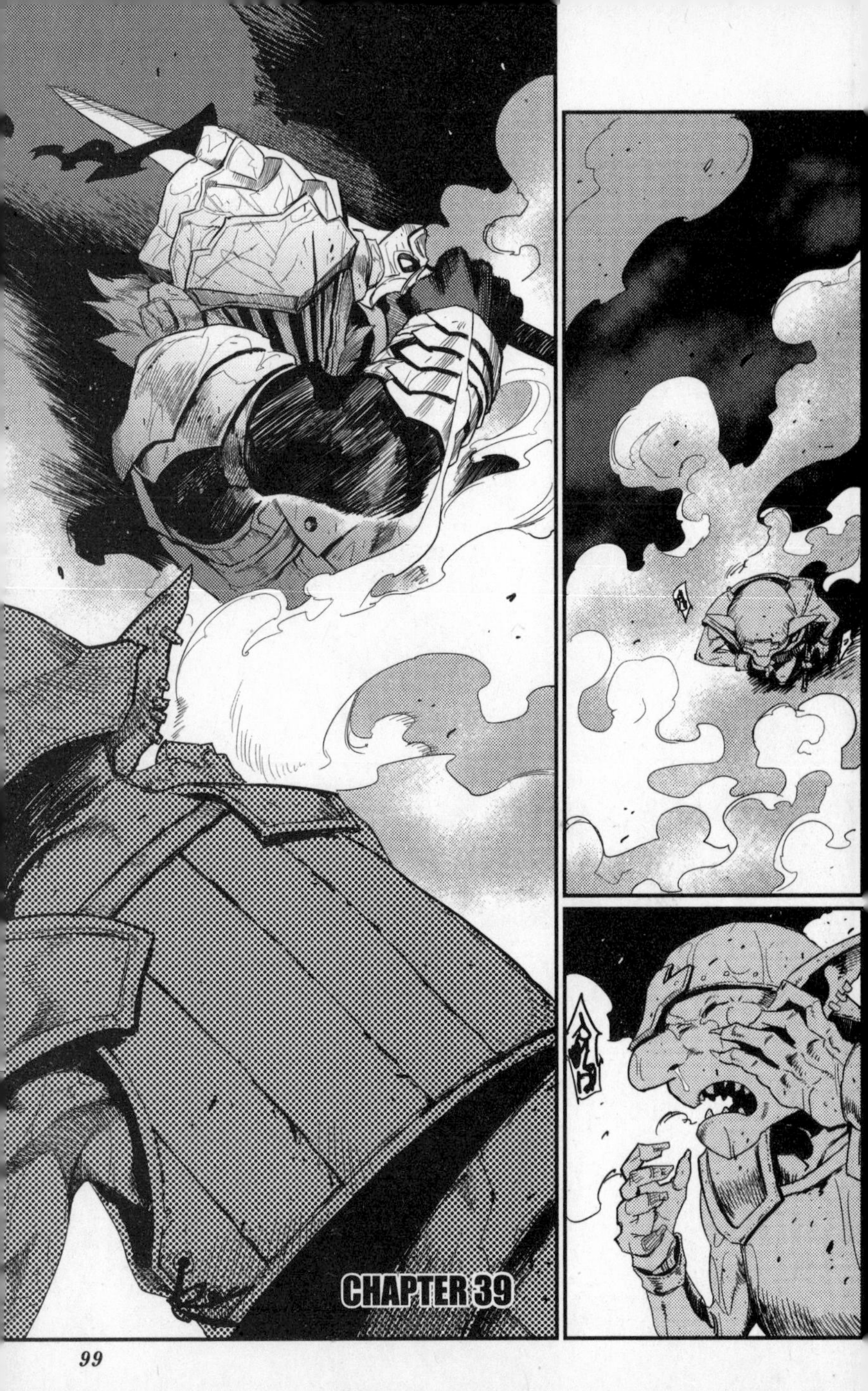
CHAPTER 39

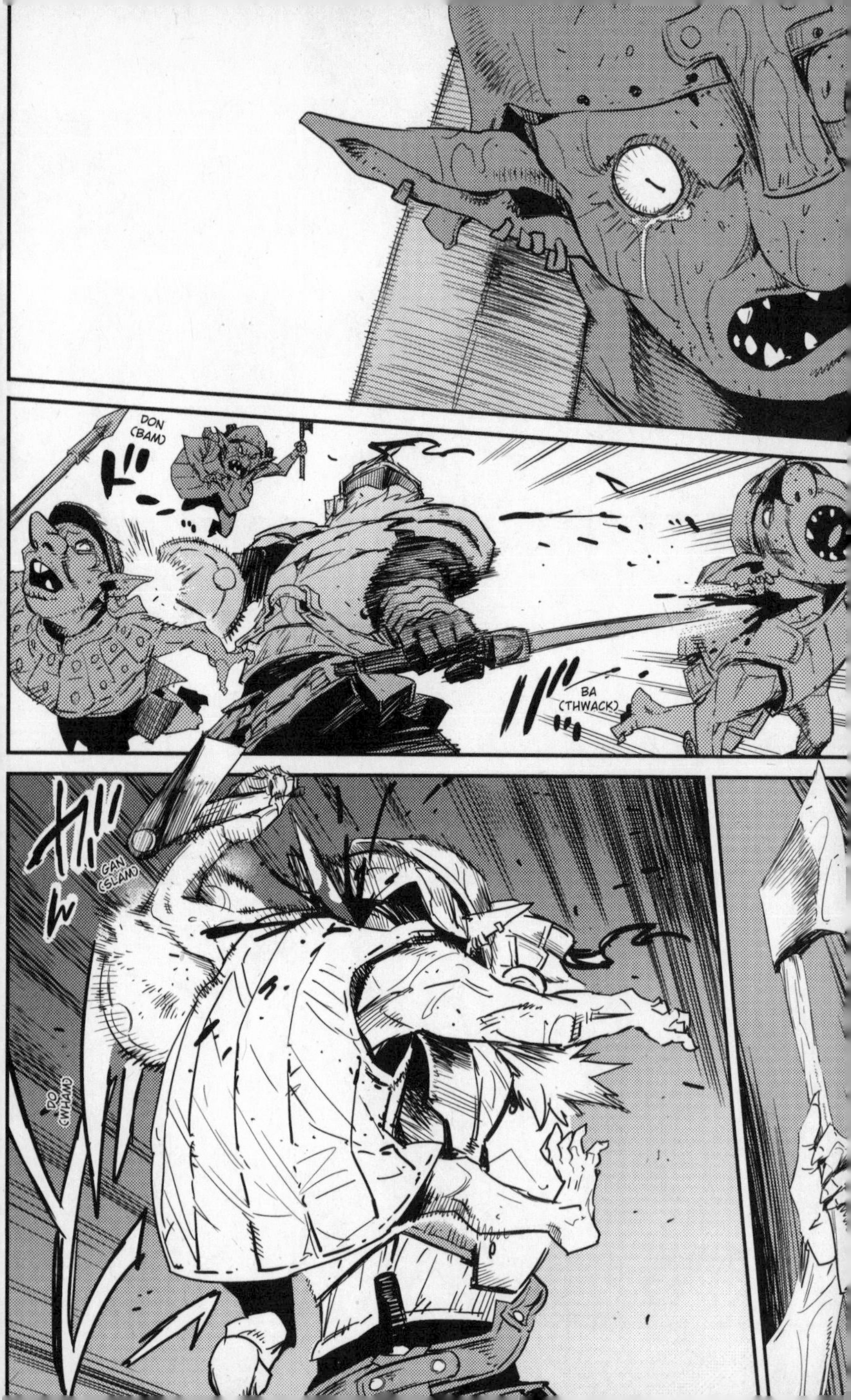
BA (THWACK)
DON (BAM)
GAN (SLAM)
DO (WHAM)

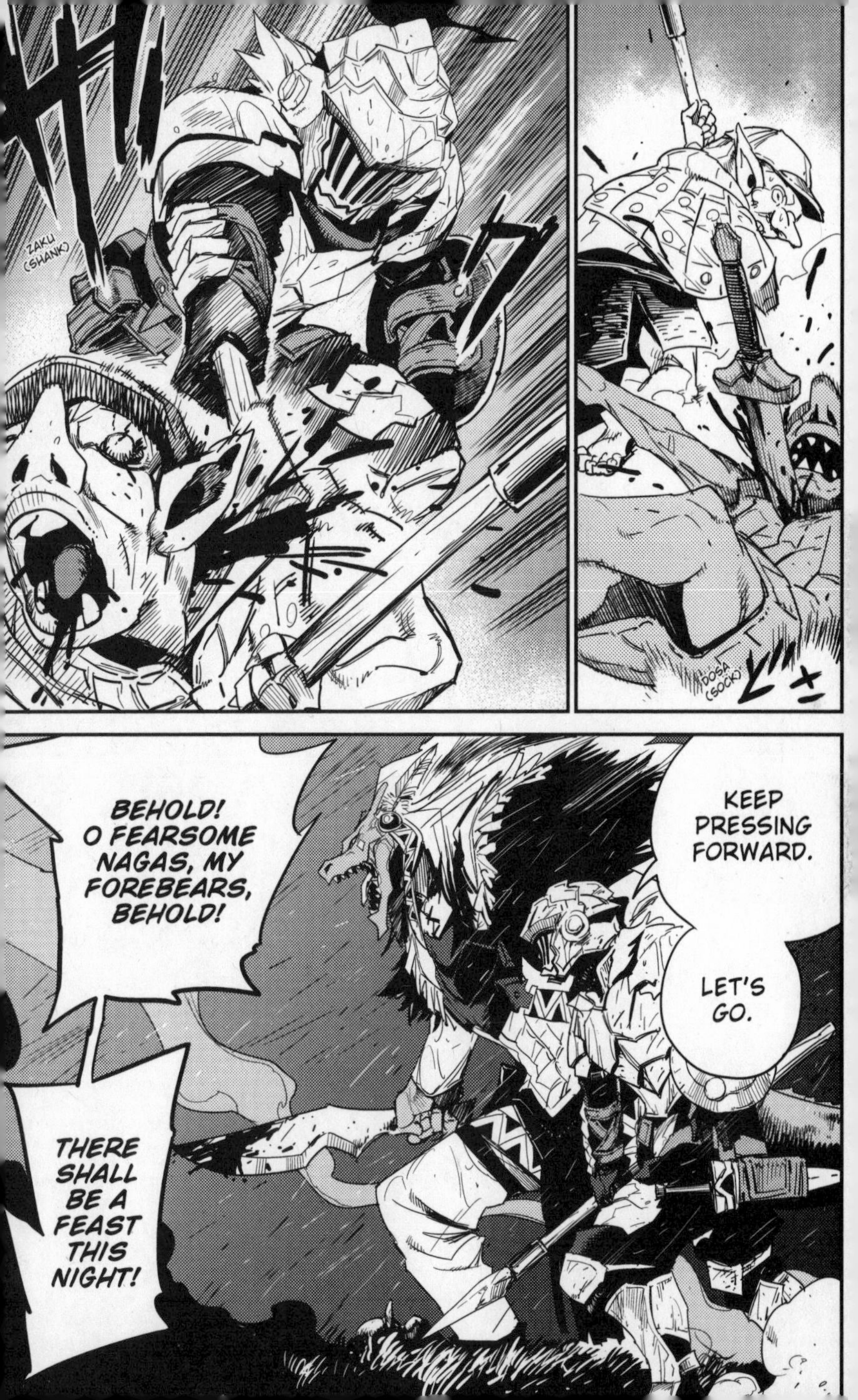
DOSA (SOCK)
ZAKU (SHANK)
KEEP PRESSING FORWARD.
LET'S GO.
BEHOLD! O FEARSOME NAGAS, MY FOREBEARS, BEHOLD!
THERE SHALL BE A FEAST THIS NIGHT!

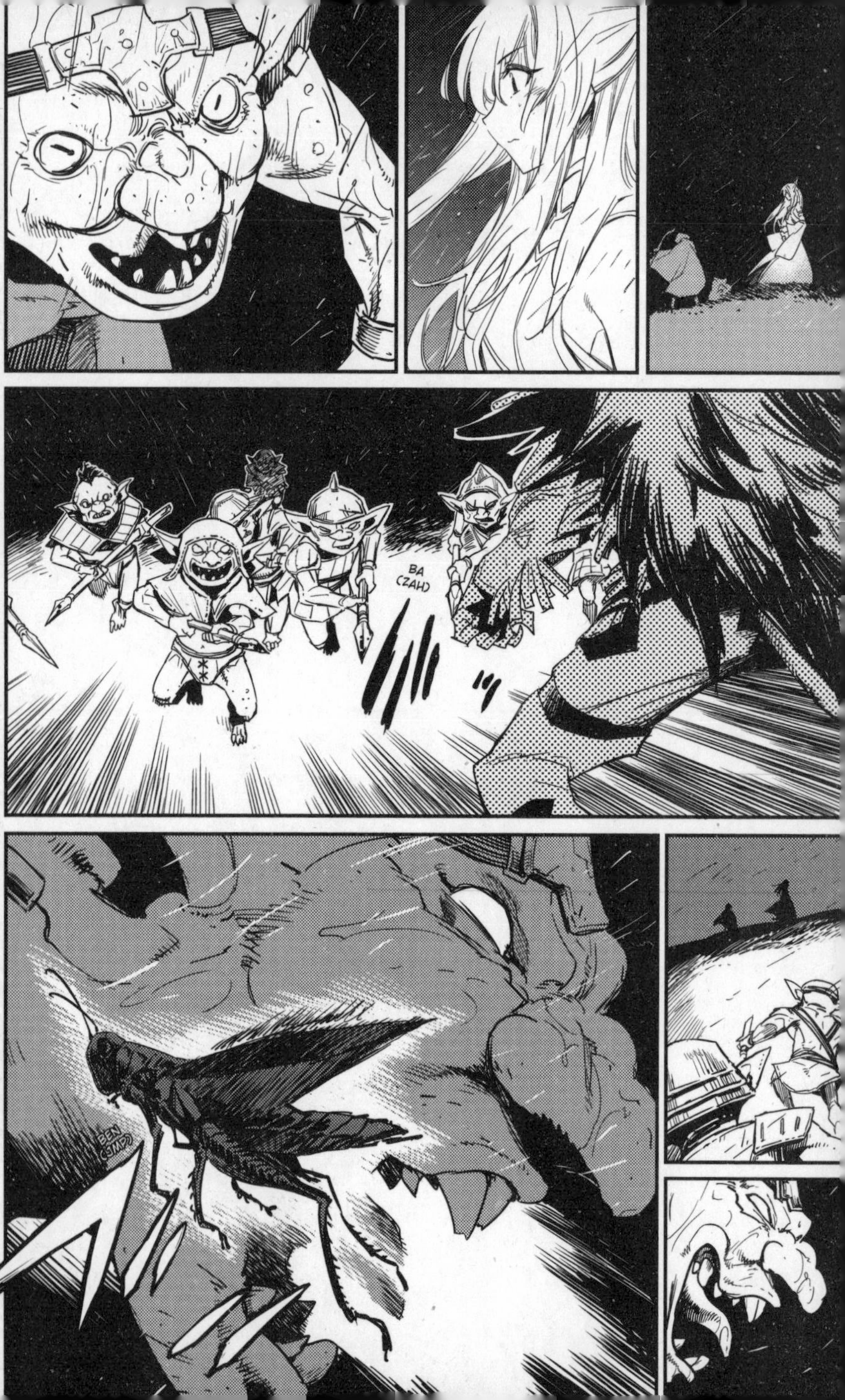
BA
(ZAH)
BEN
(JMP)

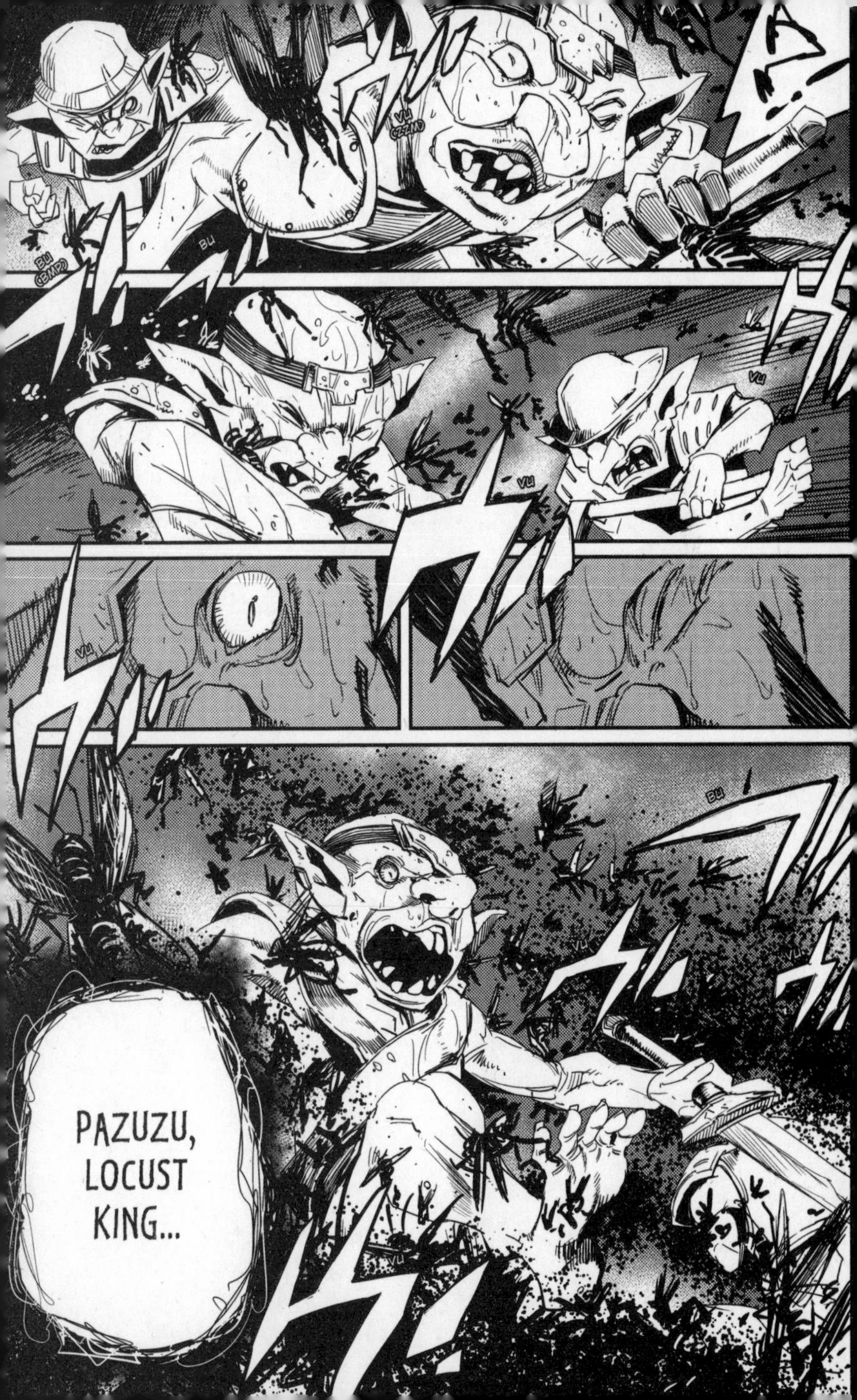
VU
(ZZM)
BU
BU
(BMP)
VU
VU
VU
BU
VU
VU
PAZUZU, LOCUST KING...
VU

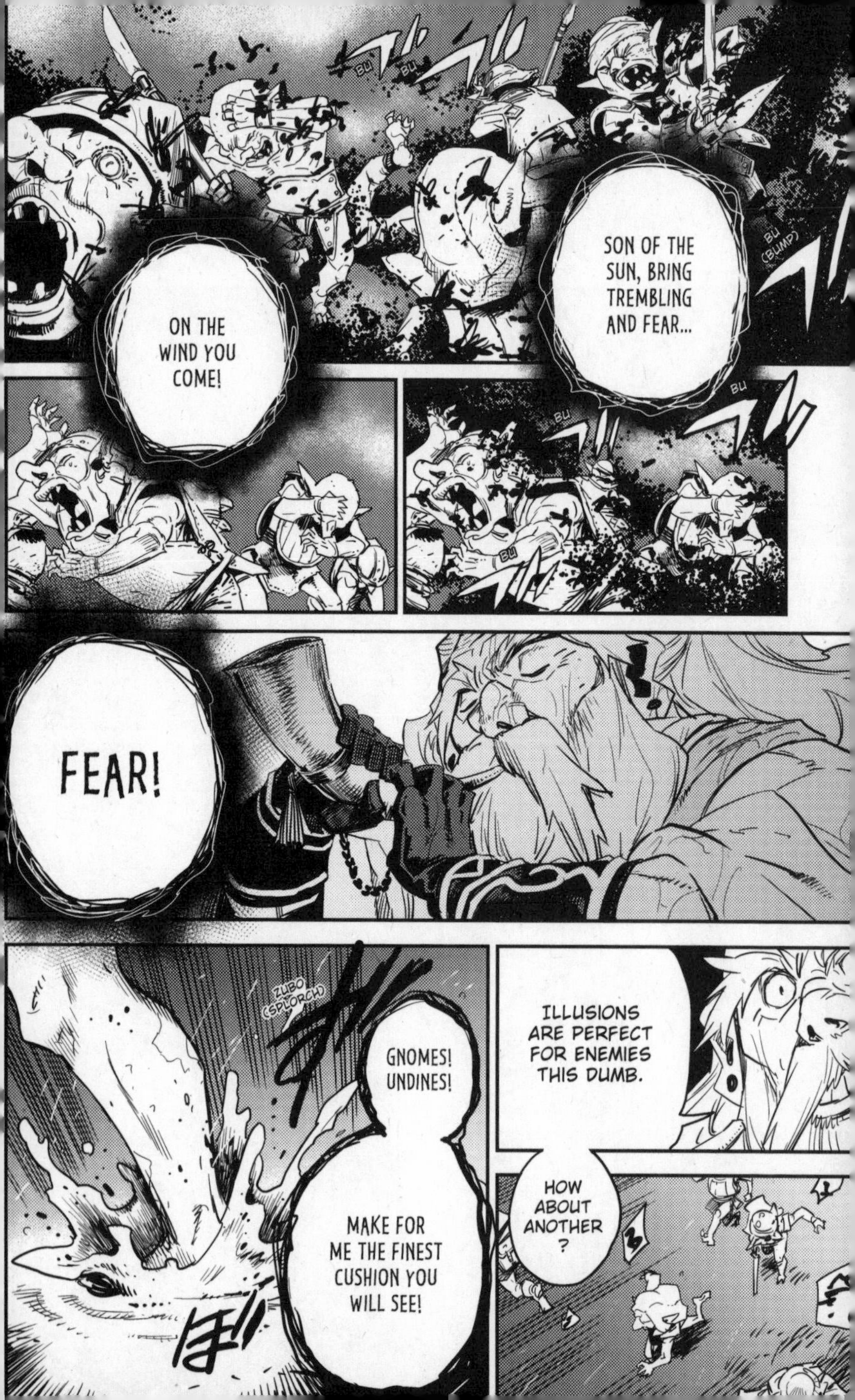

BU
BU
BU (BUMP)
SON OF THE SUN, BRING TREMBLING AND FEAR...
ON THE WIND YOU COME!
BU
BU
BU
FEAR!
ILLUSIONS ARE PERFECT FOR ENEMIES THIS DUMB.
HOW ABOUT ANOTHER ?
ZUBO (SPLORCH)
GNOMES! UNDINES!
MAKE FOR ME THE FINEST CUSHION YOU WILL SEE!

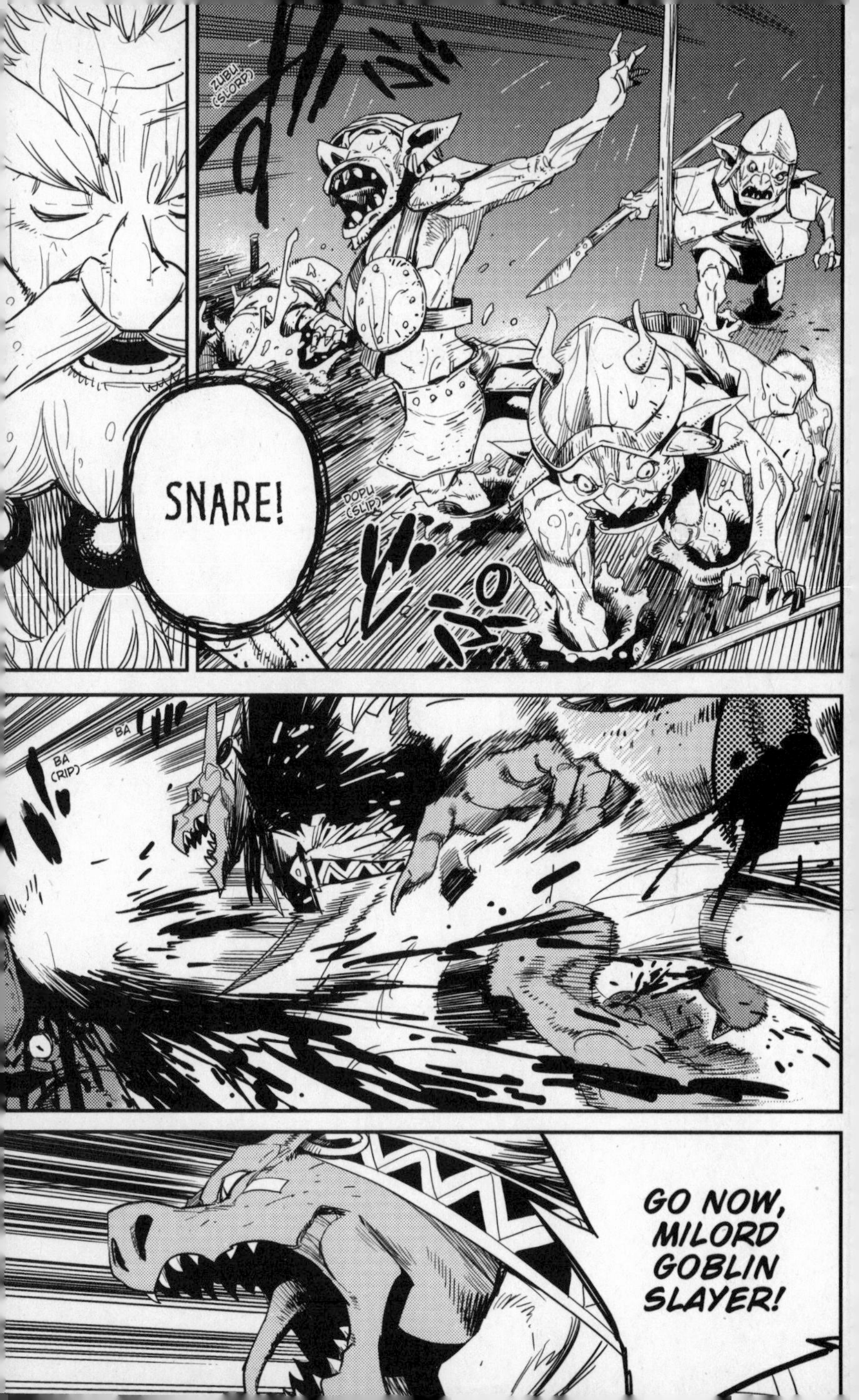
ZUBU (SLORP)
DOPU (SLIP)
SNARE!
BA
BA (RIP)
GO NOW, MILORD GOBLIN SLAYER!

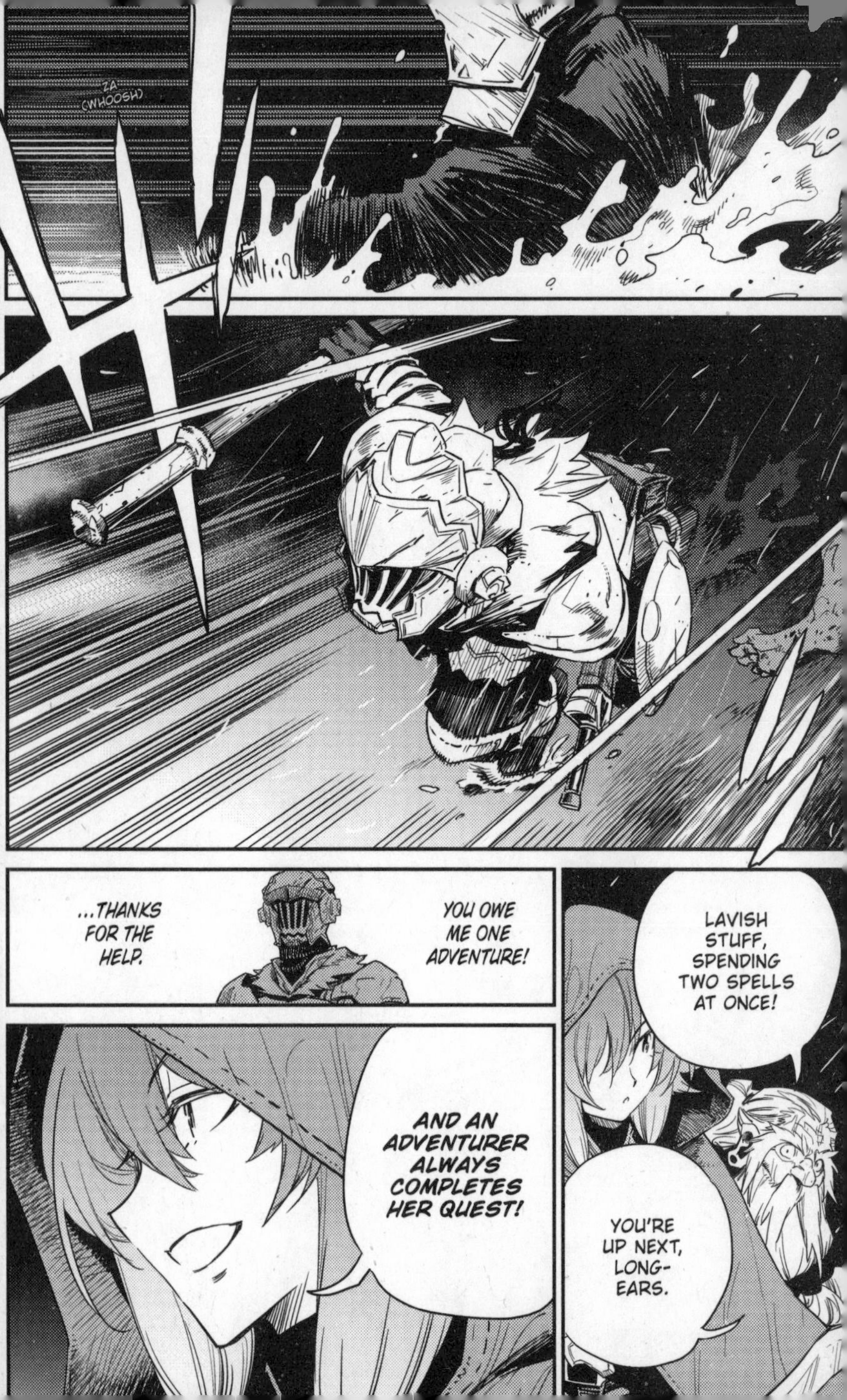
ZA (WHOOSH)
LAVISH STUFF, SPENDING TWO SPELLS AT ONCE!
YOU'RE UP NEXT, LONG-EARS.
YOU OWE ME ONE ADVENTURE!
...THANKS FOR THE HELP.
AND AN ADVENTURER ALWAYS COMPLETES HER QUEST!

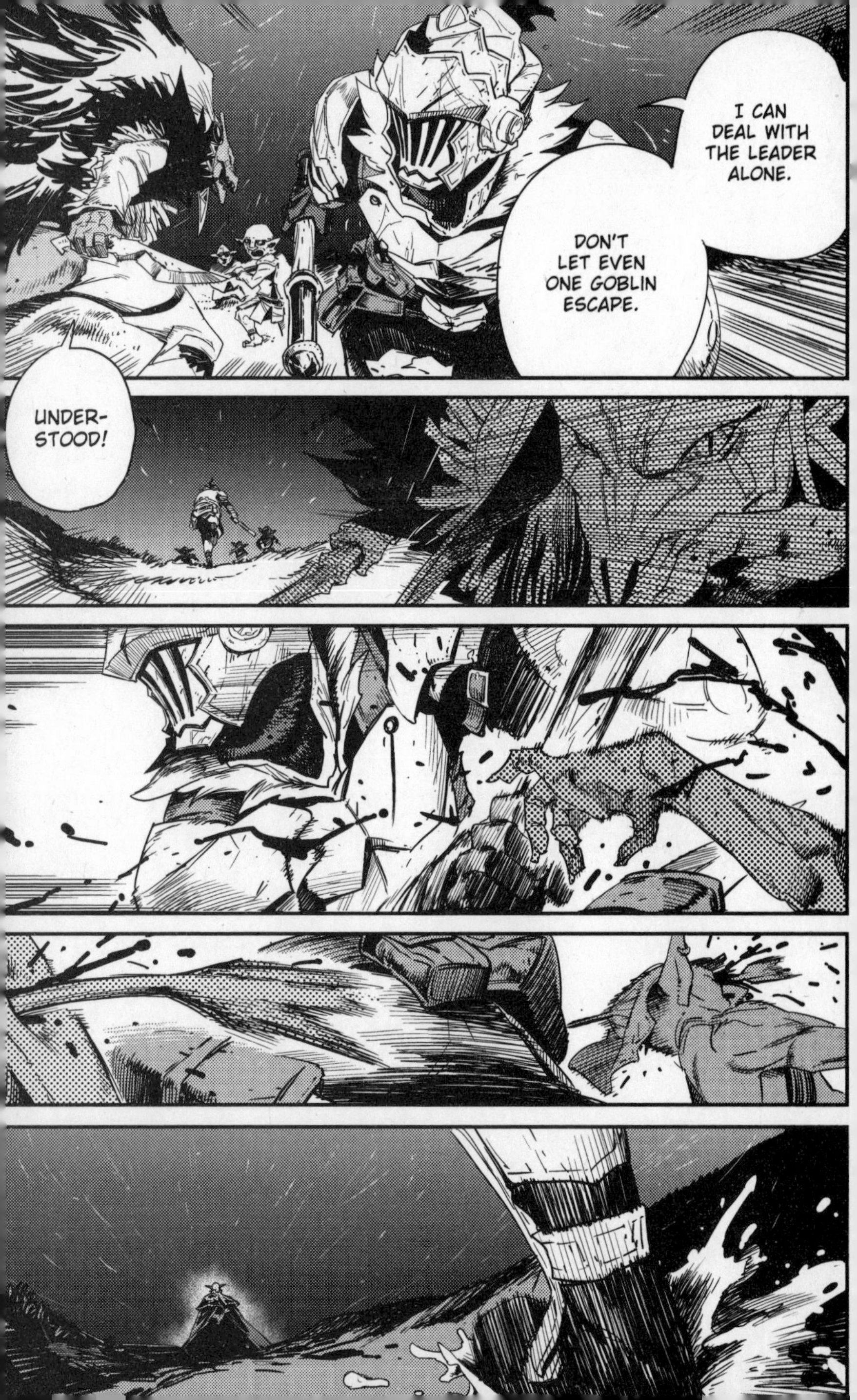
I CAN DEAL WITH THE LEADER ALONE.
DON'T LET EVEN ONE GOBLIN ESCAPE.
UNDER-STOOD!

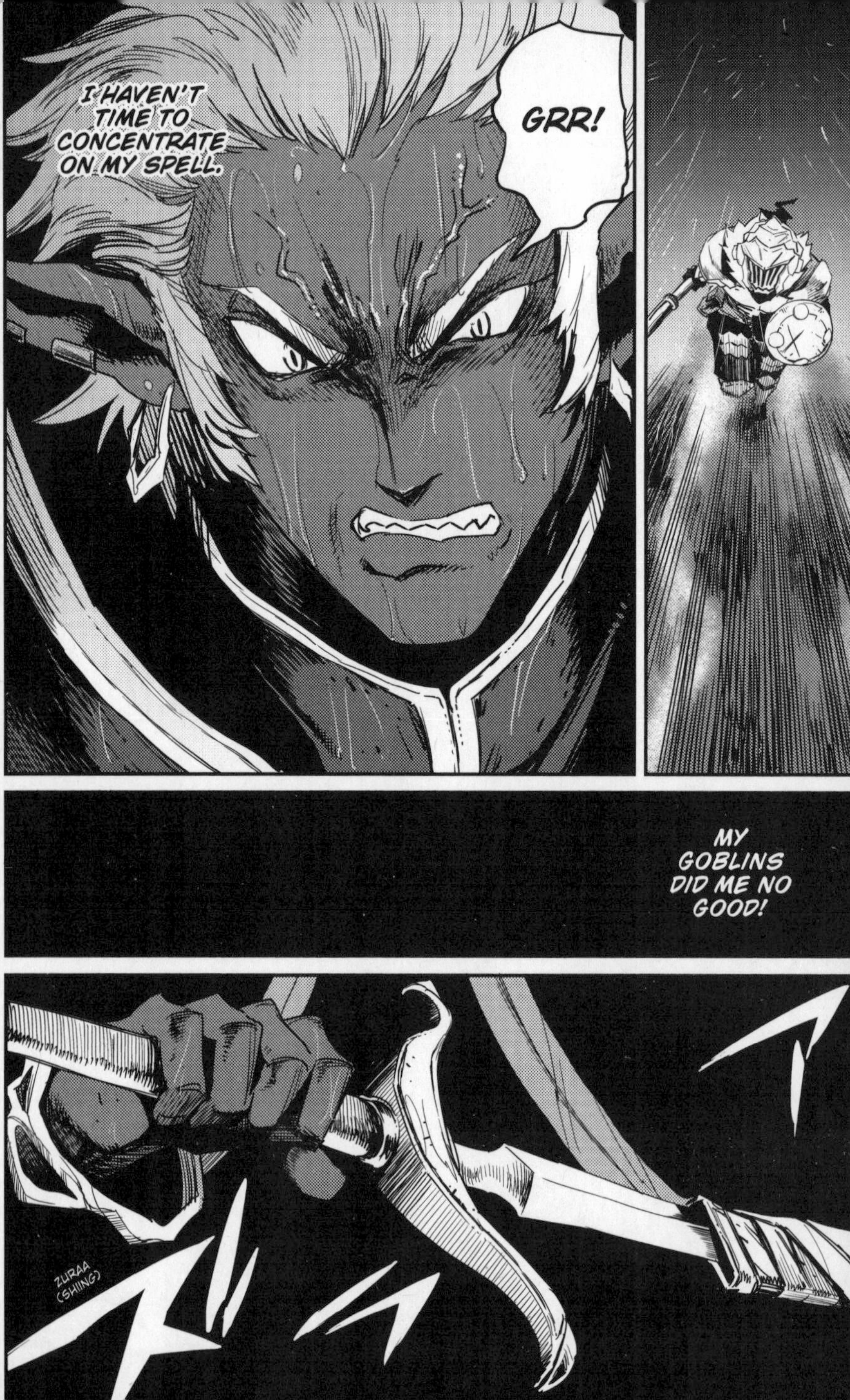
GRR!
I HAVEN'T TIME TO CONCENTRATE ON MY SPELL.
MY GOBLINS DID ME NO GOOD!
ZURAA (SHIING)

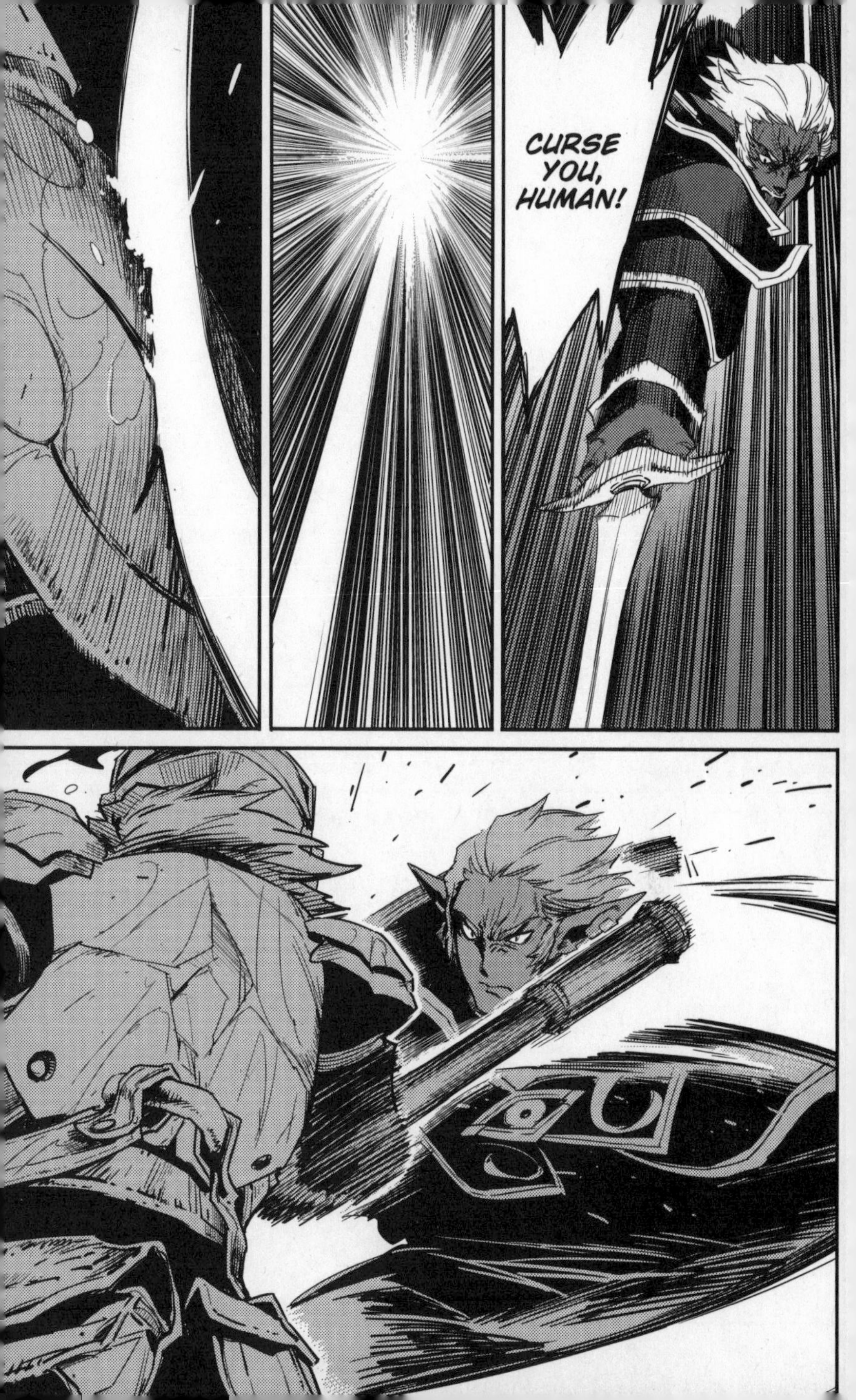
CURSE YOU, HUMAN!

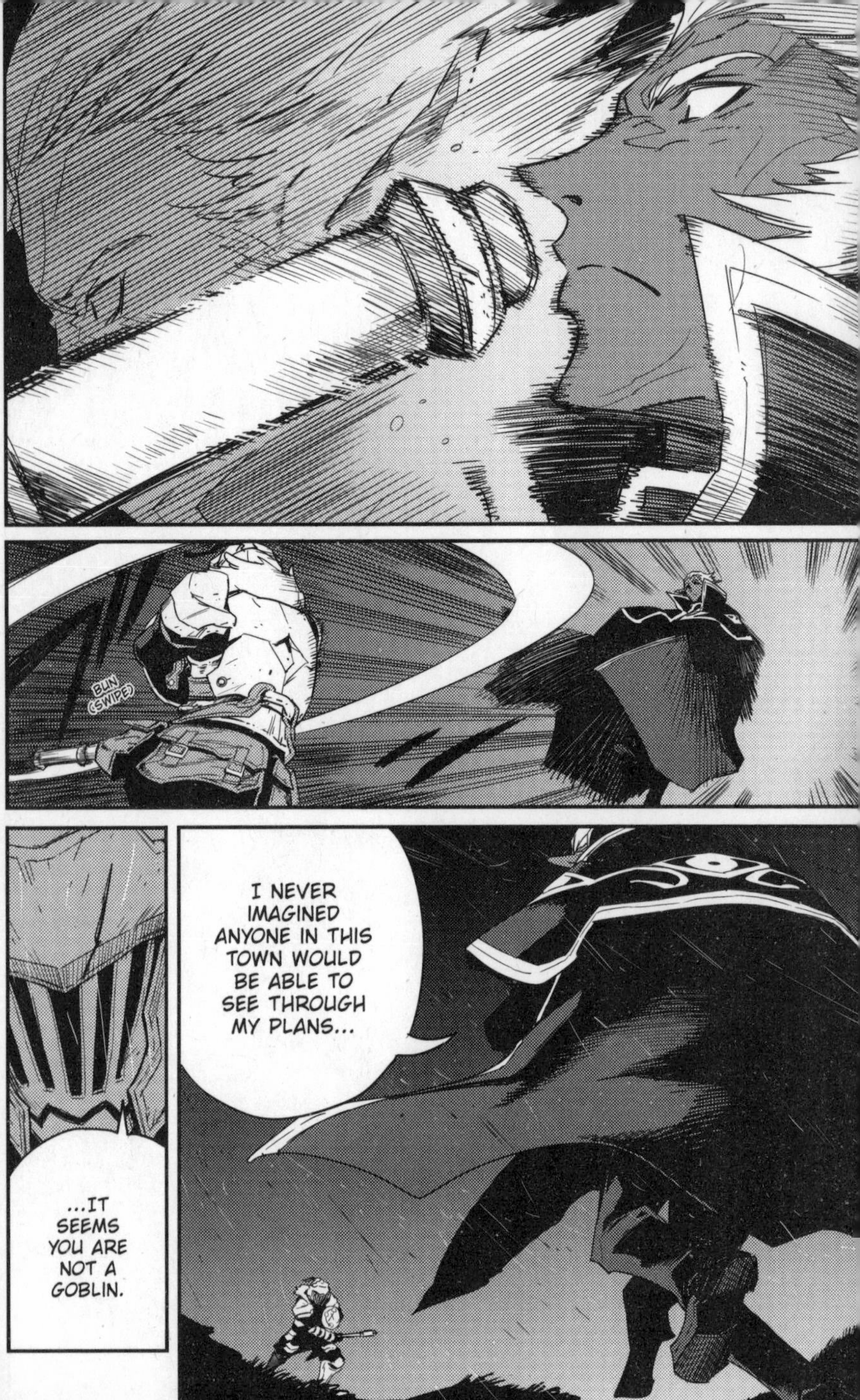
BUN (SWIPE)
I NEVER IMAGINED ANYONE IN THIS TOWN WOULD BE ABLE TO SEE THROUGH MY PLANS...
...IT SEEMS YOU ARE NOT A GOBLIN.

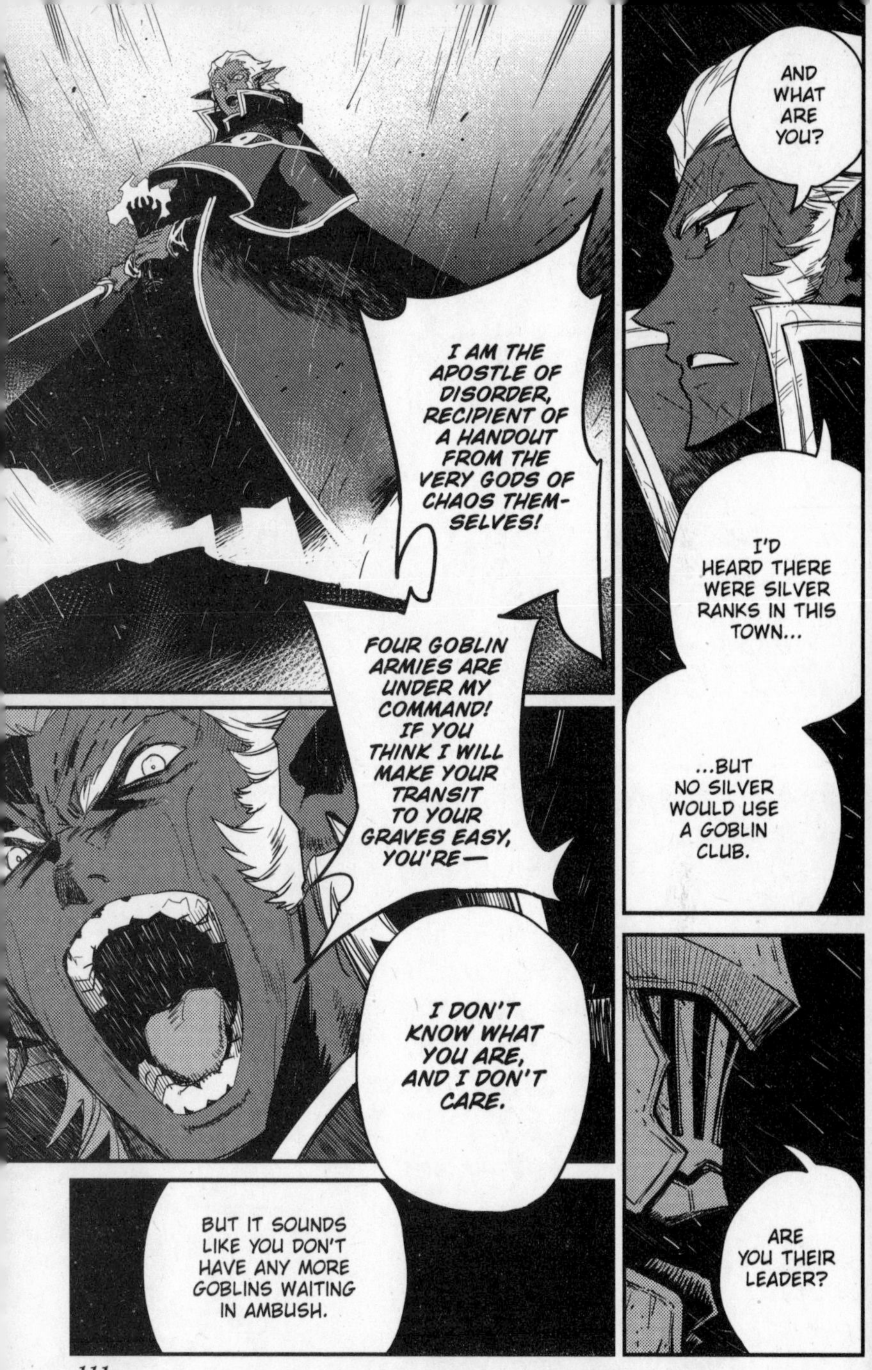
AND WHAT ARE YOU?
I'D HEARD THERE WERE SILVER RANKS IN THIS TOWN...
...BUT NO SILVER WOULD USE A GOBLIN CLUB.
I AM THE APOSTLE OF DISORDER, RECIPIENT OF A HANDOUT FROM THE VERY GODS OF CHAOS THEM-SELVES!
FOUR GOBLIN ARMIES ARE UNDER MY COMMAND! IF YOU THINK I WILL MAKE YOUR TRANSIT TO YOUR GRAVES EASY, YOU'RE—
I DON'T KNOW WHAT YOU ARE, AND I DON'T CARE.
BUT IT SOUNDS LIKE YOU DON'T HAVE ANY MORE GOBLINS WAITING IN AMBUSH.
ARE YOU THEIR LEADER?

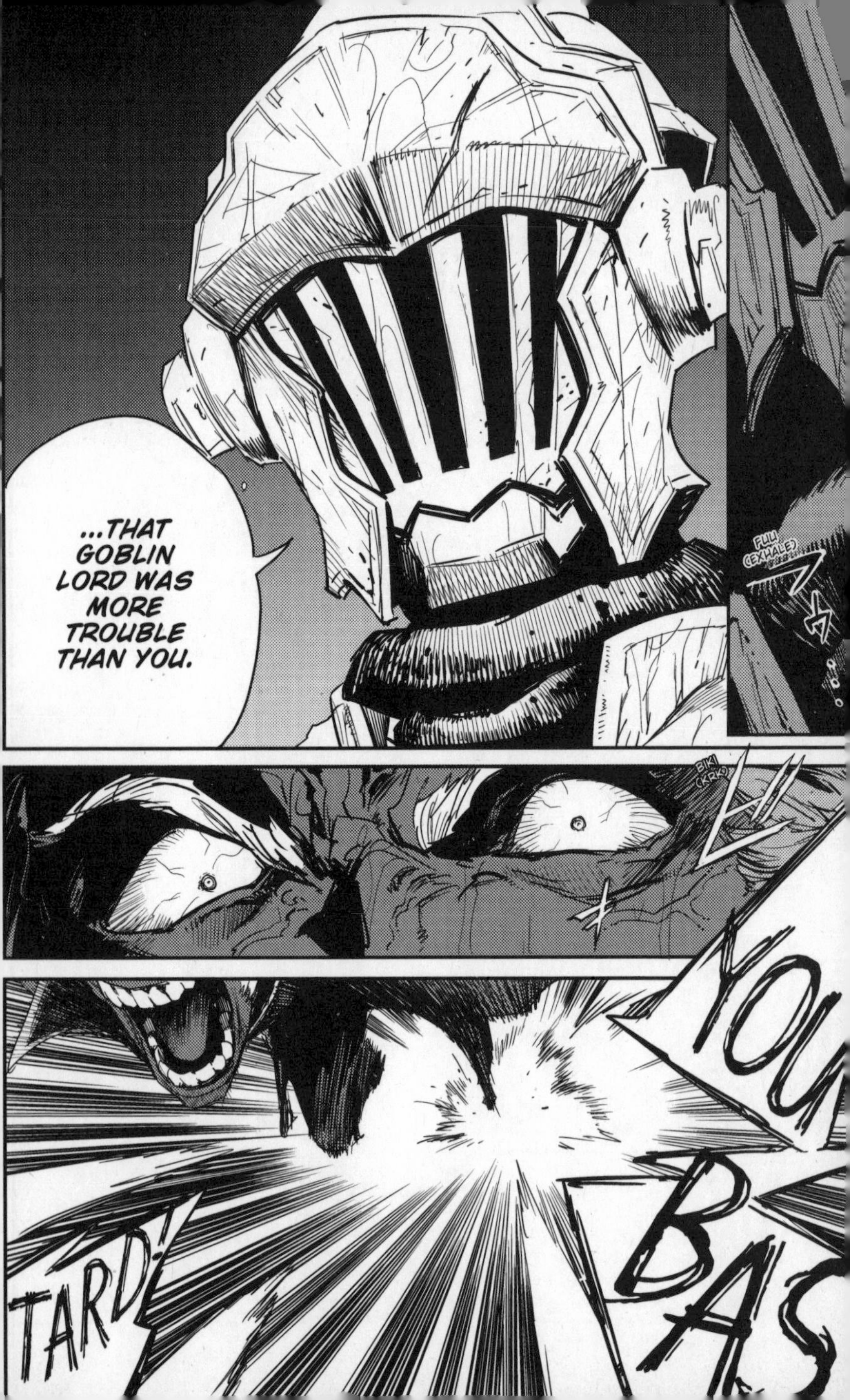
FUU (EXHALE)
...THAT GOBLIN LORD WAS MORE TROUBLE THAN YOU.
BIKI (KRK)
YOU BAS TARD!

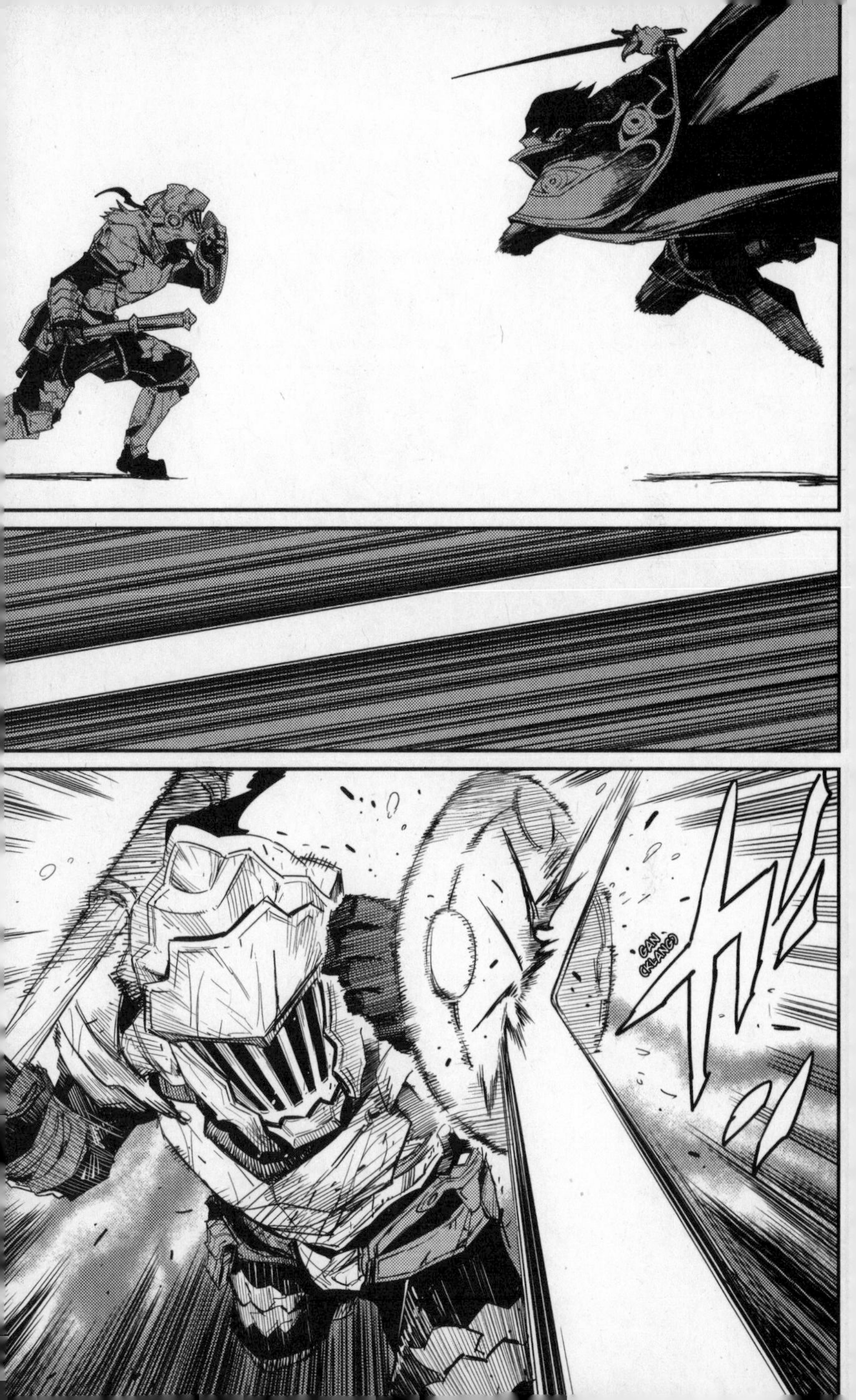
GAN
(KLANG)

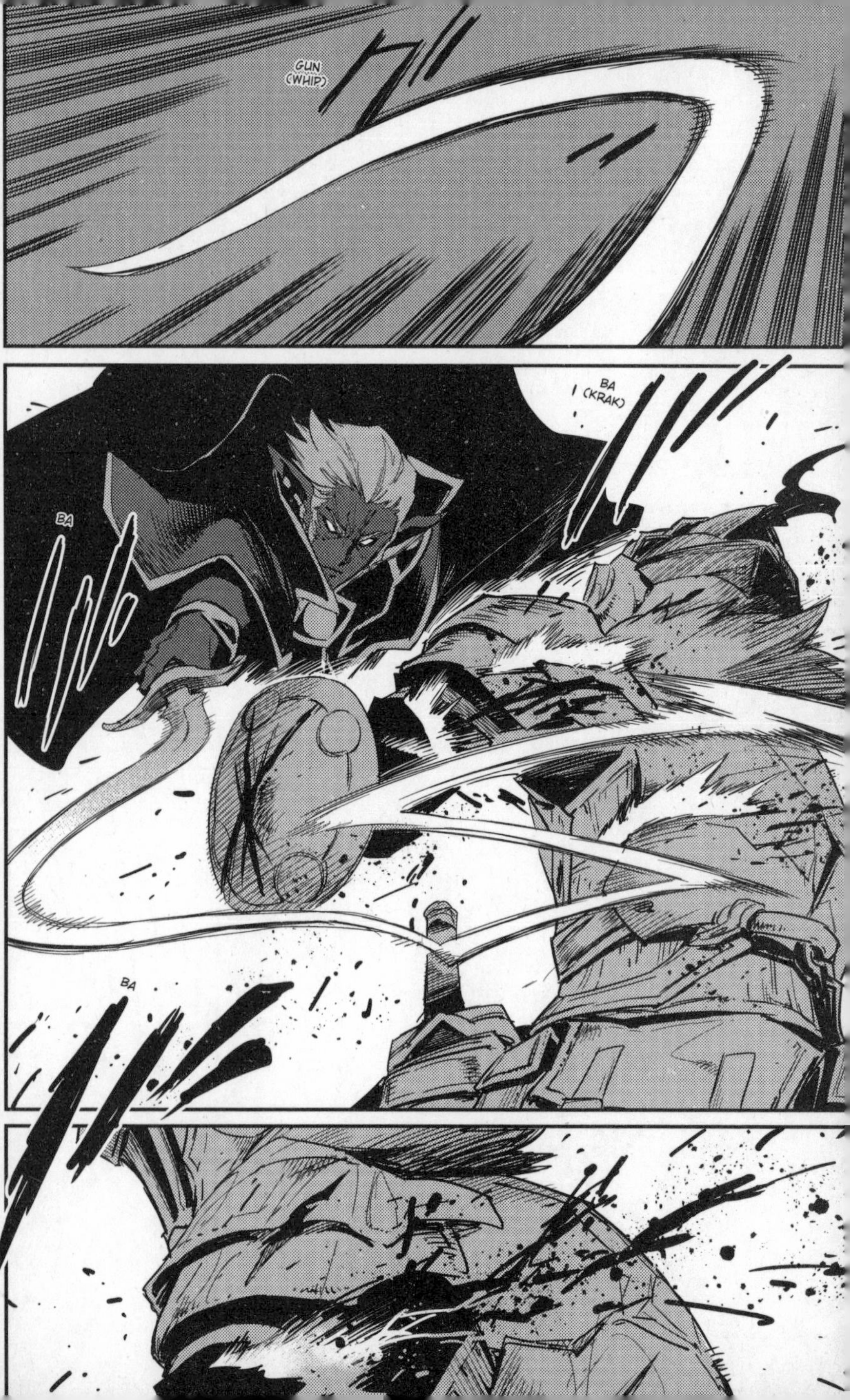
GUN (WHIP)
BA (KRAK)
BA
BA

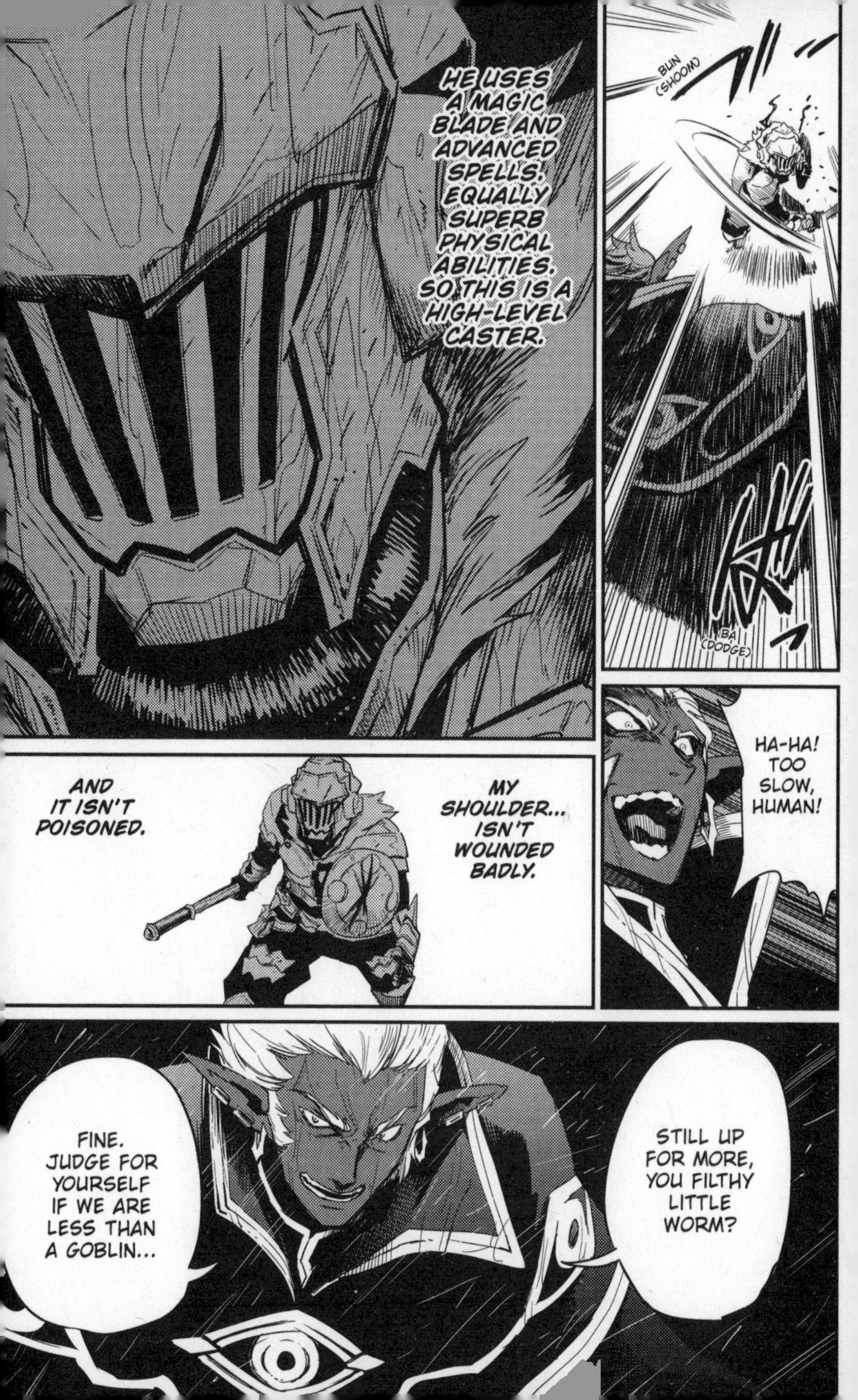
BUN (SHOOM)
BA (DODGE)
HE USES A MAGIC BLADE AND ADVANCED SPELLS. EQUALLY SUPERB PHYSICAL ABILITIES. SO THIS IS A HIGH-LEVEL CASTER.
HA-HA! TOO SLOW, HUMAN!
MY SHOULDER... ISN'T WOUNDED BADLY.
AND IT ISN'T POISONED.
STILL UP FOR MORE, YOU FILTHY LITTLE WORM?
FINE. JUDGE FOR YOURSELF IF WE ARE LESS THAN A GOBLIN...

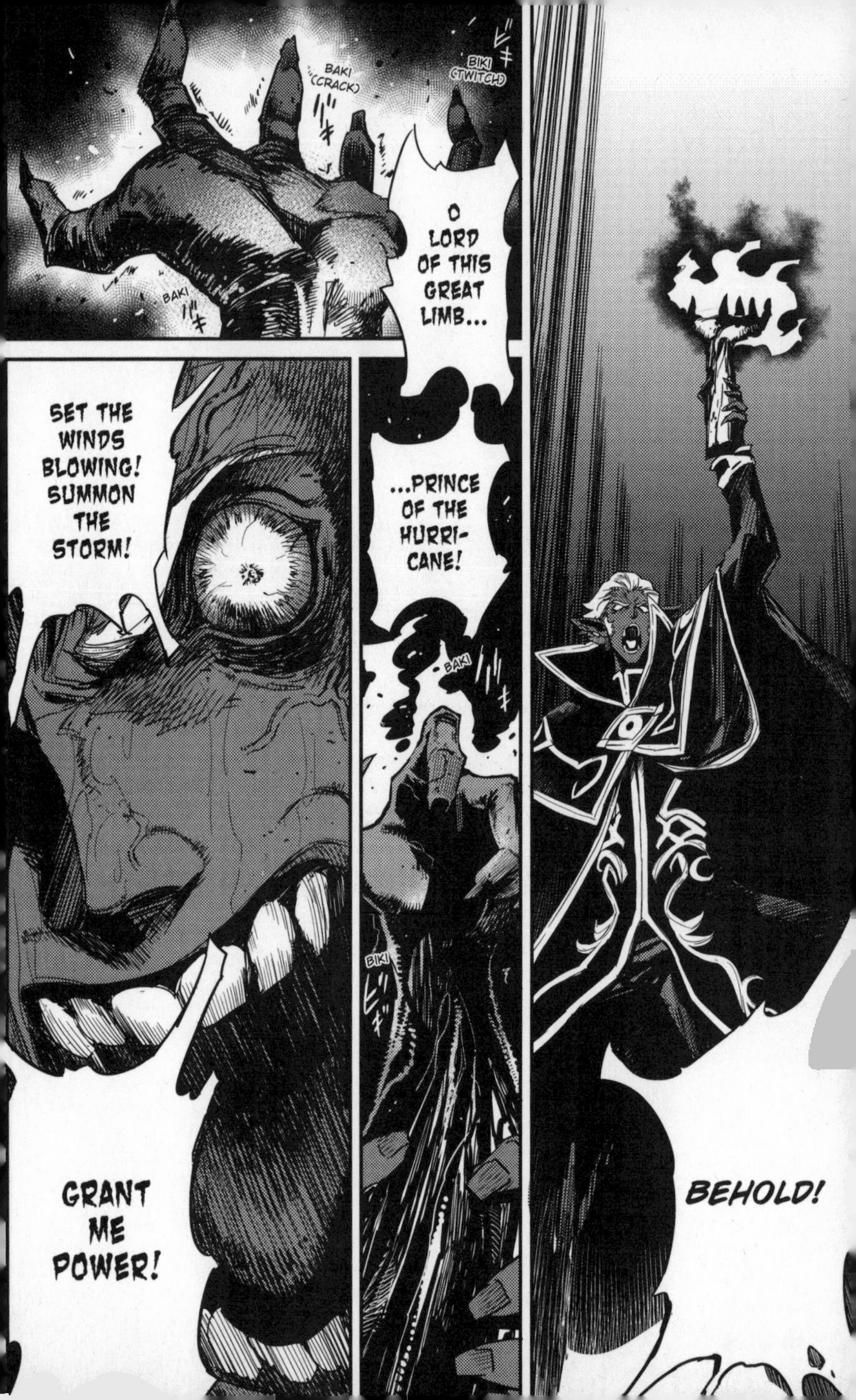
BEHOLD!
BIKI (TWITCH)
BAKI (CRACK)
O LORD OF THIS GREAT LIMB...
BAKI
...PRINCE OF THE HURRI-CANE!
BAKI
BIKI
SET THE WINDS BLOWING! SUMMON THE STORM!
GRANT ME POWER!

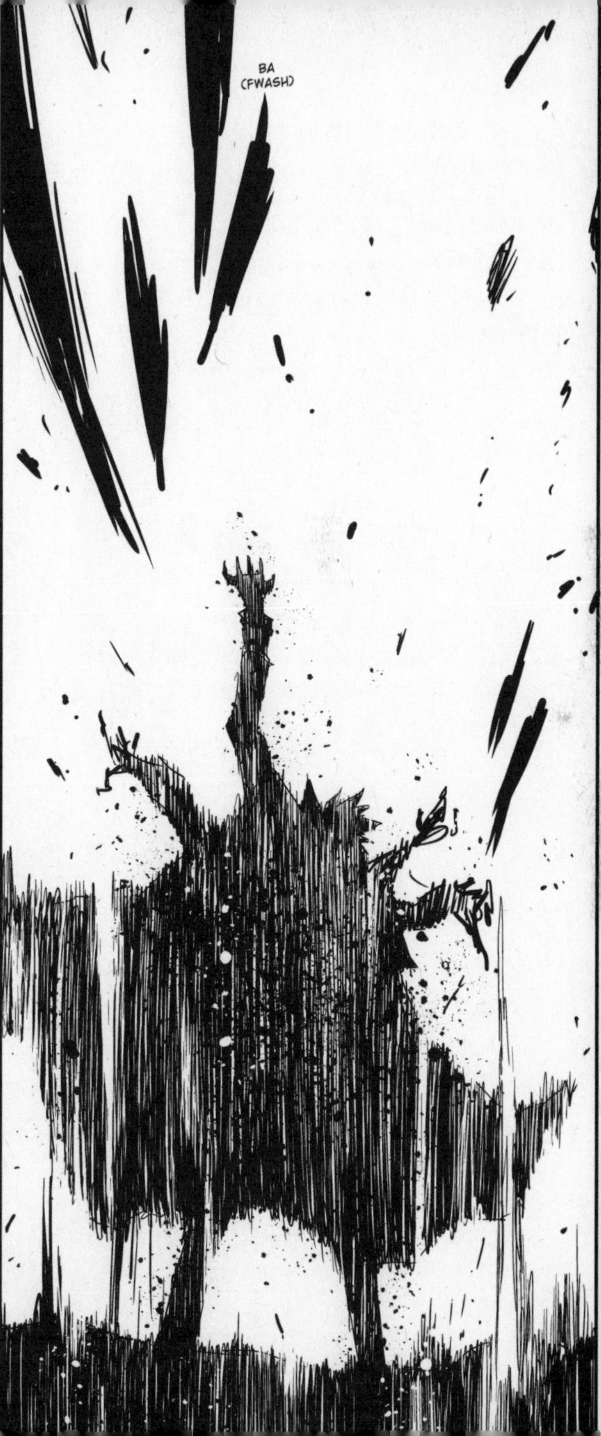
BA
(FWASH)
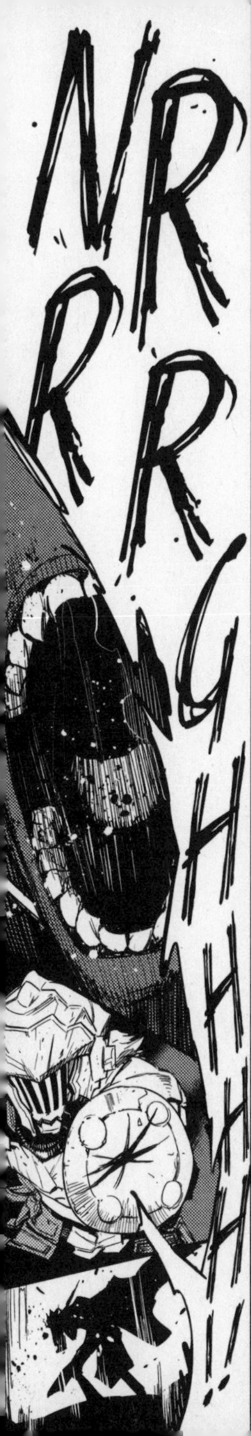
NRRRGHHHH!!

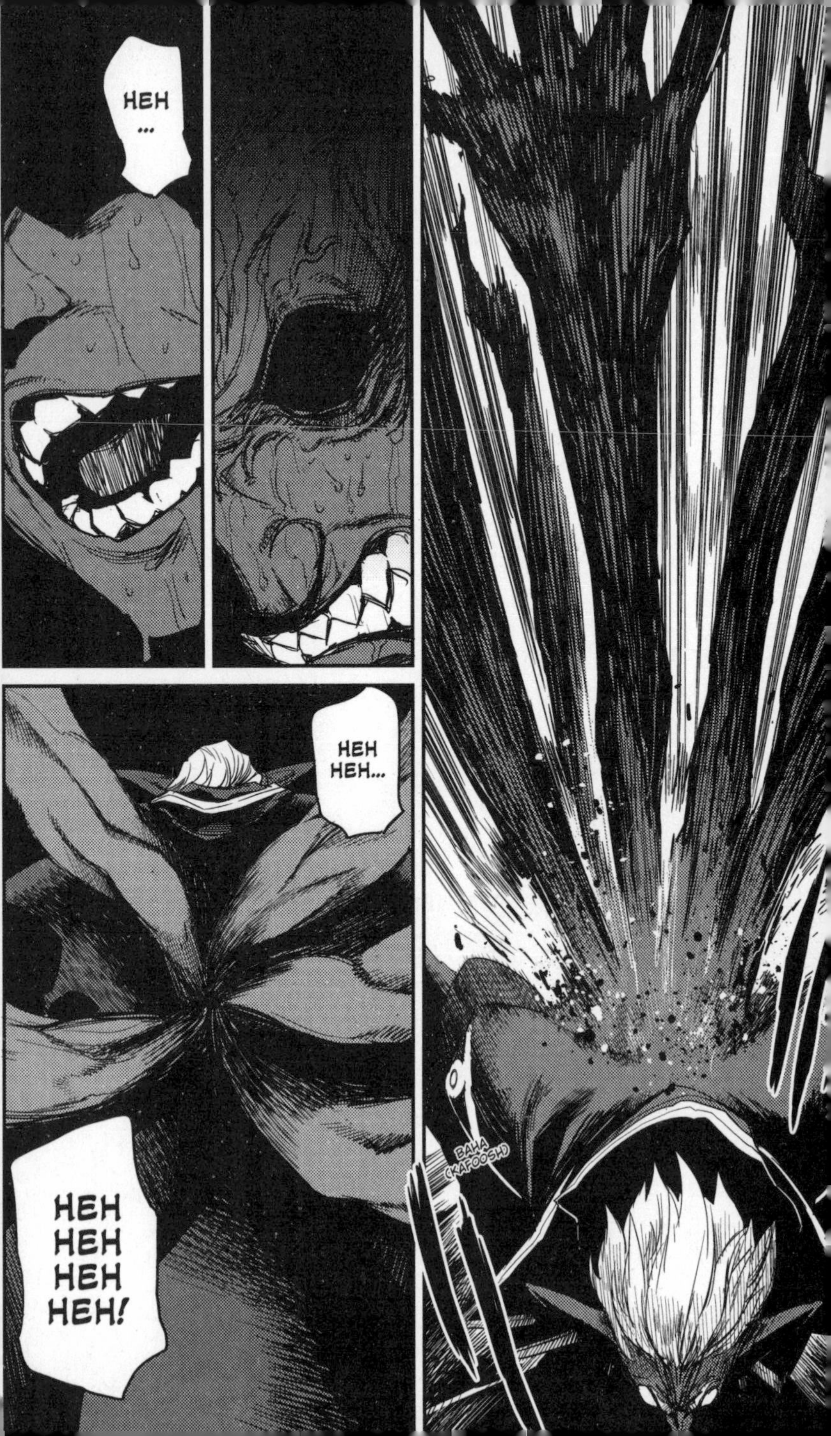
BAHA (KAFOOSH)
HEH ...
HEH HEH...
HEH HEH HEH HEH!

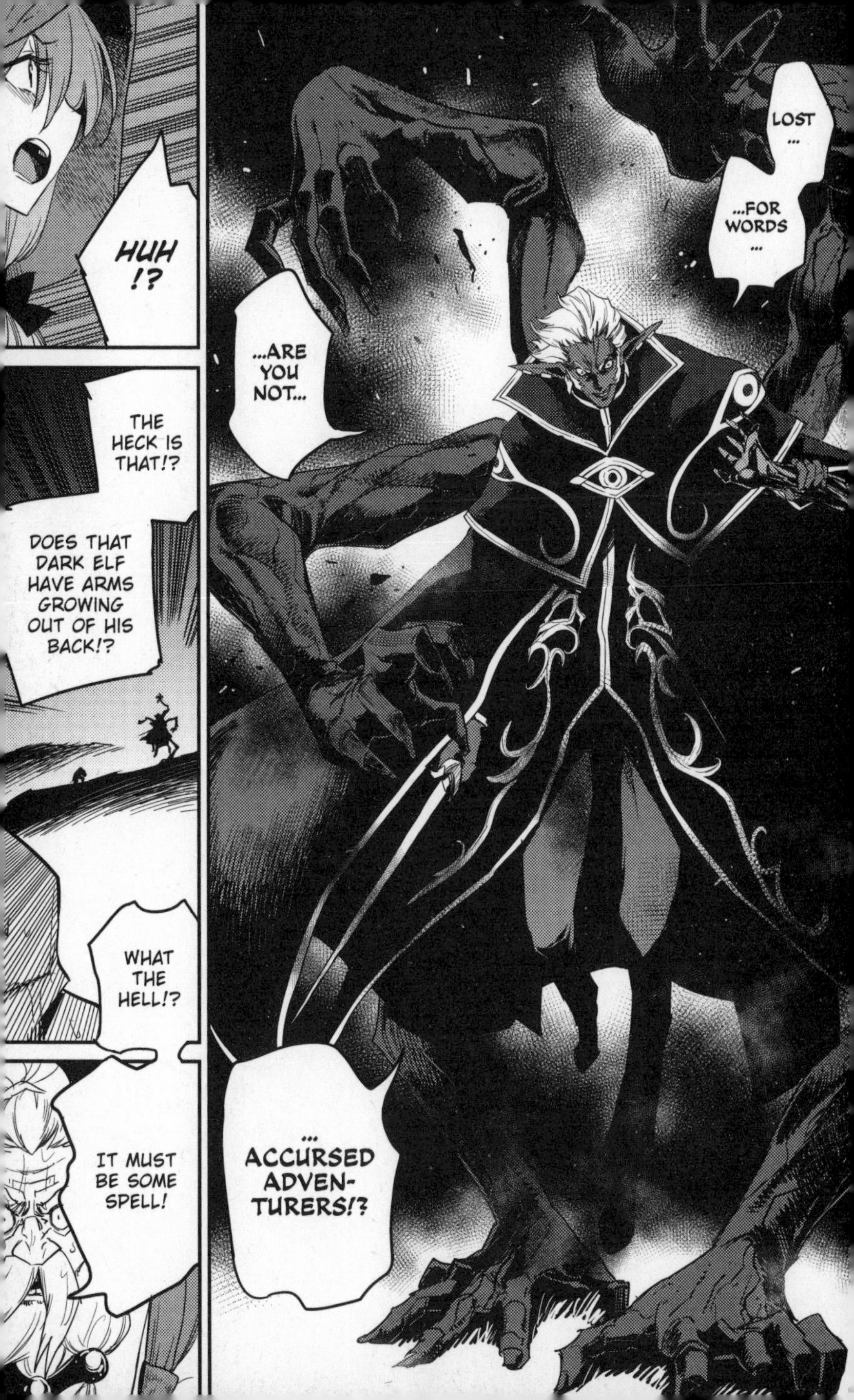
LOST ...
...FOR WORDS ...
...ARE YOU NOT...
... ACCURSED ADVEN-TURERS!?
HUH !?
THE HECK IS THAT!?
DOES THAT DARK ELF HAVE ARMS GROWING OUT OF HIS BACK!?
WHAT THE HELL!?
IT MUST BE SOME SPELL!

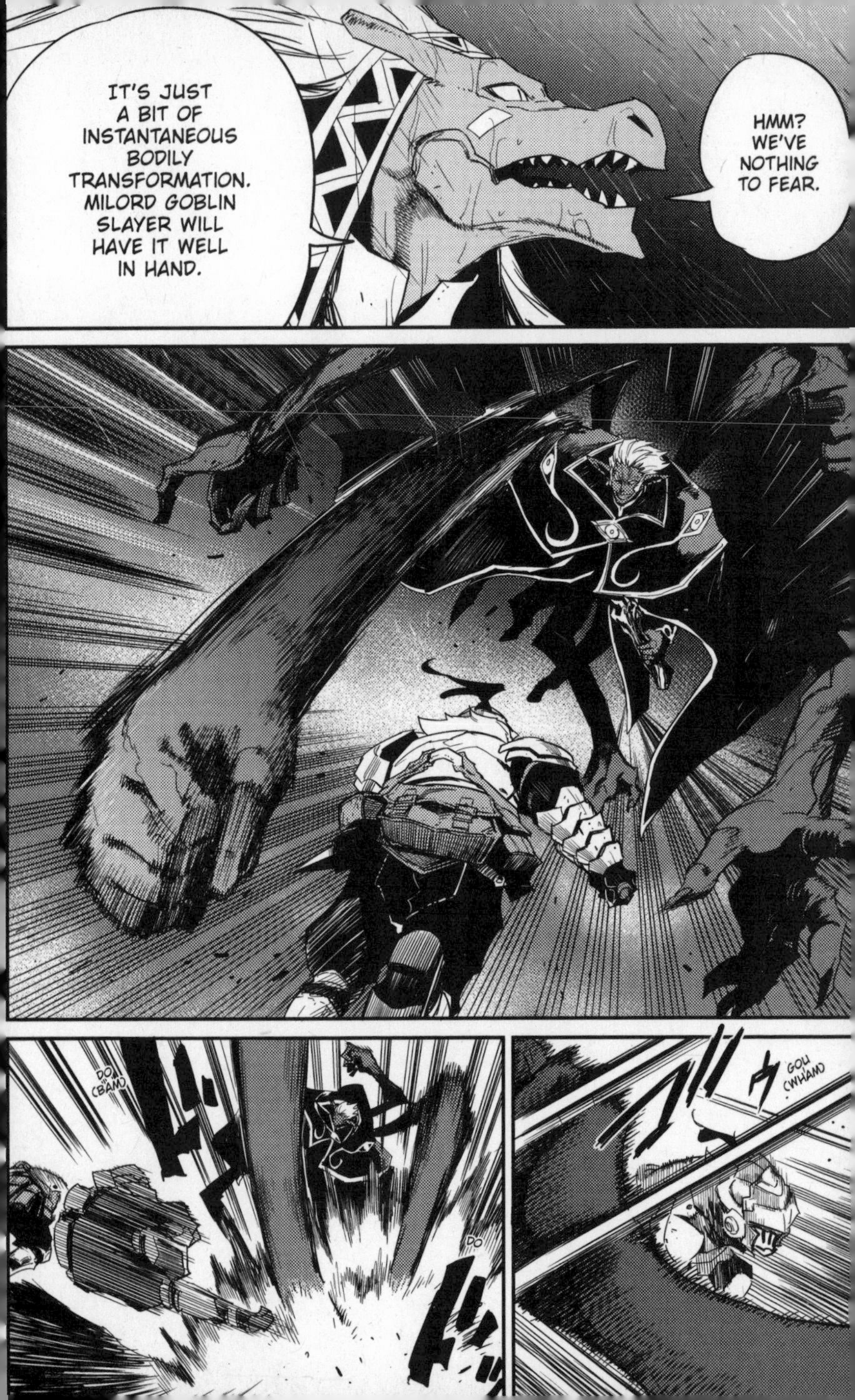
HMM? WE'VE NOTHING TO FEAR.
IT'S JUST A BIT OF INSTANTANEOUS BODILY TRANSFORMATION. MILORD GOBLIN SLAYER WILL HAVE IT WELL IN HAND.
GOU (WHAM)
DO (BAM)
DO

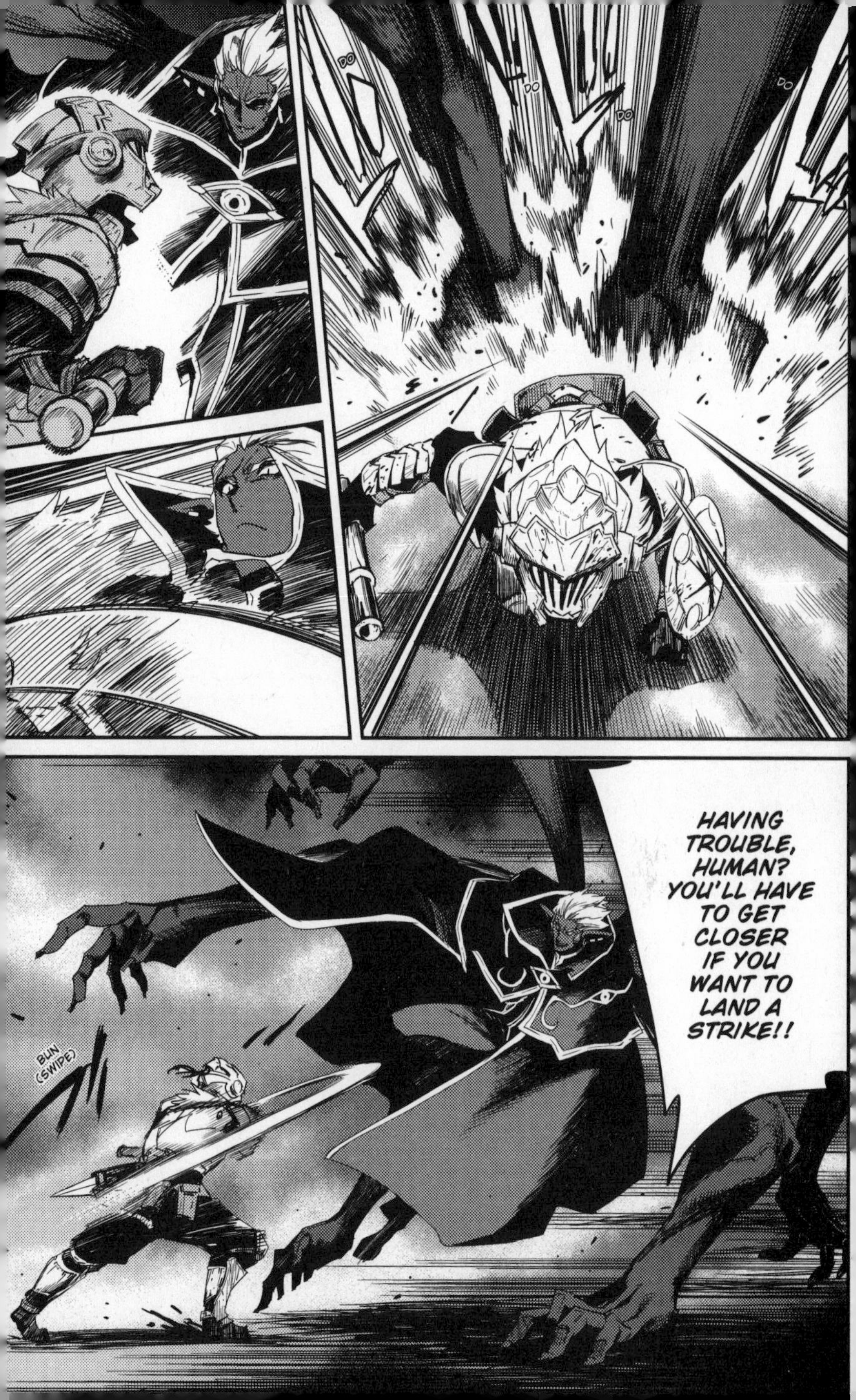
DO
DO
DO
DO
HAVING TROUBLE, HUMAN? YOU'LL HAVE TO GET CLOSER IF YOU WANT TO LAND A STRIKE!!
BUN (SWIPE)

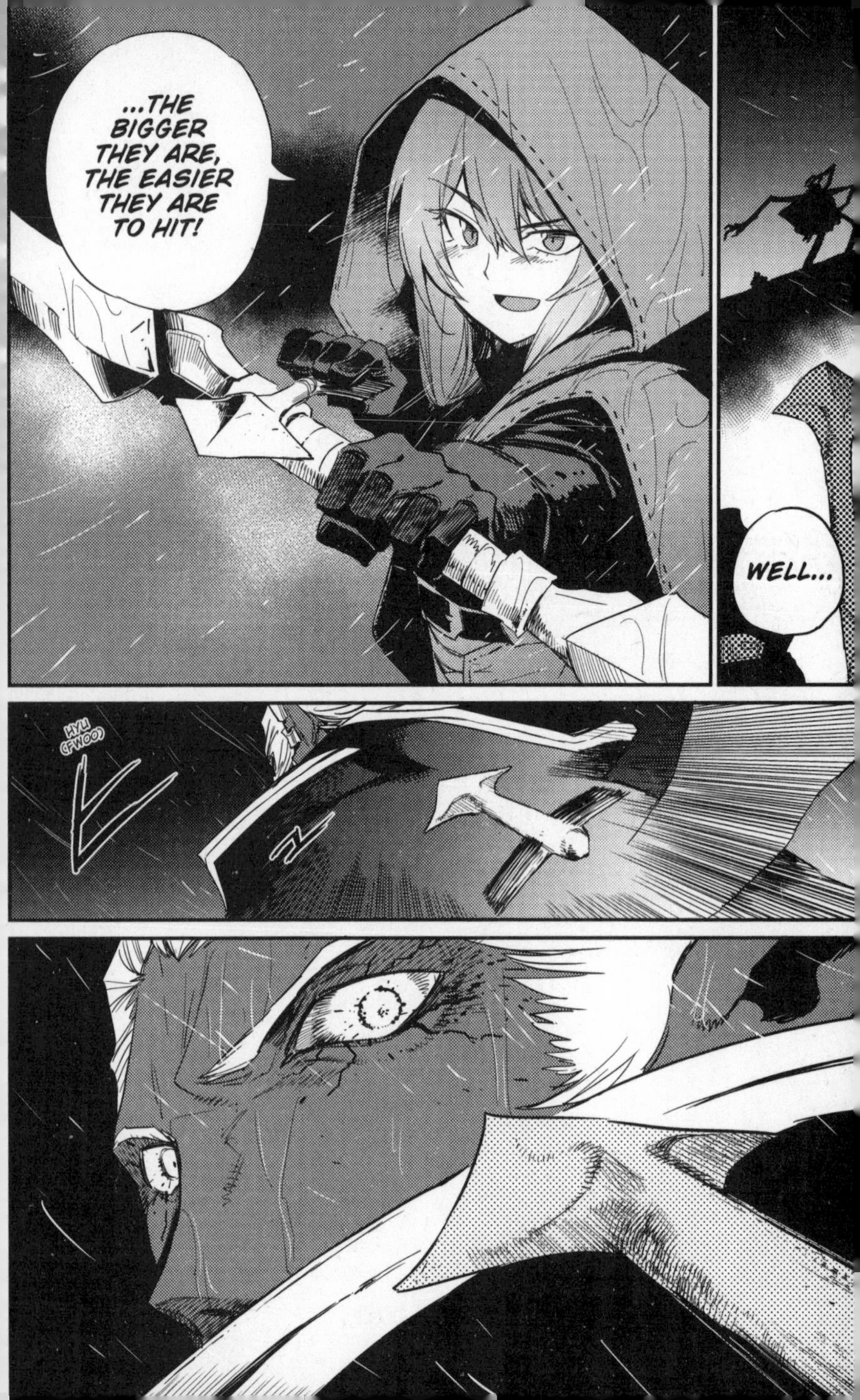
WELL...
...THE BIGGER THEY ARE, THE EASIER THEY ARE TO HIT!
HYU (FWOO)

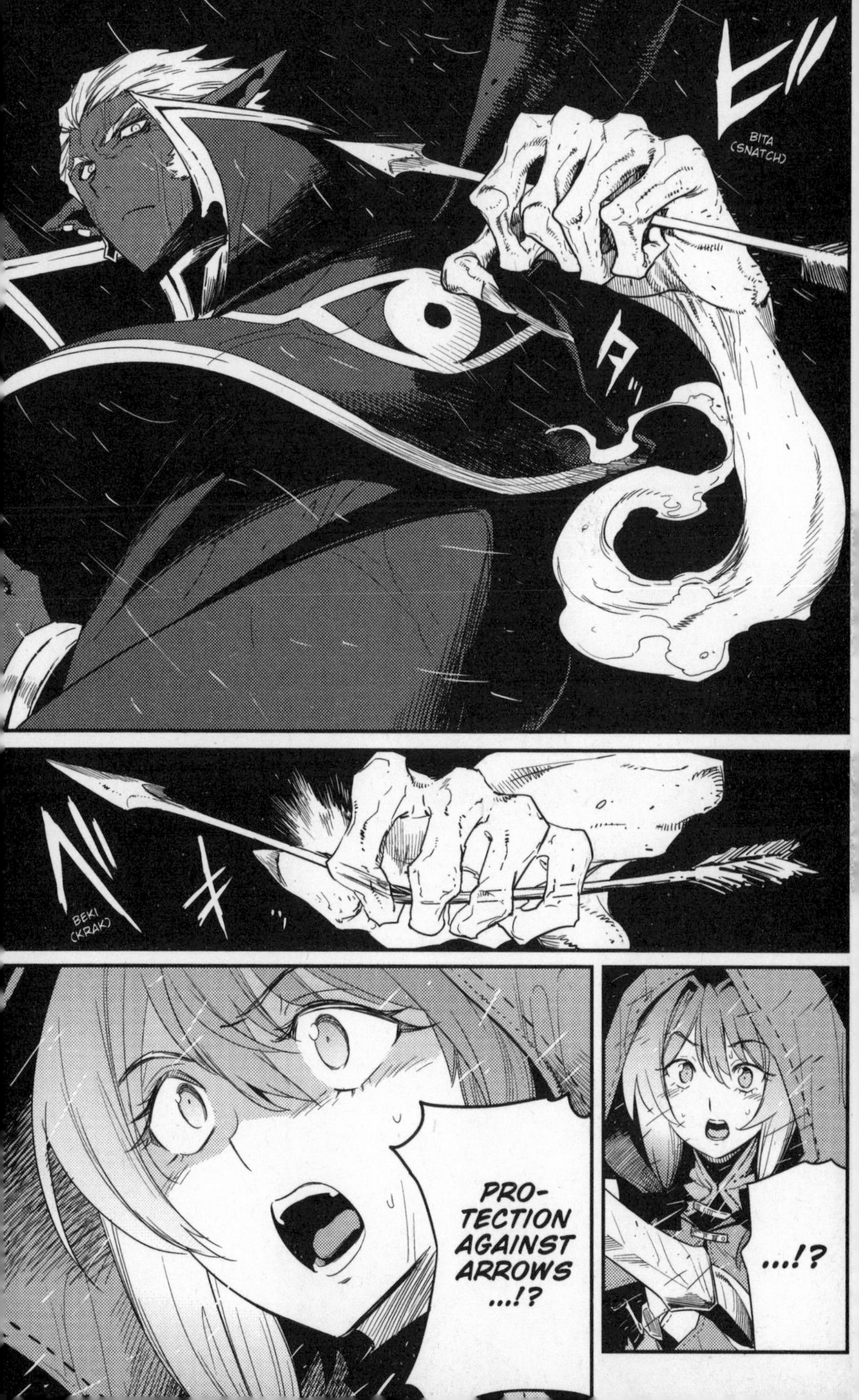
BITA (SNATCH)
BEKI (KRAK)
...!?
PRO-TECTION AGAINST ARROWS ...!?

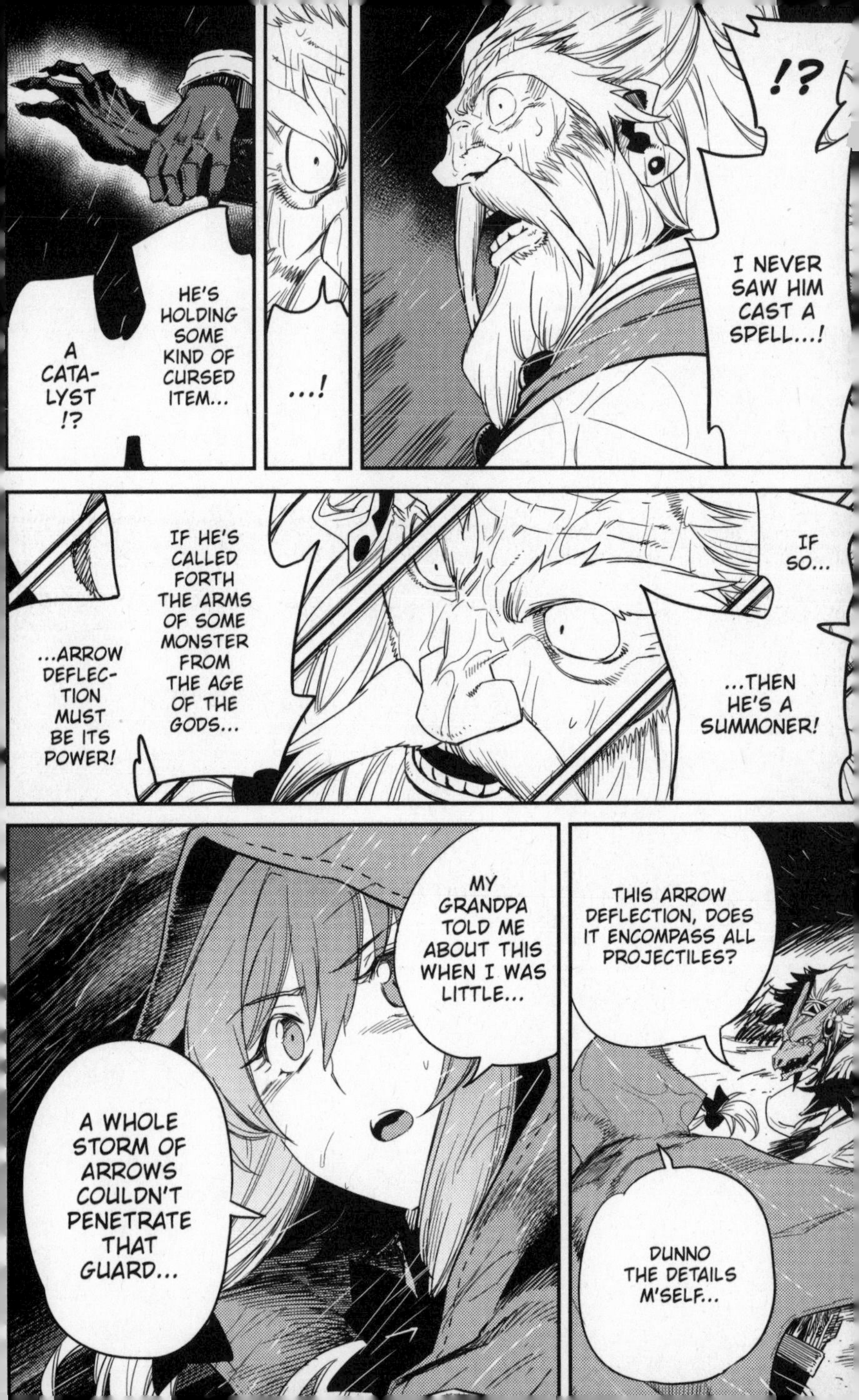
!?
I NEVER SAW HIM CAST A SPELL...!
...!
HE'S HOLDING SOME KIND OF CURSED ITEM...
A CATALYST!?
IF SO...
...THEN HE'S A SUMMONER!
IF HE'S CALLED FORTH THE ARMS OF SOME MONSTER FROM THE AGE OF THE GODS...
...ARROW DEFLECTION MUST BE ITS POWER!
THIS ARROW DEFLECTION, DOES IT ENCOMPASS ALL PROJECTILES?
DUNNO THE DETAILS M'SELF...
MY GRANDPA TOLD ME ABOUT THIS WHEN I WAS LITTLE...
A WHOLE STORM OF ARROWS COULDN'T PENETRATE THAT GUARD...

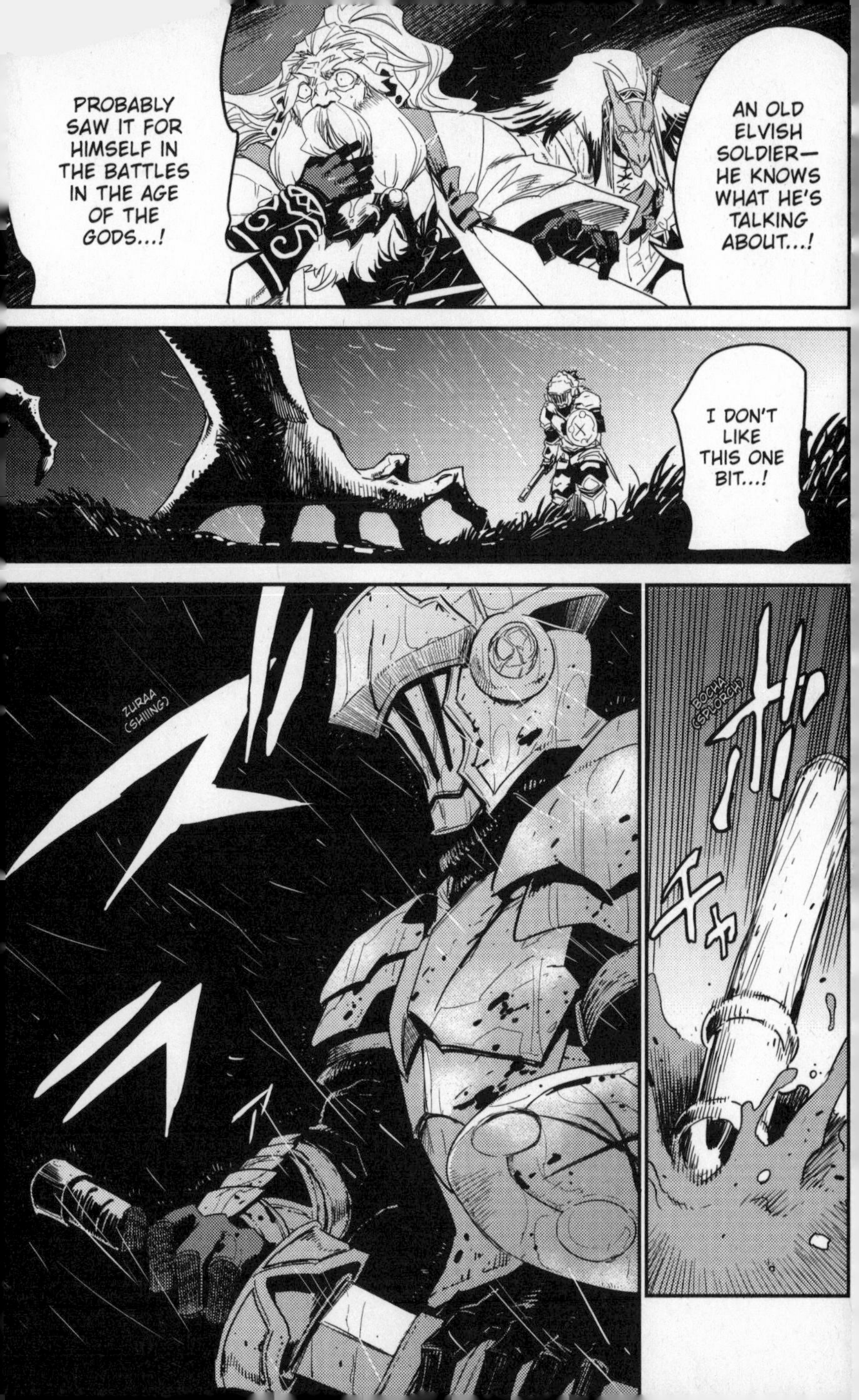
AN OLD ELVISH SOLDIER—HE KNOWS WHAT HE'S TALKING ABOUT...!
PROBABLY SAW IT FOR HIMSELF IN THE BATTLES IN THE AGE OF THE GODS...!
I DON'T LIKE THIS ONE BIT...!
BOCHA (SPLORCH)
ZURAA (SHIIING)

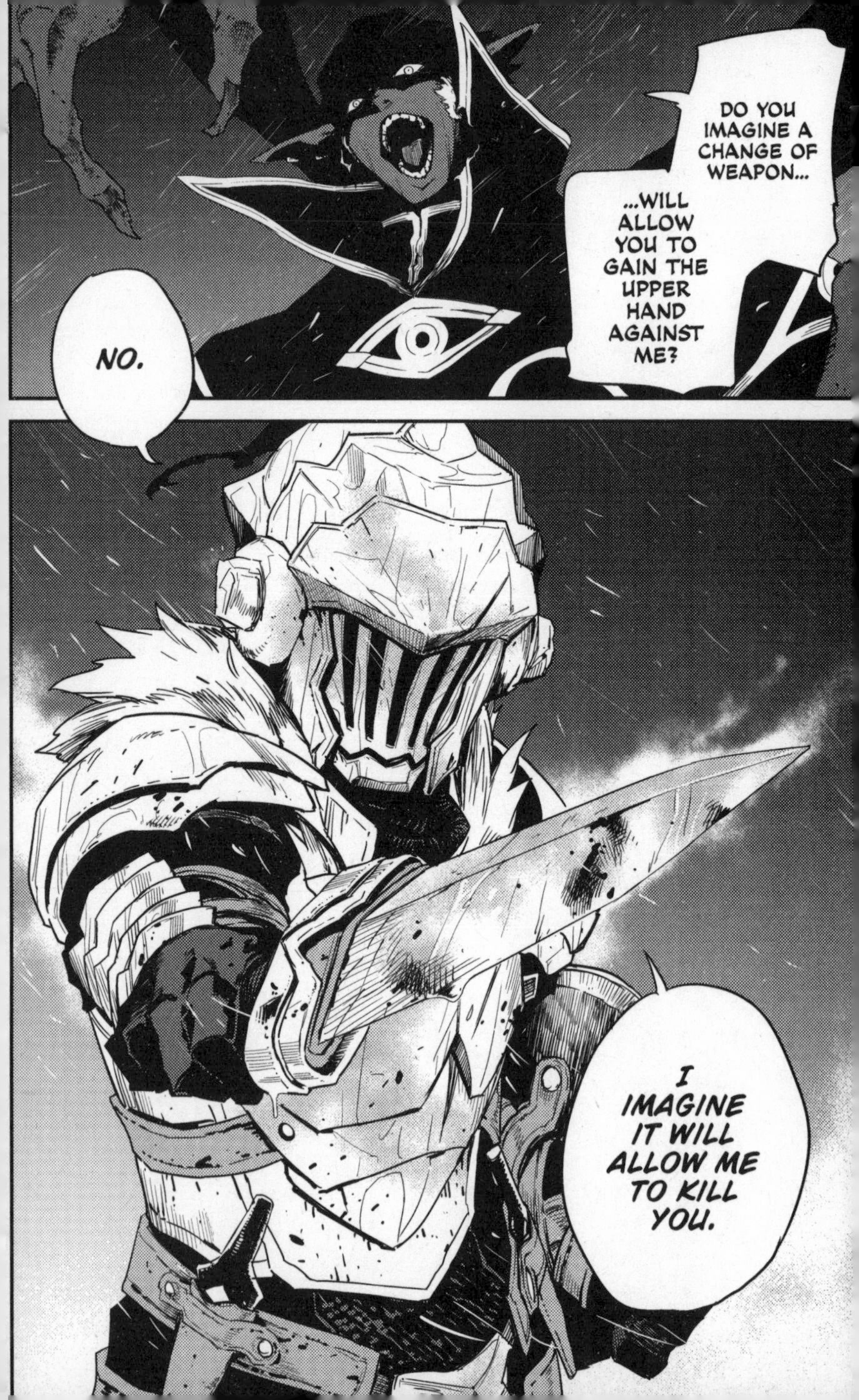
DO YOU IMAGINE A CHANGE OF WEAPON...
...WILL ALLOW YOU TO GAIN THE UPPER HAND AGAINST ME?
NO.
I IMAGINE IT WILL ALLOW ME TO KILL YOU.

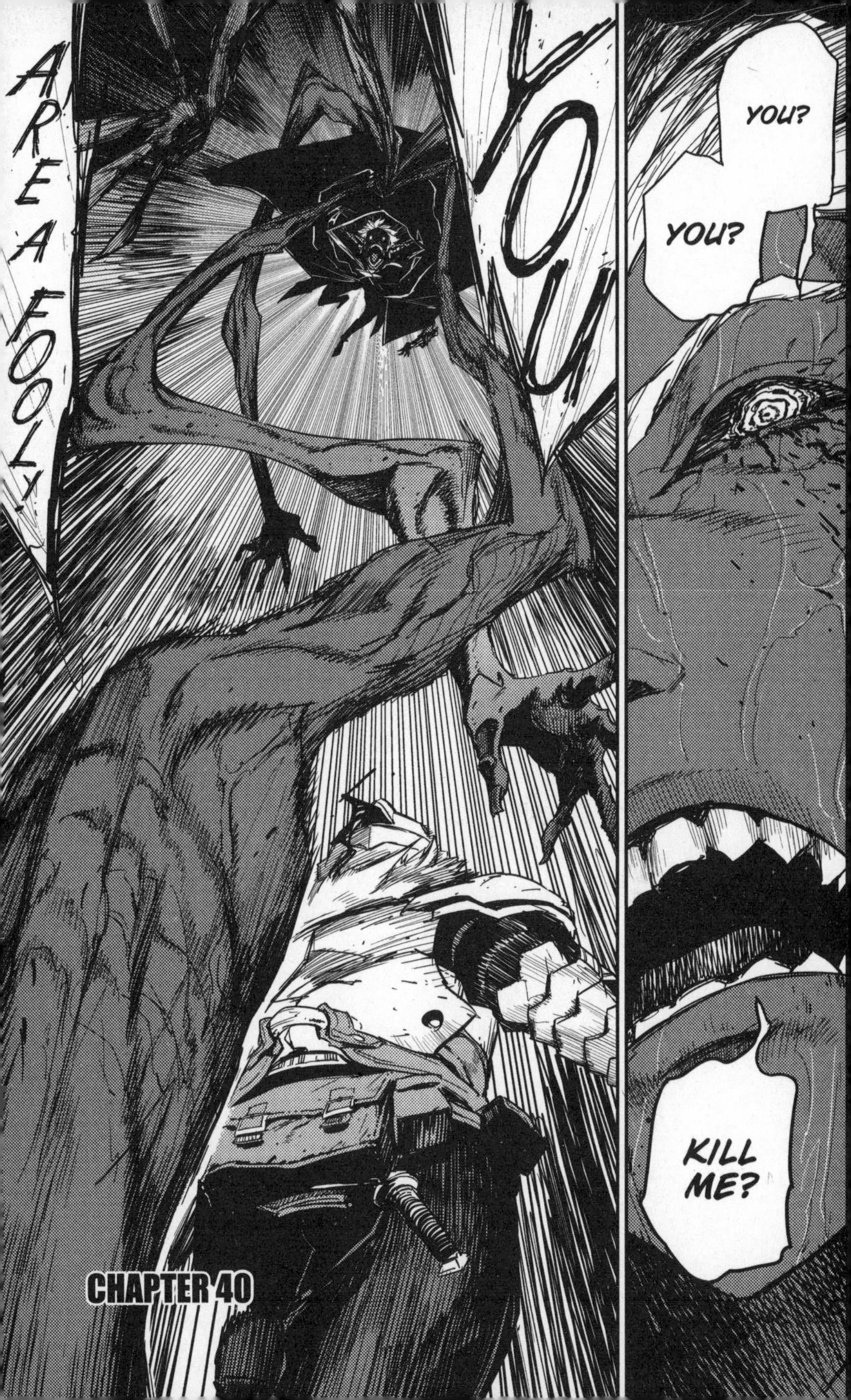
YOU?
YOU?
KILL ME?
YOU
ARE A FOOL!

CHAPTER 40

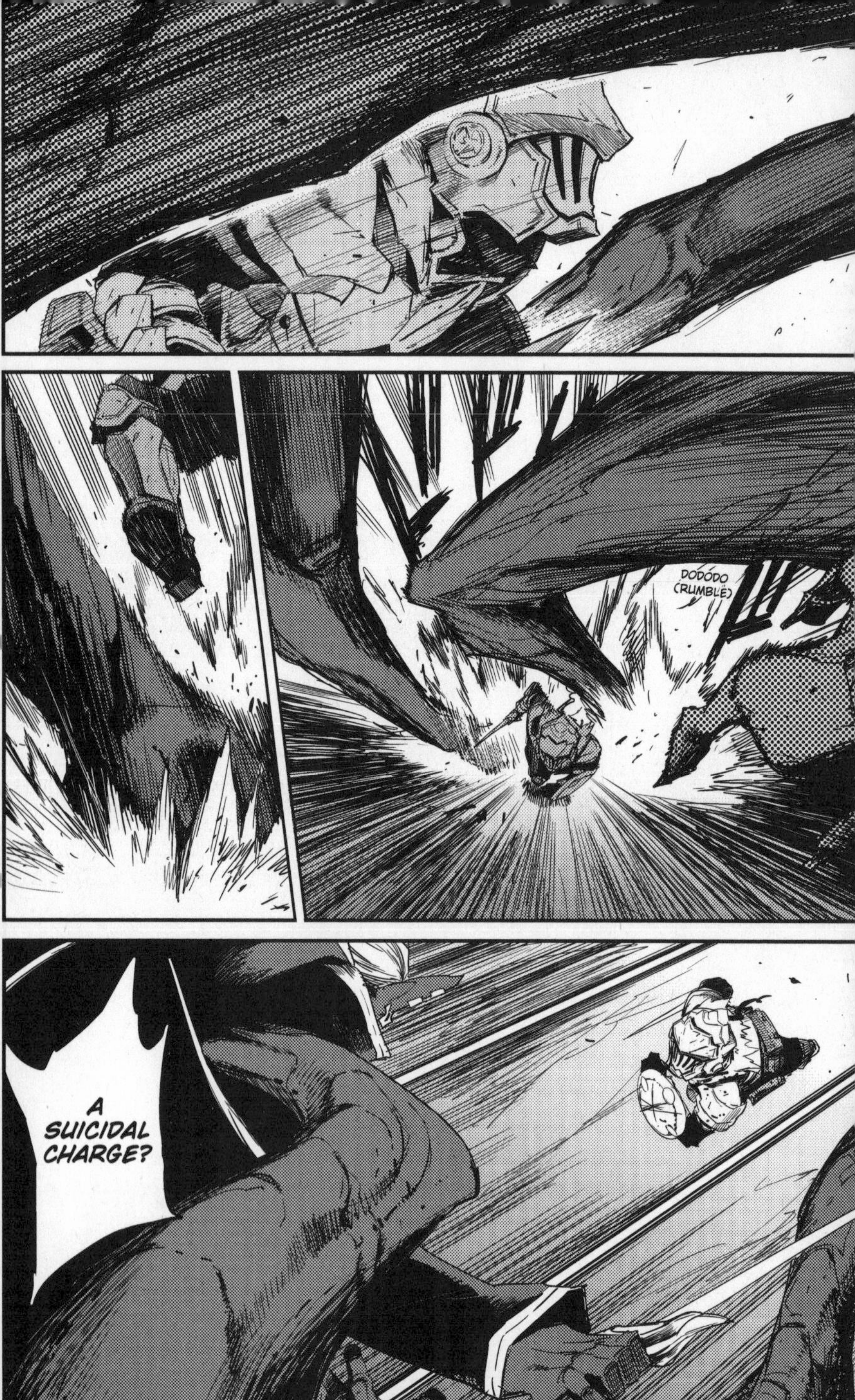
DODODO
(RUMBLE)
A SUICIDAL CHARGE?

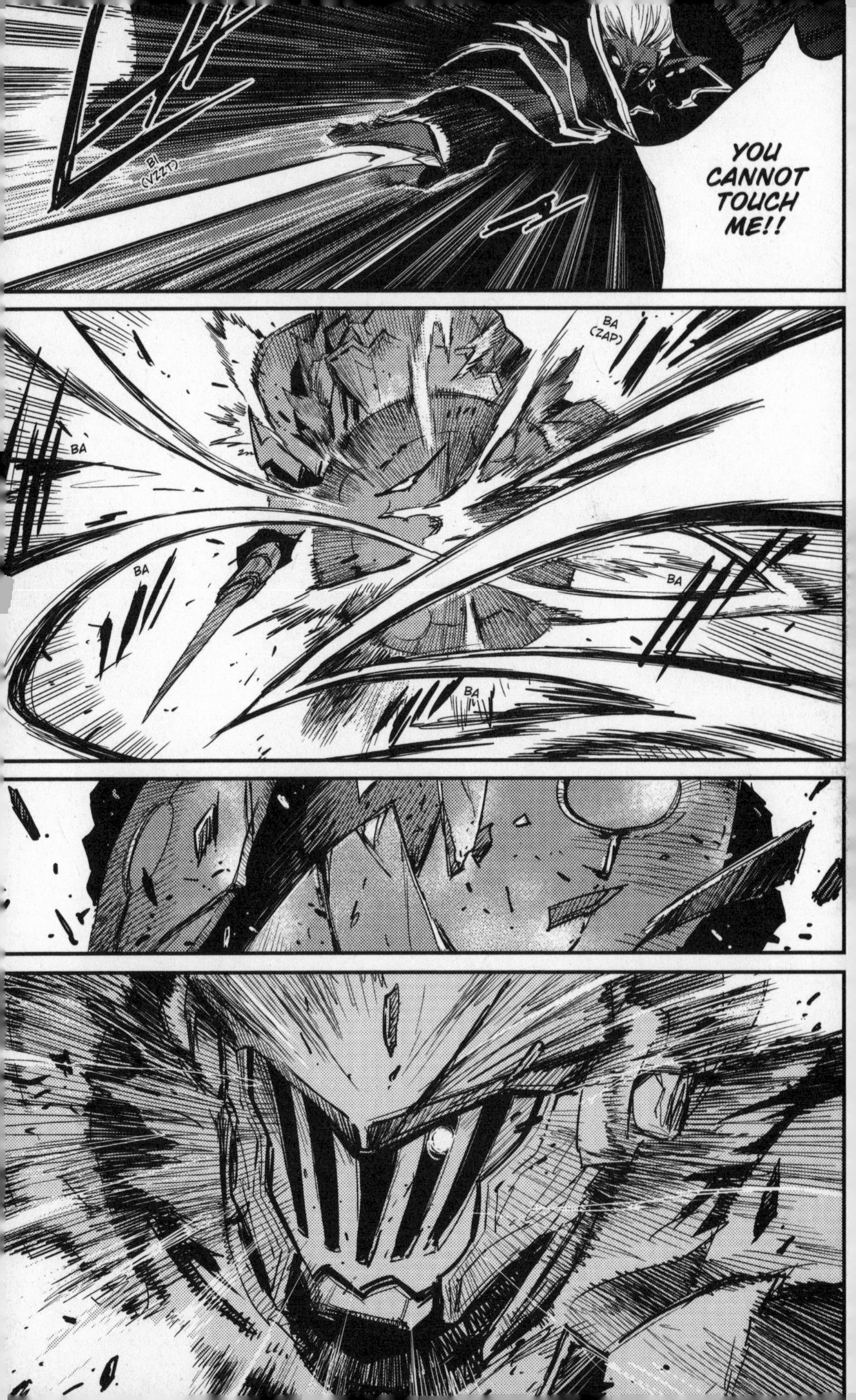
YOU CANNOT TOUCH ME!!
BI (VZZT)
BA (ZAP)
BA
BA
BA
BA

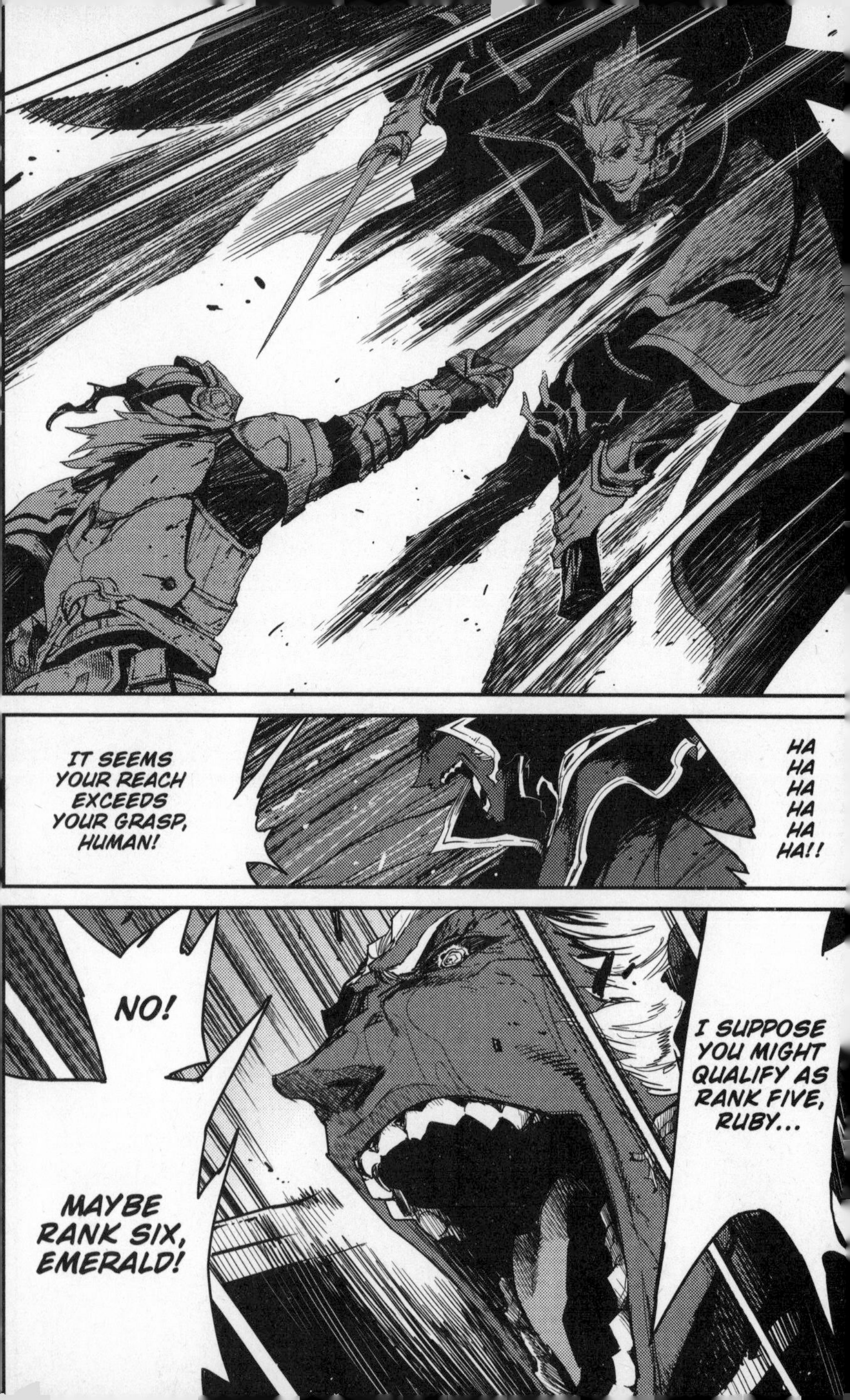
HA HA HA HA HA HA!!
IT SEEMS YOUR REACH EXCEEDS YOUR GRASP, HUMAN!
I SUPPOSE YOU MIGHT QUALIFY AS RANK FIVE, RUBY...
NO!
MAYBE RANK SIX, EMERALD!

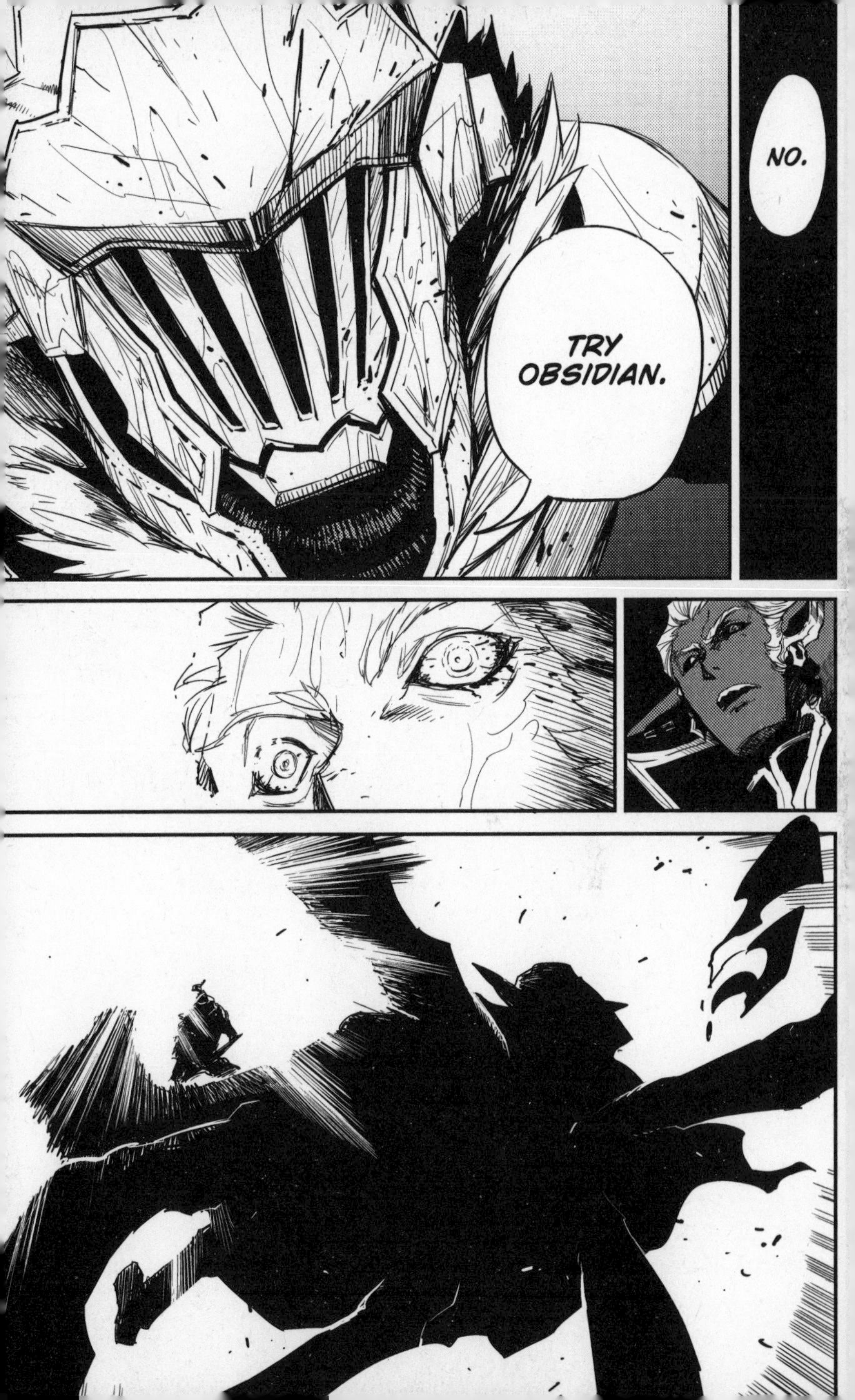
NO.
TRY OBSIDIAN.

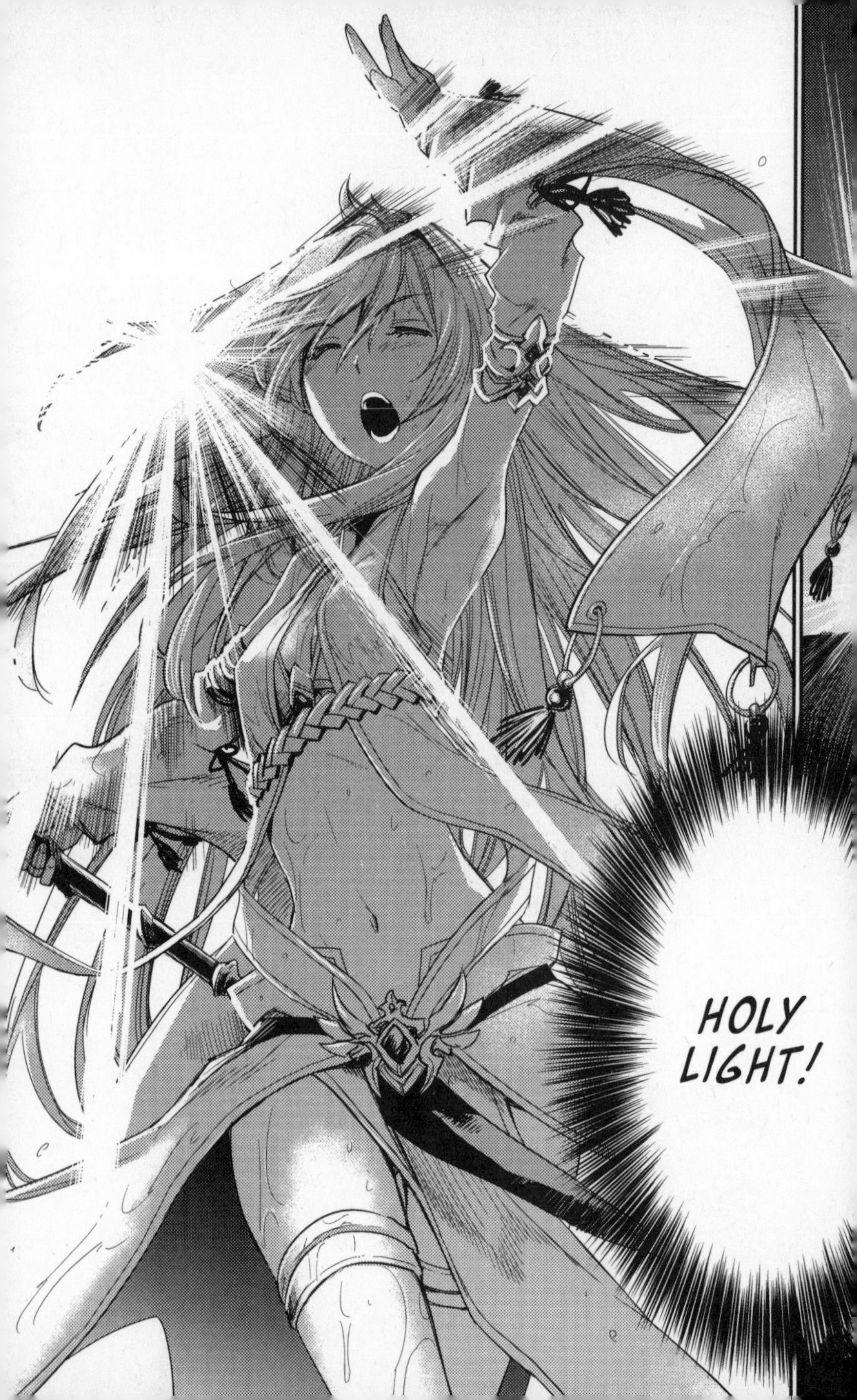
HOLY LIGHT!

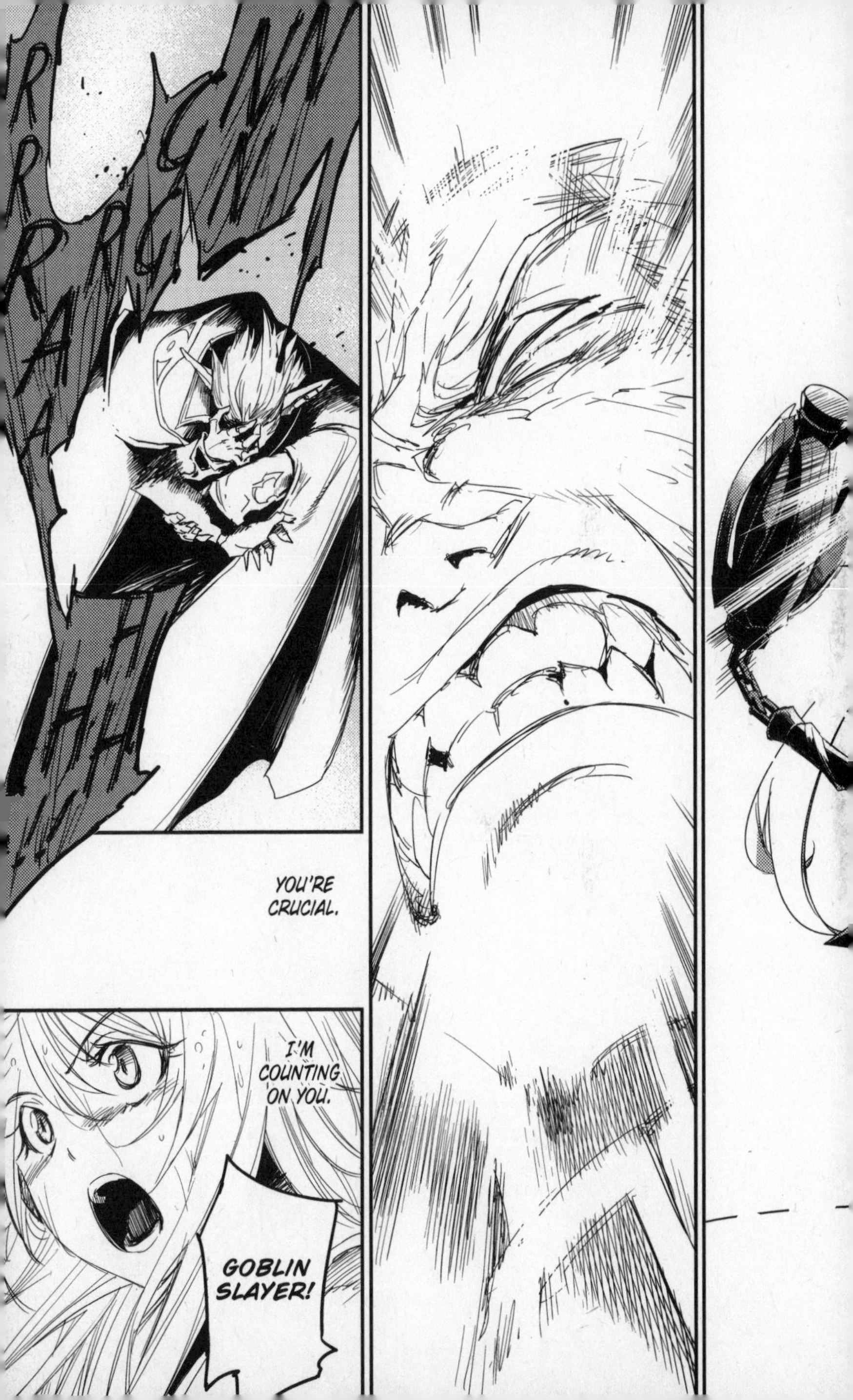
YOU'RE CRUCIAL.
I'M COUNTING ON YOU.
GOBLIN SLAYER!

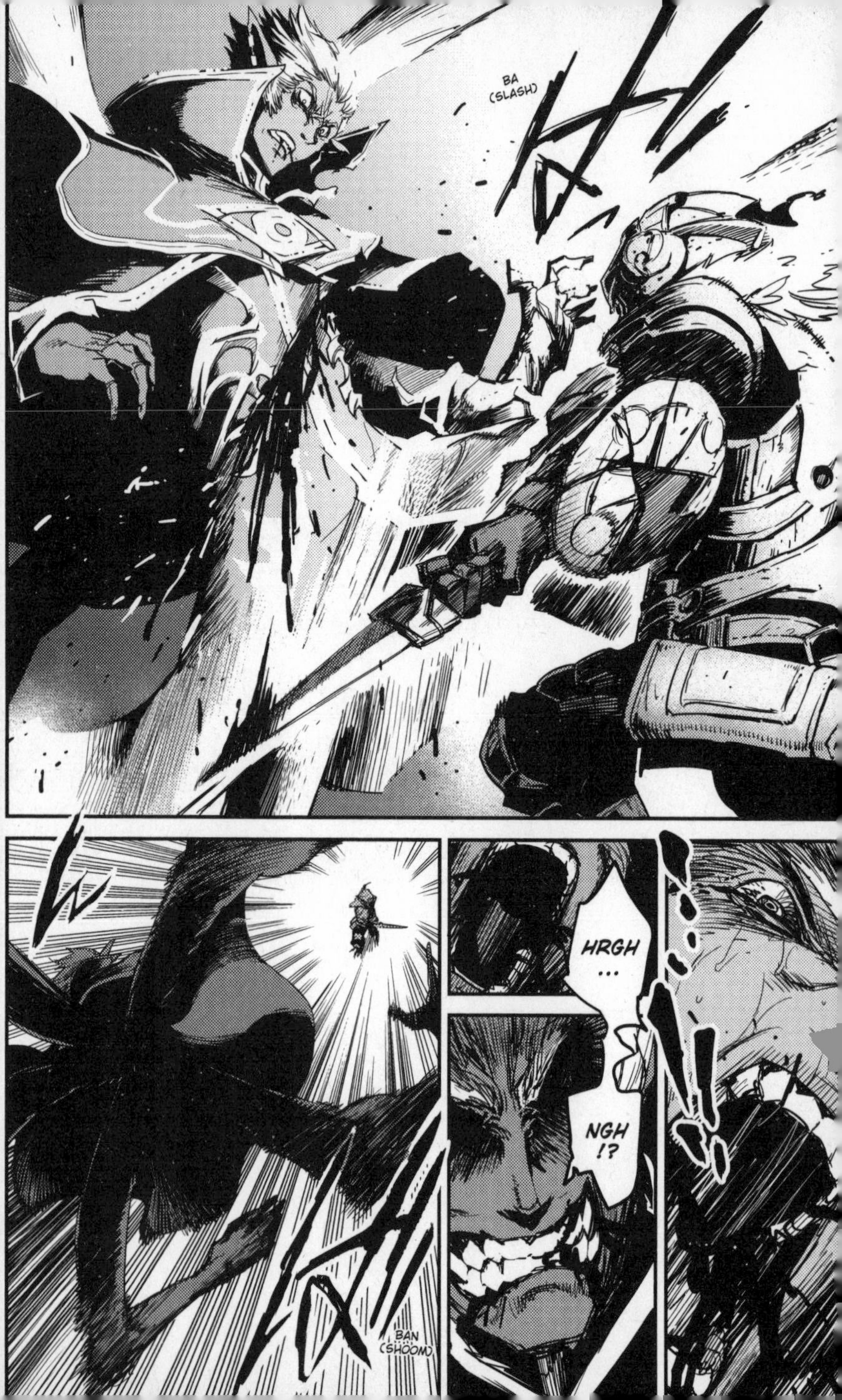
BA (SLASH)
HRGH ...
NGH !?
BAN (SHOOM)

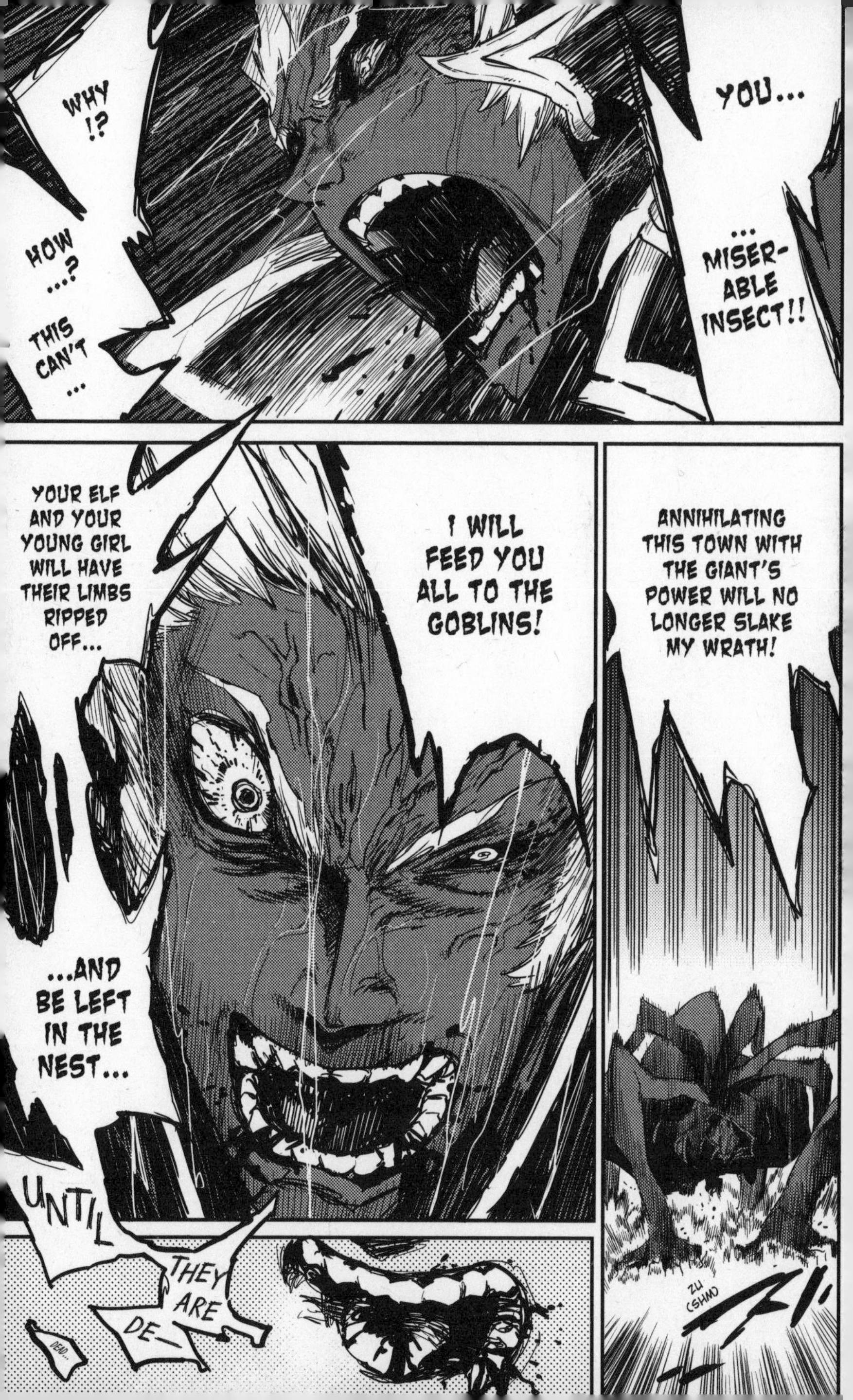
YOU...
...MISERABLE INSECT!!
WHY !?
HOW ...?
THIS CAN'T ...
ANNIHILATING THIS TOWN WITH THE GIANT'S POWER WILL NO LONGER SLAKE MY WRATH!
ZU (SHM)
I WILL FEED YOU ALL TO THE GOBLINS!
YOUR ELF AND YOUR YOUNG GIRL WILL HAVE THEIR LIMBS RIPPED OFF...
...AND BE LEFT IN THE NEST...
UNTIL
THEY ARE DE—
DEAD...

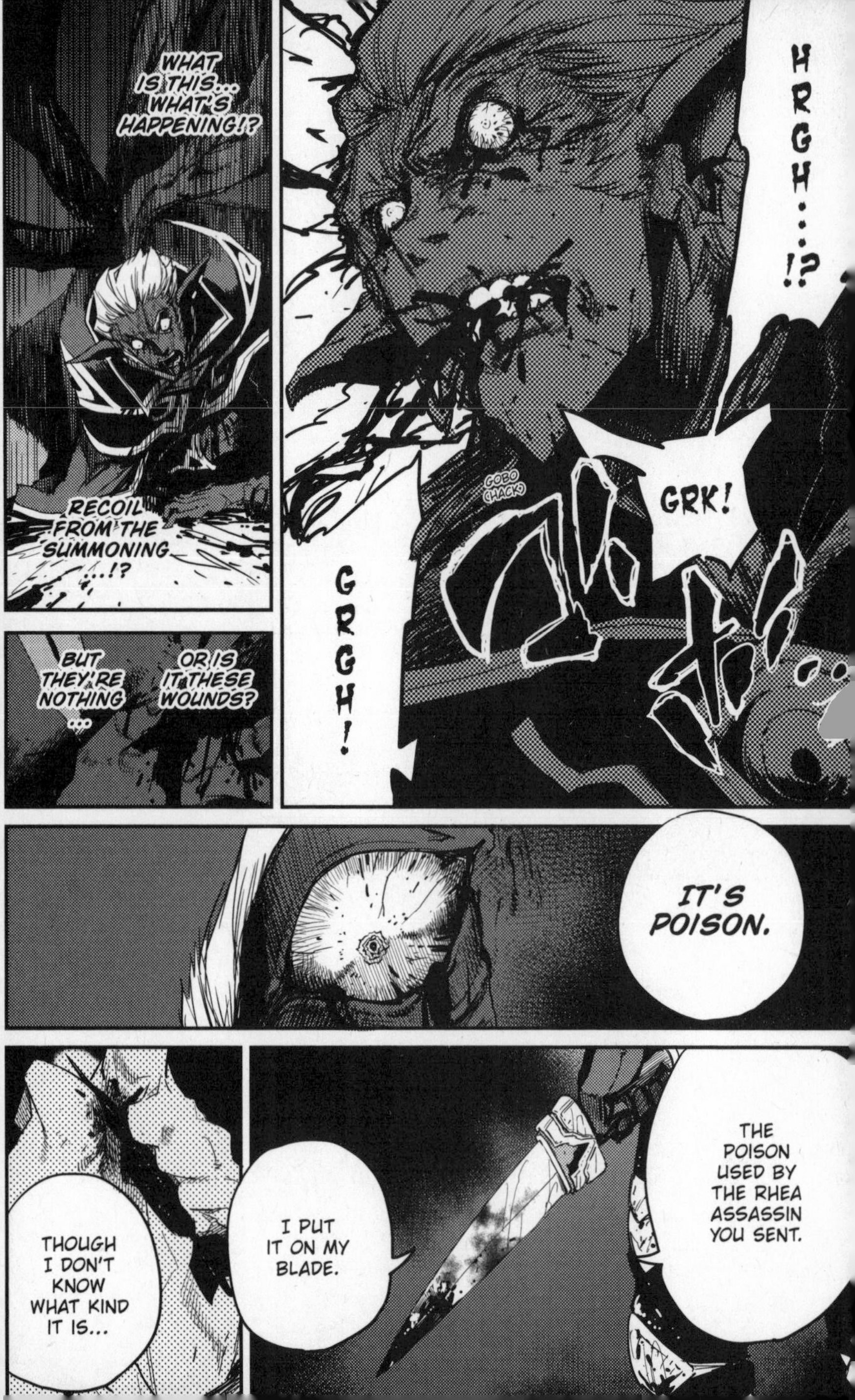
HRGH...!?
GRK!
GOBO (HACK)
GRGH!
WHAT IS THIS... WHAT'S HAPPENING!?
RECOIL FROM THE SUMMONING...!?
OR IS IT THESE WOUNDS?
BUT THEY'RE NOTHING...
IT'S POISON.
THE POISON USED BY THE RHEA ASSASSIN YOU SENT.
I PUT IT ON MY BLADE.
THOUGH I DON'T KNOW WHAT KIND IT IS...

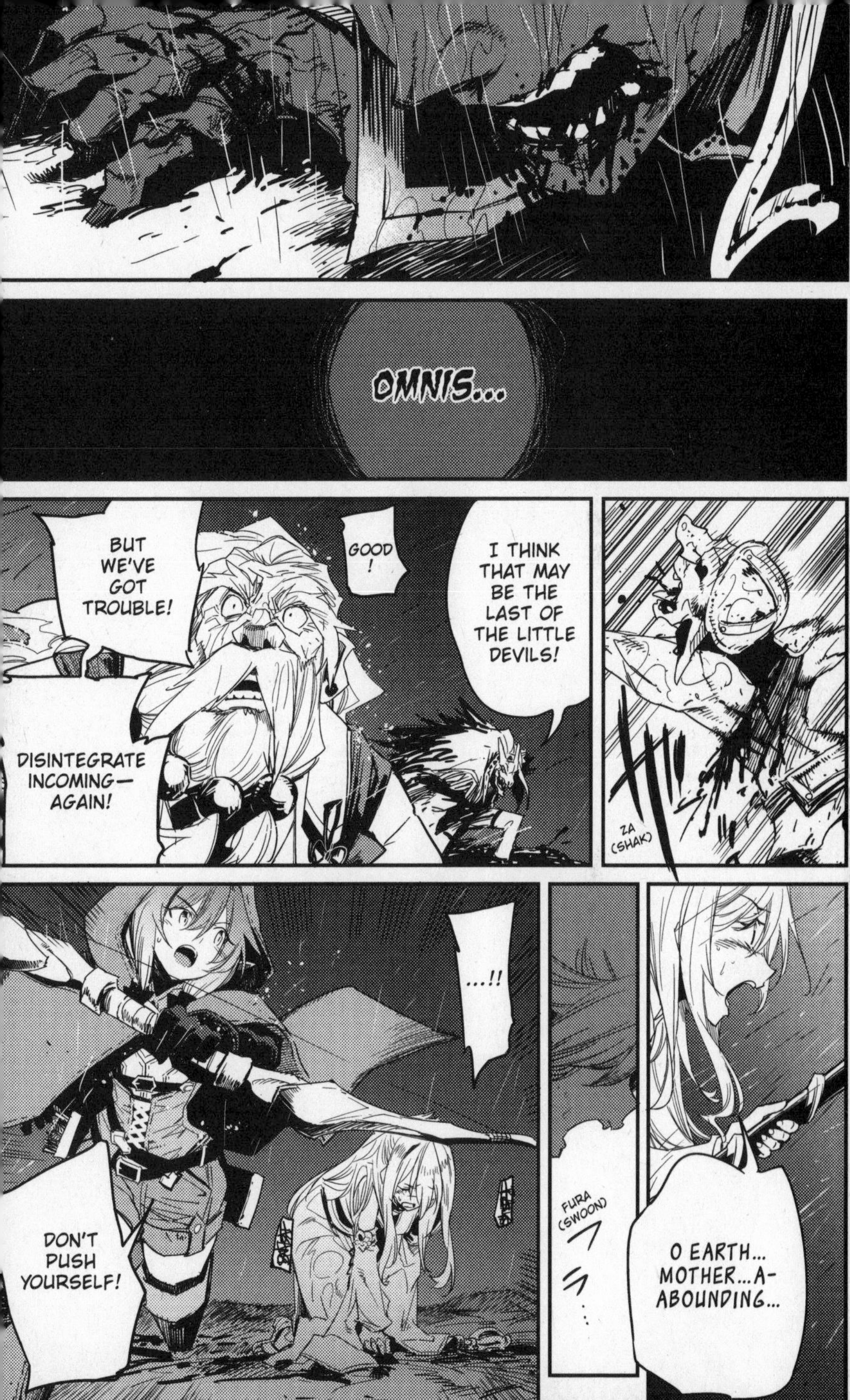
OMNIS...
ZA (SHAK)
I THINK THAT MAY BE THE LAST OF THE LITTLE DEVILS!
GOOD!
BUT WE'VE GOT TROUBLE!
DISINTEGRATE INCOMING—AGAIN!
O EARTH... MOTHER...A-ABOUNDING...
FURA (SWOON)
...!!
DON'T PUSH YOURSELF!

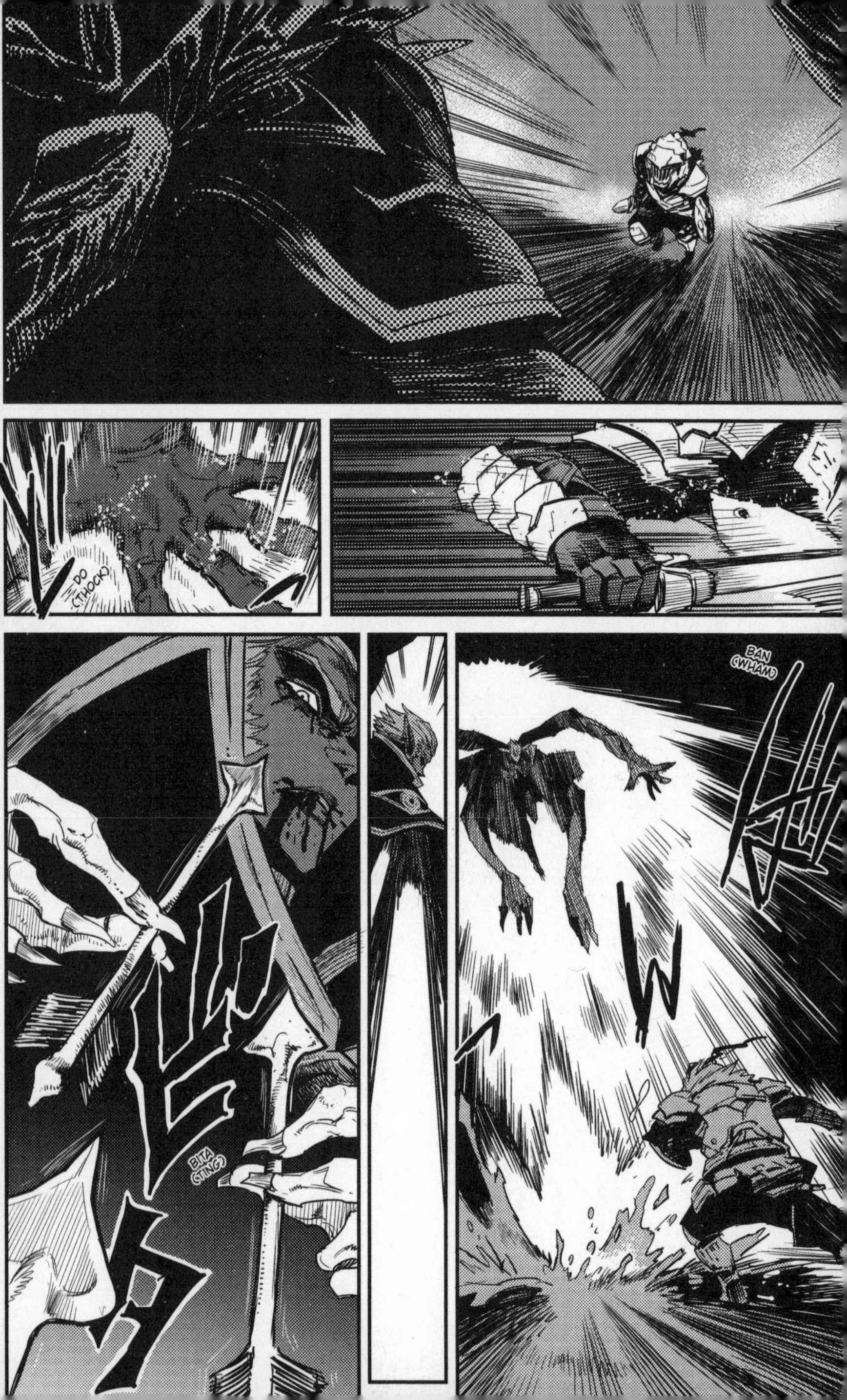
DO
(THOCK)
BAN
(WHAM)
BITA
(TING)

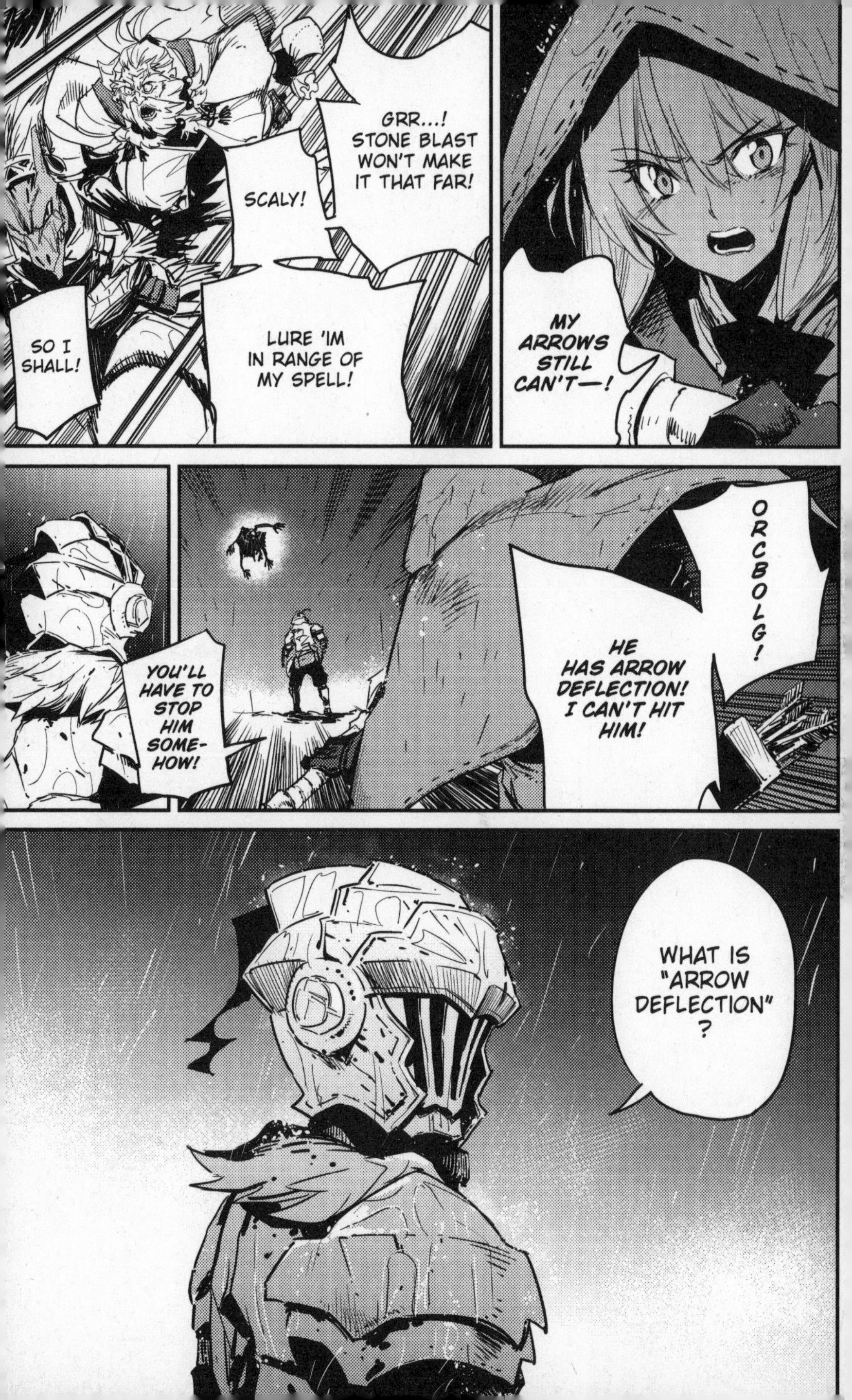
MY ARROWS STILL CAN'T—!
GRR...! STONE BLAST WON'T MAKE IT THAT FAR!
SCALY!
LURE 'IM IN RANGE OF MY SPELL!
SO I SHALL!
ORCBOLG!
HE HAS ARROW DEFLECTION! I CAN'T HIT HIM!
YOU'LL HAVE TO STOP HIM SOME-HOW!
WHAT IS "ARROW DEFLECTION"?

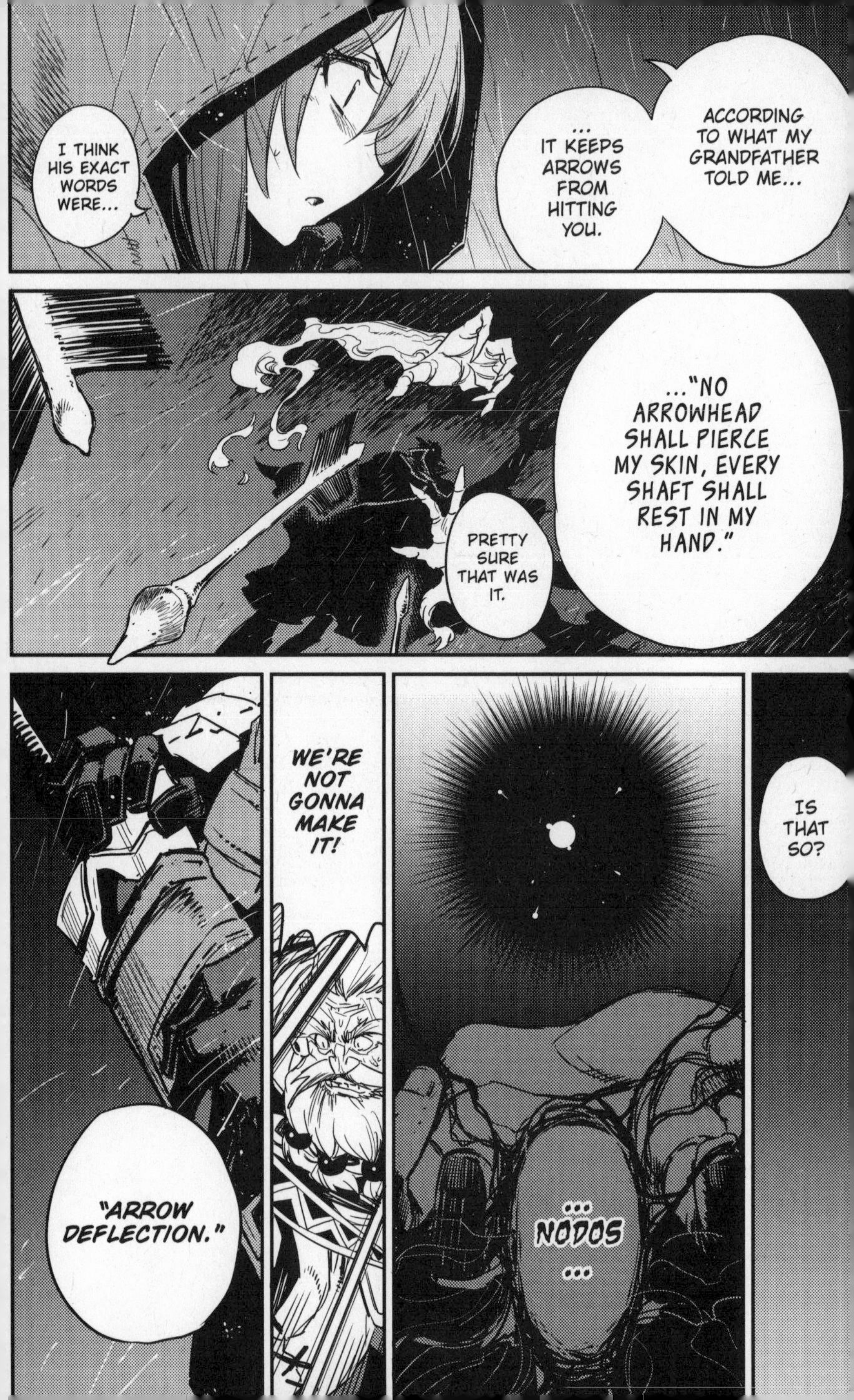

ACCORDING TO WHAT MY GRANDFATHER TOLD ME...
... IT KEEPS ARROWS FROM HITTING YOU.
I THINK HIS EXACT WORDS WERE...
..."NO ARROWHEAD SHALL PIERCE MY SKIN, EVERY SHAFT SHALL REST IN MY HAND."
PRETTY SURE THAT WAS IT.
IS THAT SO?
... NODOS ...
WE'RE NOT GONNA MAKE IT!
"ARROW DEFLECTION."

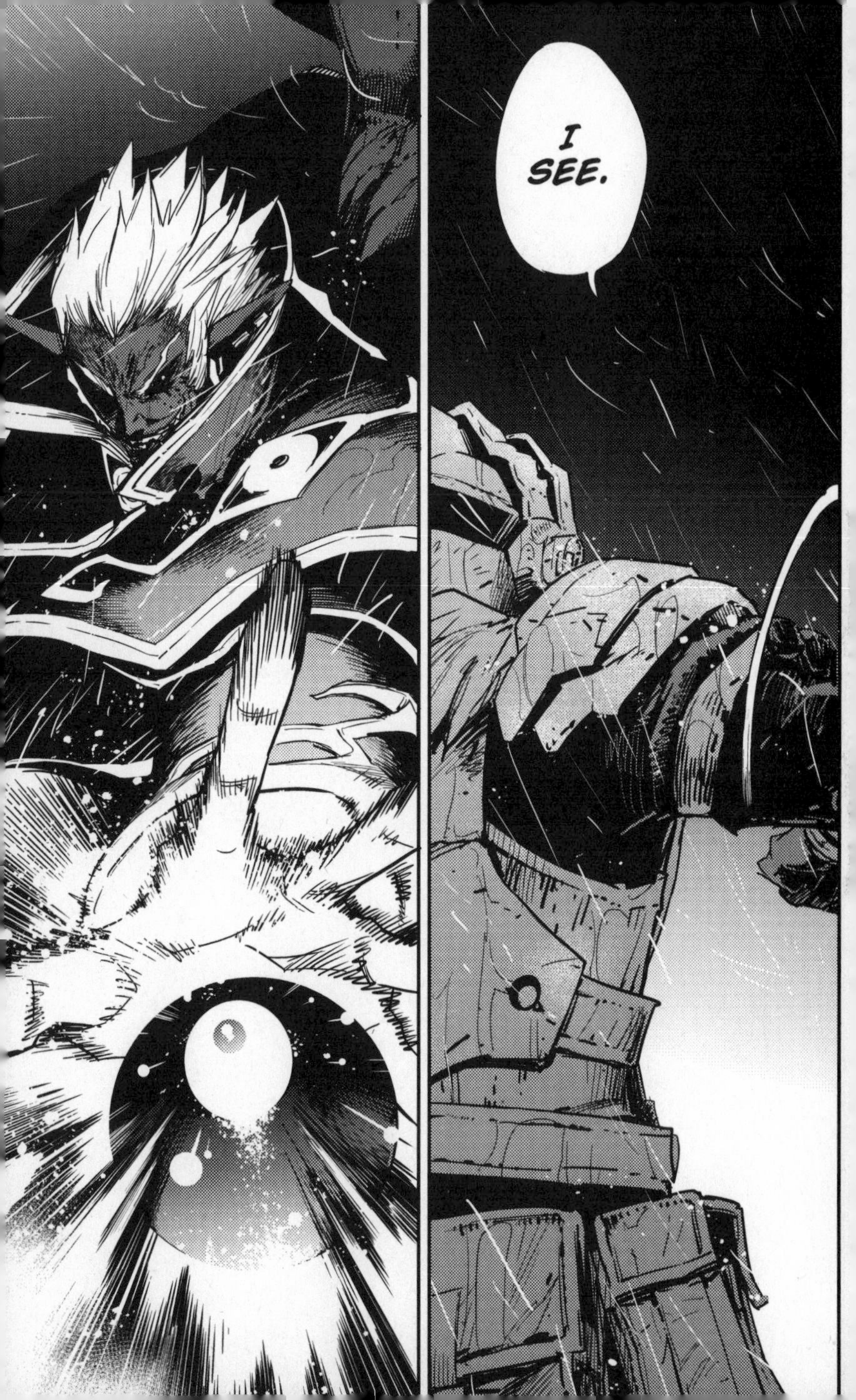
I SEE.

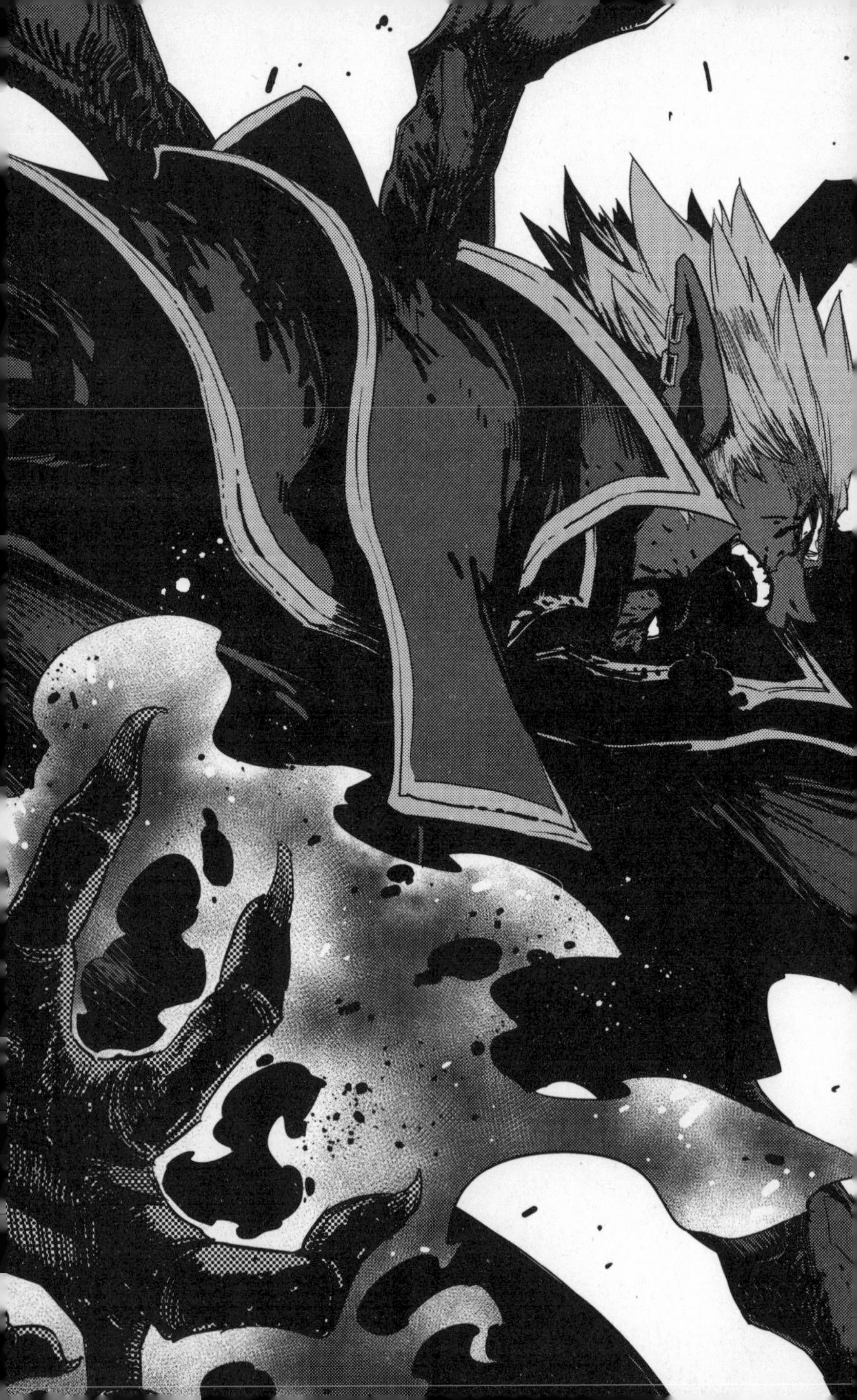

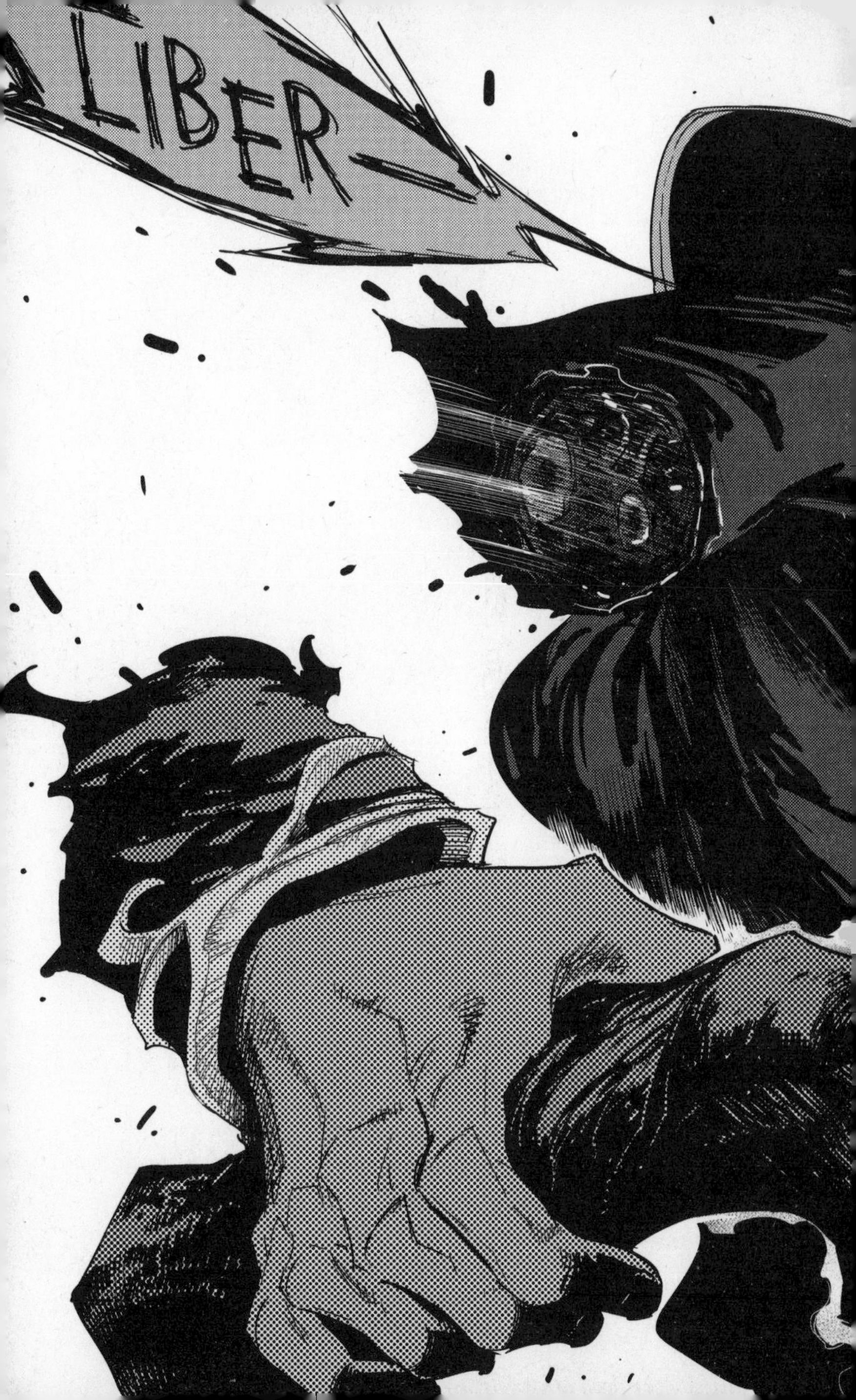
LIBER

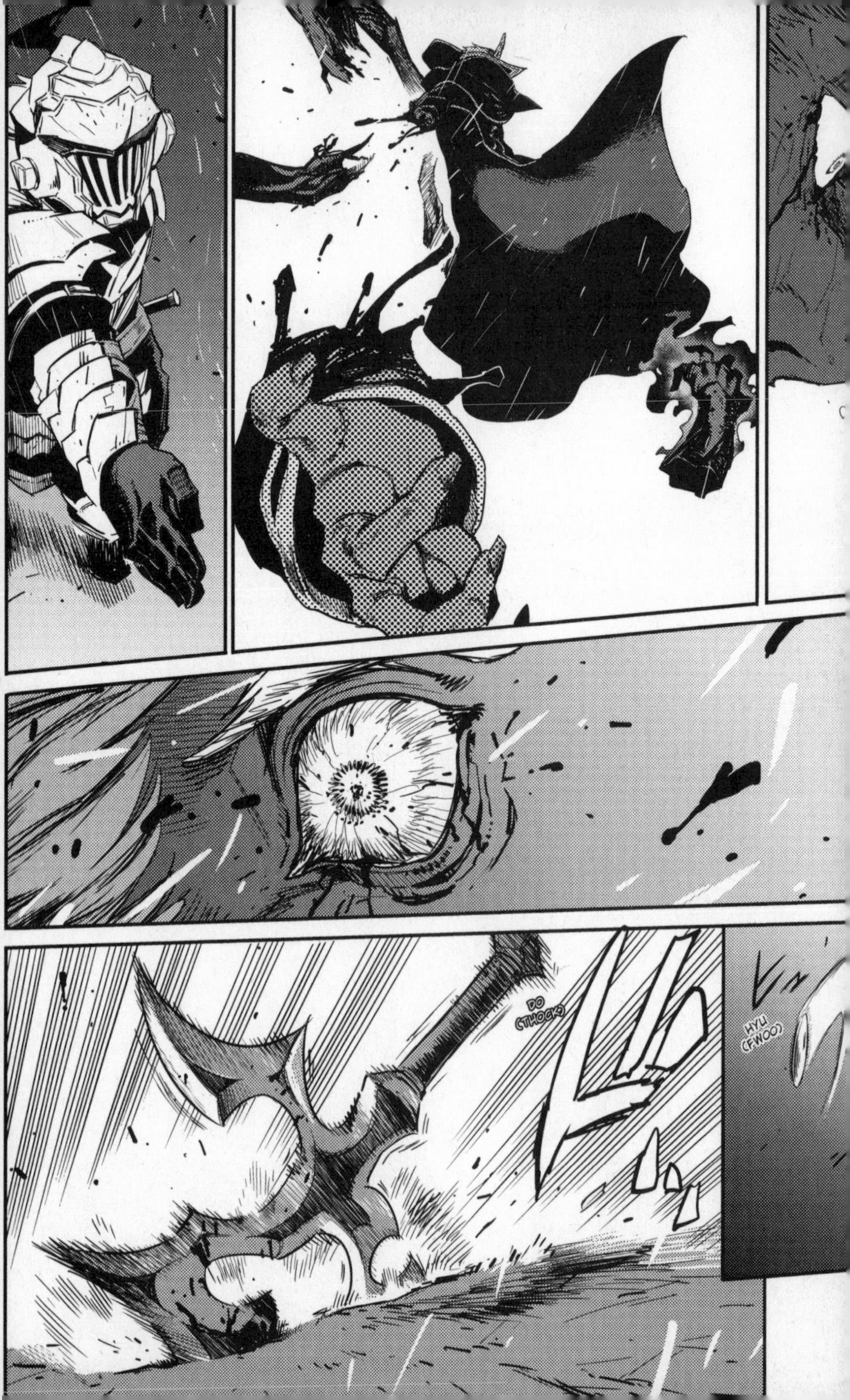
HYU (FWOO)
DO (THOCK)

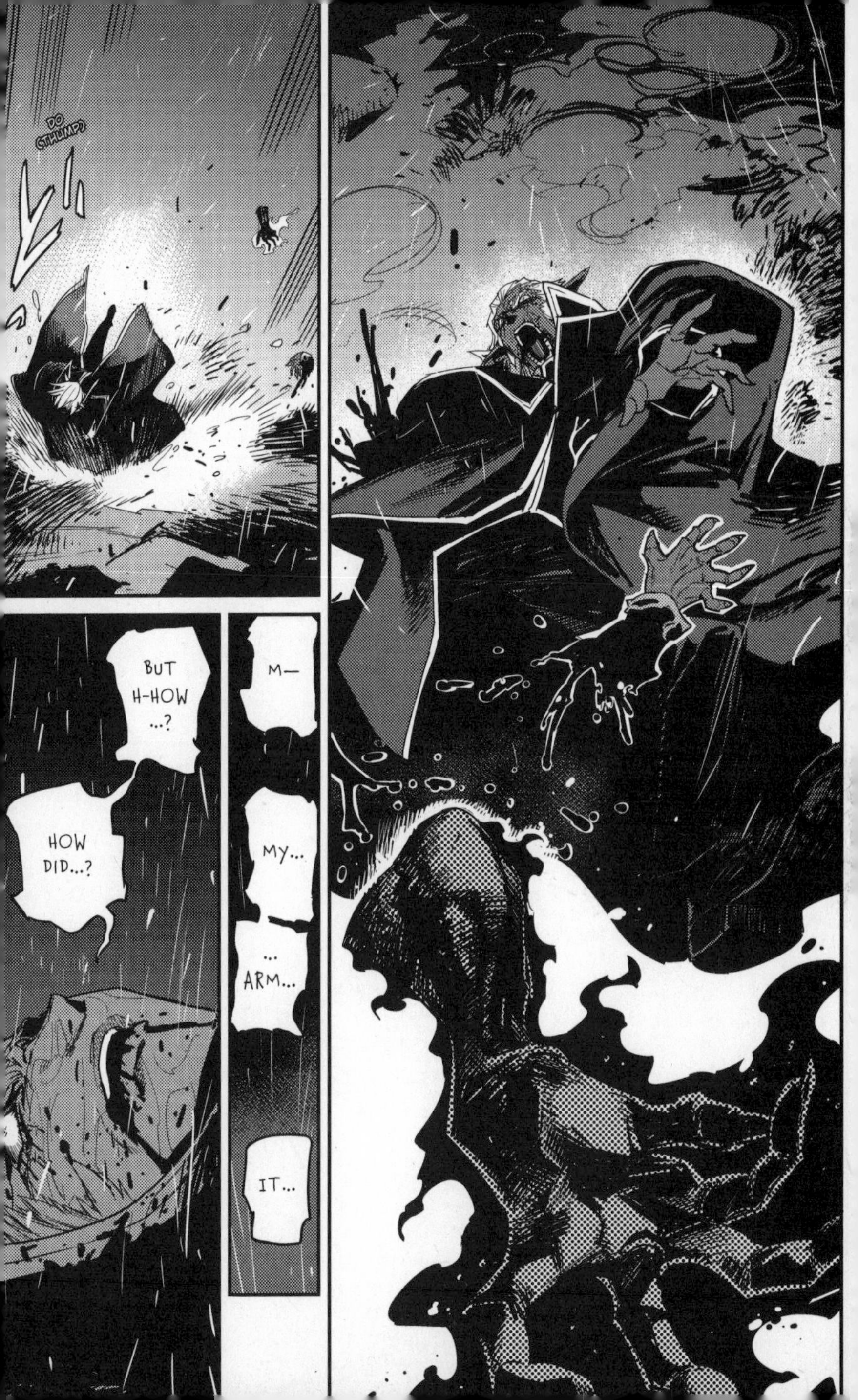
DO (THUMP)
M—
MY...
... ARM...
IT...
BUT H-HOW ...?
HOW DID...?

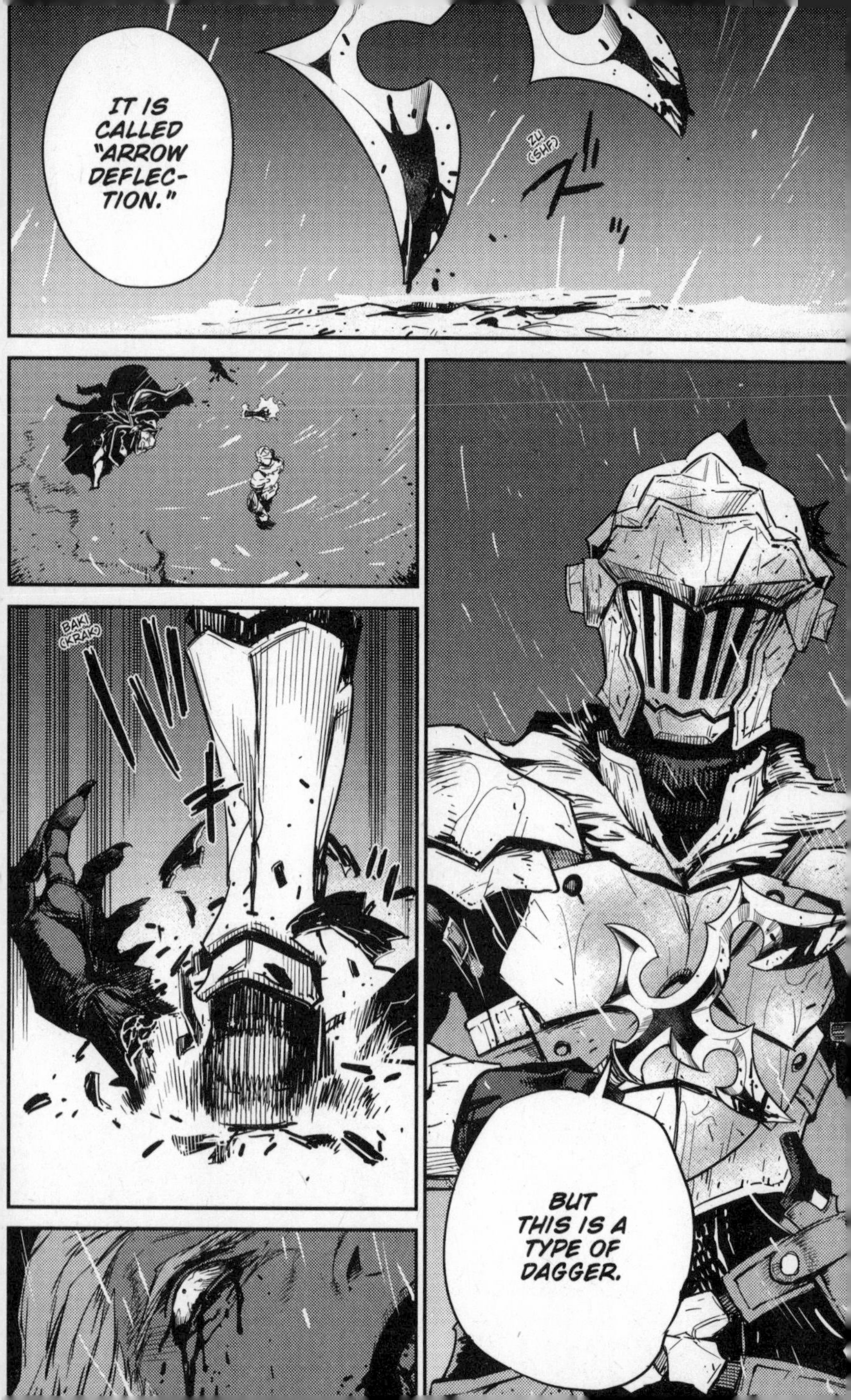
ZU (SHF)
IT IS CALLED "ARROW DEFLECTION."
BUT THIS IS A TYPE OF DAGGER.
BAKI (KRAK)

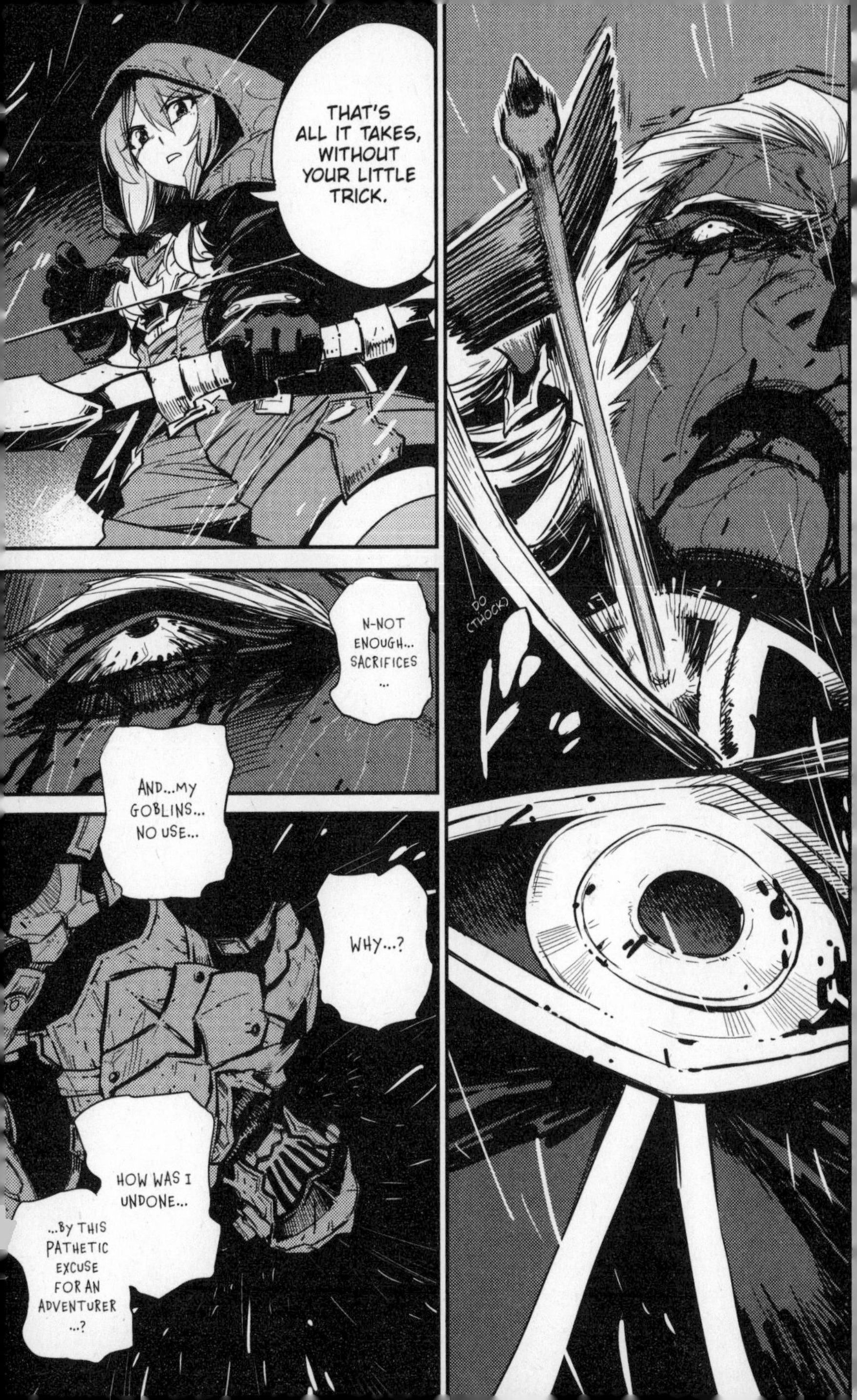
DO (THOCK)
THAT'S ALL IT TAKES, WITHOUT YOUR LITTLE TRICK.
N-NOT ENOUGH... SACRIFICES ...
AND...MY GOBLINS... NO USE...
WHY...?
HOW WAS I UNDONE...
...BY THIS PATHETIC EXCUSE FOR AN ADVENTURER ...?

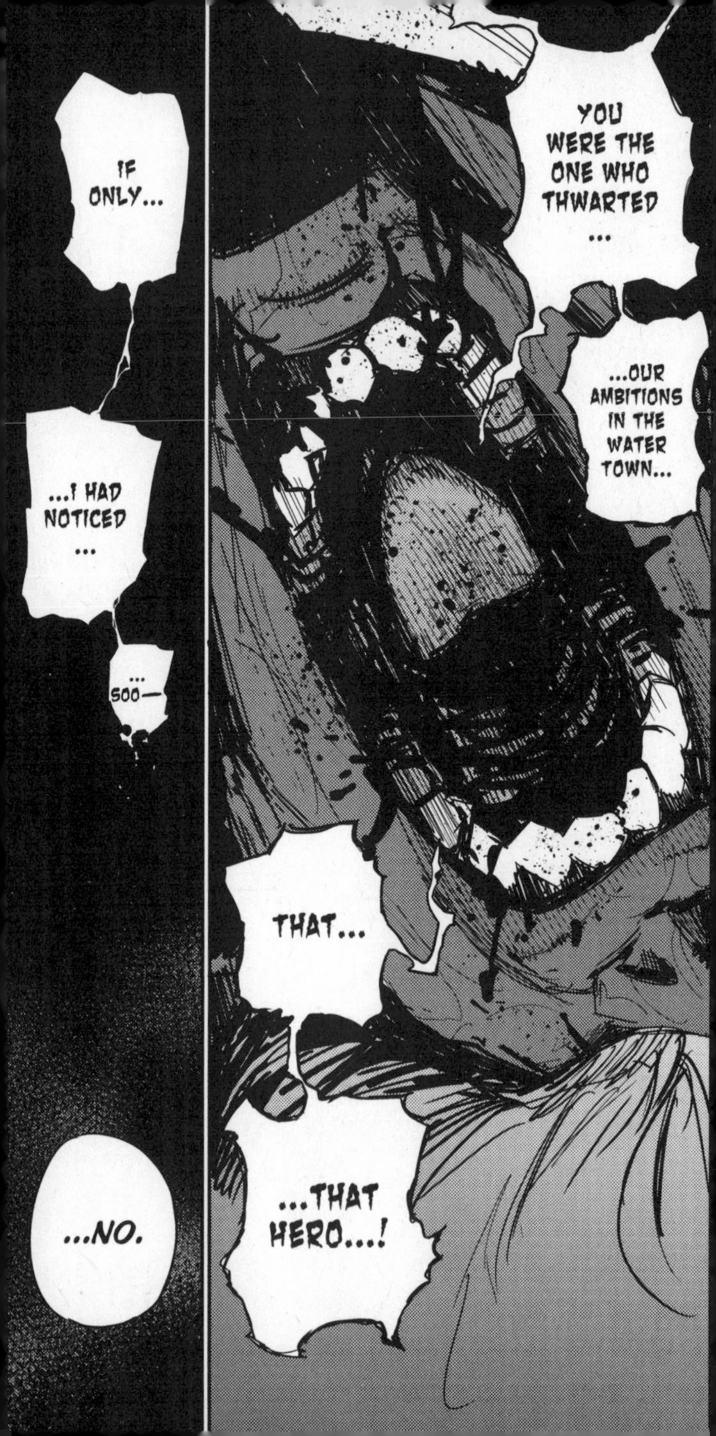
YOU WERE THE ONE WHO THWARTED ...
...OUR AMBITIONS IN THE WATER TOWN...
THAT...
...THAT HERO...!
IF ONLY...
...I HAD NOTICED ...
... SOO—
...NO.

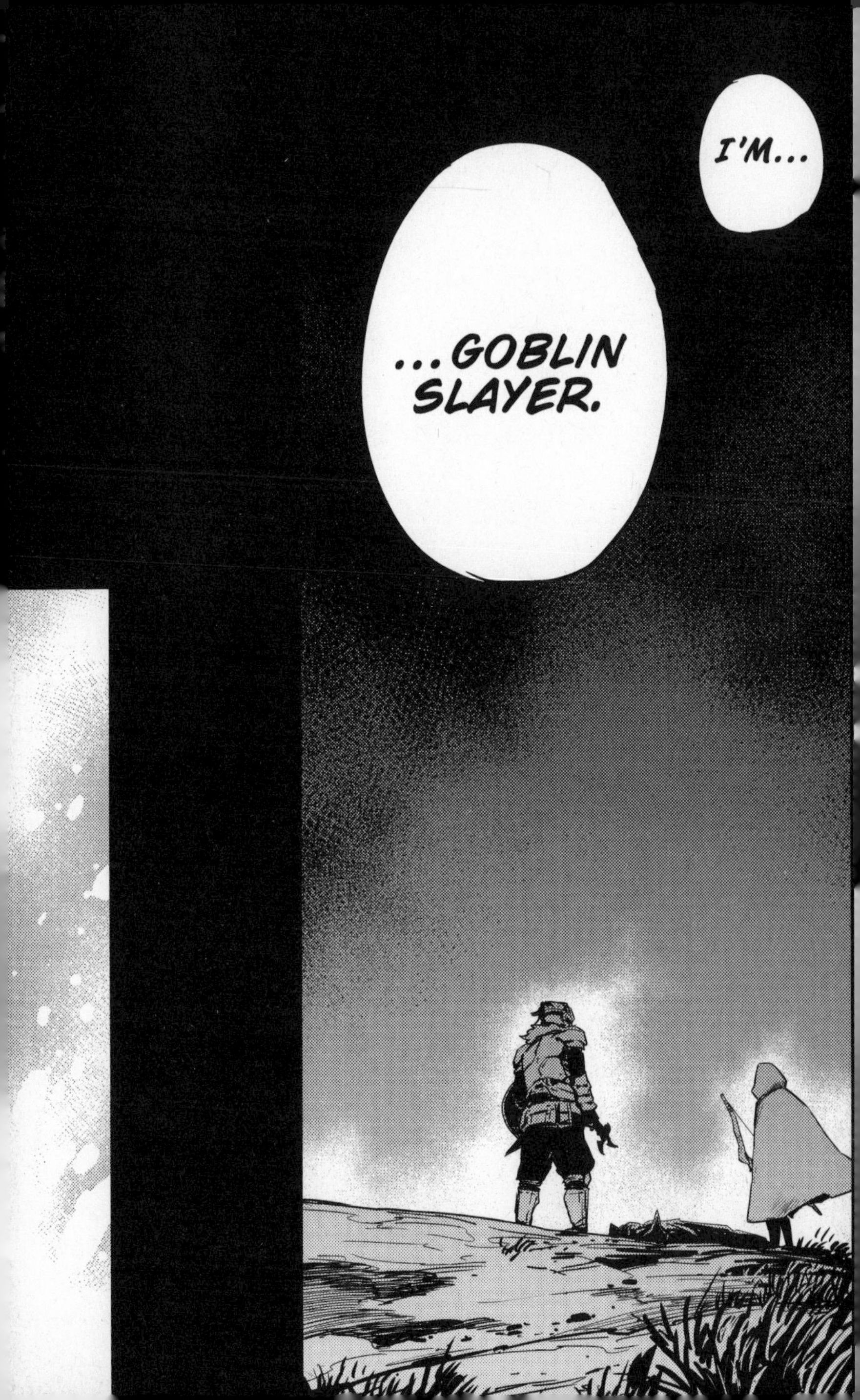
I'M...
...GOBLIN SLAYER.

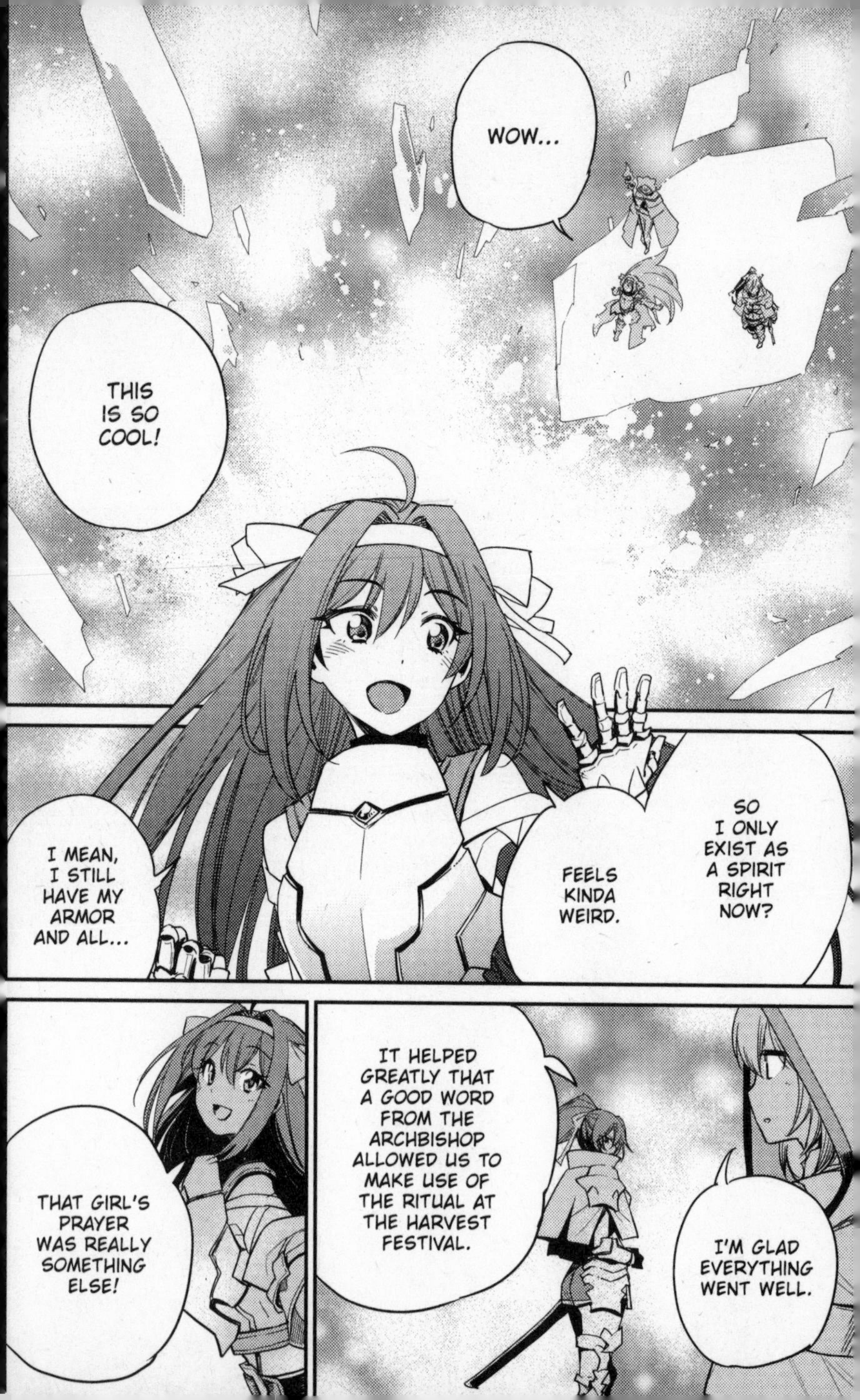
WOW...
THIS IS SO COOL!
SO I ONLY EXIST AS A SPIRIT RIGHT NOW?
FEELS KINDA WEIRD.
I MEAN, I STILL HAVE MY ARMOR AND ALL...
I'M GLAD EVERYTHING WENT WELL.
IT HELPED GREATLY THAT A GOOD WORD FROM THE ARCHBISHOP ALLOWED US TO MAKE USE OF THE RITUAL AT THE HARVEST FESTIVAL.
THAT GIRL'S PRAYER WAS REALLY SOMETHING ELSE!

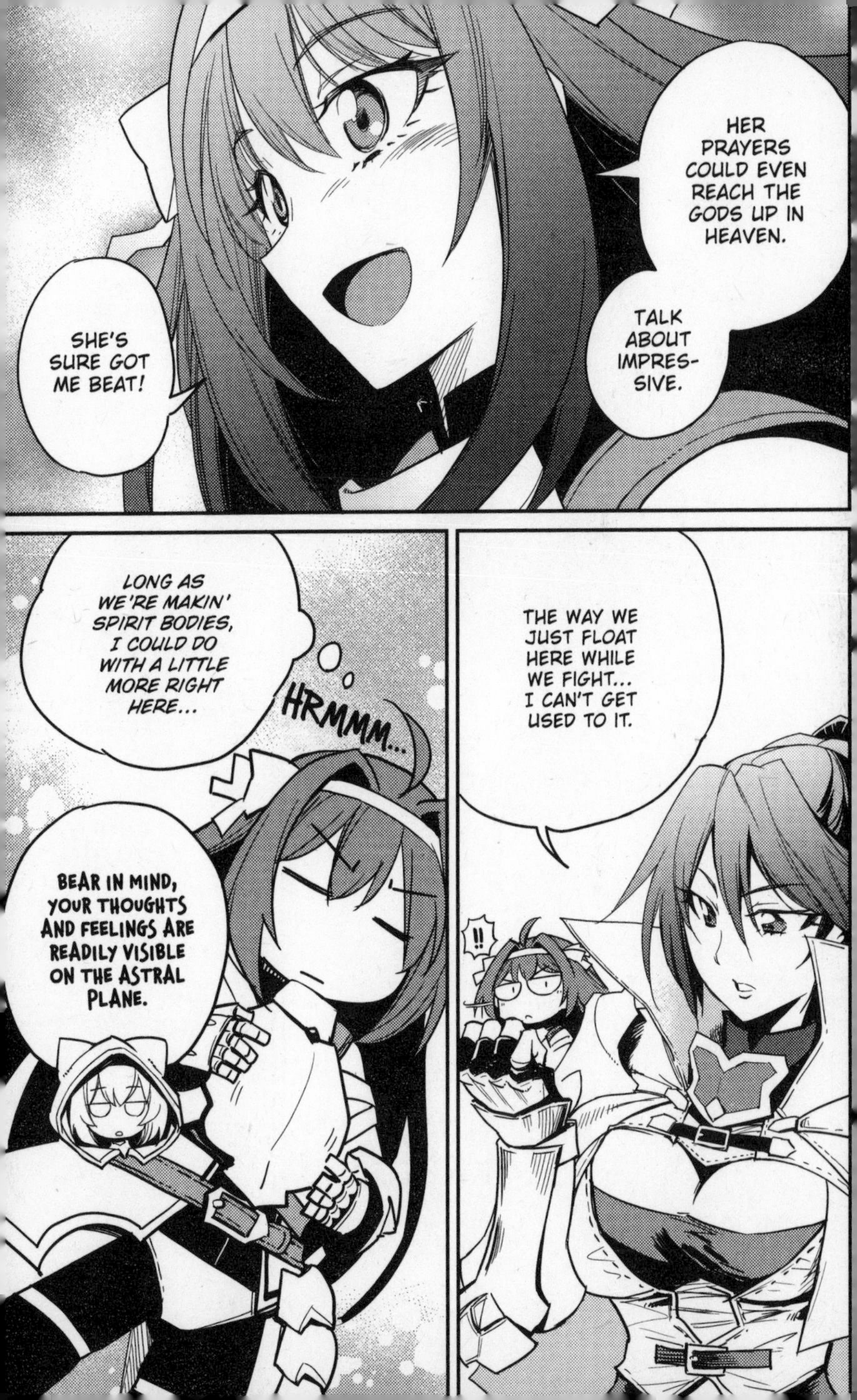
HER PRAYERS COULD EVEN REACH THE GODS UP IN HEAVEN.
TALK ABOUT IMPRES-SIVE.
SHE'S SURE GOT ME BEAT!
THE WAY WE JUST FLOAT HERE WHILE WE FIGHT... I CAN'T GET USED TO IT.
!!
LONG AS WE'RE MAKIN' SPIRIT BODIES, I COULD DO WITH A LITTLE MORE RIGHT HERE...
HRMMM...
BEAR IN MIND, YOUR THOUGHTS AND FEELINGS ARE READILY VISIBLE ON THE ASTRAL PLANE.

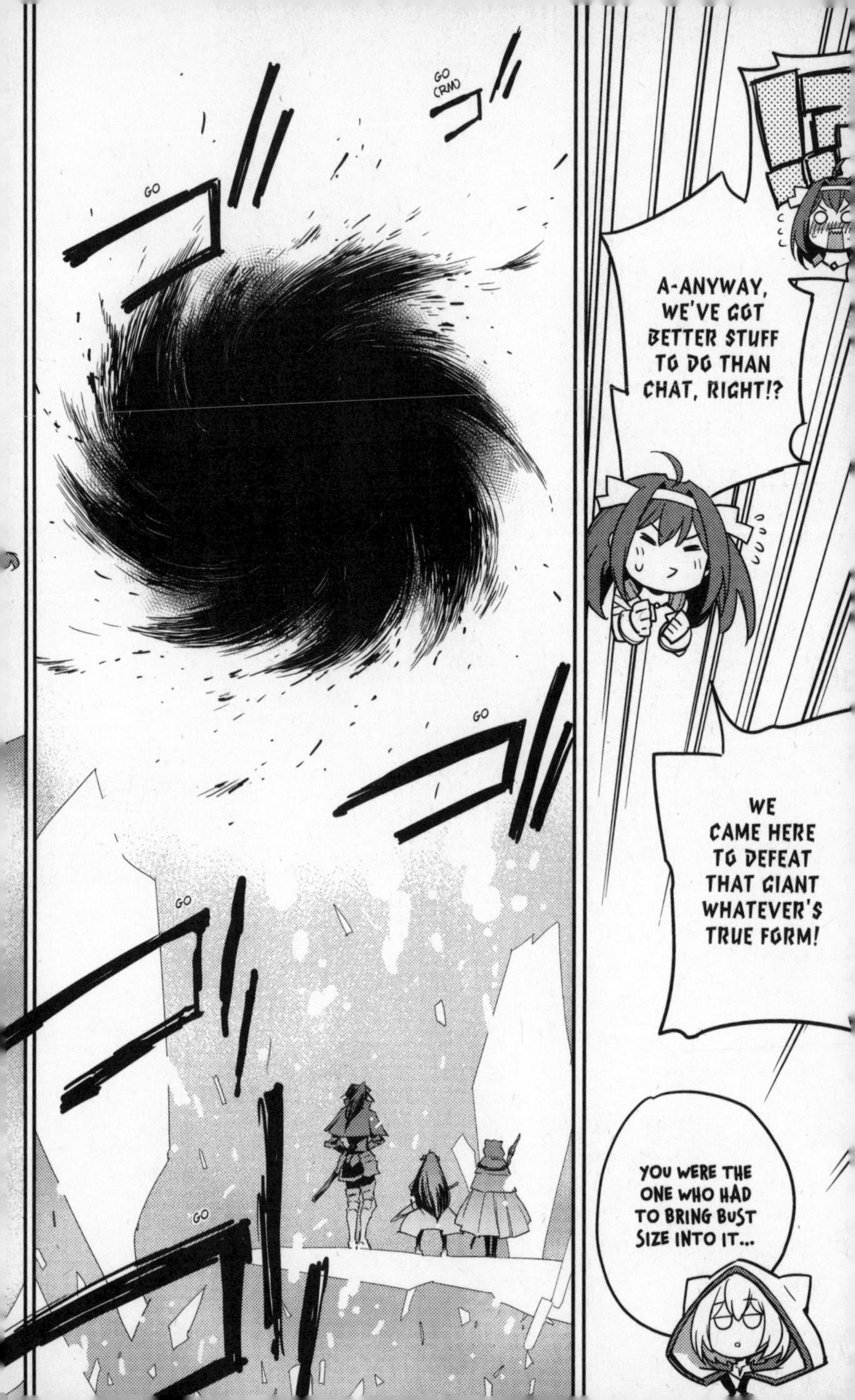
A-ANYWAY, WE'VE GOT BETTER STUFF TO DO THAN CHAT, RIGHT!?
WE CAME HERE TO DEFEAT THAT GIANT WHATEVER'S TRUE FORM!
YOU WERE THE ONE WHO HAD TO BRING BUST SIZE INTO IT...
GO (RM)
GO
GO
GO
GO

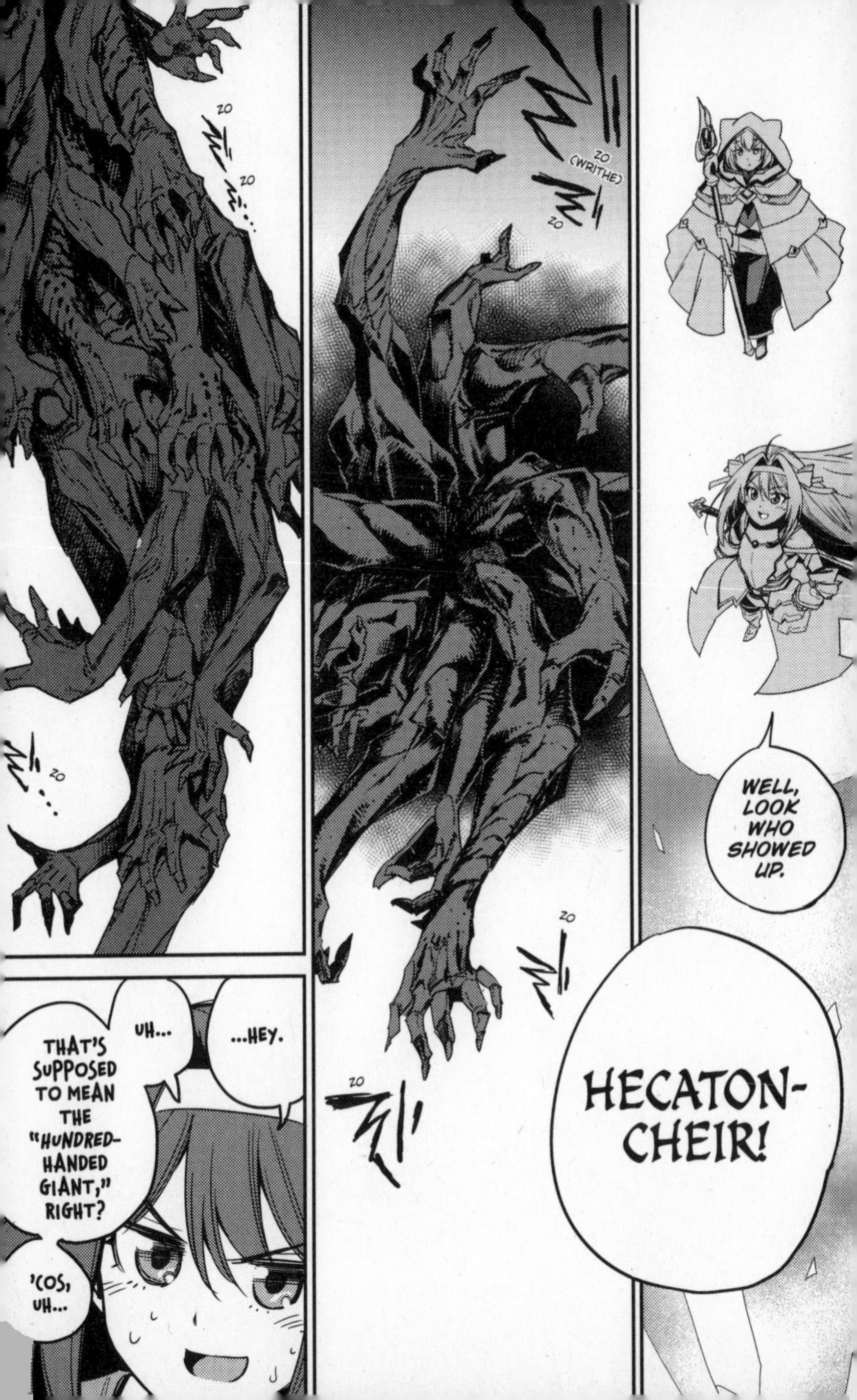
WELL, LOOK WHO SHOWED UP.
HECATON-CHEIR!
ZO (WRITHE)
ZO
ZO
ZO
ZO
ZO
ZO...
ZO...
...HEY.
UH...
THAT'S SUPPOSED TO MEAN THE "HUNDRED-HANDED GIANT," RIGHT?
'COS, UH...

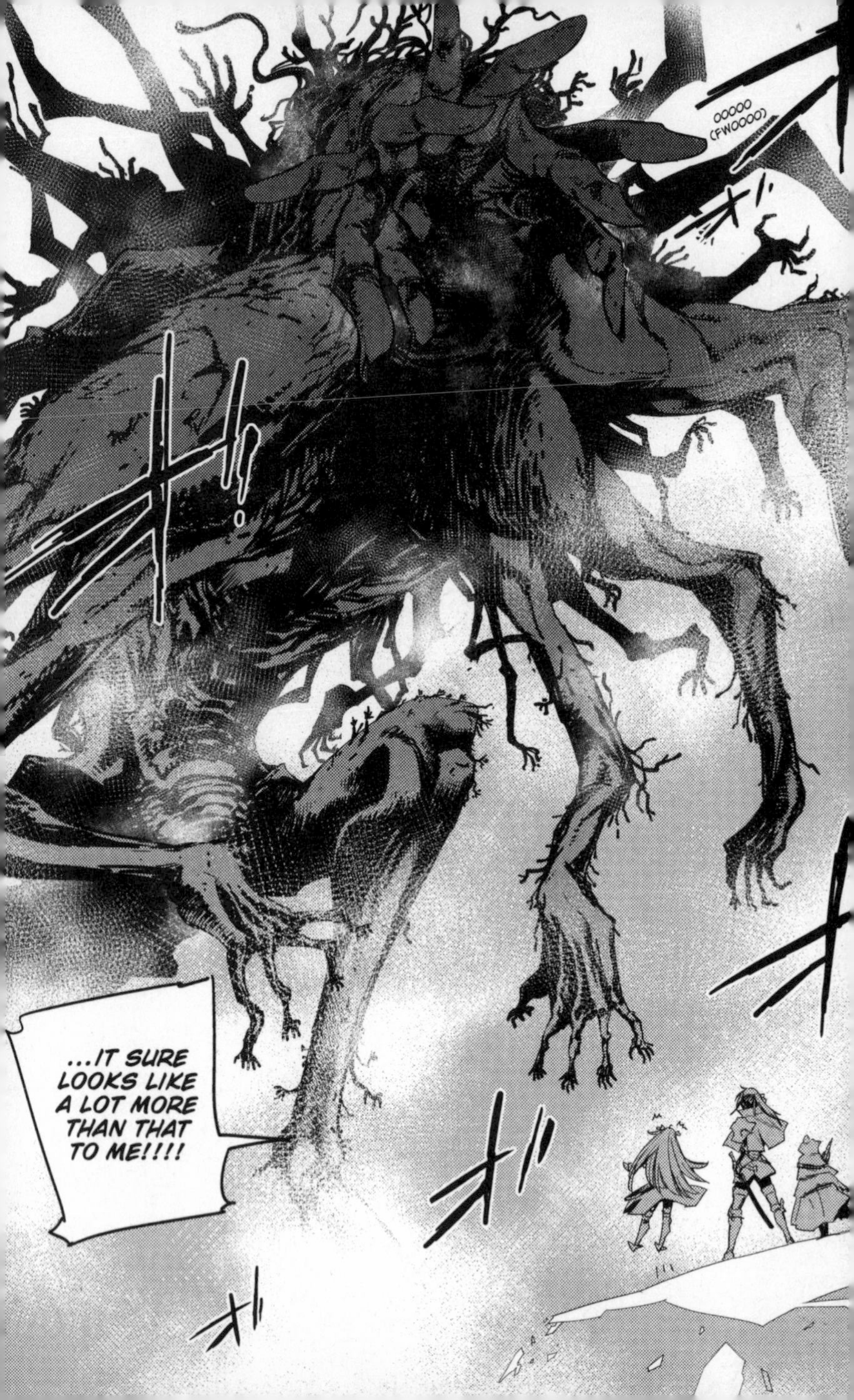
OOOOO
(FWOOOO)
...IT SURE LOOKS LIKE A LOT MORE THAN THAT TO ME!!!!

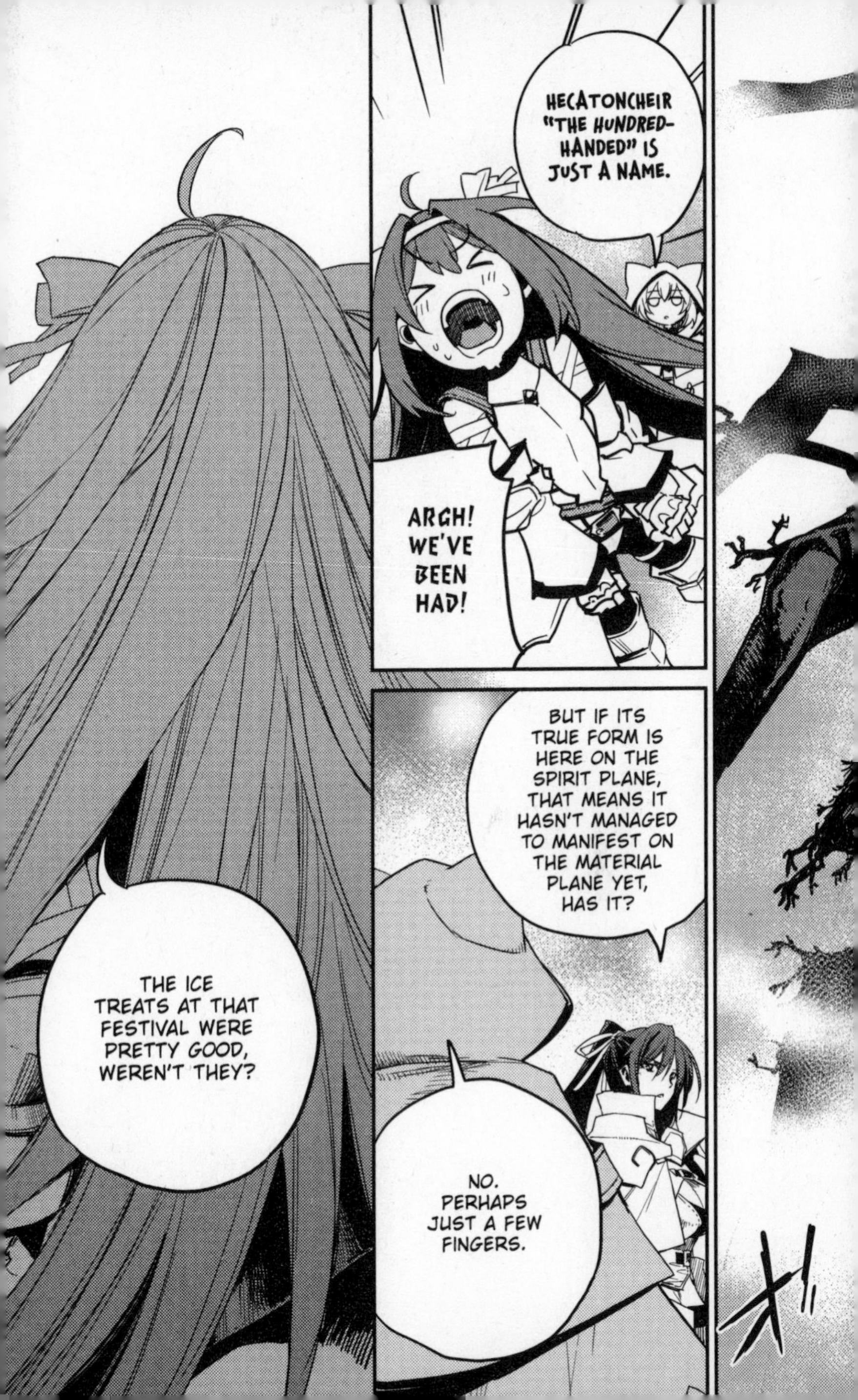
HECATONCHEIR "THE HUNDRED-HANDED" IS JUST A NAME.
ARGH! WE'VE BEEN HAD!
BUT IF ITS TRUE FORM IS HERE ON THE SPIRIT PLANE, THAT MEANS IT HASN'T MANAGED TO MANIFEST ON THE MATERIAL PLANE YET, HAS IT?
NO. PERHAPS JUST A FEW FINGERS.
THE ICE TREATS AT THAT FESTIVAL WERE PRETTY GOOD, WEREN'T THEY?

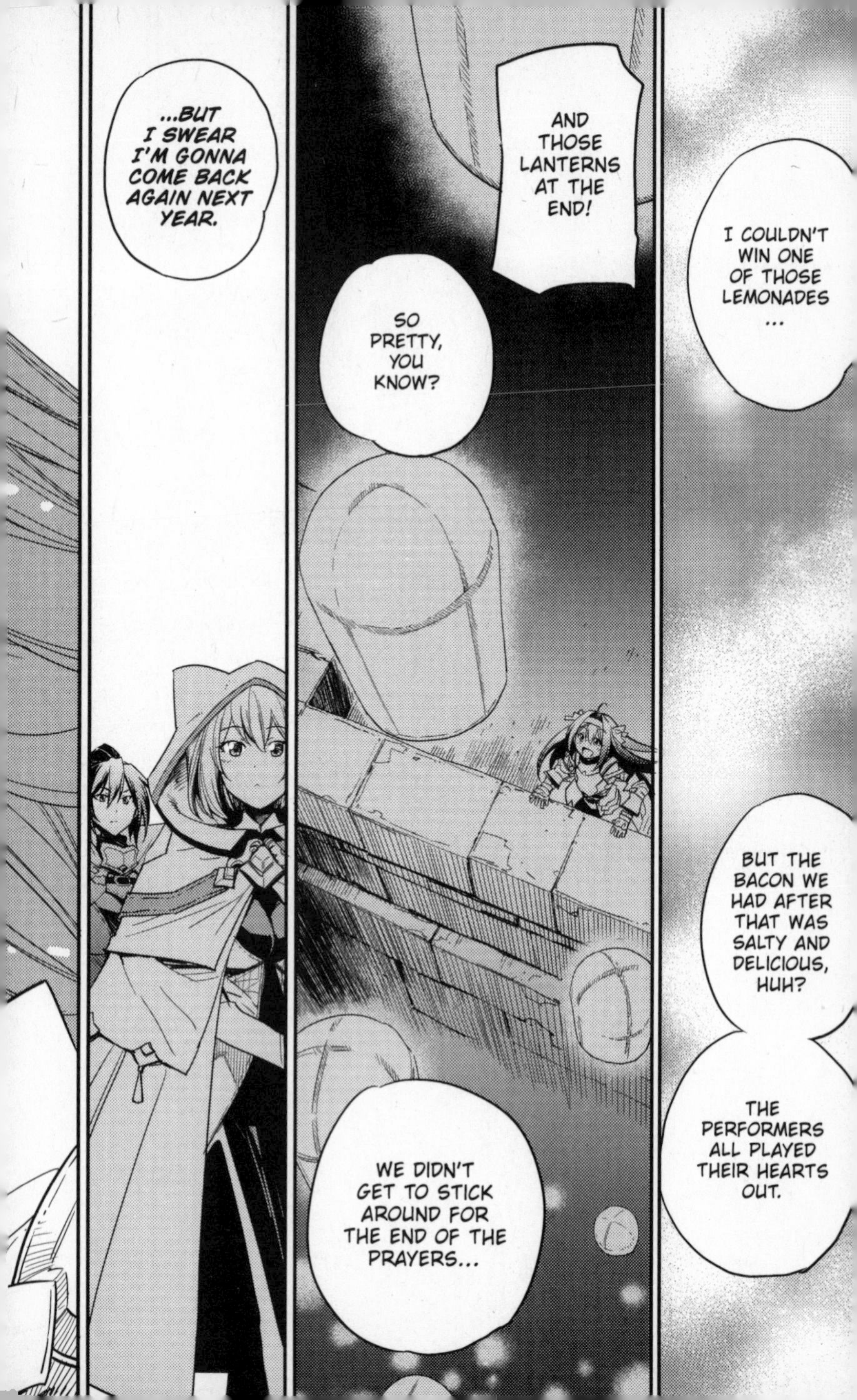
I COULDN'T WIN ONE OF THOSE LEMONADES ...
BUT THE BACON WE HAD AFTER THAT WAS SALTY AND DELICIOUS, HUH?
THE PERFORMERS ALL PLAYED THEIR HEARTS OUT.
AND THOSE LANTERNS AT THE END!
SO PRETTY, YOU KNOW?
WE DIDN'T GET TO STICK AROUND FOR THE END OF THE PRAYERS...
...BUT I SWEAR I'M GONNA COME BACK AGAIN NEXT YEAR.

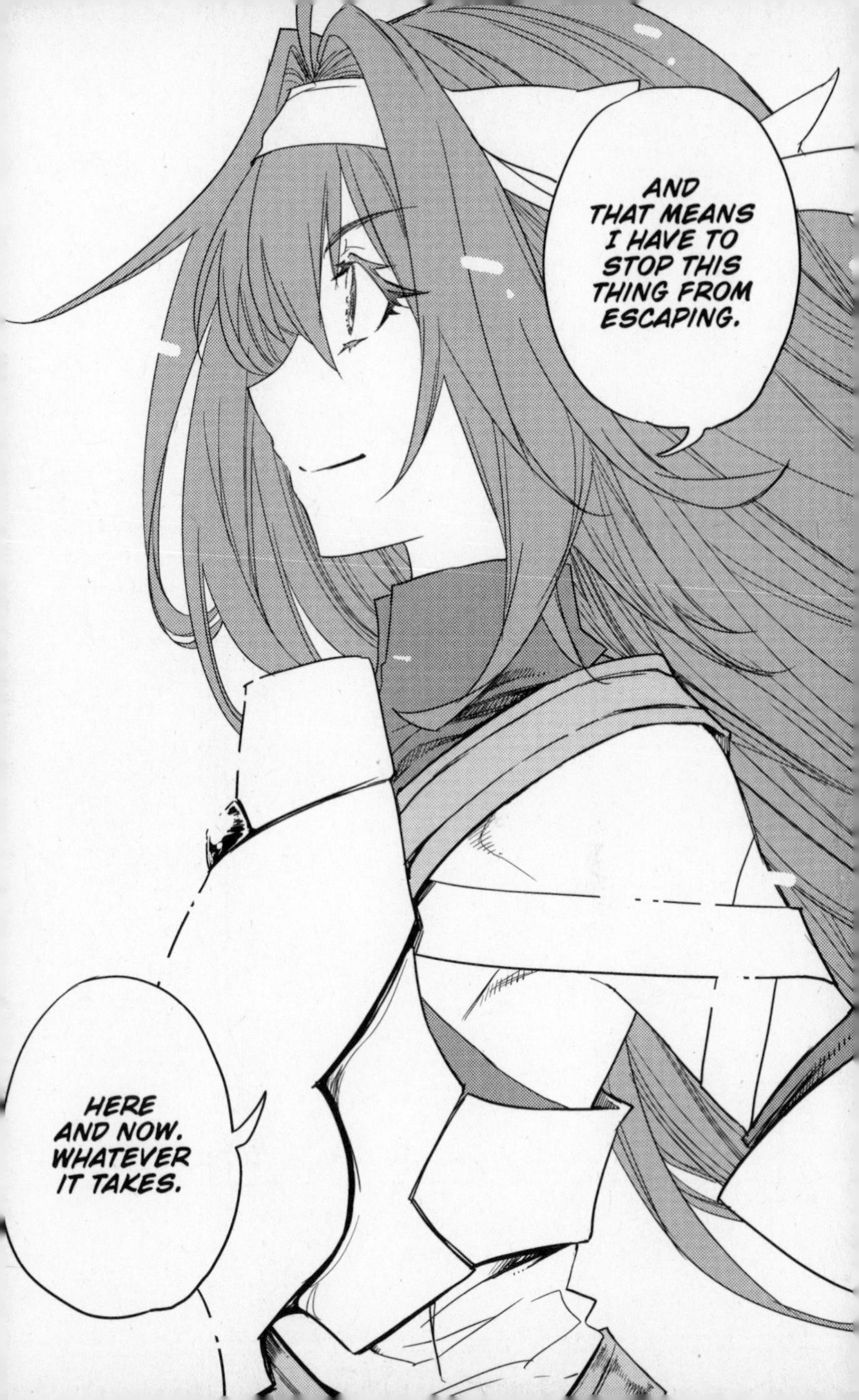
AND THAT MEANS I HAVE TO STOP THIS THING FROM ESCAPING.
HERE AND NOW. WHATEVER IT TAKES.

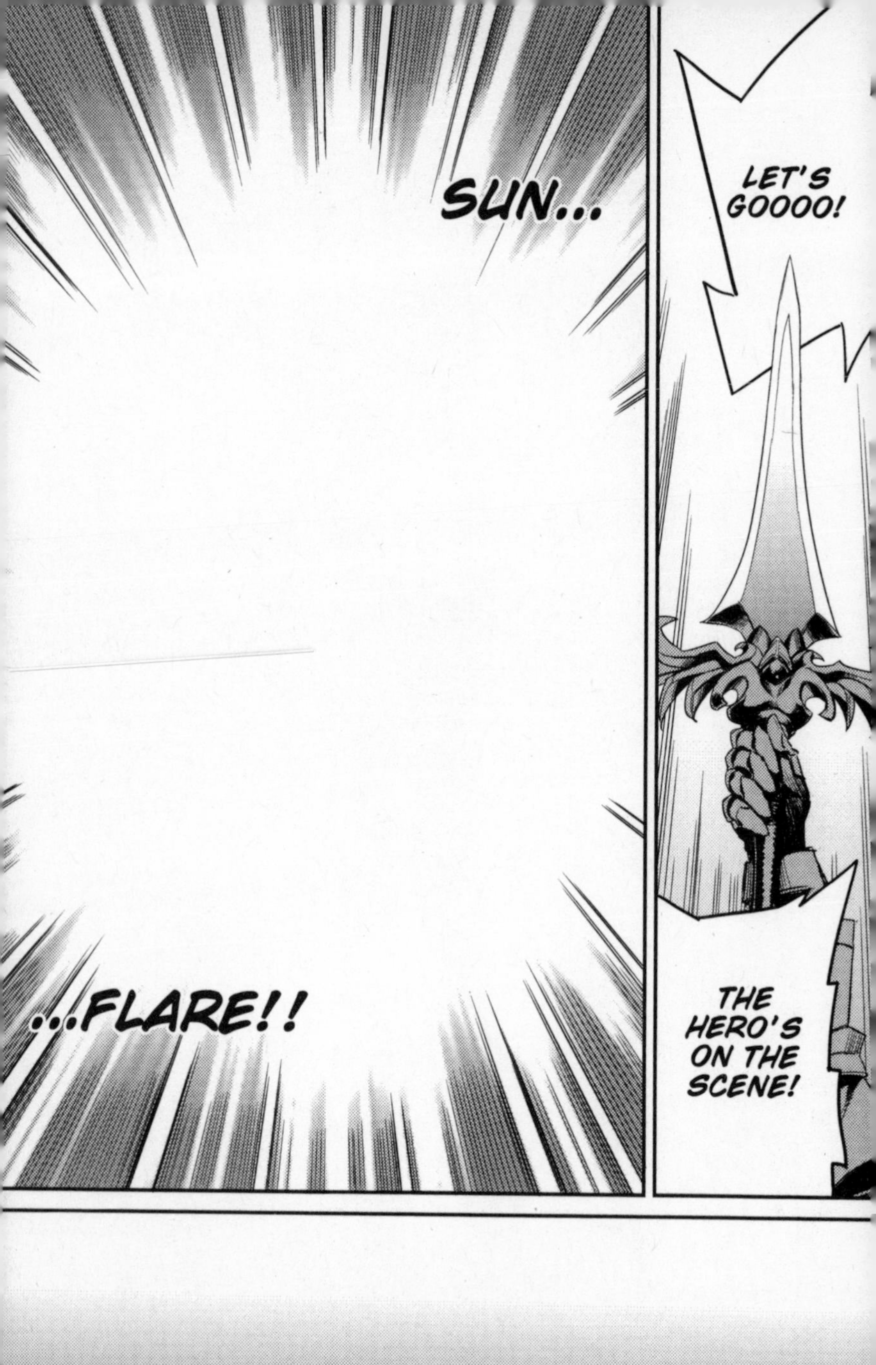
LET'S GOOOO!
THE HERO'S ON THE SCENE!
SUN...
...FLARE!!

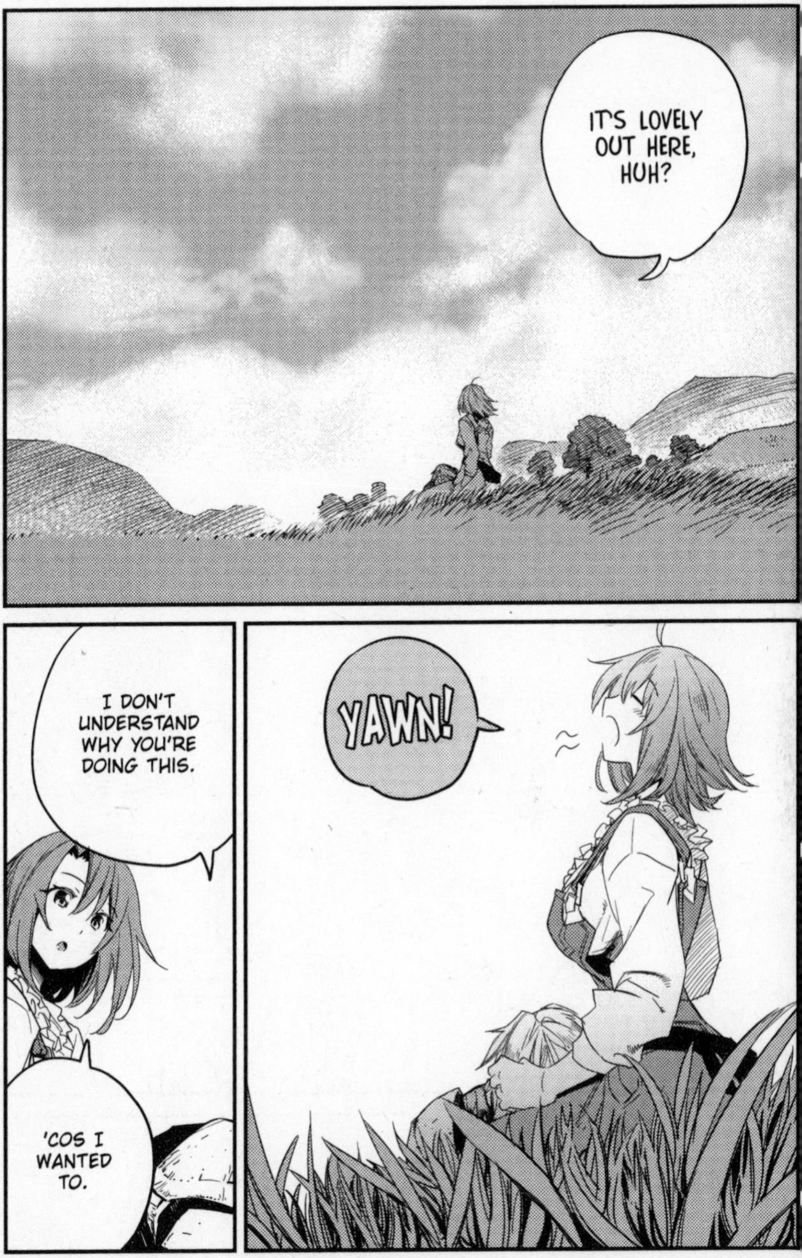
IT'S LOVELY OUT HERE, HUH?
YAWN!
I DON'T UNDERSTAND WHY YOU'RE DOING THIS.
'COS I WANTED TO.

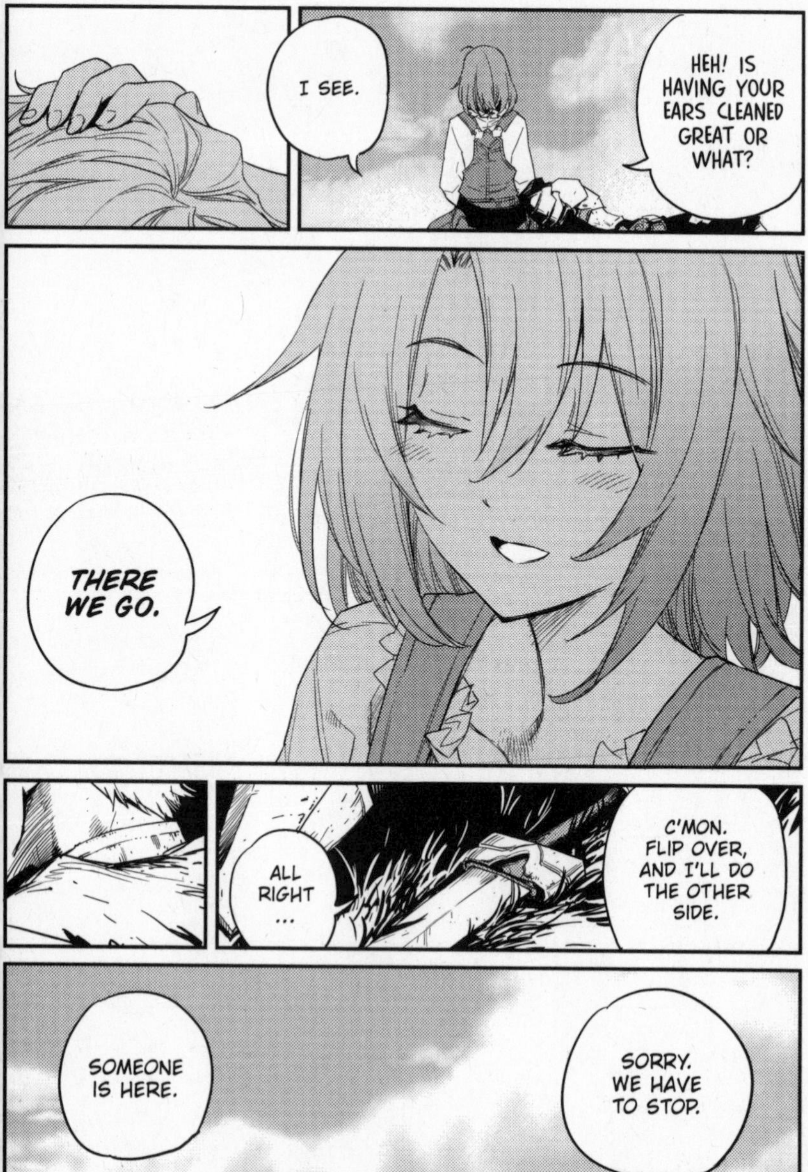
HEH! IS HAVING YOUR EARS CLEANED GREAT OR WHAT?
I SEE.
THERE WE GO.
C'MON. FLIP OVER, AND I'LL DO THE OTHER SIDE.
ALL RIGHT ...
SORRY. WE HAVE TO STOP.
SOMEONE IS HERE.

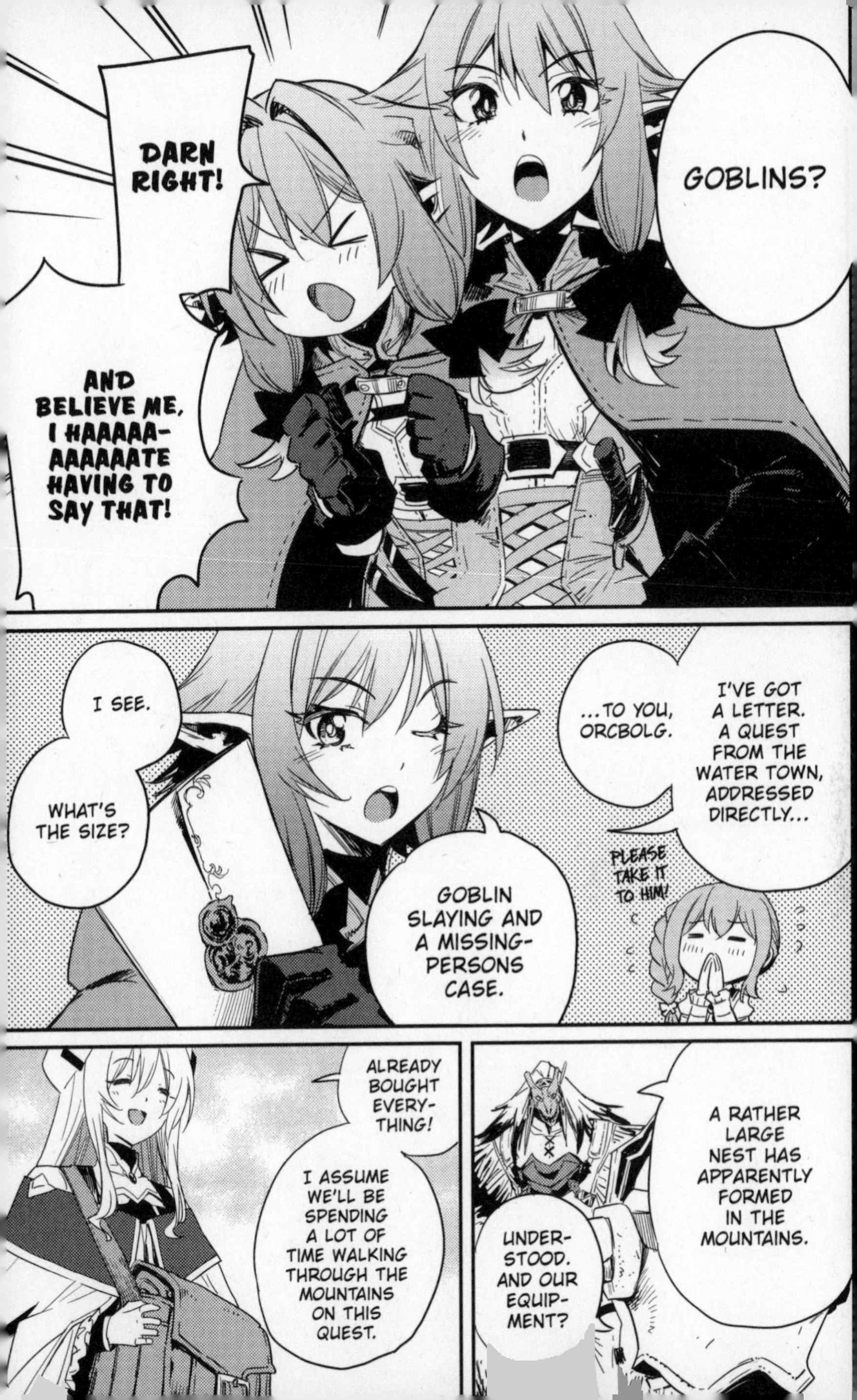
GOBLINS?
DARN RIGHT!
AND BELIEVE ME, I HAAAAA-AAAAAATE HAVING TO SAY THAT!
I'VE GOT A LETTER. A QUEST FROM THE WATER TOWN, ADDRESSED DIRECTLY...
...TO YOU, ORCBOLG.
PLEASE TAKE IT TO HIM!
GOBLIN SLAYING AND A MISSING-PERSONS CASE.
I SEE.
WHAT'S THE SIZE?
A RATHER LARGE NEST HAS APPARENTLY FORMED IN THE MOUNTAINS.
UNDER-STOOD. AND OUR EQUIP-MENT?
ALREADY BOUGHT EVERY-THING!
I ASSUME WE'LL BE SPENDING A LOT OF TIME WALKING THROUGH THE MOUNTAINS ON THIS QUEST.

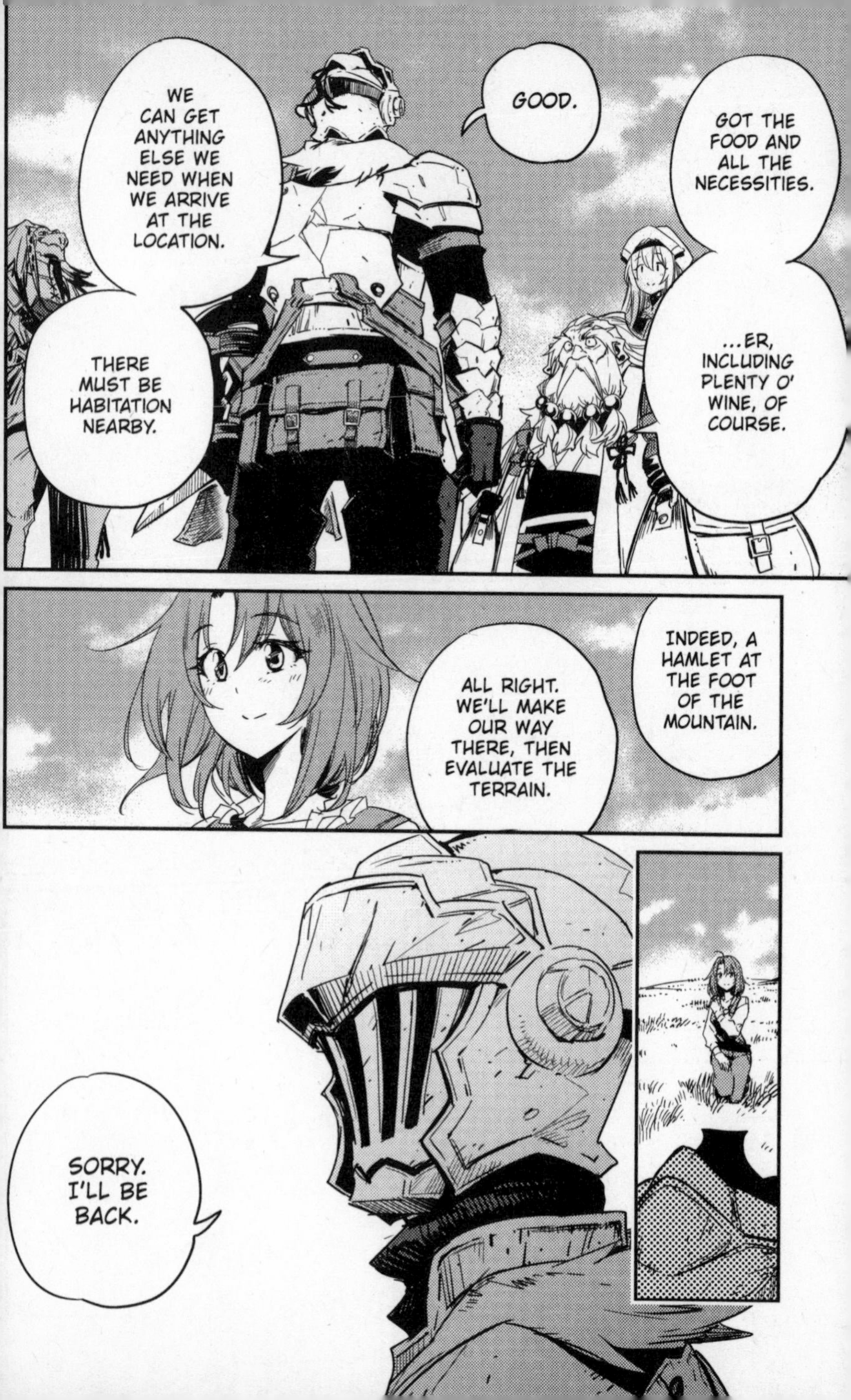
GOT THE FOOD AND ALL THE NECESSITIES.
...ER, INCLUDING PLENTY O' WINE, OF COURSE.
GOOD.
WE CAN GET ANYTHING ELSE WE NEED WHEN WE ARRIVE AT THE LOCATION.
THERE MUST BE HABITATION NEARBY.
INDEED, A HAMLET AT THE FOOT OF THE MOUNTAIN.
ALL RIGHT. WE'LL MAKE OUR WAY THERE, THEN EVALUATE THE TERRAIN.
SORRY. I'LL BE BACK.

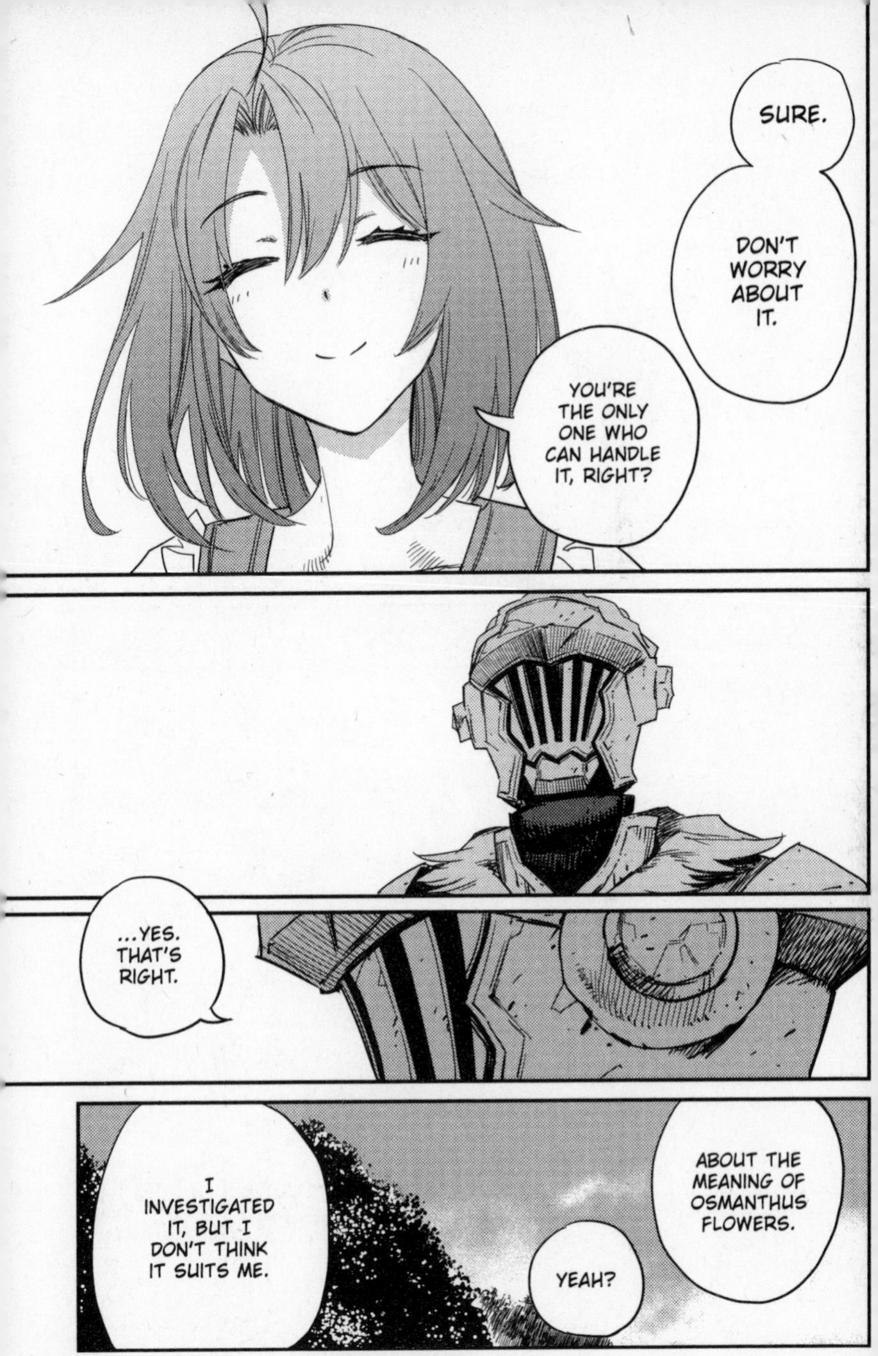
SURE.
DON'T WORRY ABOUT IT.
YOU'RE THE ONLY ONE WHO CAN HANDLE IT, RIGHT?
...YES. THAT'S RIGHT.
ABOUT THE MEANING OF OSMANTHUS FLOWERS.
YEAH?
I INVESTIGATED IT, BUT I DON'T THINK IT SUITS ME.

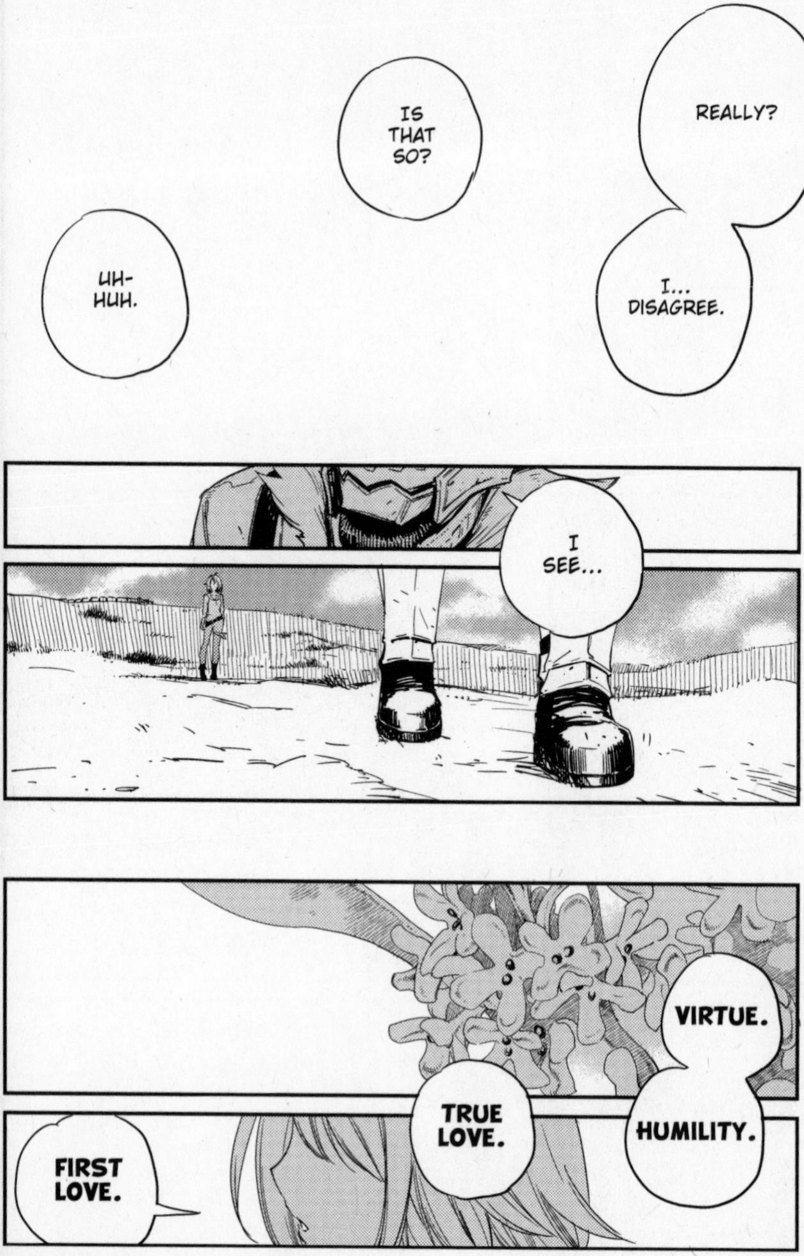
REALLY?
I... DISAGREE.
IS THAT SO?
UH-HUH.
I SEE...
VIRTUE.
HUMILITY.
TRUE LOVE.
FIRST LOVE.

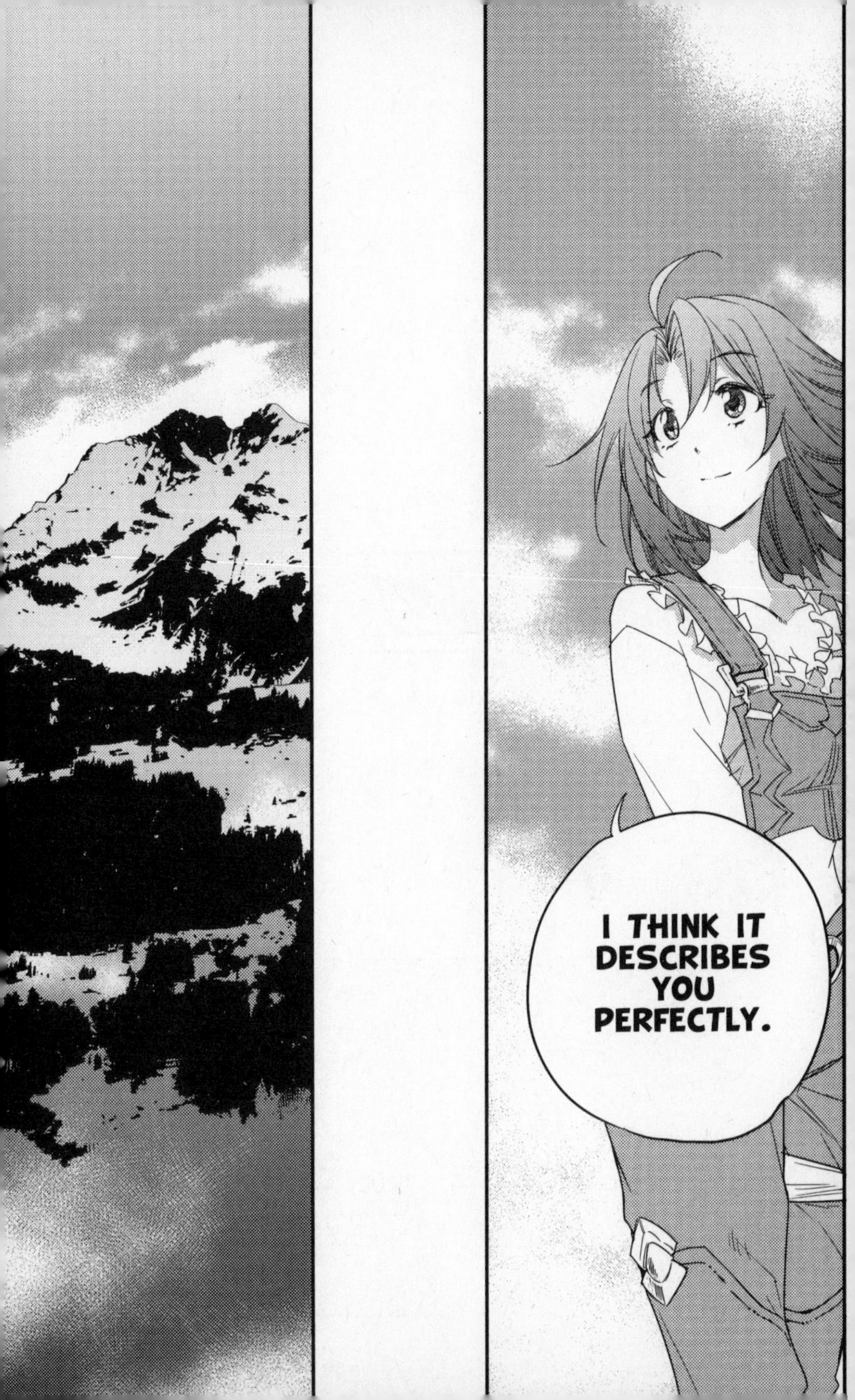
I THINK IT DESCRIBES YOU PERFECTLY.

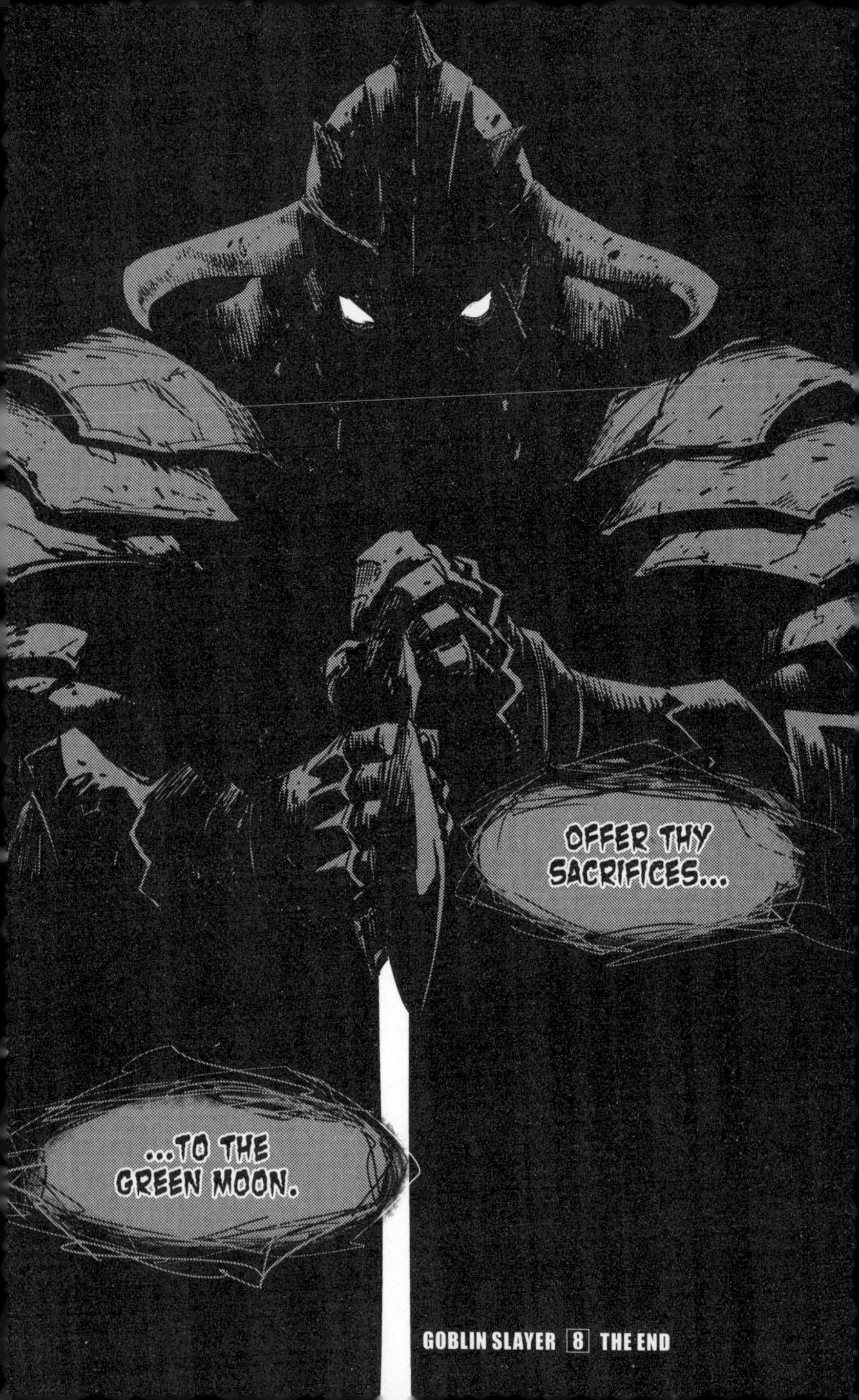
OFFER THY SACRIFICES...
...TO THE GREEN MOON.
GOBLIN SLAYER 8 THE END

Turn to the back of the
book for a short story by
Kumo Kagyu!

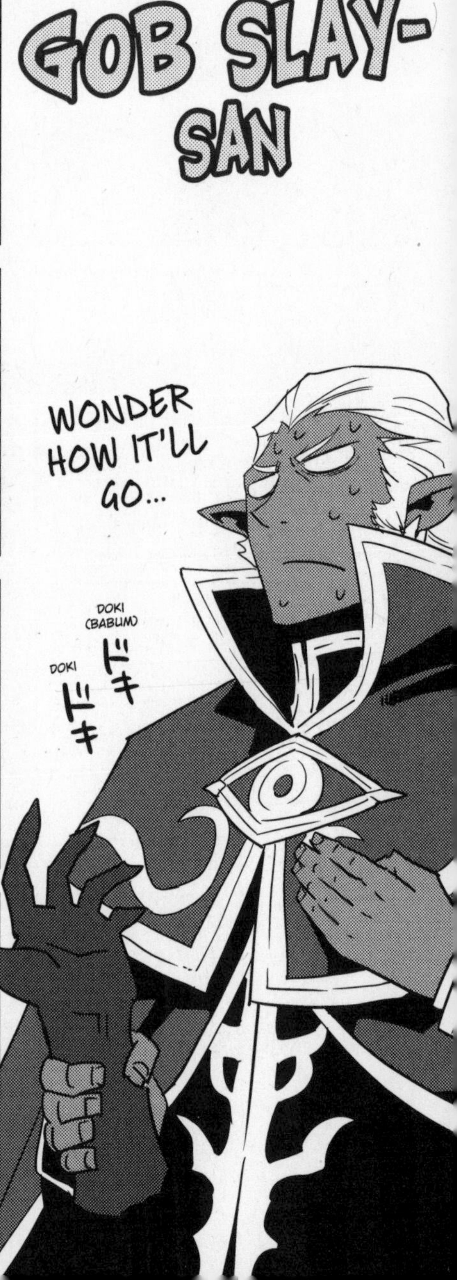
GOB SLAY-SAN
WONDER HOW IT'LL GO...
DOKI (BABUM) ドキ
DOKI ドキ

THE WORRYING TYPE

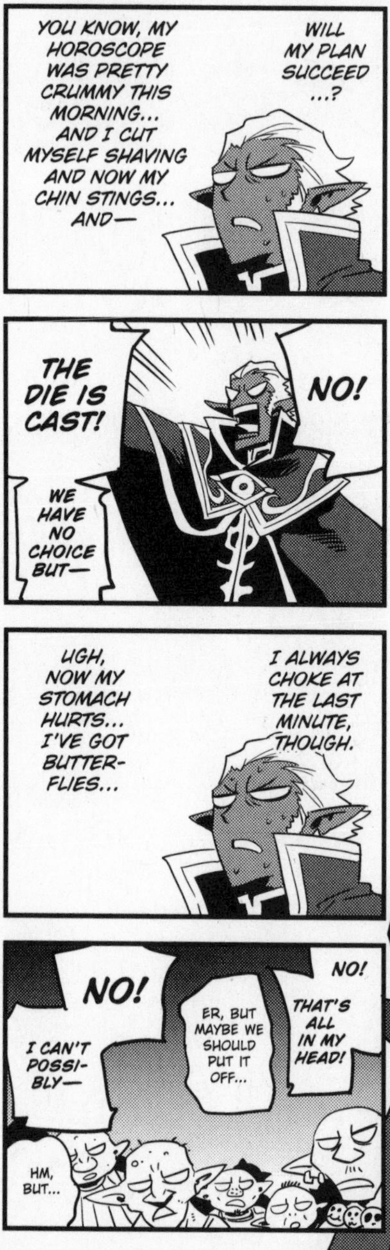
WILL MY PLAN SUCCEED...?
YOU KNOW, MY HOROSCOPE WAS PRETTY CRUMMY THIS MORNING... AND I CUT MYSELF SHAVING AND NOW MY CHIN STINGS... AND—
THE DIE IS CAST!
NO!
WE HAVE NO CHOICE BUT—
I ALWAYS CHOKE AT THE LAST MINUTE, THOUGH.
UGH, NOW MY STOMACH HURTS... I'VE GOT BUTTER-FLIES...
NO! THAT'S ALL IN MY HEAD!
ER, BUT MAYBE WE SHOULD PUT IT OFF...
NO!
I CAN'T POSSI-BLY—
HM, BUT...

OH YEAH, MY SOUVENIR

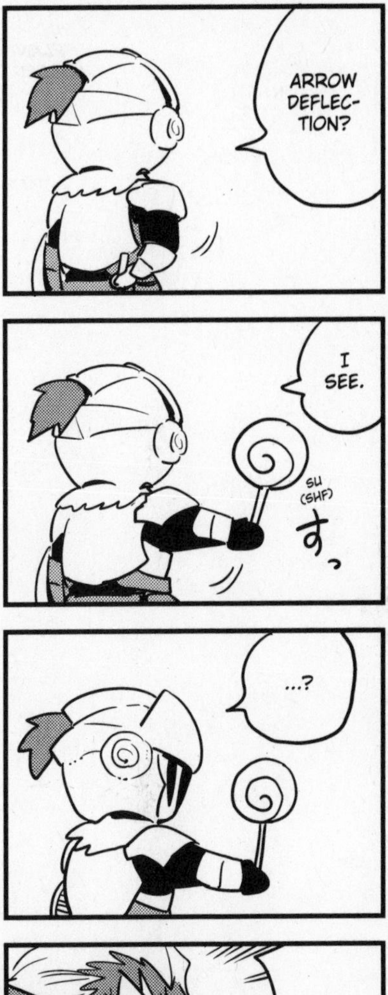
ARROW DEFLEC-TION?
I SEE.
SU (SHF)
すっ
...?
LIBE—
BLERRGH!
ドッゴォォオ
DOGOO (BADOOM)

BEATEN BY THE BEST

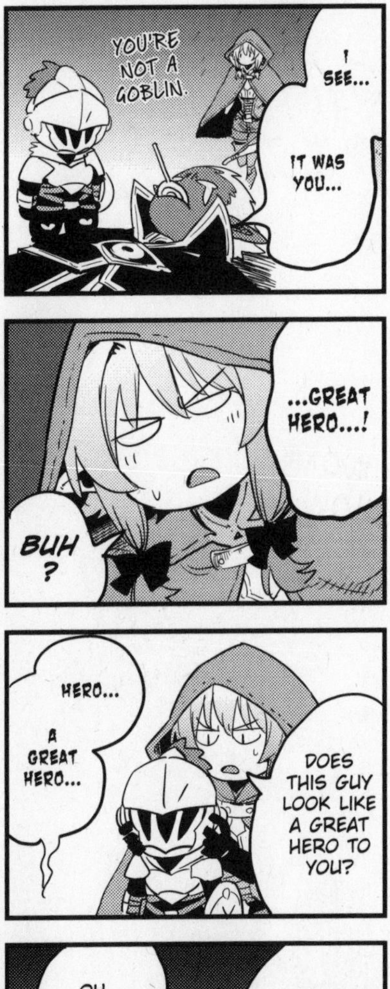
I SEE...
IT WAS YOU...
YOU'RE NOT A GOBLIN.
...GREAT HERO...!
BUH?
DOES THIS GUY LOOK LIKE A GREAT HERO TO YOU?
HERO...
A GREAT HERO...
PLEASE TELL EVERYONE... A GREAT HERO BEAT ME...
OH... YEAH.
OKAY.

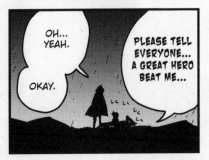

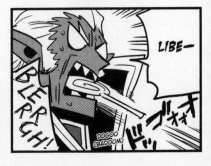

They're still my friends, though—and I still love 'em."

Priestess squinted, feeling a surge of envy that the girl could use that word, *friends*, so readily.

"Anyway, good luck with your dance, 'kay?"

"I'll give it my very best!" Happy to know that someone like her was cheering her on, Priestess wanted to offer something in return. She opened her mouth, then closed it again and thought for a second. The girl was already scrambling away, and Priestess could only come up with the most cliché reply.

"I don't know what it is you have to do, but...do your best, yourself."

At that, the girl stopped and blinked, but then she gave Priestess a firm thumbs-up and said cheerfully, "Yeah! You bet I will!" Her smile was like the sun coming out.

The girl went over to her friends, waving an apology, while Priestess let out a long breath and turned to the stage.

It was nothing more than a simple talk between two girls, hardly important.

But they, and they alone, understood perfectly: It was precisely because it had no value that it meant so much.

But that was not all there was to the world. The same die that had but a single pip on one face had six on the opposing side. You couldn't have all ones, but you couldn't have all sixes, either. She was sure of it—or at least, she thought she was.

I'll put these feelings into my dance, too.

The Earth Mother would see her...and if the souls of the dead truly came back on this night, then so would those two.

There were so many painful things in life—but not only painful things. That was what she would tell them. And then sometime, when she was finally able to go meet that girl, whose black hair was just like that of the girl in front of her...

"...Whoops!" Their carefree conversation ended abruptly.

"Sorry, there's something I've gotta do! I'd better get going." The other girl clapped her hands and peered out from behind the curtain dividing the stage from the festival. Priestess looked over in that direction and discovered two women in elaborate outfits. The other girl looked so flustered that Priestess quickly figured out what was going on.

"Your friends?"

"Uh-huh." The girl nodded without hesitation.   "One's too serious, and the other's too strict.

sprites out there, they would, she thought, come from people.

I think I know why, though.

"I'm sure it's because it's almost too delicious to bear, and the headache is a warning not to eat too much."

"Huh, maybe... Yeah, I'll bet you're right. But I wanna eat ice treats till I can't eat another bite!"

"...I think you'd get fat, wouldn't you?"

"Boo. I don't want that. My friend... Oh, this one's a warrior, see, and she's real strict about that kind of thing."

Their chat enthusiastically bounced from subject to subject. How much they had both admired the magician's sleight of hand. How they had missed out on lemonade because they couldn't throw the little balls accurately. All the mistakes in the adventure stories about former heroes at the shadow puppet play.

Suddenly, Priestess found herself thinking, *This... is nice. I hope I can enjoy the festival this much again next year.*

When she thought about it, she realized what a difficult year it had been. Not just slaying goblins but witnessing several brutal deaths—and coming close to dying herself.

"If you practiced... Well, you might get somewhere, right?"

"Which is another way of saying *you've* practiced a lot. I knew you were great at this." The girl swung her legs, using the momentum to jump down off the barrel, then spun around. Her smile was as bright as the sun. "Hey, have you been to see the festival?"

"Yes," Priestess answered, though she had been too nervous to enjoy herself much. "There were these ice treats," Priestess said, closing her eyes as if remembering the sweet flavor, "and I got one of them."

"Oooh, I know those! Those were great, huh?!" The girl leaned forward and nodded vigorously. "I had one, too! So sweet. But kinda too cold for me. Made my head hurt."

"Oh, mine, too. Why do you suppose that happens?"

"My friend—she's, like, a wizard, and she says it's the ice sprites playing tricks in your head. Swapping out cold for pain or something. I'll get them next time!" The girl snorted, but Priestess had her doubts. She had never heard her beloved high elf friend or the trustworthy dwarf shaman she knew suggest that sprites meant anyone ill. Sprites were influenced by people's hearts, so if there were evil

made her feel friendly toward the girl.

This girl must be a guest brought here by Mother Superior herself.

Was she perhaps the daughter of some particularly generous noble donor to the Earth Mother's temple, then? But she lacked the stiff manner one would expect from such a person. And the outfit was probably just a costume for the festival.

"I'm glad you think so...but honestly, I still have such a long way to go." Setting her feelings aside, Priestess had meant to be reserved and polite, yet she found herself slipping into familiar tones. Something about the girl with black hair just made her want to talk that way, and that didn't seem so bad.

"If you've still got a long way to go, that just means you can get way better, right?"

"Wha—?" blurted Priestess, and the girl burst out in a triumphant grin. Priestess had been trapped by her own modesty. The other girl laughed heartily.

"I can't dance at all, y'know? I tried at a festival once, but I just stepped on the other kids' toes." She muttered about the stupid billowy skirt that had tripped her up, tapping her foot for emphasis.

Her blushing face was just too cute, and Priestess discovered herself breaking into a smile. It really was impossible to be formal around this girl.

world love us for whatever we do...

"Wow! That was fantastic...!"

As Priestess finished dancing, putting a hand to her modest chest with a sigh of relief, a call filled with unbounded cheerfulness came from behind the stage. Priestess turned in the direction of the wild clapping to find a girl with black hair seated on the barrels in the shadows.

At first glance, one might have taken her for just another village child—but the elegance of her equipment! The young woman seemed to shimmer, like a hero from a story—but that thought caused Priestess to giggle.

If it's just a question of appearances, you could say the same of me.

Priestess was wearing her tailor-made outfit for the holy dance, and she held the ritual flail. If the other girl looked like a hero, Priestess looked like a hero's companion.

"What's the matter?" The other girl asked, looking straight at her with suspicion in her eyes, but Priestess shook her head gently.

"It's nothing."

Once Priestess gracefully walked over, she realized that if she ignored the barrel the other girl was sitting on, she was of strikingly small stature. She was sure they were the same age, and that alone

Interlude:
Of Before the Big Show —
by Kumo Kagyu

Each time she whisked the flail, a pure, clean, calming sound rang out from the ritual instrument.

The flail was not actually a weapon, but rather a farming tool for hulling grain, making it especially redolent of the Earth Mother, who ruled over fertility and abundance.

Though she had often wielded the flail for regular services, the thought of using it for the offertory dance made her especially nervous. Drawing breath into her tense body, she tried not to rush or panic—to be fluid and serene, yet not languid.

She went over the choreography she had practiced so many times in her mind, but this dance was more than just a series of steps. It was not simply about revealing the deity inside her, but about bringing warmth to the hearts of all those who attended the festival.

It was all such a contradiction.

Balancing these demands was difficult; it seemed almost impossible. But that was precisely what gave it meaning.

After all, the gods of all the four directions in this

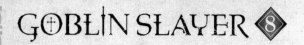

GOBLIN SLAYER 8

Original Story: Kumo Kagyu
Art: Kousuke Kurose
Character Design: Noboru Kannatuki

Translation: Kevin Steinbach ✣ Lettering: Bianca Pistillo

GOBLIN SLAYER Volume 8
©Kumo Kagyu / SB Creative Corp. Character Design: Noboru Kannatuki
©2019 Kousuke Kurose / SQUARE ENIX CO., LTD. First published in Japan in 2019 by
SQUARE ENIX CO., LTD. English translation rights arranged with SQUARE ENIX CO.,
LTD. and YEN PRESS, LLC through Tuttle-Mori Agency, Inc., Tokyo.

English translation ©2020 by SQUARE ENIX CO., LTD.

Yen Press
150 West 30th Street, 19th Floor
New York, NY 10001

Visit us at yenpress.com
facebook.com/yenpress
twitter.com/yenpress
yenpress.tumblr.com
instagram.com/yenpress

First Yen Press Edition: June 2020
The chapters in this volume were originally published as ebooks by Yen Press.

Yen Press is an imprint of Yen Press, LLC.
The Yen Press name and logo are trademarks of Yen Press, LLC.

Library of Congress Control Number: 2017954163

ISBNs: 978-1-9753-1394-4 (paperback)
       978-1-9753-1395-1 (ebook)

10 9 8 7 6 5 4 3 2 1

WOR

Printed in the United States of America